D1292792

# Lord Jesus, Hear Our Prayer

*Daily Prayers for Every Occasion*

William W. Rozek M.Ed.

WESTBOW
PRESS®
A DIVISION OF THOMAS NELSON
& ZONDERVAN

WestBow Press books may be ordered through booksellers or by contacting:

WestBow Press
A Division of Thomas Nelson & Zondervan
1663 Liberty Drive
Bloomington, IN 47403
www.westbowpress.com
844-714-3454

All cover photos are provided by Jill Allardyce Miller Photography Inc.

Scripture quotations are from the Holy Bible, King James Version (Authorized Version). First published in 1611. Quoted from the KJV Classic Reference Bible, Copyright © 1983 by The Zondervan Corporation.

ISBN: 978-1-6642-8532-3 (sc)
ISBN: 978-1-6642-8533-0 (e)

Library of Congress Control Number: 2022922489

Print information available on the last page.

WestBow Press rev. date: 01/17/2023

"For us, He was bound, beaten, and bruised

by Leather, nailed to Wood with Metal,

Died, was buried behind Hewn Stone,

yet, Rose Again, to claim Victory over

Death and all Salvation from Transgression;

Holy, Holy, Holy, is our Lord Jesus Christ!"

# Rozek, Prayer    "Lord Jesus, Hear Our Prayer"

### … Introduction and Personal Preface …

There will always be times of uncertainty in one's life, when personal trials of doubt and sadness seem to cling to the heart and soul, and it becomes difficult to see one's way through the shadows of despair (as inspired from 1 Peter 1:7); but often; a simple prayer, a small praise, or a glimmer of faith becomes a spark of hope that will rise up from a spiritual whisper and roar like a lion, awakening us to the precious truth in our Lord Jesus Christ, that he loves us and wants us to always be happy (as inspired from 1 Peter 1:8). Therefore, it is crucial to our individual happiness and spiritual growth that a sincere blessing of thanks or an offering of praise be given daily to our Lord Jesus Christ (as inspired from psalms 145:1-2 and 1 Chronicles 23:30); for a candle that does not burn, has no warmth nor gives off any radiance (as inspired from Isaiah 8:20), and if we truly consider ourselves Christians, then we are true disciples of Jesus Christ, and we must completely follow his Word (as inspired from John 10:27).

"Lord Jesus, Hear Our Prayer" is a literary composition of 366 blessings, praises, and prayers of thanks that are directed to our Lord Jesus Christ and were inspired from certain passages in "every book" of the Old and New Testament of the Holy Bible. Each inspirational composition is numbered by a cardinal number of the month that it represents and is followed by the title and the chapter and the verse that inspired its creation, which in essence, creates a "never out of date" sequential calendar of devotional and inspirational praises, prayers, and blessings.

Each daily reading is devoted to our Lord; therefore, each day becomes a daily devotion to Jesus, and may be read: aloud or silently, as a morning devotion, as a blessing before a meal, as a praise before retiring for the day, or simply as a private reading when searching for personal inspiration on any given day. Inspiration is that silent voice within; it is the Spirit of the Lord that resides in all humans and allows each and every one of us, who are willing to listen, to truly understand and accept His unspoken wisdom (as inspired from Job 32:8).

True faith is a spiritual mystery, but the results from true belief and devotion to the will of Jesus Christ are always the same: problems are resolved, questions are answered, and mysteries are solved; nothing is impossible through absolute faith and devotion (as inspired from Mark 11:24); for daily devotion is as important to our spiritual salvation as breathing is to our physical existence … and daily prayers will keep us in constant communion with Jesus Christ and act as a strengthening source of continual faith and trust in our Lord's will.

Daily praises to our Lord Jesus Christ should be as natural as a heartbeat and as regular as a sunrise; for all that we have and all that we need are obtained through the Lord's will. There is no special time, nor hour, that is set aside as the proper time to speak to the Lord; the now, the present, this is the proper time (as inspired from 2 Corinthians 6:2) The Lord Jesus Christ should be in our thoughts, in our hearts, and in our lives every hour of the day. Therefore, on a daily basis, throughout the day, throughout the year, and throughout our lives, let us keep the Lord Jesus Christ forever in our hearts and forever in our spirits, and let us glorify and praise the Lord in our minds, through our spirits, and in our spoken words.

## "Lord Jesus, Hear Our Prayer"

Pray for us, Lord Jesus, and shield us from all that is false; for if we believe a lie, then the lie will surely become our reality; but if we trust in your Perfect Will, Lord Jesus, our faith will always reside in the truth, for the truth is always right! Help us, Lord, to obtain purity of faith, for only through the Good Graces of your Divine Love will we learn to have absolute trust and absolute faith in what was, what is, and what will be, according to the glorious Word of your Holy Spirit, born of flesh, our Lord and Savior, Jesus Christ (as inspired from John 1:14); and this, Lord Jesus, we accept through pure faith!

Please note that the previous devotional praise, as are all the readings, prayers, and blessings in "Lord Jesus, Hear Our Prayer" is in first person plural, as inspired from Matthew 6:9, "After this manner therefore pray ye: 'Our' Father who art in heaven, hallowed be thy name. Thy kingdom come, thy will be done, on earth, as it is in heaven. Give 'us' this day our daily bread. And forgive 'us' 'our' debts, as 'we' forgive 'our' debtors. And lead 'us' not into temptation, but deliver 'us' from evil," and by Luke 11:1, "And it came to pass, that as he was praying in a certain place, when he ceased, one of his disciples said unto him, Lord, teach 'us' to pray, as John also taught 'his' disciples," and in 1 Thessalonians 5:25, "Brethren, pray for 'us,'" and in Numbers 21:7, "Therefore the people came to Moses, and said, 'We' have sinned, for 'we' have spoken against the LORD, and against thee; pray unto the LORD, that 'he' take away the serpents from 'us.' And Moses prayed for the people," and in 1 Samuel 12:19, "And all the people said unto Samuel, Pray for 'thy' servants unto the LORD 'thy' God, that 'we' die not: for 'we' have added unto all 'our' sins this evil, to ask 'us' a king," and in Jeremiah 42:2, "And said unto Jeremiah the prophet, Let, 'we' beseech thee, 'our' supplications be accepted before thee, and pray for 'us' unto the LORD thy God, even for all this remnant; (for 'we' are left but a few of many, as thine eyes do behold 'us:');" and so many other examples and passages throughout the whole Bible. The Lord resides in each and every one of us. We are never alone with our problems; for the memories and the souls of all who love the Lord will transcend time and space and will continue forever. Hence, when reading a praise, a blessing, or a prayer from this book, let us each one of us think of ourselves as a unique and blessed member in a timeless and limitless family of the Lord Jesus Christ, and "All that the LORD has spoken, 'we' will do (Exodus 10:8).

## "Just One of the Flock"

And now, speaking from a layperson's point of view, I would first like to establish the fact that I am not a professional cleric, nor have I ever been ordained, nor do I possess any authority to pronounce absolution or administer any of the sacraments. But first and far most, I am a Christian who proudly confesses that Jesus Christ is our Lord and Savior (as inspired from Philippians 2:11). My profession for over thirty years is that of a public school English teacher; and the entire perspective for the inspired creation of this book, giving "thanks and reverence" to our Lord Jesus Christ, is based on the fact that it was formulated and written from the view point and rationale of "one of the flock". As a concerned Christian, as an experienced teacher, and simply, as a parent, I have observed, through the years, an ever increasing decline in family values and traditions. This strange apathetic-phenomenon towards family values is challenging many of our society's time honored beliefs that are found in numerous Christian households; and it seems to be sweeping through the very fiber of our moral stability, everywhere in the world, at an alarming rate! It is now prevalent and most noticeable in the entertainment realms such as those found in the motion picture industry and the movies they produce, in the so called "family-oriented" programs on television, in the lyrics of popular songs, in commercials, and yes, even in the cartoons that children watch, and the comics that appear in the Sunday newspapers; truly, there is a clear tendency to remove "goodness" from our culture and replace it with "ungodliness". This obvious and discernible trend away from "family traditions" is not chiseled in stone and is reversible and forgivable (Numbers 14:18), but it will take a conscious effort by individuals, people who cherish the values of virtue, to morally decide and determine "what, where, when, and how" to draw the proverbial "line in the sand" when they have had enough ungodliness in their lives. Reversing a negative is only possible when individuals make a personal choice in their lives to no longer participate in a "negative trend" but to make a determined effort to do something about it; and through prayer, faith, and perseverance, everything is possible through our Lord Jesus Christ.

Throughout my many years of teaching, I have subtly questioned multitudes of students concerning their family traditions such as the blessing before a meal, giving thanks for all they have, the saying of grace, and so forth. Unfortunately, through each passing decade, time honored practices of reverence towards our Lord Jesus Christ and giving thanks to Him for abundant blessings are greatly on the decline; and whether families of individuals know it or not, ignoring the "thanks and reverences" for any blessing is an irreverence towards the Lord (as inspired from Ephesians 5:20 and Hebrews 13:16). And whenever the occasion has presented itself to share in a blessing of a meal, I have also noticed that the words of the blessing are often hurried, or said in a "matter-of-fact" way and did not spiritually nor emotionally impact a single person at the table. It was at this personal awaking, a crossroads in my religious convictions, that I made a decisive and personal resolution in my life on the "what, where, when, and how" and drew my "line in the sand" and decided to write this book; hence, the inspiration for "Lord Jesus, Hear Our Prayer."

So often, family members and individuals become weary of the same blessing that is offered time and again before each meal. And a blessing that is overused will often create an uneasy feeling of commonplace and fails to deliver the true spiritual zeal of its original intent; end results, the blessing is eventually hurried, forgotten, or totally eliminated. But in this book of blessings, a different and unique prayer has been created (inspired) for each and every day of the year (including Leap Year); and each blessing was an inspiration from either the Old Testament or the New Testament; thereby, engaging and inviting the reader's interest to possibly investigate and research the Scripture reading.

"Chapters and Verses that were used as Inspirations for the Preface"

1) 1 Chronicles 23:30 … And to stand every morning to thank and praise the LORD, and likewise even;

2) 2 Corinthians 6:2 … (For he saith, I have heard thee in time accepted, and in the day of salvation have I succoured thee: behold, now is accepted time; behold, now is the day of salvation.)

3) Ephesians 5:20 … Giving thanks always for all the good things unto God and the Father in the name of our Lord Jesus Christ:

4) Hebrews 13:16 … But to do good and to communicate not: for with such sacrifices God is well pleased.

5) Isaiah 8:20 … To the law and to the testimony: if they speak not according to this word, it is because there is no light in them.

6) Job 32:8 … But there is a spirit in man: and the inspiration of the Almighty giveth them understanding.

7) John 1:14 … And the Word was made flesh, and dwelt among us, (and we beheld his glory as the only begotten of the Father,) full of grace and truth.

8) John 10:27 … My sheep hear my voice, and I know them, and they follow me:

9) Mark 11:24 … Therefore I say unto you, what things soever ye desire, when ye pray, believe that ye receive them, and ye shall have them.

10) 1 Peter 1:7 … That the trial of your faith, being much more precious than of gold that perisheth, though it be tried with fire, might be found unto praises and honour and glory at the appearing of Jesus Christ:

11) 1 Peter 1:8 … Whom having not seen, ye love; in whom, though now ye see him not, yet believing, ye rejoice with joy unspeakable and full of glory:

12) Psalms 145:1-2 … I will extol thee, my God, O King; and I will bless thy name for ever and ever. (2) Every day will I bless thee; and I will praise thy name for ever and ever.

13) Numbers 14:18 … The LORD is longsuffering, and of great mercy, forgiving iniquity and transgression …

14) Philippians 2:11 … And that every tongue should confess that Jesus Christ is Lord. …

Please note: Scripture quotations were taken from the King James version of the Holy Bible …

# "Lord Jesus, Hear Our Prayer"

The Following Table of Contents

is arranged by

Month

and

Day

and

Title ...

# January

Day: Title of blessing: Chapter and verse of inspiration:
One: "We Seek Renewed Direction" Genesis 1:5
Two: "Your Magnificent Heart" Matthew 28:19
Three: "Within The Love Of Your Living Spirit" 2 Corinthians 6:16
Four: "You, Lord, Conquer All" Matthew 22:37-39
Five: "We Sing Praises To You, Lord" Judges 5:3
Six: "Your Divine Spirit" Nehemiah 8:6
Seven: "A Day That Was Made For Us" Mark 2:27-28
Eight: "Glory And Acclaim To You, Lord" 1 Corinthians 6:20
Nine: "You Hear And Answer All Prayers" Romans 15:4
Ten: "Your Divine Plan For Us" Ecclesiastes 3:1
Eleven: "Family And Friends Are True Blessings" Job 42:10-11
Twelve: "Your Love Is The Eternal Light" Psalms 23:1
Thirteen: "Only You, Lord, Have Fulfilled Our Prayers" Jeremiah 31:13
Fourteen: "You Are The Perfect Truth" Psalms 25:5
Fifteen: "Become The Marrow Of Our Strength" Hosea 14:9
Sixteen: "We Honor You, Lord" Daniel 4:37
Seventeen: "Show Us The Paths Of Mercy And Truth" Psalms 25:10
Eighteen: "Lord, The Creator Of Truth" Isaiah 40:28
Nineteen: "You Are The True Meaning Of Life" Proverbs 8:35
Twenty: "Through You, Lord, We Are Complete" Nahum 1:7
Twenty-One: "Cleanse And Enlighten Our Spirits" 2 Samuel 22:4
Twenty-Two: "May We Forever Rejoice In Our Faith" Ephesians 5:19
Twenty-Three: "May You Find Us Obedient To Your Will" 2 Chronicles 7:14
Twenty-Four: "Continually Bless Us With Fellowship" 1 John 1:7
Twenty-Five: "Creator Of All Creation" Malachi 1:11
Twenty-Six: "You Have Given Freely Of Your Love" Micah 7:19
Twenty-Seven: "Let Everyone Come Together, Lord" John 3:21
Twenty-Eight: "Your Immaculate Heart" Lamentations 5:19
Twenty-Nine: "Your Love Exists Everywhere" Genesis 1:29-30
Thirty: "Lord, May Our Spirits Overflow With Love" Psalms 118:28-29
Thirty-One: "Touch Our Hearts, Lord" Revelation 1:17-19

# February

Day: Title of blessing: Chapter and verse of inspiration:
One: "The Higher We Reach" Genesis 28:12
Two: "Allow Us To Become Warriors Of Virtue" Luke 6:19-20
Three: "Lord, Hear Us As We Pray" Joshua
Four: "We Bear Witness To Our Blessings" John 15:27
Five: "Lord, We Await The Day" 1 Chronicles 16:35
Six: "Glory Be To You, Lord" Matthew 4:4
Seven: "You Have Delivered Your Faithful, Lord" Exodus 13:3
Eight: "Lord, We Pray To You In Unspoken Words" 1 Peter 3:4
Nine: "We Exalt You In Our Prayers" 1 Chronicles 16:29
Ten: "Help Us, Lord, To Endure" Galatians 6:2
Eleven: "May Our Intentions Always Be Sincere" 2 Thessalonians 2:3
Twelve: "There Is No Other Truth But Yours" Deuteronomy 4:39
Thirteen: "Lord, We Will Venerate Your Word" 1 Thessalonians 5:14
Fourteen: "Your Love, Lord, Is All Abundant" Jude 21
Fifteen: "A World Of Eternal Peace" Ezekiel 37:26
Sixteen: "Peace In Our Neighborhoods" Leviticus 19:18
Seventeen: "Accept Our Confession Of Faith" Deuteronomy 6:5
Eighteen: "A New Dawning" Mark 16:15
Nineteen: "It Is Your Perfect Wisdom, Lord" Malachi 3:6
Twenty: "Darkness Cannot Pierce The Light" 1 John 1:5
Twenty-One: "The Lord Of All That Is" Matthew 10:32
Twenty-Two: "Lord, Bless The Family" Ephesians 3:14-15
Twenty-Three: "All Things Are Possible" Luke 17:19
Twenty-Four: "Lord, We Are As One Voice" 2 Chronicles 5:13
Twenty-Five: "How Quickly You Answer" Acts of the Apostles 2:25-26
Twenty-Six: "Lord, Help Us To Become Worthy" Psalms 18:3, 6
Twenty-Seven: "Darkness Lost To The Light" 2 Timothy 4:6-7
Twenty-Eight: "Lord, All We Really Need Is You" Revelation 19:5-7
Twenty-Nine (A prayer for Leap Year): "Lord, Grant Us Many Days" Ruth 1:16

# March

Day: Title of blessing: Chapter and verse of inspiration:

One: "A Creation That Was Created For All" Genesis 9:16-17

Two: "Sheaves Of Faithful Souls" Isaiah 58:8-9

Three: "A Heavenly Home Of Glory" 1 Samuel 2:8 and John 14:2

Four: "Teach The Truth" 2 John 4

Five: "Your Wondrous Creation Of Love" Philippians 3:20

Six: "The Gift Of Life" Ecclesiastes 5:18

Seven: "All Are Welcomed" Matthew 13:23

Eight: "Lord, We Gloriously Belong To You" Matthew 5:28 and Hebrews 11:9-10

Nine: "Through Daily Devotions, We Will Grow" 1 Kings 8:38-39

Ten: "We Belong To You, Lord" Psalms 34:3-4

Eleven: "We Have Become Pillars Of Faith" Mark 8:36

Twelve: "Send Your Guiding Light, Lord" Jeremiah 29:13

Thirteen: "We Pray, Lord, That We Will Never Falter" Jonah 4:2

Fourteen: "We Give Thanks For This Day" Esther 9:19

Fifteen: "Your Law Of Love" 2 John 5-6

Sixteen: "The Light Of The World" John 3:16

Seventeen: "Become True Reflections" 1 Samuel 12:24

Eighteen: "Lord, We Pray For A Vision" 2 Thessalonians 2:16-17

Nineteen: "Begin The Resolution Of World Strife" 2 Peter 1:2-3

Twenty: "A Visible Force Of Spiritual Energy" Ezra 3:11

Twenty-One: "Promise Of Eternal Life" Ezekiel 34:26-27

Twenty-Two: "May We Stand Perfect And Whole" James 2:5

Twenty-Three: "We Lift Our Praises To You, Lord" Psalms 34:1-2

Twenty-Four: "Lord, Let Us Mirror Your Image Of Love" Colossians 3:8-10

Twenty-Five: "We Are Never Too Lost To Be Found" John 8:31-32

Twenty-Six: "We Do Not Have To Look Very Far" Isaiah 45:6

Twenty-Seven: "The Lord Of All Creation" Psalms 100:4-5

Twenty-Eight: "May They Be Humbled" 3 John 11

Twenty-Nine: "Please, Remember Our Supplications" 2 Kings 20:3

Thirty: "Through The Lessons Of Life" Revelation 2:2-3

Thirty-One: "For All Bonded Souls" Isaiah 61:1

# April

Day: Title of blessing: Chapter and verse of inspiration:
One: "Your Creation Is A Sculptured Work Of Art" Genesis 1:27, 31
Two: "A Treasure From Heaven" Romans 8:27-28
Three: "You Are The Light Of The World" John 8:12
Four: "Lord, We Pray For Your Perfect Blessing" Titus 3:7
Five: "We Will Forever Worship" Obadiah 15
Six: "Lord, Your Gifts Are Perfect And True" Zephaniah 3:17
Seven: "Our Bond Is Sealed" Haggai 1:13, 2:4, 2:23
Eight: "Allow Your Wisdom, Lord, To Govern" Colossians 1:9-10
Nine: "Your Love Is The Power Of Life" Philemon 5-7
Ten: "Teach Us How To Forgive And Forget" Daniel 9:9
Eleven: "The Family Is Truly Blessed" Luke 15:32
Twelve: "We Call Upon You, Lord" 1 Kings 18:24, 37-38
Thirteen: "The Daily Miracles Of Life" Hebrews 2:4
Fourteen: "We Are Servants To Your Glorious Word" 1 Corinthians 7:22, 24
Fifteen: "Your Power Is Absolute" Zechariah 10:12
Sixteen: "The Lord Of All Glory And Wisdom" 1 Corinthians 2:5, 7
Seventeen: "We Exalt And Acclaim Your Excellence" 1 Samuel 2:1
Eighteen: "Your Word Of Life" 1 John 1:1-2
Nineteen: "You Understand" James 2:23
Twenty: "You Seek Those Who Are Lost" Ezekiel 34:15-16
Twenty-One: "A Oneness With All Life" Galatians 3:28
Twenty-Two: "We Will Follow Your Infinite Wisdom" Matthew 19:26
Twenty-Three: "We Enter This World With Nothing" Hebrews 3:14
Twenty-Four: "We Seek Your Truth, Lord" Job 36:4-5
Twenty-Five: "You Are The Perfect Wisdom" Proverbs 14:5-9
Twenty-Six: "Lord, Help Us To Understand" The Acts of the Apostles 2:21
Twenty-Seven: "You Are The Eternal Flame" 2 Corinthians 4:18
Twenty-Eight: "Open Their Eyes" Amos 5:8
Twenty-Nine: "Where There Is Truth, There You Are, Lord" Exodus 34:6
Thirty: "Lord, Remain With Us" Revelation 22:11

# May

Day: Title of blessing: Chapter and verse of inspiration:
One: "In The Beginning Of Time" Genesis 1:24-25
Two: "Calm Our Passions And Open Our Eyes" Ephesians 3:16, 20
Three: "Let Us Never Lose Confidence" Hebrews 10:35-36
Four: "Our Lord Of Everlasting" Amos 4:13
Five: "The Wisdom Of The Ages" James 3:17
Six: "Blessed Be Your Unbounded Holiness" Deuteronomy 7:9
Seven: "May Every Soul Be Delivered" Titus 3:5
Eight: "The Holy Spirit Will Intercede" Romans 8:24-26
Nine: "Our Faith Is Always In You, Lord" 2 Thessalonians 3:2-3
Ten: "You Are Our Refuge, Lord" 2 Samuel 22:2-3
Eleven: "Forever Abide Within Our Lives" 2 Peter 1:19, 21
Twelve: "We Are Endlessly Grateful To You" Romans 8:32
Thirteen: "A Life In Harmony With Itself" Colossians 1:14
Fourteen: "Your Word, Lord, Is Love" 1 John 4:7-8
Fifteen: "Restore And Make Whole The Shattered" 3 John 2
Sixteen: "A Constant Utterance Of Praise" Jude 24-25
Seventeen: "We Thank You, Lord, For Everything" Deuteronomy 8:3
Eighteen: "On A Mission From You, Lord" Hebrews 13:1-2
Nineteen: "With You, Nothing Is Impossible" Luke 1:36-38
Twenty: "We Search The Depths Of Our Emotions" 1 Timothy 2:7-8
Twenty-One: "We Shall Forever Maintain Our Faith" Esther 10:1-2
Twenty-Two: "Proven In Every Place" 2 Corinthians 2:14
Twenty-Three: "Life Is A Blessed Gift Of Love" Isaiah 45:17-18
Twenty-Four: "Most Gracious Lord, Receive Us" Hosea 14:2
Twenty-Five: "You Do Great Things Everyday" Joel 2:21, 26
Twenty-Six: "Hear Our Words Of Praise" Acts of the Apostles 17:27-28
Twenty-Seven: "Love Conquers All" Hebrews 13:4 and Genesis 2:24
Twenty-Eight: "Deliver Us, Lord" Exodus 6:6
Twenty-Nine: "Servants Of Your Gentleness" 2 Timothy 2:19, 24
Thirty: "Remember Those Who Have Gone Before Us" 1 John 3:1, 14
Thirty-One: "Show Us The Way, Lord" Revelation 22:16

# June

Day: Title of blessing: Chapter and verse of inspiration:

One: "Your Promises Are Forever Kept" Genesis 9:12

Two: "Lord, You Are The Rock Of Truth" Deuteronomy 32:4

Three: "You Are The Lord, Our God" Ezekiel 34:30-31

Four: "The True Power Of Peace" Exodus 15:2

Five: "We Disavow The World And Avow Your Love" Titus 2:12-13

Six: "Please, Lord, Hear Our Endless Prayers" 1 Thessalonians 5:17

Seven: "Change The Direction Of All Nations" Amos 5:14-15

Eight: "Your Love, Lord, Is Always With Us" Nehemiah 1:5

Nine: "Lord, We Will Never Waver" Ephesians 3:8-9

Ten: "Faithfully Obedient To Your Word" Daniel 7:27

Eleven: "The Footpaths Of Our Destinies" Joel 2:8

Twelve: "We Aspire To Serve Your Will On Earth, Lord" Ezra 9:8

Thirteen: "We Pray For Spiritual Charity" Matthew 10:8

Fourteen: "Lord, We Have Chosen Your Way In Life" Isaiah 58:11

Fifteen: "Love And Reverence Towards You, Lord" 2 Corinthians 5:1, 6-7

Sixteen: "Lord, Shower The World" Habakkuk 3:2, 18

Seventeen: "Lord, We Seek Your Love And Protection" 2 Chronicles 15:2

Eighteen: "Grant Us Wisdom Of The Heart" Zechariah 8:16-17

Nineteen: "We Humble Ourselves Before You, Lord" Isaiah 23:9

Twenty: "Your Triumphant Love" Acts of the Apostles 20:24

Twenty-One: "The Season Of Fulfillment" Luke 21:30-31

Twenty-Two: "Your Great Love" Joshua 22:5

Twenty-Three: "In Universal Peace And Harmony" Philemon 3, 12, 17

Twenty-Four: "All Life, Everywhere, Gives Praise" Habakkuk 2:14

Twenty-Five: "The Child Is The Seed Of Hope" Zechariah 8:12

Twenty-Six: "Heal Us, Lord" Jeremiah 17:13-14

Twenty-Seven: "Your Spirit Is Continually With Us" 2 Corinthians 3:16-17

Twenty-Eight: "We Are Shepherded By Your Goodness" Micah 7:7

Twenty-Nine: "Everything Occurs At Its Own Time" Ecclesiastes 3:11

Thirty: "You Continue Forever" Revelation 1:8

# July

Day: Title of blessing: Chapter and verse of inspiration:

One: "Protect And Proclaim The Miracle Of Life" Genesis 9:2-3

Two: "The Fullness Of Our Faith" 2 John 8-9

Three: "There Is Love In The Whole Of The Universe" Deuteronomy 4:29-31

Four: "Willful Servants Of Your Supreme Will" 1 Timothy 2:1-4

Five: "Guide Our Intentions, Lord" Job 33:16-17

Six: "Holy! Holy! Holy Are You, Lord!" Acts of the Apostles 4:24

Seven: "We Rejoice In Our Hearts" Mark 10:21-22

Eight: "Forgive Us Our Weaknesses, Lord" 1 Corinthians 2:5

Nine: "The Family Will Come Together" Ephesians 2:18-19

Ten: "Calm Their Troubled Spirits" Luke 6:27-28

Eleven: "Our Lord Of Perfect Compassion" Mark 11:24

Twelve: "Watch Over The Innocence Of The Newborn" Exodus 23:7

Thirteen: "Wonderful Blessings Of Friendship" Proverbs 18:24

Fourteen: "Love Abounds In Our Lives" Philippians 1:9

Fifteen: "From Generation To Generation" Daniel 4:3

Sixteen: "Make Calm The Storms Of Frustration" Lamentations 3:21-22

Seventeen: "Shield Our Loved Ones" Ephesians 6:15-16

Eighteen: "Lord, We Rejoice In Your Righteous Authority" Leviticus 26:3-4, 9

Nineteen: "Within Our Spiritual Lives" Romans 6:23

Twenty: "There Are No Shadows In The True Light" John 1:4-5

Twenty-One: "Your Spirit Touches Our Lives" Malachi 4:2

Twenty-Two: "The Absolute Fulfillment Of Joy" Philippians 2:1-3

Twenty-Three: "Living In Your Words Of Peace" Numbers 6:24-26

Twenty-Four: "We Pray To You, Lord, Our Souls To Keep" 1 Corinthians 4:4, 7

Twenty-Five: "Born Again" John 3:3

Twenty-Six: "The Perfect And True Destination" 1 Peter 3:10-12

Twenty-Seven: "The Whispers Of Innocent Praises" Ephesians 1:3, 11

Twenty-Eight: "We Will Find Your Voice Within" 2 Kings 22:19

Twenty-Nine: "We Have Completely Turned To You, Lord" Jonah 3:10

Thirty: "Help The World To Understand" Deuteronomy 30:15-16

Thirty-One: "Through Zealous Love" Revelation 3:16, 19

# August

Day: Title of blessing: Chapter and verse of inspiration:
One: "Guided By Your Glowing Radiance" Genesis 49:18
Two: "Bless This Simple Temple Of Faith" 2 Corinthians 6:16
Three: "The Creation Of Love" Galatians 5:22-23
Four: "One Table, Together In One Common Faith" 1 Corinthians 10:21
Five: "We Believe In Faith" Galatians 3:22 And Matthew 17:20
Six: "Your Sheltering Arms" John 11:25-26
Seven: "There Is No Greater Authority" Nehemiah 9:5 and Exodus 20:7
Eight: "Towers Of Compassion" Luke 20:17
Nine: "Everyday Miracles" Deuteronomy 29:2-6
Ten: "Children Of Faith" 2 John 1-3
Eleven: "Your Love, Lord, Remains Constant" Micah 6:8
Twelve: "We Declare The Glory Of Your Compassion" Judges 5:31
Thirteen: "Fill The Void In Their Hearts" Acts of the Apostles 26:18 and John 13:34
Fourteen: "Uncertainties Will Cast Shadows" Luke 11:17
Fifteen: "We Follow No Other" Luke 4:8
Sixteen: "Greet One Another With Peace" 1 Peter 5:14
Seventeen: "You Will Always Provide" Luke 18:27
Eighteen: "Our Purpose On Earth" Romans 9:17
Nineteen: "We Are Faithful And True Believers" Joshua 24:14
Twenty: "Your Divine Words Will Fulfill" 1 Thessalonians 2:12-13
Twenty-One: "All Time Is Of Your Design" Psalms 119:108-109
Twenty-Two: "The Rewards Of Trust" Ruth 2:12
Twenty-Three: "An Edifice Of Goodness" Hebrews 11:32-34
Twenty-Four: "True Blessings Of Mercy" Acts of the Apostles 8:22
Twenty-Five: "You Are The Lord Of Love" Ezekiel 11:19-20
Twenty-Six: "Never Render Empty Promises" James 5:12
Twenty-Seven: "We Have Direction And Promise" Acts of the Apostles 27:23-24, 44
Twenty-Eight: "We Greatly Praise You" 1 Corinthians 10:13
Twenty-Nine: "Your Word Will Endure Forever" 1 Peter 1:24-25
Thirty: "Lord, We Thank You For Everything" Hebrews 13:15
Thirty-One: "Victory Is Yours, Lord" Revelation 6:2

# September

Day: Title of blessing: Chapter and verse of inspiration:
One: "The Power Of Your Word" Genesis 24:26-27
Two: "The True Path Of Life" Proverbs 4:11, 18
Three: "Lord, There Is Much To Marvel" Mark 10:6-8
Four: "All Power Is Given" Romans 13:1
Five: "You, Lord, Are Eternity" 1 Corinthians 15:52
Six: "Bless Our Young People" Leviticus 10:10-11
Seven: "Honor And Receive Others" Galatians 5:14
Eight: "The Delights Of Mercy" Ephesians 4:31
Nine: "You, Lord, Are Holy" 1 Peter 1:16
Ten: "We Shall Reap What We Sow" Galatians 6:7
Eleven: "Love Dwells Within Love" 1 Chronicles 16:8
Twelve: "You Stand Alone In Greatness" 1 Chronicles 17:19-20
Thirteen: "The Wisdom Of Scripture" 2 Samuel 7:28-29
Fourteen: "True Love Offers True Forgiveness" Matthew 6:14
Fifteen: "The Lessons Of Your Love" 2 Thessalonians 2:13
Sixteen: "Gifts From The Holy Spirit" 1 Corinthians 12:1, 3
Seventeen: "Purify Our Hearts" 2 Chronicles 29:18
Eighteen: "In Their Innocence" Isaiah 11:6
Nineteen: "Hosanna In The Highest" Luke 19:40
Twenty: "The Season Of Maturity" Acts of the Apostles 14:17
Twenty-One: "Comfort Us With Your Compassion" Psalms 27:8-9
Twenty-Two: "Your Path Of Righteousness" 2 Samuel 22:2 and Revelation 3:12
Twenty-Three: "Seek Goodness And Virtue" Daniel 2:20-21
Twenty-Four: "Circle Of Love" James 5:16
Twenty-Five: "The God Of All" Ephesians 4:5-6
Twenty-Six: "They Will Find The Light" 1 John 2:10-11
Twenty-Seven: "No Light Shines Brighter" Ephesians 5:13-14
Twenty-Eight: "Family And Friends" John 15:12-14
Twenty-Nine: "Our Spirits Are Restored" Micah 7:8
Thirty: "You Are The Power And The Glory" Revelation 4:11

# October

Day: Title of blessing: Chapter and verse of inspiration:
One: "Guardians Of Their Care" Genesis 1:28
Two: "Your Word Has Delivered Us" Jeremiah 20:13
Three: "Be Thankful For Every Blessing" 2 Kings 19:15
Four: "How Enduring Your Love Is, Lord" Numbers 14:18
Five: "Pour Out Your Blessings, Lord" Jeremiah 26:13
Six: "Lord, Your Love Is Forever" 2 Thessalonians 1:11
Seven: "Increase Our Wisdom, Lord" Proverbs 3:35
Eight: "The Power Of Prayer" James 5:15
Nine: "In The Steps Of Your Righteousness" Proverbs 12:28
Ten: "Holy And Divine Is Your Glorious Name" 1 Chronicles 16:10-11
Eleven: "Immersed In Your Heavenly Love" 1 Corinthians 12:13
Twelve: "A True Reflection Of Your Goodness" 2 Corinthians 3:18
Thirteen: "You Are The Eternal Holiness" Habakkuk 1:12
Fourteen: "In The Total Radiance Of Pure Light" Job 22:27
Fifteen: "Created Within Our Souls" Obadiah 3-4
Sixteen: "Only You, Lord, Can Intervene" Isaiah 42:16
Seventeen: "Blessed Are Your Gifts That Heal" 2 Samuel 22:7
Eighteen: "Your Precious And Perfect Love" 1 Chronicles 16:34
Nineteen: "Your Power, Lord, Radiates Truth" Jude 9
Twenty: "Bless Our Household" Proverbs 3:33
Twenty-One: "In Your Name And Glory, Lord" 1 John 5:1
Twenty-Two: "You Are God Eternal" 1 Timothy 1:17
Twenty-Three: "Through Every Moment Of Time" 2 Peter 3:8
Twenty-Four: "The Way Of The Soul" John 14:6
Twenty-Five: "The Circle Of Faith" Psalms 5:12
Twenty-Six: "You, Lord, Are The Giver Of Truth" Daniel 2:22-23
Twenty-Seven: "If It Were Not For You, Lord" Solomon 1:1, 2:1
Twenty-Eight: "Reflections Of All That Is Righteous" 1 Corinthians 15:49
Twenty-Nine: "We Beseech Your Mercy" 14:19-20
Thirty: "God Of All Redemption And Salvation" Lamentations 3:25-26
Thirty-One: "You Are The Lord Of Holy Truth" Revelation 7:12

# November

Day: Title of blessing: Chapter and verse of inspiration:

One: "Through Faith In Your Spirit" Genesis 1:1-2

Two: "All Futures Begin Today" Deuteronomy 4:10

Three: "True Word Of Grace" Deuteronomy 15:7, 11

Four: "Through The Darkened Barriers"

Five: "To A New Freedom" Luke 1:78-79

Six: "Your Word Is Never Broken" Numbers 30:2

Seven: "Fill Their Spirits To Capacity" Daniel 9:18

Eight: "Our Lamp Unto The Darkness" 2 Samuel 22:29 and Isaiah 45:2

Nine: "Together As One, In One Belief" Exodus 24:3

Ten: "The Truth Is Always Right" Mark 10:15 and Deuteronomy 4:13

Eleven: "The Armor Of Our Righteousness" Ephesians 6:10-11

Twelve: "We Attest To Our Belief" John 10:41-42

Thirteen: "In Faith, We Trust" Job 24:22

Fourteen: "Forever Shall Your Power Reign" Exodus 15:18

Fifteen: "You Touch Each Life" 1 Peter 3:8-9

Sixteen: "All Paths Lead Directly To You!" Matthew 3:3

Seventeen: "Defeat The Enemies Of Truth" Colossians 1:16

Eighteen: "Given A Special Gift" Daniel 1:17

Nineteen: "Make Our Hearts Pure And Good" 2 Peter 3:18

Twenty: "Award Us Peace Of Mind" Romans 12:19

Twenty-One: "You Are The Crowned Glory" Jeremiah 4:2

Twenty-Two: "We Have Humbled Our Hearts" James 4:10

Twenty-Three: "Our Past Generations" Ezekiel 18:4

Twenty-Four: "Show Compassion And Tolerance" Zechariah 7:9-10

Twenty-Five: "Let All Conflict End" Esther 9:22

Twenty-Six: "Lord, Enable Us To Grow As Individuals" 2 Chronicles 20:21

Twenty-Seven: "Our Fears Are Conquered" Nahum 1:3

Twenty-Eight: "Lord, You Transcend Time And Space" Exodus 15:11

Twenty-Nine: "Your Benevolent Goodness" Ephesians 5:20

Thirty: "King Of Kings" Revelation 19:16

# December

Day: Title of Blessing: Chapter and verse of inspiration:
One: "May The Quest For Peace Begin" Genesis 4:8-9
Two: "May We Continue To Spiritually Grow" Proverbs 3:1-2
Three: "Blessed Are The Moments Of Truth" Luke 1:46-47
Four: "Whatever You Bless, Is Blessed Forever" 1 Chronicles 17:27
Five: "We Confess This Truth As Absolute" 1 John 4:2
Six: "Judge The Worthiness Of Our Needs" 1 Timothy 4:10
Seven: "In You, We Trust" Numbers 15:28
Eight: "You Are All That We Need" Philippians 4:19
Nine: "In Your Name, Lord, There Is Victory" 1 Chronicles 29:10-11
Ten: "The Will Of Your Holy Spirit" Acts of the Apostles 2:4
Eleven: "In The Name Of Your Love" Isaiah 65:25
Twelve: "Your Eternal Power" Romans 1:20
Thirteen: "From Darkness To Light" Deuteronomy 32:39
Fourteen: "In Your Name And For Your Glory" Romans 1:4-5
Fifteen: "Your Words Of Life" Colossians 3:16
Sixteen: "The Heavenly Chimes Of Joy" Deuteronomy 30:2
Seventeen: "Your Evangelizing Love" Mark 1:17
Eighteen: "Love Is Unconditional" Haggai 1:5, 2:5
Nineteen: "The Blessing Of Innocence" 1 Timothy 4:12
Twenty: "The Season Of Challenge" 1 Kings 8:57-58
Twenty-One: "We Will Follow You" Matthew 19:21
Twenty-Two: "True And Perfect Adoration" Psalms 51:10-11
Twenty-Three: "Home Again For The Holidays" Acts of the Apostles 20:35
Twenty-Four: "We Await The Birth Of Peace" Daniel 7:14
Twenty-Five: "Peace On Earth" Luke 2:13-14
Twenty-Six: "Fill The World Forevermore" 1 John 4:18
Twenty-Seven: "Lord, You Chose Us" Deuteronomy 4:32
Twenty-Eight: "We Denounce All Worldly Possessions" Matthew 6:24 and 2 Corinthians 4:15
Twenty-Nine: "Your Benevolent Spirit" Joel 2:12-13
Thirty: "The Word Of Your Anointed Love" 1 Timothy 1:4-5
Thirty-One: "Gathered Together Under One Roof" Revelation 21:4

# January One: "We Seek Renewed Direction"

(As inspired from Genesis 1:5 and Romans 15:15)

Lord Jesus, hear our prayer …

Boldly, we step forward into a new year of Hope and resolutions, and we, as true believers in our Lord Jesus, welcome, once again, the opportunity to challenge ourselves as Good Christians; for the most difficult resolve in the world, is to become a True Christian, in that Absolute Goodness requires total forbearance of heart, mind, and soulful obedience to His Glorious Word, and to always follow in the Footsteps of Our Lord Jesus Christ!

Blessed are you, O Lord, for creating the Creation! Lord God, you made the evening and the morning and you called it the first day. And so, on this special occasion, the first day of this New Year, we joyfully pray for the Spirit of your Holy Guidance to direct us throughout the coming year. Lord Eternal, may every day and every new month bring us the Blessings of Peace on earth.

Help us to resolve our difficulties and our dissatisfactions that we may have for any family member, or friend, or stranger. Inspire us to learn and to understand the true meaning of "Good Will" towards all. And as we seek a renewed direction from you, Our Lord Christ, guide us to become of one accord with your Heavenly Saints that we too may learn to follow your Ways of Love and Forgiveness here on earth. Allow each day of the new year to bring us closer to you, Lord Jesus, and closer to one another as family or friend. And may the new year also bring about a jubilant awareness of our own personal Christian faith.

Now and throughout the year, Lord Jesus, we will resolve to always seek your Heavenly Blessings. Now and throughout all life, Lord Jesus Christ, we will pray for your Divine Intervention into our lives. And as it was in the beginning of days, is now, and will be forevermore, we individually give thanks to you for your Beautiful Love that is constantly with us, Our Lord and God of Creation; for we give continual praise to your Magnificent Spirit of Salvation: Blessed are all True Believers in your Hallowed Existence!

Amen …

Chapter and verse that inspired prayer:

Genesis 1:5     And God called the light Day, and the darkness He called Night. And the evening and the Morning were the first day.

Romans 15:15    Nevertheless, brethren, I have written the more boldly unto you in some sort, as putting you in mind, because of the grace that is given to me of God.

# January Two: "Your Magnificent Heart"

(As inspired from Matthew 28:19)

Lord Jesus, hear our prayer …

Our Lord and God, we extol your Immaculate Perfection, and in our sincerest acclaim for you, we hold your Great Glory in the highest of esteem! Through generations and generations of time, your Glorious Goodness remains prevalent, your Unbounded Love for us is constant, and your Miraculous Mercy far exceeds our expectations! As faithful Christians, may we always be worthy enough to understand and worship the Divine Power of your Triumvirate Godhead that eternally rules the heavens above and the earth below and all who abide within! Lord Jesus, allow the whole world to gain and experience your Wonderful Wisdom of Kindness so that this Righteous Knowledge may be imparted to all future generations yet to come: Blest is the Trinity of The Father, The Son, and The Holy Spirit, all of Whom are One, even unto eternity!

Thank you, Lord Jesus, for our blessings that we receive daily! We are most grateful to you for our spiritual gifts and for the unceasing care that you bestow upon us from the Bounty of your Magnificent Heart! Our Precious Lord Jesus Christ, you are worthy of all honor and acclaim! And with joyful praise on our lips, we proclaim and praise this wondrous knowledge to the world and to the heavens above: In the name of The Father, The Son, and The Holy Ghost, we ask of you, Our Most Hallowed One, that you will send an Outpouring of Compassion unto this good earth, into all nations, baptizing every human alive with the Great Love of your Divine Spirit!

Amen …

Chapter and verse that inspired prayer:

Matthew 28:13    Go ye therefore, and teach all nations, baptizing them in the name of the Father, and of the Son, and of the Holy Ghost:

# January Three: "Within The Love Of Your Living Spirit"

### (As inspired from 2 Corinthians 6:16)

Lord Jesus, hear our prayer …

We are wonderfully created in your image, Lord of Creation, which makes all of us sons and daughters of Our Living God; but we are also in constant rejection of our Heavenly Father's Will by following our own will, and it is from here, resides the division of heaven and earth, of Spirit and flesh, and of Eternal Life and death! Enlighten us, Lord God, and hear our supplication: It is our hope and prayer, Dear Lord, that you will forever abide within our hearts, continually shepherd our thoughts, and always be present within our lives; and then, Our Lord Jesus Christ, we will become living temples for your Most Holy Spirit to dwell.

Each and every day belongs to you, Lord Jesus, and everyday we will give thanks to you for our health and happiness! We pray that you will hear our praises on this day and on all the days of the coming year: Bless those who love you and adore you with all of their might! And with resounding praise in our voices, we proudly confess, Lord Jesus Christ, that we love and adore you with all of our spiritual presence, our physical strength, and our mental awareness!

By your name, Our Good Lord Jesus Christ, are your faithful followers called! O Lord, as the sky shelters the earth, as the house shelters the person, and as the body shelters the soul, happy are we, as Christians, to reside within the Pure Love of your Living Spirit; for truly, Lord of Heaven and earth, we have found the Absolute Essence of your Salvation dwelling within our own hearts; blessed is your Ever Compassionate Heart of Mercy!

Amen …

Chapter and verse that inspired prayer:

2 Corinthians 6:16    And what agreement hath the temple of God with idols? For ye are the temple of the living God; as God hath said, I will dwell in them, and walk in them: and I will be their God, and they shall be my people.

# January Four: "You, Lord, Conquer All"

(As inspired from Matthew 22:37-39)

Lord Jesus, hear our prayer ...

Pure faith is the absolute conquest of all doubt! We trust only in your Judgment, Lord Jesus; for human justice is frail, but Divine Justice is Spiritual Knowledge that is pure! And in our hearts, and from our souls, and within our minds, we firmly avow, Lord of Mercy, that we love you and that we trust in no other Power but you! And just as the sun overcomes the evening, our deep faith in you, Lord Preserver, allows us to overcome unfounded fears that we may have gained for others. Help us, Our Lord of Salvation, to develop true confidence in other people and to resolve our unwarranted feelings of intolerance towards one another. As the light conquers the darkness, and as love conquers adversity, you, O Lord, conquer all; and we pray to you, Lord Christ, that you will enlighten our minds and our spirits to recognize the goodness that is in every person, everywhere! And through your Eternal Wisdom, we will learn to pierce the dark shadows of our own spiritual ignorance as we step forward into the Light of your Holy Truth! Resolve, dissolve, and conquer our fears, Lord Jesus Christ! For joyfully, we have opened our eyes and our hearts to the truth of your Great and Wonderful Commandment that asks us to love God and to love one another as we love ourselves, with every molecule of heart, mind, and soul! Dear Lord, hear our prayer request: We are faithful believers who are completely enraptured with our wonderful faith of Christianity; bless us and all who absolutely follow your Word of Compassion every moment of life!

Amen ...

Chapter and verse that inspired prayer:

Matthew 22:37-39   Jesus said unto him, Thou shalt love the Lord thy God with all thy heart, and with all thy soul, and with all thy mind. (38) This is the first and great commandment. (39) And the second is like unto it, thou shalt love thy neighbor as thyself.

# January Five: "We Sing Praises To You, Lord"

(As inspired from Judges 5:3)

Lord Jesus, hear our prayer ...

There is within every human being, O Lord, a beautiful soul that was formed by your Hallowed Hands of Creation! And we not only pray for ourselves, but also for the countless multitudes of faithful people that exist in this world and who adore you and praise you daily for their lives and their many blessings! From every continent on earth, there are true followers of your Holy Word, Lord God, and will remain thankful and honorable to you, Lord Jesus Christ, until the end of time! Please hear our prayers. Lord of Heaven and Earth: From out of the midst of every nation, hold fast in your Loving Embrace all those who love you and who fervently follow your Commandments! Save us. Lord Christ, from all destructive forces, whether it is constructed by human hands or it comes from nature; please, Lord Jesus, champion your worldwide ministry of Christians and inspire all nations to make amends with one another in order that we may all live and worship you in Godly Peace, surrounded by a loving fellowship of family, friends, and even strangers!

Great is the Charity of your Heart, and Blest are all who receive of it! Lord God, the world and all of creation exalts your Holy Name and celebrates the wonderful gifts of your Bountiful Love! And in our own words of thankfulness, Lord Jesus, we give all glory and honor to you for our Christian faith and for all the blessings that you have so graciously bestowed upon us. When our hearts are filled with joy, we give thanks to you, Lord Christ! When our spirits are uplifted, we sing praises to you, Lord God! And when we are filled with the Glorious Spirit of your Love, we hear no other voice but yours, Lord Jesus Christ Our Savior!

Amen ...

Chapter and verse that inspired prayer:

Judges 5:3     Hear, o ye kings; give ear, O ye princes; I, even I, will sing unto the LORD; I will sing praise to the LORD God of Israel.

# January Six: "Your Divine Greatness"

## (As inspired from Nehemiah 8:6)

Lord Jesus, hear our prayer …

Praise upon praise, do we offer you, Our Lord and God, for all that we have! We believe and we testify that everything good comes through you and from your Infinite and Glorious Compassion, Lord Christ. And only through your Boundless Glory, are we able to realize and accomplish our most challenging goals in life. Great is your Glory, Lord Jesus, and greatly have we been blessed! With lifted hands, we worship you, O Lord! And with bowed heads, we show our steadfast reverence for you, Lord Jesus Christ, because, your Hallowed Magnificence is Eternal and Divine and redeems all who ask for your Cleansing Mercy!

Wherever and whenever we gather in your name, Lord Jesus, we proclaim our spiritual salvation as a Heavenly Gift from your Precious and Sacred Heart; for we realize that Eternal Life is not possible without full forgiveness of all transgression, and that nothing miraculous in life will ever be achieved without you. And without your Profound Presence in our lives, Lord Christ, nothing lasting may ever be attained. Surely, all who understand and believe in your Divine Greatness, Lord Jesus Christ, will forever be blessed by you! Therefore, we ask that you bless us, Our Lord and God, bless our family and friends, and bless all people, throughout this wonderful world, who proudly worship and honor your Name! And now, into your Protective Care, Our Risen One, do we place our total well-being and spiritual safekeeping! Receive us, Dear God, as you receive our soulful words of adoration: All Holy and Good are you, Our Great Lord of Salvation, and with all adoration, we Revere and Love You!

Amen …

Chapter and verse that inspired prayer:

Nehemiah 8:6    And Ezra blessed the LORD, the great God. And all the people answered, Amen, Amen with lifting up their hands: and they bowed their heads, and worshiped the LORD with their faces to the ground.

# January Seven: "A Day That Was Made For Us"

### (As inspired from Mark 2:27-28)

Lord Jesus, hear our prayer ...

Throughout your Heavenly Kingdom, there is a continuous and glorious praise of happiness and thanksgiving for the Blessing of Eternal Life! And, here on earth, we too worship you, Our Lord and God, for every blessing that we receive!

In the beginning, we know and believe that when the heavens and the earth were finished, you rested on the Seventh Day, O Heavenly Father: Blessed is your Wisdom, Lord of Creation, and how wonderful your day of Sabbath is! Dear Lord, you have created for us, a day that we may call our own. A day to give all the glory and all the power to you, Our Lord Jesus Christ Most High! It is a day to reflect and to meditate upon your Glorious Works! For us, believers of the Sabbath, this is truly a time of spiritual thanksgiving and a time to remember all the Good Blessings that you have bestowed upon us as a people, as a nation, and as faithful, individual Christian followers of your Most Immaculate Word of Life!

Because we love you and respect you so much, Lord God, we will forever bear witness in mind, in body, and in spirit to your Praiseworthy Intervention into our lives. And through a total adoration for you, Lord Jesus, we will give thanks to you for this day, a day of rest and worship that we have received from your Bountiful Love. May we forever honor you in praise and in prayer, Lord God, as The Son of Man, on this, the Seventh Day of the new year, a day to recall our blessings, a day that was made for us; a holy day of remembrance for the entire world to cherish and honor into infinity! All glory and praise to Our Lord of the Sabbath, to you, Lord Jesus Christ!

Amen ...

Chapter and verse that inspired prayer:

Mark 2:27-28    And he said unto them, The sabbath was made for man, and not man for the sabbath: (28) Therefore the Son of man is Lord also of the sabbath.

# January Eight: "Glory and Acclaim To You, Lord"

## (As inspired from 1 Corinthians 6:20)

Lord Jesus, hear our prayer …

Worthy are you in heaven and on earth, for our very souls were redeemed by God the Father with the payment of a Perfect and Incorruptible Life, your life, Our Emmanuel Christ Lord Jesus! And because of your Unselfish Sacrifice, we, as humans, must also pray for one another: O Lord, because their futures and destinies are shrouded in obscurity and doubt, we pray for all people who do not wholeheartedly accept you, Lord Christ, as their Personal Savior! They see, but do not believe; they hear, but are unable to understand; therefore, we pray for their souls and for their futures and for the destinies of all humans who refuse to see and hear your Wonderful Message of Salvation!

Thank you, Lord, for saving our lives; through your Incorruptible Death, our corruptible souls were released from all bondage by the ransom of your Innocent Blood and Life! Receive us, Lord Eternal, as members of one family, united under one belief that you are The Only Way to The Father! Accept our praises, Lord Jesus, as one voice, committed to the Endless Glorification of your Perfect Goodness. Lord of Purity, we are all members of your Immaculate Spirit; for you are the Heart and the Soul of our Christian faith! And only through a total commitment of mind, body, and spirit, do we extol you, Lord Jesus Christ, as The Absolute and Complete Fulfillment of our spiritual and physical lives!

Lord Jesus, we praise you with undying faith; for what our eyes can see, our spirits give continual praise! And for what our ears can hear, our voices loudly ring out, giving all glory and acclaim to you, Lord Jesus Christ, Our Everlasting God of Perpetual Love and Mercy.

Amen …

Chapter and verse that inspired prayer:

1 Corinthians 6:20    For ye are bought with a price: therefore glorify God in your body, and in your spirit, which are God's.

# January Nine: "You Hear And Answer All Prayers"

(As inspired from Romans 15:4)

Lord Jesus, hear our prayer …

Our Heavenly Father, make us courageous in all things: Remove any unfounded fear that may haunt the heart and allow doubt and suspicion to enter and thrive; for only through constant and patient faith in your Sacred Word, Lord God, have we come to know that Hope and Comfort are truly obtainable by the faithful soul. Lord of Scripture, because we believe in your Word of Life, we know that you have the power to enrich all lives. Because only you, Lord Jesus Christ, can change the destinies of those who actually believe and accept in the reality of true faith as a testimony throughout chapter and verse of the Old and New Testaments; which were personally witnessed through the eyes of God's Holy Prophets!

O Lord, there is such great joy in life knowing that you hear and answer all prayers of deep sincerity; and through a personal Christian commitment of long-suffering, we realize that all things in life are possible through total faith. And only through the attainment of pure faith, will all physical and spiritual needs be atoned for according to your Glorious Will. Therefore, Lord Jesus, it is our hope and our prayer that you will continually strengthen our Christian faith and increase our patience in life. Please, Lord Jesus Our Savior, now and forevermore, help us to remain steadfast and faithful to our individual convictions that we have spiritually vowed to keep in our personal relationship with you! Allow no one to deviate from the Truth of the Gospels nor lead a single soul astray; permit us, instead, to forever remain fixed in our ardent belief that through you, Christ Our King, all things are possible!

Amen …

Chapter and verse that inspired prayer:

Romans 15:4   For whatever things were written aforetime were written for our learning, that we though patience and comfort of the scriptures might have hope.

# January Ten: "Your Divine Plan For Us"

(As inspired from Ecclesiastes 3:1)

Lord Jesus, hear our prayer …

Life is not an accident, and no person on earth is born spiritually inept! Blessed is your Heavenly Plan for all creation, Lord; for our lives, as with all life, is truly Sanctified by the Holy Design of your Perfect Understanding. And although your Vision and True Intention for our individual lives may be hidden from our eyes, everything under the sun and in the heavens has meaning and purpose; and all we have to do as Christians, is accept! And just as the sun will set in the evening and rise again in the morning, we are just as certain of your Divine Plan for us! Lord Jesus Christ, hear our prayers and guide us along the proper path of our true meaning and reason for our existence in life: Prepare our way in life, O Lord, clear our future courses of all obstructions, detours, and failures!

Just as newborns naturally accept the world in which they are born, without knowledge and without question, we too, as faithful followers, must learn to reason our spiritual lives through the attainment of Pure Faith in you, Our God Almighty! O Lord, that everyone may continue to follow the Way of your Heavenly Inspirations, permit your Divine Spirit to guide the heart and fill the soul of every spiritually passionate person that so desires to complete their mission on earth! Lord Jesus, your design and resolution for us in life is Flawless, it is of Perfect Accord; Divine Inspiration that is set for all ages, for all lives, and for all generations, forever and ever, in a world without end. Hear us, Our Lord of All Truth, for we trust and we believe in your Eternal Wisdom to direct our individual lives and destinies towards the Unflawed Purpose of your Unconquerable Will! Help us to succeed in every way; help us to find you in our lives everyday, Lord Jesus Christ Our Eternal Life!

Amen …

Chapter and verse that inspired prayer:

Ecclesiastes 3:1   To everything there is a season, and a time to every purpose under the heaven:

# January Eleven: "Family And Friends Are True Blessings"

(As inspired from Job 42:10-11)

Lord Jesus, hear our prayer …

During your mission on earth, Lord Jesus, when you lived among your chosen people, you ate and feasted with publicans, transgressors, and various dignitaries, and all were called friends by you; all who would listen to your Word and were willing to follow the teachings of your Gentle Way! Lord Christ, we too pray for the well-being of our family and friends. And whenever we welcome family or friend into our homes and into our hearts we are actually embracing your Divine Gift of Kindness; for family and friends are true blessings, Heavenly Gifts of Compassion from you, Lord Jesus Christ; and for this, we are eternally grateful!

O Lord, forever and ever, our hearts and our homes are open to you. Please, Our Lord and Christ, reside and dwell within our existence, and there, remain forever as the Greatest Blessing that our human lives could ever receive! And with you in our lives, in our hearts, and in our destinies, we will find Everlasting Peace within our souls!

Through family and friends, we find harmony and security in life. With the love of family and friends, we find accord and happiness in our individual lives. And when relatives and neighbors, throughout the world, gather together in your Blessed Name, Lord Jesus Christ, you are glorified in all corners of the world! Blest are you, The Lamb of God, He, who comes in the name of Peace and Friendship!

Amen …

Chapter and verse that inspired prayer:

Job 42:10-11   And the LORD turned the captivity of Job, when he prayed for his friends: also the LORD gave Job twice as much as he had before. (11) Then came there unto him all his brethren, and all his sisters, and all they had been of his acquaintance before, and did eat bread, with him in his house: and they bemoaned him, and comforted him over all the evil that the LORD had brought upon him: every man also gave him a piece of money, and every one an earring of gold.

# January Twelve: "Your Love Is The Eternal Light"

(As inspired from Psalms 23:1)

Lord Jesus, hear our prayer ...

Blessed are you, Our Guardian and Good Shepherd of Life! Lord Jesus, never, do we feel alone, for you are always with us, watching over us, protecting our very footsteps, guiding us through the darkness, shepherding our spirits as we journey through life; and every person and every soul that accepts you, Lord God, as their Personal Savior, becomes a part of your faithful fold, forever enclosed in the safety of your love. For whenever we are filled with doubt and depression, we know that your Spiritual Strength will enshroud and protect us. When the long shadows of despair close in upon us, we know that your Lamp of Love will light the way. And when we feel lost and alone, we know that you will always find us, Lord Jesus Christ, to show us the Way to the Calm Waters of Compassion, beside the Promising Pastures of Spiritual Fulfillment!

From the beginning of time, Lord Jehovah, your faithful have praised and blessed your Supreme Existence, for your Love is the Eternal Light that radiates throughout creation, and we realize that you will never abandon us; because only we, through freewill and poor choices, can remove ourselves from the Safety and Protection of your Glory! Blessed are you, Lord Jesus Christ, for your Magnificent Radiance will forever lead us into the Light of Our Salvation; and Blessed are the Beckoning Fires of Our Creator that call us to find redemption by the Peaceful Shores of Forgiveness and Deliverance! We ask of you, please, gather your chosen on earth, Our Good Shepherd, and lead us to the Promised Land of our Heart's Desire, where we will wander no more.

Amen ...

Chapter and verse that inspired prayer:

Psalms 23:1    THE LORD is my shepherd; I shall not want.

# January Thirteen: "Only You, Lord, Have Fulfilled Our Prayers"
### (As inspired from Jeremiah 31:13)

Lord Jesus, hear our prayer …

When all transgression is forgiven, the shadows of sadness quickly wither into the Light; for our hearts and souls are uplifted and magnified by the Wonderful Virtue of the Holy Spirit that exists in everything Good! Blest are you, O Lord, because, your Love and Joy always brings happiness to the human spirit, and throughout the world, all the adoration and acclamation belong to you, Lord Jesus Christ! You have turned away all sorrow in our lives, Dear Lord, and we rejoice in your Word! Our spirits leap and dance with the greatest of joy for the continued blessings that you have so generously bestowed upon us. Your wondrous gifts of life, love, and spiritual liberty gives us reason to pause daily and acclaim your Absolute Existence throughout the creation: Our Never Ending Lord, life's praise and adulation are constantly echoed throughout the Heavenly Heavens of your Kingdom Above and on your Earthly Kingdom below! For all life adores you, because, all life is adorned by your Complete Compassion for Goodness!

Our Bountiful Lord, your Unselfish Goodness and Abundance are vast and boundless! Beyond our needs, beyond our expectations, only you, O Lord, have fulfilled our prayers! We are in spiritual oneness with you, Lord Jesus Christ, and we are together in our concurrence for you as Our Lord of Infinite Power; and now, we celebrate our blessings of life, for in the heavenly unity of love, we know and understand that all life is as one, together in harmony with the creation and its Creator! And if the trees could sing and the mountains rejoice, then all of earth and the universe would immediately resound its jubilation for you, Lord Jesus, in a loud and continuous exultation of living and loving praise!

Amen …

Chapter and verse that inspired prayer:

Jeremiah 31:13    Then shall the virgin rejoice in the dance, both young men and old together: for I will turn their mourning into joy, and will comfort them, and make them rejoice from their sorrow.

# January Fourteen: "You Are The Perfect Truth"

(As inspired from Psalms 25:5)

Lord Jesus, hear our prayer …

Through patience and soulful comfort of the Scriptures, we learn solace and hope, and we will wait an eternity, if we must, for you to lead us to your Wonderful Truth, O Lord; because only you, Our True Messiah, can guide us and teach us correctly, all that we must learn, in order to be Spiritually Saved and Delivered from our misgivings and misdirections! Everyday, we lift our spirits up to you, Dear Lord, for you are the Veritable Existence of All that is Holy, and only through your Sacred Word is there life in one's soul! We give praise and thanks to you, Lord Jesus, and ask that our prayers will be answered, but only if it is your Will, not ours, Our God of Total Salvation!

Our True Lord, your Glorious Word is the Supreme Perfection in every way, infallible and all powerful, you are the Perfect Truth! You are the spiritual source of our Christian strength, for your Gentle Word inspires us towards morality and goodness. Lord Christ, you are the Spiritual Wisdom for all ages, and throughout the ages, your Gospel of Love lives on and on!

Enlighten us, Lord Jesus, for you are the Eminent Truth for all generations! Spiritually enliven us, Lord Christ, and inspire our hearts to always accept the Ways of Goodness. Empower us with patience, grant us virtue, and encourage us to be obedient to your every Word, Lord Jesus Christ, that we may know and find and remain on the Unparalleled Path of your Spiritual Salvation! O Gentle Lord, we ask of you, direct our footsteps through life, and teach us the lessons that we must learn in order to achieve Eternal Life; and like hammered-steel upon the anvil of life, temper our individual Christian Convictions and strengthen our personal determination to lead a righteous existence through the Hallowed Power of your Commanding Name!

Amen …

Chapter and verse that inspired prayer:

Psalms 25:5   Lead me in thy truth, and teach me: for thou art the God of my salvation; on thee do I wait all the day.

# January Fifteen: "Become The Marrow Of Our Strength"

### (As inspired from Hosea 14:9)

Lord Jesus, hear our prayer …

As with all faithful and mature Christians, there is a sharp feeling of uneasiness when our own decisions lead us to trespass against your Commandments of Life; thank you, Our Lord of Truth, for our individual consciences; to morally know the difference between right and wrong in our personal acts and motives is truly a blessing from you! Because, without a guiding conscience, our Eternal Existence would be in utter jeopardy! But through Scripture, you have shown us, O Lord, that the ways of all transgression lead away from your Heavenly Light; and only through perseverance of prayer and soulful compunction, will everyone find that their Personal Path to Salvation leads directly to your Forgiveness!

The Ways of Goodness are Mercy and Kindness; and to individually follow in your footsteps, Lord God, is our prayer and Way of Life! Confer upon us, Lord, the knowledge to understand and to fulfill the ordained design that you have reserved for each and every one of us. Make us wise in practical matters of morality and encourage us to be prudent in our actions. Lord Christ, your love is always with us, for you have allotted to us a perfect proportion in life. Merciful and Gentle is your Forgiveness, Lord Jesus, and Swift and Exact is your Reward!

When all hope seems lost, the spirit becomes weak. But through you, Lord Jesus, we find the courage and fortitude to survive! When the heart is filled with sorrow, the shadows of grief can blind one to the Light. But through you, Lord of Redemption, the darkness of despair disappears into the Brilliant Radiance of Joy! We pray for your Inner Spiritual Energy, Lord Jesus Christ, that it may become the Marrow of Our Strength and the Radiant Beacon that will guide us and fill our lives with the Brilliance of Overflowing Happiness!

Amen …

Chapter and verse that inspired prayer:

Hosea 14:9    Who is wise, and he shall understand these things? prudent, and he shall know them? For the ways of the LORD are right, and the just shall walk in them: but the transgressors shall fall therein.

# January Sixteen: "We Honor You, Lord"

## (As inspired from Daniel 4:37)

Lord Jesus, hear our prayer …

Heavenly Father, thank you for imparting your Wisdom unto us concerning heaven and who shall be heirs in your Kingdom! We pray for strength in character that each and every one of us will use Christian Common Sense to be fully aware of any personal decisions that might be contrary to the Word of God! Lord Jesus, you have taught us that we must have the heart of a child, embraced by a blameless soul, before we will be able to receive full inheritance of your Sacred and Promised Domain; for your Great Judgments are Exceedingly True, and we are individually responsible for our personal actions! O Lord, we pray to you: Remove all earthly pride from our hearts that you may hear and receive our truest words of love that we so humbly offer to you. And because your works are Ordained and Deserving, we honor you, Lord God, for our blessings; and we praise you for all that you do! Throughout the ages of all existence, since the beginning of time, and until the end of times, your Wonderful Works are extolled, Lord Jesus Christ, by kings and rulers, by free and bond, by rich and poor, by the loving acclaim of young and old alike, and by all people who desire to faithfully follow your Path to Personal Salvation and Spiritual Redemption; for the Writing is on the Wall!

Lord, we extol upon you our love and our promise of obedience; for all that we do, we do for your Righteousness. We praise you, Our Prince of Peace, in soulful adoration; for all that we are, we owe to your Glory. And we exalt you, Our Good King of Heaven and Earth, through loving acclamation and devotion; for all that we have received, we have received from your Merciful Bounty! Therefore, Lord Christ, within our hearts, we earnestly pray to you! Within our individual Christian lives, we live only for you! And within our spirits, we give continual praise and honor to your Infallible Splendor; for where there is love for you, Lord Jesus Christ, the obedient and faithful soul will also be found, proudly carrying your Banner of Truth in the Wisdom of Ages, by all who have accomplished Complete Happiness through Total Redemption and Atonement of spiritual offense!

Amen …

Chapter and verse that inspired prayer:

Daniel 4:37    Now I Nebuchadnezzar praise and extol and honour the King of heaven, all whose works are truth, and his ways judgment: and all those that walk in pride he is able to abase.

# January Seventeen: "Show Us The Paths Of Mercy And Truth"

### (As inspired from Psalms 25:10)

Lord Jesus, hear our prayer ...

From the moment we are born, our lives are filled with stumbling blocks; and it is only through Divine Intervention that our pathways are cleared. Therefore, we pray to you, O Lord, show us the paths of mercy and truth that we, as faithful followers, must pursue in life. From our youthful innocent beginnings and throughout our entire earthly existence, we must learn to greet and comprehend all the trials and spiritual lessons of this world! And for that reason, as each lesson or trial approaches, we ask of you, Lord of All Wisdom, that you will intercede into our lives and enlighten us to accept the bitter with the sweet; for we know that you, Our Lord and Protector, are always there to give us the inner strength to meet and defeat any and all challenges! And we thank you, Lord Jesus Christ, for we realize that all challenges met and conquered will give us experience, confidence, and a deeper Christian faith!

To every person who keeps your Holy Word within their heart and abides in your Teachings of Love, your Unending Mercy will forever protect and direct their spiritual path! O Lord, lead us to your Truth and Wisdom, give us a genuine understanding of Christianity that we may conscientiously learn to confront and discern all the difficult lessons and trials of life! Please, Lord Jesus, teach us to prevail, to endure, and to persevere during difficult times as well as prosperous times. And remove any hurtful vanity and pride that may exist within us, so that we may be able to forgive one another our transgressions towards one another. But most of all, Lord Jesus Christ, in our heart of hearts, above and beyond our individual prayerful requests, we humbly ask: How best may we serve you!

Amen ...

Chapter and verse that inspired prayer:

Psalms 25:10    All the paths of the LORD are mercy and truth unto such as keep his covenant and his testimonies.

# January Eighteen: "Lord, The Creator Of Truth"

### (As inspired from Isaiah 40:28)

Lord Jesus, hear our prayer …

As followers and believers of our Christian faith, we profess and openly admit with heart and soul that we accept you, Our King of Kings, as the Absolute Giver of All Knowledge, Truth, and Judgment! Everyone that has ever lived, everyone that is now living, and everyone that is yet to be born, owes continuous devotion and homage to you for their existence, Lord God Creator of All That Is! Only you, Our Lord and Savior, are worthy of total tribute and emulation from every generation that has ever been or will ever be! You are the only One, Lord Christ Redeemer of Souls, who deserves our complete obedience and reverence; for you alone, Lord Jesus Christ, suffered, died, and conquered death for our transgressions and for our salvation! To you, Lord of the Resurrection, we bind and promise our souls and our absolute belief to your Most Hallowed Existence, now and forever!

Because of your Immaculate Heart, Lord Jesus, the world has an Eternal Fire of Purity and Truth to follow! And as life can only create life, and light can only radiate light, the truth can only produce that which is pure and true! For everything that exists is a creation of your Word, O Lord The Creator of Truth! Therefore, throughout life, we will praise you and we will extol you, Lord, as Our God of Infinite Understanding! Blessed are all who fervently believe in you and all who honestly worship and acclaim you in heart, mind, and soul; for the True Believer needs no proof of your Physical Hallowed Existence, they simply know, from the heart of their hearts, that You Are!

Amen …

Chapter and verse that inspired prayer:

Isaiah 40:28    Hast thou not known? Hast thou not heard, that the everlasting God, the LORD, the Creator of the ends of the earth, fainteth not, neither is weary? There is no searching of his understanding.

# January Nineteen: "You Are The True Meaning Of Life"

(As inspired from Proverbs 8:35)

Lord Jesus, hear our prayer …

The Biblical kings of the Old Testament, with God's help, defeated every Godless nation after nation, but in the end, lost it all to pride. Ancient Rome also conquered the world, but lost it all to civil disobedience. Even the fierce Barbarians subdued the known world, but they too could not remain in power because of greed. Only Jesus Christ, The Living Son of God, without an army, without a weapon, without bloodshed, other than His own, conquered the whole world, and to this day, has kept it as His own, through love and peace!

Lord, life is a blessing that comes from the unblemished virtue of your Never Ending Love. And there is but one rightful purpose in life, one meaning for being born, one reason to exist in this world, and that is to find you, Lord Jesus Christ, for you are the True Meaning of Life! Only through you, Our Lord and Messiah, will we find sincere happiness. Only with you in our lives, Lord King of Glory, are we able to conquer our fears. And only by your Divine Intervention, Lord of Providence, will we individually find our true purpose and meaning in life; for life would have no meaning without you.

Lord Jesus, please grant us the power to receive insightful meanings of your Beautiful and Holy Word that we may share our living testimony with others. Glory to you, Lord Christ, Giver of All Life! Righteous is the Way that leads everyone to you, Lord Emmanuel, and blessed are those who follow your Path to their Personal Redemption! And now, in one accord, we herald the absolute acclaim and conviction of our Christian faith: Behold, Our Living God, The Son of Man, and The Spirit of Love, All of Whom are One in Compassion, Mercy, and Forgiveness; for it is in you, Our Lord Jesus Christ, that resides All Spiritual Salvation!

Amen …

Chapter and verse that inspired prayer:

Proverbs 8:35   For whoso findeth me findeth life, and shall obtain favour of the LORD.

# January Twenty: "Through You, Lord, We Are Complete"

## (As inspired from Nahum 1:7)

Lord Jesus, hear our prayer ...

When we diligently pray to you, Our Immutable Lord, prayers are always answered! Lord God, you are Forever Good, The Unparalleled Stronghold against all worldly and spiritual adversity, and we beseech you in praise and sincere supplication: Lord, we trust in the Judgment of your Divine Will, because we know that you desire us to be fulfilled in spirit, mind, and body. And in all that we do, and in all that we are, and in all that we can be, we forever give thanks to you, Lord Jesus Our Heavenly King, for allowing us to achieve our personal goals in life!

Your Love within our lives becomes a Fortress of Hallowed Might! And we have absolute trust in you, Lord Christ Our Prince of Peace, for you alone defeat adversity, overcome disorder, subdue doubt, conquer confusion, and triumph over all chaos! Blessed are you, Our Venerable Lord Jesus!

Our Good Lord, please, give consideration to our prayerful petition, for we are united in one voice that proudly proclaims to the world and to the heavens above: Through your Commanding Love, Dear Lord, we are fulfilled in spirit, mind, and body! And it is through one Christian voice of strength and agreement that we offer this heartfelt praise of gratitude to you: Thank you, Lord Jesus Christ, for your Flawless Love and Spiritual Protection; thank you for guiding us through this day and all the days of our lives; and thank you for allowing the blessings of joy and happiness to enter our hearts! Through you, Our Great and Mighty Lord, we are made complete!

Amen ...

Chapter and verse that inspired prayer:

Nahum 1:7    The LORD is good, a strong hold in the day of trouble; and he knoweth them that trust in him.

# January Twenty-One: "Cleanse And Enlighten Our Spirits"
### (As inspired from John 9:31 and Samuel 22:4)

Lord Jesus, hear our prayer …

Lord, we pray that our prayers will be received by you. And as it must be, all prayers, petitions, and praises that are offered to you, have to be offered with sincerity of mind and purity of spirit. Please, Lord Jesus, hear and receive our words as sincere and spoken in all truth and honesty; for we know that the words of a deceiver never reach heaven. Therefore, we call upon you, Lord Jesus Christ, who is benevolent and merciful, to purify our living spiritual vessels that our prayerful words of need and praise may reach your Heavenly Kingdom, for we are worshipers of the Living God!

That we may be worthy in your eyes, Lord Jesus, forgive us any transgression and disobedience. Lord of Mercy, we are truly sorry and repentant for ever having offended you in word or action. And that no family member, friend, or stranger may ever hold any personal feelings of resentment towards us as individuals, from any spoken word or deed, we ask that you soften their hearts, Lord of Forgiveness, that we may all be able to reconcile our individual differences with one another!

Your Peaceful Heart calls out to the world, and we are honored to hear the Holy Inspirations that aspire everyone to rise above temporal allurement and material attainment and seek, instead, your Imperishable Love! O Merciful Lord, that our spiritual offerings may be pure, cleanse and enlighten our loving souls as we continually pray to you for salvation; for we realize that no shadow is able to remain in the Light of your Great Truth, Lord Jesus Christ! Hear us, forgive us, and bless us, Our Forever King!

Amen …

Chapter and verse that inspired prayer:

John 9:31        Now we know that God heareth not sinners: but if any man be a worshiper of God, and doeth his will, him he heareth.

2 Samuel 22:4   I will call on the LORD, who is worthy to be praised: so shall I be saved from mine enemies.

# January Twenty-Two: "May We Forever Rejoice In Our Faith"
### (As inspired from Ephesians 5:19)

Lord Jesus, hear our prayer …

We are always thankful to you, Lord, for everything in the creation, and we keep our hearts continually filled with love and spiritual praise for you! All around us, everywhere, there are wonderful reflections of your Grand and Divine Design of Magnificence; for they are the natural sights and sounds of nature that serve as a constant reminder and a melody of love for you: The falling snow, a gentle spring breeze, the warming earth, a tumbling autumn leaf; these are but a few memories of life that forever sing out your Glorious Name in perfect praise! May every birth, every drawn breath, and every life-giving heartbeat become a vast symphony of love and adoration unto you, Lord Christ, as every voice in the world rises up to become a united chorus of continuous exaltation to you, Our Lord and God Jesus Christ!

O Lord, as our souls sing out words of love in our hearts for you, may we forever rejoice in our faith as Christians. And we pray that you will forever rejoice in us, Lord Jesus, as we spiritually strive to become a new song unto you: Bless this earth and bless every man, woman, and child, Lord God, with a deep Spiritual Understanding of just how precious our Hallowed Gifts of Life are in this world! Compose in everyone's heart, Lord Jesus Christ, a New Dawning of Compassion, a silent soulful song that will be continually sung to your Holy Spirit of Love and Forgiveness! To Our King of Kings, Our Lord of Lords, He, who is Mightier Than All, we submit our lives and our souls and our truest words to your Never Ending Melody of Spiritual Passion that clearly and constantly encircles the whole of creation: Love is all there is; Love is all that matters; for Pure Love is the Life Giving Blood of our Living God, of you, Christ Our King!

Amen …

Chapter and verse that inspired prayer:

Ephesians 5:19    Speaking to yourselves in psalms and hymns and spiritual songs, singing and making melody in your heart to the LORD.

# January Twenty-Three: "May You Find Us Obedient To Your Will"

(As inspired from 2 Chronicles 7:14)

Lord Jesus, hear our prayer …

Lord of All Generations, we are proudly called by your wonderful name, and as Christians, we follow the Only True Light of the World; because, through your Sacred Name, we are spiritually saved! Pray for us, Lamb of God, that we may remain strong. With our heads bowed, we, your faithful, do humble ourselves before you, Lord Jesus; for in you, we seek refuge. And through your name, we seek The Ways of Righteousness; and through soulful prayer and obedience, we ask of you, Lord Jesus Christ, to keep us in the Protective Radiance of your Holy Love, away from the terrible shadows and pitfalls of this world.

With our hearts lifted and our spirits soaring, we give thanks and honor to you, Our Good Shepherd of Life! May you find us worthy of your blessings, may you find us obedient to your will, and may the Bounty of your Compassion be upon us and all who believe in the Perfection and Beauty of your Hallowed Name!

O Lord Jesus Christ, how generous you are! How glorious you are! How wonderful and merciful you are! And how secure and complete we are in the Abundance of your Benevolent Love! Thank you, Lord, for allowing us to share, to witness, and to find shelter in your Great Goodness! Please, hear our praise: Glory! Glory! Glory unto you, Our Lord and Savior of Souls! Bless us and keep us safe in your Immaculate Heart of Holiness, and please, forgive us our trespasses, Merciful God, as we forgive all who have trespassed against us: Heal our hearts, heal our homes, and heal all unwarranted hardships from our individual lives!

Amen …

Chapter and verse that inspired prayer:

2 Chronicles 7:14    If my people, which are called by my name, shall humble themselves, and pray, and seek my face, and turn from wicked ways; then will I hear from heaven, and will forgive their sin, and will heal their land.

# January Twenty-Four: "Continually Bless Us With Fellowship"

### (As inspired from 1 John 1:17)

Lord Jesus, hear our prayer …

Heavenly Father, we thank you for your Only Begotten Son, for your Word Made Flesh, for His Great Sacrifice, and for our Spiritual Salvation of Love; Lord God, we pray to you: Through your Redeeming blood, Lord Jesus, through your Stripes, and through your Death and Resurrection, we, as Christians, are spiritually cleansed from all earthly and bodily transgression of mind, body, and soul! O Lord, bless our families, bless our friends, and bless this prayer that we offer up to you as a sign of our love and gratitude for our many relationships that you have given us: Help us, Lord Christ, to obtain and maintain a richness and a fulness in life with others that is only acquired through faith, through heartfelt compassion and through a genuine regard for other people. And now, through love and true fellowship, Lord Jesus Christ, we begin to move closer to you and closer to one another as sincere Christians, devoted to following your Commandments of Love!

Lord of Intercession, through your Spiritual Guidance, we will reach a fulness in life that is undaunted by jealousy, anger, or fear of one another. Our Lord of Goodness, you embody the True Spirit of Kindness, and through your Infinite and Unceasing Wisdom, we pray for the ability to always trust one another in a loving embrace of friendship and respect. Lord Jesus Christ, we pray that you will continually bless us with fellowship and a deep regard for one another; and we thank you, Lord God, for all of your blessings that we receive throughout all our days and nights: You are the Way and the Light to all Truth, and on your Path of Righteousness do we desire to walk!

Amen …

Chapter and verse that inspired prayer:

1 John 1:7     But if we walk in the light, as he is in the light, we have fellowship one with another, and the blood of Jesus Christ his son cleanseth us from all sin.

# January Twenty-Five: "Creator Of All Creation"

(As inspired from Malachi 1:11)

Lord Jesus, hear our prayer …

When this beautiful morning began, we blessed you, O Lord. As the afternoon proceeds, we ask of your Divine Protection and Guidance. And when the evening comes, we will give praise and thanks to you for our well-being and for our total happiness! Lord God, we know that each day, when we see the rising sun, or drifting clouds, or a midnight moon, or even a quiet starry night, that we are gazing upon the everyday miracles of your creation! Great is your name upon our lips, Our Lord and God, Creator of Creation! For each day that we witness your Wondrous Works, Lord, we give thanks and praise for being a part of your Glorious Miracle! And as we see and perceive the perfection of your creation, we are also assured that you see and perceive those who are faithful followers, Lord Jesus Christ, of your Magnificent Word of Life; which is found throughout the whole of creation and throughout all the beautiful generations that have been blessed by you! Please, hear our supplication of love: Invincible and Everlasting is your Heavenly Kingdom, Lord, because, you are the Throne of Existence!

Lord God, when we consider the infinite magnitude of the universe, a solitary prayer is but one small utterance in your Grand and Vast Creation; but we also know that at the very mention of your Glorious Name through prayer and praise, all of heaven, Our Creator of All Creation, immediately unites into one thunderous shout of joy, giving endless glory to you, Lord Jesus Christ! Blessed is your Holy Name, Lord of Hosts, among the nations of the world, by all the people, and throughout every single language that is spoken on earth! Those who have truly found you, Lord Jesus, have most definitely found the Treasure of Heaven, the Riches of Life, and the Blessings of Eternal Love!

Amen …

Chapter and verse that inspired prayer:

Malachi 1:11    For from the rising of the sun even unto the going down of the same my name shall be great among the Gentiles; and in every place incense shall be offered unto my name, and a pure offering: for my name shall be great among the heathen, saith the LORD of hosts.

# January Twenty-Six: "You Have Given Freely Of Your Love"

(As inspired from Micah 7:19)

Lord Jesus, hear our prayer …

Dear Lord, from the beginning of time, you have always given freely of your Love: Compassionate are you, Joyous and Everlasting is the Grace Within You! And with each new morning, we pray for your Divine Wisdom and Guidance to watch over us and to protect us throughout the day from the iniquities of this world! What a wonderful assurance there is in life, Lord Jesus Christ, knowing that you bless your faithful with a love that is Never-ending! Our hearts are overjoyed, for we are so very thankful that you remain in our lives, now, and forevermore!

Our Sovereign of Love, we pray that you will pray for us, your faithful: Bountiful are you, Lord Jesus, Generous and Wonderful is your Spirit! And throughout the day, Our Lord and Savior, we will keep you in our hearts and in our thoughts, because there is no one else like you, we have no other King but you; for you are the Unequaled Authority of Heaven and Earth and The Infinite Universe!

Forgive us, O Lord, and do not turn away from us, but to us! Allow the Tender Mercies of your Sacred Heart to flow outward from your Holy Throne and fill our souls and drive out the dark shadows of deception from within our hearts, our minds, and our spirits! Increase our faith, Our Lord and God, as we pray: Have Great Compassion upon us, release us from the stronghold of adversity and cast out all doubt and fear from our lives! Beloved are you. Lord Jesus, Merciful and Kind is your Sacred Heart! And with each day's end, Lord, we will give exaltation and thanks to you for everything that we have received throughout the day.

Amen …

Chapter and verse that inspired prayer:

Micah 7:19    He will turn again, he will have compassion upon us; he will subdue our iniquities; and thou wilt cast all their sins into the depths of the sea.

# January Twenty-Seven: "Let Everyone Come Together, Lord"

(As inspired from John 3:21)

Lord Jesus, hear our prayer …

Most Merciful Lord, we praise you, we honor you, and we love you! Please, bestow upon all who ask in your name, Lord Jesus, a blessing of Spiritual Strength to overpower, subdue, and vanquish all worldly transgression against your Holy Word and Righteous Commandments! We ask you, God Almighty, command the Rains of Compassion to fall from the heavens and flood the earth with peace and good will! Allow the winds of harmony to begin in every place and port of this wonderful planet, which will reach deeply into all the souls of those who desire spiritual change and resolution in their lives. Bring forth the radiance of a new dawning in this world, Lord Christ, that will open the eyes of all to an Imminent and Beautiful Understanding of your Hallowed Presence in everyone's life! Lord Jesus Christ, sanction the Sun to never set upon our spiritual existence, and encourage every human to become a faithful follower in your Every Word of Truth Through Salvation: To love God with all of our heart, and to love our neighbor as we would love ourselves! And if everyone sincerely follows these two truths, there would be Immediate Salvation for everyone, everywhere, throughout the world!

Our Lord and God, your Gifts of Grace are Pure, and your gifts are to be shared by everyone who believes in you and asks you to come into their lives as their Own Personal Savior! Therefore, let everyone come together, O Lord, in a Christian Fellowship of faith and render their thanks unto you! Let everyone yield unto you, Lord Jesus Christ, their absolute obedience, their complete adoration, and their sincere belief that you are the Corner Stone of Christianity, Our Complete Love, and Our Absolute Salvation in this life and the life to follow!

Amen …

Chapter and verse that inspired prayer:

John 3:21    But he that doeth truth cometh to the light, that his deeds may be made manifest, that they wrought in God.

# January Twenty-Eight: "Your Immaculate Heart"

(As inspired from Lamentations 5:19)

Lord Jesus, hear our prayer …

We ask that your Heavenly Inspirations will fill every waking moment of our day: Allow your faithful to see and understand that even though this world is filled with complex problems, you, Our Lord and God, hold all the answers, merely for the asking!

Days come and go, years come and go, even mountain ranges and great civilizations come and go, but only you, Our Lord God, endure forever! O Lord, you fill our spirits with Light, and you fill our hearts with Delight! We exalt and praise the Power of your Love; for your Might is Right, and your Right is Everlasting! Lord Jesus, the Purity in your Love is the Majestic Force that rules and governs the entire universe; all glory belongs to the Triumphant Perfection of your Divine Goodness! No other power is greater than you, Lord Christ, for your Perfect Will is the Sovereign Force of All that exists! Lord Jesus Christ, you will Reign Forever and ever, and your Heavenly Throne will endure unto all generations into eternity!

It is our personal confession and soulful prayer request, Lord of All Life, that you accept our truthful praise of acknowledgment and admission of faith: Hear us, Lord Jesus, for we are but servants of Your Immaculate Heart who willingly submit to your Loving Authority as Absolute and Supreme! For you, Lord Jesus Christ, we forgo all earthly and temporal powers and do humbly ask for your Infinite Goodness to protect and watch over us, today, tomorrow, and forevermore into eternity, unto all generations of faithful and endearing Christians!

Amen …

Chapter and verse that inspired prayer:

Lamentations 5:19   Thou, O LORD, remainst for ever; thy throne from generation to generation.

# January Twenty-Nine: "Your Love Exists Everywhere"

(As inspired from Genesis 1:29-30)

Lord Jesus, hear our prayer …

If we are to truly follow you, Our Lord Jesus, we must deny ourselves and take up your cross upon our shoulders, and then, you alone, Our Lord and God, will help each one of us to bear our burdens in our personal and individual journeys through life!

We pray to you, O Lord, that we may devote our entire lives to the Loving and Living Glory of your Giving Heart; for we know that you have dedicated everything that exists to us! Every tree, every fish, every fowl, every creature, and every living thing and nonliving part of the physical universe has been acclaimed for us by you, Lord Jesus Christ! And we offer this deep soulful praise of gratitude for such a Wondrous Wonderful Gift: There is no one like you, Lord God, for you are the Power of the Universe, you are the Source of All Light, you are Supreme Love, Pure and Innocent, present in all Perfection and Goodness!

From the beginning of time, age after age, era after era, and season after season, your Spiritual Love for us, Lord Jesus Christ, reigns foremost and eternal in the creation; for the whole of creation is the intention of life, and the resolution of life is the continuation of your Endless Creation! Our Living God, we give thanks to you for all the happiness in life; for the joy of life is knowing that your Boundless Love exists everywhere, throughout the universe, O Lord of Creation, and may be seen, and touched, and enjoyed by every human soul who stands upon this miraculous planet, even, until the end of times!

Amen …

Chapter and verse that inspired prayer …

Genesis 1:29-30    And God said, Behold, I have given you every herb bearing seed, which is upon the face of all the earth, and every tree, in the which is the fruit of a tree yielding seed; to you it shall be for meat. (30) And to every beast of the earth, and to every fowl of the air, and to everything that creepth upon the earth, wherein there is life, I have given every green herb for meat: and it was so.

# January Thirty: "Lord, May Our Spirits Overflow With Love"

### (As inspired from Psalms 118:28-29)

Lord Jesus, hear our prayer …

When we individually pray, we will pray to you, Dear Lord, from the heart, from a Sacred Dwelling Place devoted only to you. Therefore, we will build an altar for worship and adoration within ourselves; for you are truly our Lord and God! And when we pray, we will offer up to you, Our Lord Jesus, only the purest of prayers, only the most perfect of praises, only the greatest of exaltations, and only the truest of thanks! Lord Jesus Christ, your Benevolent Mercy embraces our very existence, and will endure forever; please, receive the following words that we submit to you, for they are purely, perfectly, and precisely from the center of our prayerful hearts: We love you and we are obedient to your Holy Word!

Our spirits are enraptured by your Never-failing Promise of Mercy and Deliverance regarding our lives and destinies; because only you, Lord Jesus, are forever present on the Beckoning Shores of Salvation, guiding each and every one of us to Eternal Life with you! And we give thanks unto you, Our Great Lord and God, because without you, we surely would not exist! O Lord, let our hearts truly be an altar of worship to your Everlasting Mercy, as we individually pray to you for personal redemption: Lord God, may our spirits overflow with love and compassion. May kindness become our natural way of life. And may your Holy Presence continually be within us, Lord Jesus Christ, as we create in our lives a Hallowed Dwelling place for the Goodness of your Perfect Love! Bless us, Lord of Our Faith, forever and a day, and pray for us to always remain strong and firm in our Christian beliefs and convictions! Find us worthy, Lord of Mercy, to receive your Great Blessings of Love, by strengthening each and every one of us in our individual faith and courage!

Amen …

Chapter and verse that inspired prayer:

Psalms 118:28-29    Thou art my God, and I will praise thee: thou art my God, I will exalt thee. (29) O give thanks unto the LORD; for he is good: for his mercy endureth for ever.

# January Thirty-One: "Touch Our Hearts, Lord"

### (As inspired from Revelation 1:17-19)

Lord Jesus, hear our prayer …

Heavenly Father of All That Is, we individually confess to you our love and our obedience to your Magnificent Word: Our Lord and Gentle Prince, you are the Life Force in all that is alive, your Majestic Love is the proof of our Creation, for there is nothing in this world nor in the next that may Live Eternal without You in its existence!

Our Merciful Lord and God, if we were to actually witness you before our very eyes, the Image of your Resplendent Glory would be beyond our human comprehension; and for this reason, you have given our hearts love, faith, and the promise of Eternal Life, where all earthly mysteries are resolved!

Lord Christ, your Beautiful Compassion abides within the lives and souls of those, who in all truthfulness, believe in you and follow your teachings of Love and Forgiveness, without question! Blessed is everyone who knows and accepts you in their lives, Lord Jesus Christ, as the Living Word of God! Enliven our spiritual knowledge, Lord of All Inspiration, to do what is right in life, not for punishment nor reward, but simply because it is the right thing to do! Allow us to devote our individual lives to your Indelible Will of Everlasting Truth; please, touch our very souls, O Lord, that we may obtain a wonderful and lasting Christian faith! Because, with you in our lives, Lord Jesus, fear and doubt will no longer exist! And through your Living Loving Presence within our lives, we will learn to have complete trust and unwavering faith in your Most Holy Spirit of Love, according to what was, what is, and what will be; and this, Our Lord and Savior, we avow daily and accept wholeheartedly through pure faith in you!

Amen …

Chapter and verse that inspired prayer:

Revelation 1:17-19    And when I saw him, I fell at his feet as dead. And he laid his right hand upon me, saying unto me, Fear not; I am the first and the last: (18) I am he that liveth, and was dead; and, behold, I am alive for evermore, Amen; and have the keys of hell and of death. (19) Write the things which thou hast seen, and the things which are, and the things which shall be hereafter;

# February One: "The Higher We Reach"

### (As inspired from Genesis 28:12)

Lord Jesus, hear our prayer …

Dear Lord, you hold the world in the palm of your hand, you direct all things to occur, and our spiritual and physical lives are infinitely indebted to your Immeasurable Love! Our strength is in you, Our Beloved One, please help us, for we cannot make it alone. Our faith is a spiritual ladder to your Holy Spirit, Lord Jesus, and as we individually climb towards you, we must reach each rung of the ladder by ourselves, one rung at a time; for as we ascend, we each must carefully move at our own haste and at our own measure. And the higher we reach, the greater our Christian faith becomes! Pray for us, Lord Jesus Christ, that everyone will eventually reach the summit of their Own Spiritual Salvation!

We pray to you, O Lord, that if we should slip in our climb, our faith will not permit us to completely fall; for we know that there is always someone there with open arms, reaching out to us; and without question, we are reassured in knowing, Lord Jesus, that it is you who is forever there! Blessed are you, Lord Jesus Christ, for you are invariably there with outstretched hands, ready to safely return us to our true destination in life.

In our visions and in our dreams, we envision a tranquil world at peace, where everyone lives a life in harmony; therefore, we pray to you, Our Merciful God: Let the future we see for all generations begin today through your Everlasting Accord and Compassion! Lord of Our Salvation, we thank you for your Unconditional Love; please, inspire us to be there for others, as you have been there for us!

Amen …

Chapter and verse that inspired prayer:

Genesis 28:12    And he dreamed and behold a ladder set up on earth, and the top of it reached to heaven: and behold the angels of God ascending and descending on it.

# February Two: "Allow Us To Become Warriors Of Virtue"

(As inspired from Luke 6:19-20)

Lord Jesus, hear our prayer ...

All praise to Our Victorious King who conquered the shadows of darkness with the Glowing Radiance of Love! O Lord, our spirits reach out to touch the Redeeming Compassion of your Valiant Virtue: Blessed is your Unbounded Mercy, Lord Christ, and praised is the Living Power of your Divine Grace; for your Exalted Goodness will always be Victorious! Lord Jesus, unanimously, we have completely devoted all loyalty to you, and we will faithfully follow the Paramount Truth of your Holy Heavenly Authority, now and forevermore, unto your Kingdom Most High! For with a mere touch of your Holy Spirit, our physical and spiritual lives are made whole; hear us, Our Good Lord Jesus Christ, as we pray for your Wonderful Presence in our individual lives: Glory to you, Most Gracious Lord, for you remove all doubt, confusion, and fear from within the soul and fill the heart with a Vibrant Desire to be Totally Submersed in the Hallowed Promise of your Healing Powers!

Our Dear Lord, sanction our souls and encourage us to become Warriors of Virtue! Allow our spiritual swords and shields to be forged from the Mettle of your Truth and Justice. Empower the faith we possess to become a Banner of Godliness. And through your Supreme Goodness, Lord Jesus, our Heavenly Armor will radiantly shine, suffering no foe to hinder the truth nor defeat our true purpose in life; for only you, King of Glory, are the Steadfast Truth and the Perfect Purpose of All Life! Lord Christ, let it be proclaimed throughout all the lands of creation, that the honor of all praise and power belongs solely to you; for only you, Lord Jesus Christ, conquered all the ills and imperfections of this world and are worthy to wear the Glorious Crown of Victory!

Amen ...

Chapter and verse that inspired prayer:

Luke 6:19-20   And the whole multitude sought to touch him: for there went virtue out of him, and he healed them all. (20) And he lifted up his eyes on his disciples, and said, Blessed be ye poor: for yours is the kingdom of God.

# February Three: "Lord, Hear Us As We Pray"

(As inspired from Joshua 1:9)

Lord Jesus, hear our prayer …

We praise your Holy Commandments, Lord God, and we accept your Word as the Divine Truth in heaven and on earth! Lord Christ, we pray for all who are in need of spiritual strength and courage in their lives; please; inspire their knowledge to be filled with the Great Wisdom of your Love! Strengthen their hearts with the security of your Gentle and Compassionate Spirit. And through the Positive Powers of your Loving Grace, Lord Jesus, we ask you to break the bonds of anything negative that may have become strongholds in their lives; for you will never fail nor forsake anyone who seeks your Endless Salvation!

O Lord, let all who are restless, find lasting contentment in your Loving Embrace. Let all who are troubled, find peace in your Perfect Word. And, Lord Jesus, let all who are weak in body and spirit, find their spiritual and physical strength in the power of your Steadfast Love and Mercy! And whether we meekly walk through the shadows of life or proudly follow the Lighted Path of your Righteousness, we give Great Praise and Honor to you, Our Lord and God, simply, because, you are forever with us!

Dear Lord, hear us as we pray for your Ever Flowing Love to continually fulfill the days of our lives and the lives of all who seek to know and to become aware of your Wonderful Truth; for truly, Lord Jesus Christ, your Love Commands in the Kingdom of Heaven above and on the earth below, forever into all eternity: Give us inner strength, Our Lord and God, because, with you in our lives, we become physically, mentally, and spiritually robust, strong enough to endure and advance through any ill-fated situation that may personally befall us!

Amen …

Chapter and verse that inspired prayer:

Joshua 1:9    Have not I commanded thee? Be strong and of good courage; be not afraid, neither be thou dismayed: for LORD thy God is with thee whithersoever thou goest.

# February Four: "We Bear Witness To Our Blessings"

(As inspired from John 15:27)

Lord Jesus, hear our prayer …

We give to you our deepest of heartfelt thanks, O Lord of Heaven and Earth, for all that you have Spiritually and physically provided us. From the inception of time unto the end of time, you have always been and you will always be, there is no beginning nor ending of your Infinite Love for us! Blessed are you, Lord Jesus Christ, for shepherding our wants and our needs as so deemed necessary by the Good Graces of your All Knowing Wisdom and Will!

Dear Lord, our needs have been met, our dreams have become reality, and our blessings have been revealed through the Manifestation of your Divine Intervention into our lives; blessed are you, Lord Jesus, and Hallowed are your Divine Works throughout the creation!

Good Lord, we bear witness to our blessings when we give testimony and praise to all that you have done for us in life. And as you have so blessed us, permit us also to show our reverence for you, Lord Jesus, by voicing aloud our Christian faith and by sharing our testimony with all who will listen: Thank you, Almighty Lord, for blessing those that hear and receive and accept your Wonderful Word of Peace, and thank you, Lord Christ, for being the Good Shepherd of our immortal souls! We are but a few of your worldwide flock who seek your Great Love and Safe Passage through life's ongoing tribulations and from those whose intentions are to purposely do wrong. Bless all who treasure harmony in their hearts, Lord God, and shelter all souls that sincerely pray for your Heavenly Protection; because, our spirits have been with you, Lord Jesus Christ, since the beginning of time, and we will faithfully remain with you until the end of all time!

Amen …

Chapter and verse that inspired prayer:

John 15:27    And ye also shall bear witness, because ye have been with me from the beginning.

# February Five: "Lord, We Await The Day"

### (As inspired from 1 Chronicles 16:35)

Lord Jesus, hear our prayer …

Hallowed and Exalted is your Holy Name, Lord Jesus Christ, for you protect and redeem your faithful among all the nations of this great earth; and blessed are the Comforting Mercies that the whole world receives because of you! We greatly extol you, Lord Jesus, for your Liberating Love has rescued us and freed us from the spiritual entrapments of pride and vanity, from the physical limitations that are caused by anxiety and uncertainty, and from all confusing choices of right and wrong! We thank you, Our Lord of Heavenly Hosts, for saving our spiritual lives, which will one day exist in eternity; for your Divine Redemption belongs to all who follow and rejoice in your Everlasting Word of Love and Forgiveness! Lord Jesus Christ Our Savior, we ask for your Intercession: Spiritually strengthen and encourage the personal determination of all people who earnestly desire to bring about positive change in their lives and in the lives of people around them; fill their hearts with the Unconquerable Resolution of your Judgment!

Lord Jesus, we pray for the future time when all darkness will become Light. We long for the moment when all the shadows of doubt and ignorance will be suddenly vanquished by your Radiant Righteousness. Dear Lord, we await the day when every tongue in every nation will speak your Glorious Name in praise, when every heart in the world will leap with joy at the very mention of your Name, and when every soul on earth will be filled with the Holy Spirit of your Love! Lord God, we pray that today will be that Day of Deliverance! Return to us, Lord Jesus Christ, deliver us from the ills of the world and become the Rightful One of Authority over all nations, He, who will judge the faithful and the unfaithful, the rich and the poor, the great and the humble; oh, please, Lord Almighty and Forgiving, let that day be today!

Amen …

Chapter and verse that inspired prayer:

1 Chronicles 16:35    And say ye, Save us, O God of our salvation, and gather us together, and deliver us from the heathen, that we may give thanks to thy holy name, and glory in thy praise.

# February Six: "Glory Be To You, Lord"

(As inspired from Matthew 4:4)

Lord Jesus, hear our prayer …

All good words and all loving thoughts grow out of Heaven's Blessings on earth! The staples of life may give our bodies sustenance, but it is only by and through the Blessed Word of God, which created all nourishment, upon which we truly exist and thrive! We thank you, Lord, for fulfilling our worldly needs, but we continue to hunger for your Sacred Spiritual Blessings; for our spiritual needs are great and we cannot survive life through temporal fulfillment alone. Therefore, Christ Our Savior, we are all in one agreement, united as a single voice, when we proclaim our immortal trust in your Unblemished Truth! Lord Jesus, we remove all fear and anxiety from our hearts and place our problems into the Peaceful Palms of your Merciful Hands! Glory be to you, Lord Jesus Christ, and to every Hallowed Word that you deliver into the hearts and lives of all humankind! And so, we pray: Open our eyes, open our ears, and open our hearts to receive the Glorious News of Salvation!

When we are filled with fear, we trust in you, Our Prince of Peace, and all worry disappears! When there is sadness in our lives, we call upon you, The Son of God, and happiness returns once more! And when doubt overshadows our dreams, we pray to you, Lamb of God, and our faith rises like the morning sun; for we have accepted your Word, Our Anointed Christ, as Absolute! Because only through your Calming Word, Lord God, will we ever have a tranquil heart, a life filled with harmony, and a world blessed by your Peace. Glory be to you, Lord Jesus Christ, and to your Holy Spirit that is proclaimed throughout all time and throughout the entire world of your faithful Christian followers!

Amen …

Chapter and verse that inspired prayer:

Matthew 4:4    But he answered and said, It is written, Man shall not live by bread alone, but by every word that proceedeth out of the mouth of God.

# February Seven: "You Have Delivered Your Faithful, Lord"

### (As inspired from Exodus 13:3)

Lord Jesus, hear our prayer …

You have delivered your faithful, Lord God, from all forms of judgment: From out of bondage in distant lands, through pestilence, through famine, saved from the ravages of a world flood, and freed from the terrible consuming flames of a fiery furnace, you are always there to deliver your faithful, Lord God, through centuries of time and trouble! Blest are you, Lord Jesus, for the countless blessings you give to the world that conquer our innumerable problems in life!

With total conviction in our hearts and in our souls, Lord Christ, we acknowledge and believe in your Glorious Holy Spirit of Life! We greatly extol you and thank you, Lord All-powerful, for our very existence! Lord Jesus, you are the One and Only True God in our Christian lives, no other power stands before you, and no other power will ever take your place! Into your Lovingkindness we indenture our lives and our souls! Bless us, O Lord, when we sincerely profess our personal belief in you and in all that you have done for your people throughout the ages!

From out of the darkness of ignorance and into the Golden Light of your Enlightenment, you have brought us, God of Abraham, to our Spiritual Salvation! And now, with every fiber of our existence, we exalt your Name above all others and rejoice in you, Lord Jesus Christ, for no greater power exists in our lives nor throughout the universe than you! Thank you, Lord, for bringing us to this very day, to this moment in time, to this Wonderful Day of Deliverance!

Amen …

Chapter and verse that inspired prayer:

Exodus 13:3    And Moses said unto the people, Remember this day, in which ye came out from Egypt, out of the house of bondage; for by strength of hand the LORD brought you out from this place: there shall no leavened bread be eaten.

# February Eight: "Lord, We Pray To You In Unspoken Words"

### (As inspired from 1 Peter 3:4)

Lord Jesus, hear our prayer ...

How wonderful it is to know that we are always in your sight, Our Blessed Lord Jesus, and we are always within your tender reach; even if we whisper in the wind, or speak softly in the night, or quietly confess our individual love and trust in you, your Holy Spirit of Great Compassion will forever hear us.

O Lord, there are times when we must silently speak to you, sharing only with you, the spiritual passions of the heart; for these are the private times and prayers of our inner most personal intentions. Therefore, Lord Christ, please hear our silent prayers, our intimate requests of the soul, a spiritual entreatment that is meant only for you to hear, Lord Jesus Christ Our Eternal Holiness! Thank you, Lord God, for knowing all matters of the heart, thank you for being so aware of our individual needs, and thank you for being so selfless and considerate concerning those things that are so personally important to us and to our individual needs.

God the Father, you hear all the sounds of your creation; every thought and every whisper reaches you. And as all sincere concerns of the heart, given in Absolute Reverence, will surely reach you, Lord Jesus, we know that you will hear the requests of our silent supplications. We pray to you, Our Incorruptible Lord, through the Holy Ghost in secret utterances, deep from within our spirits, giving thanks and praise for your Never Ending Mercy. In silence, do we individually ask of you, Lord Jesus Christ, our most passionate of concerns. Please, Lord God, approve of our personal petitions, but only if it is of your Will, and not ours; and now, O Lord, we pray to you in unspoken words, words that stem from the hidden reaches of the heart and from feelings that are solely reserved for you, Our Personal Savior and Creator! Thank you, Lord Infinite, for your Reverential Concern.

Amen ...

Chapter and verse that inspired prayer:

1 Peter 3:4   But let it be the hidden man of the heart, in that which is not corruptible, even the ornament of a meek and quiet spirit, which is in the sight of God of great price.

# February Nine: "We Exalt You In Our Prayers"

(As inspired from 1 Chronicles 16:29)

Lord Jesus, hear our prayer ...

We bestow upon you, Our Hallowed Lord, a soulful praise of adoration: Honored from the beginning of eternity and cherished throughout all generations, it is your presence, Lord Jesus Christ, that is magnified everywhere in the creation! Lord of All that is Holy, we bring to you, our spiritual offering of obedience! And in our greatest expression of thanks, we offer our heartfelt praises of love and adoration; may our exaltations, Lord of Scripture, be in accordance with the Beauty and the Holiness of your Miraculous Name as it is perpetually known throughout the whole of creation and throughout every Word of the Old and New Testament for the Salvation and Redemption of Life!

All glory and praise goes to you, Lord Jesus; for when we exalt you in our prayers, we pray to you with an absolute certitude in our hearts. When we glorify you in our inner thoughts, Lord Eternal, we venerate your Most Holy Spirit to the highest of acclaim! And when we reflect upon your Holiness, Lord Jesus Christ, we joyously celebrate the beauty and the perfection of your Majestic Magnificence as it is so reverently worshiped throughout all of life within the living universe of your creation; for by your Glorious Name do we call ourselves true Christians, faithful and loyal followers of your Loving Grace and Peaceful Heart! And now, we humbly bring to you, O Lord, a personal offering of love and peace, for we understand and accept that your Hallowed Message of Compassion belongs to all humans on earth! Therefore, we individually commit our lives to the Sanctity of your Every Word, which is given to us in chapter and verse, through Heavenly Inspirations from your Kingdom above!

Amen ...

Chapter and verse that inspired prayer:

1 Chronicles 16:29     Give unto the LORD the glory due unto his name: bring an offering, and come before him: worship the LORD in the beauty of holiness.

# February Ten: "Help Us, Lord, To Endure"

### (As inspired from Galatians 6:2)

Lord Jesus, hear our prayer ...

Lord God, life takes us on a myriad of journeys, and in our individual lifetimes, there are times when we are unable to carry our burdens alone; for the weight of our suffering is sometimes too difficult to tolerate by ourselves. But it is during these times of personal challenge and conflict, that we know we are never alone! And therefore, we are so thankful to have you in our lives, Lord Christ, for you are always there to help us survive our hardships and afflictions that we must bear in life. We pray to you, Lord Jesus, that you will also fill our hearts with Christian empathy, so that we will be naturally impassioned to help others who are also troubled or in need, just as you have helped us and blessed us so many times!

Lord of Mercy, take away our misfortunes and sufferings. Eliminate every worldly pressure that may cause stress and frustration in our lives. Help us, Dear Lord, to endure and to conquer the demands of our responsibilities and the weight of any taxing obligation that we must personally bear. And that we may all gain insight into difficult situations and learn how to avoid future trials and tribulations, empower us, Lord God, with the True Spiritual Knowledge of Discernment to build upon the lessons of life!

O Lord, no task is too difficult nor any demand too great when you are there to ease our burdens. All the praise and glory in the universe belongs to you, Lord Jesus Christ, for your Holy Spirit is forever with us! Bless you, Our Lord of Ages, for your Constant Love and Support.

Amen ...

Chapter and verse that inspired prayer:

Galatians 6:2    Bear ye one another's burdens, and so fulfill the law of Christ.

# February Eleven: "May Our Intentions Always Be Sincere"

### (As inspired from 2 Thessalonians 2:3)

Lord Jesus, hear our prayer ...

Lord God, you were born without blemish, and you never transgressed once in your beautiful life! Bless us and Spiritually Strengthen us, Dear Lord, to remain faithful to the values of our Christian Morals of Goodness. That our intentions will always be sincere, Lord Jesus, we pray: Inspire our thoughts, our words, and our deeds, that we will never practice to deceive! And that we may never fall under the influence of false affections or godless promises, allow us the courage to always speak the truth to one another! Lord Christ, remove any haughty pride and arrogance from our hearts so that we will never be blinded from your Heavenly Sight! Pray for us now, Lord Jesus Christ, that we, as faithful Christians, will truly become spiritual role models for those who will one day follow in our footsteps!

Through the eyes of innocence, the world becomes clearer. Our Lord God, please, forgive us our transgressions, so that we may clearly see all truth through the veil of any faithless pretense. Shelter us, O Lord, from the dark reaches of deceit and deception. Bless us, that we should never be fooled by false witnesses, insincere words, or by hollow works. Shield us from the treacherous pitfalls of disguised truths, deceiving and unholy allurements, and even little white lies; for a lie is a lie, no matter how small it is! Please, Lord Jesus Christ, enlighten us to perceive and recognize the inner light of all people who are spiritually good, as you protect us from those whose inward purpose is set merely to deceive the innocent soul. Pray for us now, Our Lord and God, that we will never fall away from the Directing Light of your Goodness, nor backslide from our true course and direction in life, or revere any faithless or unholy cause: Let no person deceive us by any form of persuasion!

Amen ...

Chapter and verse that inspired prayer:

2 Thessalonians 2:3    Let no man deceive you by any means: for that day shall not come, except there come a falling away first, and that man of sin be revealed, the son of perdition.

# February Twelve: "There Is No Other Truth But Yours"

(As inspired from Deuteronomy 4:39)

Lord Jesus, hear our prayer …

Our Heavenly Father of Justice and Purity, we have come to realize, through the study of Scripture, that all deception is merely a lie that promises to be true; but real truth cannot falter and stands alone, without any reassurance! Lord Jesus, we remain faithful to the Way of your Immaculate Word, because you are the Living God in the heavens above and on the earth below, and in your footsteps do we desire to walk! Perfect is the Way of the Lord! And as we pass through the light of each day, and through the dark of each night, we know there will be many things that we must experience, and we pray to you, Our Lord Jesus, that our personal paths will always be guided by the Unrestricted Perfection of your Word! Lord Jesus Christ, there is no other Truth but yours, and there is no other way to find Eternal Happiness except through you; for every individual soul that exists, you, Lord of Our Faith, are the Only Way to Spiritual Salvation!

Our Lord in Heaven, we have humbled our hearts and we have turned from our indiscretions and pray to you with all of our might: Forgive us and heal us! Please, O Lord, bless all who seek to discover your Holy Way of Truth! And for all who desire to follow your Unparalleled Path of Glory, we hope and pray that your Innocent Love will become their sole goal and purpose in life! Lord Jesus, we ask that your Righteous Word will guide our days as we individually seek The Divine Gifts of your Great Wisdom throughout our Christian lives! For our singular passion and quest in life, Lord Jesus Christ, is the continual pursuit and attainment of your Most Perfect and Holy Word; therefore, we pray to none other than you: Safeguard our individual steps along the Pathway of Life, ensure the course that will lead us directly and forever to you, Our Lord and God!

Amen …

Chapter and verse that inspired prayer:

Deuteronomy 4:39   Know therefore this day, and consider it in thine heart, that the LORD he is God in heaven above, and upon the earth beneath: there is none else.

# February Thirteen: "Lord, We Will Venerate Your Word"

## (As inspired from 1 Thessalonians 5:14)

Lord Jesus, hear our prayer ...

In an honest and faithful measure of spiritual fellowship, O Lord, that we have firmly established in ourselves through your tenets and teachings, we ask that you will bless and keep together the unity of all true friendships that we have created! We pray to you, Lord Jesus, to increase our individual faith that we have in one another. And during times of personal need, may we freely give comfort to family, friends, and even strangers, through a sincere feeling of Christian fellowship. Pray for us, Lord of Mercy, and encourage us to become more supportive and patient with one another, both the strong and the meek. Instill in us, Lord God, the innate knowledge to treat others as we would want to be treated! Lord Jesus Christ, please, allow all who seek deserving friendships in their lives to come together in a steadfast and faithful accordance of your Heavenly Love and Respect!

As love and life were created by you to be shared in a moral and virtuous way, Lord God, may we also learn, in all humility, to share our deepest friendship with one another, as you have shared your friendship with the entire world! Therefore, in everything we do we and say, Christ Jesus Our Lord, we will venerate your Word as we learn the real value of harmony and faith and goodwill towards one another! For only through a genuine gain of respect and trust, will a lasting and loyal friendship ever be created and continued between two or more people. And if just two people can honestly care about one another, their natural affection will flow outwardly to others, and others to others, and so on, and then, in time, everyone in the whole world will be respectful of one another!

Amen ...

Chapter and verse that inspired prayer:

1 Thessalonians 5:14    Now we exhort you, brethren, warn them that are unruly, comfort the feebleminded, support the weak, be patient toward all men.

# February Fourteen: "Your Love, Lord, Is All Abundant"

(As inspired from Jude 21)

Lord Jesus, hear our prayer …

You have taught us through Scripture and Gospel, O Lord, that genuine Forgiveness and Deliverance are granted only to the soul that personally seeks your Redemption from their own spiritual transgression! All true repentance must come solely from the heart of the person who searches their own conscience and truly acknowledges having offended your Commandments; Our Merciful Lord, hear our sincere words of petition: Remember our iniquities and misjudgments no more, Dear Lord, for we were spiritually mislead, but now, we see and understand the terrible mistake of not following your every Commanding Word for Spiritual Survival!

Bless the faithful witnesses that exist throughout the world! And if the world could speak as one voice, Lord Christ, it would proudly announce and commend its total existence into the greater care of your Loving and Gentle Spirit! Lord Jesus Christ, your Sacred Love is an unselfish love, an unconditional love, a love that is reserved for everyone who seeks true salvation from the ills of the world! For your love, Lord, is all abundant, all merciful, all forgiving, eternal unto all time! Blest and Holy is the Infinite Compassion within your Sacred Heart!

Life exists because love exists! And as evidence of your Miraculous Love for us, Lord of Creation, all that anyone ever has to do is to see, observe, and testify to all the countless and diverse blessings of life that prevails on earth; for no greater love exists, than the Love that we receive from you, Lord Jesus Christ! You alone, O Lord, are the only one who really knows us, who really sees us, and who really cares about us! Thank you, Our Lord Divine, for showing us what True Love and Mercy is. Thank you, Lord God, for giving us the greatest gift in the whole of the universe, Eternal Life through your Divine Salvation!

Amen …

Chapter and verse that inspired prayer:

Jude 21    Keep yourselves in the love of God, looking for the mercy of our Lord Jesus Christ unto eternal life.

# February Fifteen: "A World Of Eternal Peace"

(As inspired from Ezekiel 37:26)

Lord Jesus, hear our prayer ...

Throughout this planet, Lord God, there is a vast fellowship that is spiritually connected and unified by your Glorious Word, and we thank you, Lord Jesus, for in your Holy Name is the Promise of Peace. And as followers of your Infallible Truth, our testimonies and our praises have become a spiritual vow for harmony throughout the nations! Lord of All Who Live, it is our deepest desire to exist in a nation without chaos and turmoil. Our thoughts and our prayers are united deeply into a single plea of Everlasting Hope, Lord Jesus Christ, that you will touch the heart of every man, woman, and child on earth, so that each person may have the opportunity to live in a land of eternal peace, now, and forevermore!

O Gracious Lord, throughout this glorious world, and throughout the centuries, your faithful may have developed separate doctrines and tenets of Christian faith, but we are all still brothers and sisters, steadfast believers in you, Lord Jesus! And it is through your Covenant of Peace, Lord Christ, that unites every Sincere Christian; because, all true believers in you, Lord Jesus Christ, are of one family and of one mind! Please, hear our prayer of unity: O Prince of Peace, allow the olive branch of your love to be planted deeply into our hearts and souls, so that compassion may grow and prosper throughout our individual lives. And as faithful members of your vast Christian Congregation, Lord Jesus, everyone will then become as one family of true believers, united in a sanctuary of one thought, in one faith, in a wonderful understanding that you, Lord Jesus Christ, are the Supreme and the Eternal Peacemaker for all people, for all nations, and for all eternity! And in this, we proudly profess to the world as The Solemn Truth of God The Father, through the life and death and Resurrection of the Son of Man Lord Jesus Christ, as revealed to us through the Divine Inspirations of the Holy Spirit!

Amen ...

Chapter and verse that inspired prayer:

Ezekiel 37:26   Moreover I will make a covenant of peace with them; it shall be an everlasting covenant with them: and I will place them, and multiply them, and will set my sanctuary in the midst of them for evermore.

# February Sixteen: "Peace In Our Neighborhoods"

(As inspired from Leviticus 19:18)

Lord Jesus, hear our prayer …

We are aware, Lord Jesus, that through the gaining of Spiritual Knowledge, the lives of all people will grow in a Positive Light, making the Ways of Harmony and Accord accessible to one and all! Bless this community in which we live, O Lord, and help us to personally resolve and end any situations and individual problems within our lives and within our own neighborhoods; please, hear our prayer request for peace: Bring resolution to all strife, malice, unrest, and personal resentment that we may hold for one another. Elevate our feelings for other people, Lord God, that will make it possible for every citizen to realize their Christian duty, and to do whatever is humanly possible to aid those in distress. Using sound judgment and common sense, let us also watch over the well-being of one another's children; for you have truly taught us, Dear Lord, that the good neighbor is a blessing of Heavenly Fellowship, and we sincerely pray for peace in our neighborhoods, in our own homes, and in our individual hearts. Help us to learn how to respect each other as we would regard ourselves. Lord Jesus, Spiritually Encourage people, everywhere, to come together in a new and enlightened awareness, to appreciate the differences that exist between people, and to never purposely infringe upon the rights or comforts of others through ignorance or personal spite! Let all neighbors on earth be of good-will and be inspired to understand that every person is a child of God and is therefore a brother or a sister to one another! Lord Christ, bless all neighbors and neighborhoods and fill all hearts with a New Love of total compassion and resolution for each other! Please, Lord Jesus Christ, make it possible for people, all around the world, in every nation, state, city, and hamlet, to come together in a lasting fellowship of faith, through the unity of friendship, by the Enacting Power of your Everlasting Love and Mercy!

Amen …

Chapter and verse that inspired prayer:

Leviticus 19:18    Thou shalt not avenge, nor bear any grudge against the children of thy people, but thou shalt love thy neighbor as thyself: I am the LORD.

# February Seventeen: "Accept Our Confession Of Faith"

(As inspired from Deuteronomy 6:5)

Lord Jesus, hear our prayer …

Lord of Divine Right, you are The First Cause, The Supreme Being who has brought about all that exists, and in this, there is no denying! We give thanks to you, Our Lord and Savior, for our lives have been wonderfully graced with the blessings of your Almighty Love! And as you are forever and without end, so too is your compassion forever and without end! Lord Jesus Christ, you have always been, and we know that your Unceasing Love will always be! For we, as committed Christians, who truly believe in you, are totally in agreement in this single belief: That we truly love you, Our Divine Jesus, with every fiber of our existence! Bless us and watch over us, Our Good Shepherd of Life!

Our Sacred Lord, from your Holy Spirit, all love is created and is manifested through the miracle of life. And our love for one another, Lord Jesus, is our visible, living testimony of our Christian faith! Therefore, we pray to you, O Lord, to accept our confession of faith as an outward reflection of our spiritual love for you and for all that exists throughout this incredible creation: Dear Lord, when the shadows of obscurity prevail around us, we search for you; when we are confused or in doubt, we turn to you, Our God of Infinite Wisdom; and when we are sad and lonely, we call out to you, Our Lord Christ! Therefore, in good times as well as in bad times, we will always call upon your Majestic Name, Lord Jesus Christ! As in times of peace or in times of great turmoil, we continually find our spiritual redemption through the Ever Present Love that you have for us; because, you are The Comforter and The Strength of our physical bodies and our immortal souls, forever and ever into eternity!

Amen …

Chapter and verse that inspired prayer:

Deuteronomy 6:5    And thou shalt love the LORD thy God with all thine heart, and with all thy soul, and with all thy might.

# February Eighteen: "A New Dawning"

(As inspired from Mark 16:15)

Lord Jesus, hear our prayer ...

You have given to us, O Heavenly Lord, through Hallowed readings from the Bible, a deep and realistic understanding of all things that are an abomination to your Word; therefore, as you have stated, no human shall judge, least they be judged, and that we, your faithful followers, must, through example, teach repentance and remission of all transgression! For the last thing you said to your disciples was to pass unto all nations the Knowledge of your Word, to instruct one another in the Ways of the Lord; because you, Our Lord and Teacher, and only you, will one day return to earth, to judge the faithful and the non-believers! All praise and glory to you, Our Lord Jesus Christ!

The Good News of Our Messiah and Savior has encompassed the planet and is known in every nation and is spoken about in every language! We earnestly pray to you, Dear Lord, that every man, woman, child, and living creature will begin to freely follow along the pathway of your Divine Design that you have created for the Creation! Intercede, Lord Jesus, in the spiritual pilgrimage of the world. Illuminate the path for all people that they may clearly see and follow the True Way of your Righteous Perfection; Lord of the Beginning, you are the Only Light in a darkened and troubled world! Please, Lord Christ, allow the good that is in everyone, everywhere, to radiate towards your Unerring Will. Grant the whole world and all of creation the ability to understand the beauty of your Ordained Destiny for us! For in all sincerity, Lord Jesus, only you are able to bring about the Miraculous Beginnings of World Deliverance! And that peace on earth may actually be achieved in everyone's lifetime, we ask you to inspire a deep passion within every person to develop a spiritual desire to serve, to the best of their Christian ability, your Glorious Will on earth. And then, O Lord, allow this desire to blossom and grow and fill every corner of the world! For a world that follows the Perfection of your Truth, Lord Jesus, will no longer be in darkness, but will radiate brightly in a New Dawning of World Salvation and Deliverance!

Amen ...

Chapter and verse that inspired prayer:

Mark 16:15    And he said unto them, Go ye into all the world, and preach the gospel to every creature.

# February Nineteen: "It Is Your Perfect Wisdom, Lord"

### (As inspired from Malachi 3:6)

Lord Jesus, hear our prayer ...

The sun sets, the moon rises, the stars form definite patterns overhead in the midnight sky; O Lord, we realize that there is a purpose for everything, and there is a reason for all change; because, seasons change, people change, all life is restless and must change: Babies are born, children grow and learn, people mature, fall in love, marry and have families of their own, and the beautiful cycle of life continues. Year after year, day by day, minute to minute, everything in this wonderful creation changes, Lord Christ. Great mountains erode away, moving rivers alter their courses, and even deep valleys fill in; all things that exist are in forever motion, unsettled. But the phases of change are natural, for it is your Perfect Wisdom, Lord Jesus, that everything must evolve, everything that is, except for you, Lord Jesus Christ, for only you remain constant in an ever transforming universe! We give tribute and acclaim to you, Our Lord and God, for your Unremitting Love and Longsuffering Patience as you wait for everyone in the world to change from their secular concerns to unmovable, incorruptible souls of pure faith and goodness; Lord of Heaven and Earth, give us the spiritual determination to be worthy of Eternal Life and the everlasting inheritance of your Beautiful Heavenly Kingdom of Love as we offer the following prayer to you: Because Love changes not, establish in our hearts and minds, Dear Lord, the Knowledge that the riches of this world cannot turn transgression into virtue, that all the power on earth will not save a single person; help us to realize, Our Lord of Light, that gold and silver are of little or no concern to our immortal souls! Therefore, because of your Spiritual Perfection, Our Lord and God Jesus Christ, we will change our personal lives, by individually adorning ourselves in prayer, praise, and peaceful embraces of love and fellowship!

Amen...

Chapter and verse that inspired that prayer:

Malachi 3:6   For I am The LORD, I change not; therefore ye sons of Jacob are not consumed.

# February Twenty: "Darkness Cannot Pierce The Light"

### (As inspired from 1 John 1:5)

Lord Jesus, hear our prayer …

Immeasurable and Never-ending is the Magnificent Power and Protection of the Holy Spirit! In the Unblemished Light that radiates from the Son, there is no darkness, there are no shadows, there is no fear, there is only the Goodness of God! We give thanks for the Glorious Guardianship in which we securely stand, and we give eternal acclaim to you, Lord Jesus Christ, for you are the source of all Heavenly Light! Lord God, your Everlasting Radiance is the core of all love, of all life, and of all spiritual happiness and joy! Pray for us, Our Lord of Pure Enlightenment, that we may always abide in the brilliance of your Holy and Sacred Illumination of Love!

O Lord, you are the Sunrise of All Existence, and your Resplendence is the Hallowed Spear that pierces all darkness! But if we remove ourselves from the Light of your Spiritual Safekeeping, then, and only then, are the dark shadows of this world able to draw near and cover us. Therefore, we beseech you, Lord Jesus Savior of All Souls, that we may eternally remain in the Heavenly Guardianship of your Immaculate Radiance; for the long reaching shadows of darkness cannot pierce the Light from the Son of God Almighty! Pray for us to remain diligent in our Christian values and morals. Increase our principles of right and wrong. Warrant True Compassion into our lives as a standard of behavior! And bless every soul who comes to you, Lord Jesus, in the name of Peace! Thank you, Lord Almighty, for our lives and for the unbounded joy that shines down upon us from your Heavenly Throne!

Amen …

Chapter and verse that inspired prayer:

1 John 1:5    This then is the message which we have heard of him, and declare unto you, that God is light, and in him is no darkness at all.

# February Twenty-One: "The Lord Of All That Is"

(As inspired from Matthew 10:32)

Lord Jesus, hear our prayer …

O Lord, you know every person that has ever been, is, and is yet to be. You know their name, their heart, and their spiritual intentions. In life, it is us who must first find and acknowledge you, Christ Our Lord, for you know exactly where we are at all times! And it is for this reason, as faithful Christians, Lord Jesus Christ, that we glorify your Hallowed Name, that we testify and bear witness to your Beautiful Love, and that we confess our complete devotion and love to your Holy Spirit before all people and before all the nations of the world! Lord God, open the eyes and ears of everyone on earth to the marvelous knowledge of your Incredible Presence on earth! Fill their hearts and minds to totally accept you as Lord and God of their existence! Let the Miracle of Belief begin today!

From now until forever, we openly admit and proudly proclaim you, Lord Jesus, to everyone, as the True Lord, The Only Lord, The Lord of Our Total Creation, The Lord of All That Is! In all corners of the world, people exalt your Grand and Glorious Name, Lord God. And in every country, state, city, village, and county corner, we pray that new conversions, far and near, will eternally venerate you, Lord Jesus Christ, as their Personal Lord of Spiritual Salvation! Bless those who believe, bless those who search for The Unblemished Truth in their lives, and bless every man, woman, and child who truly confesses that Jesus Christ, The Promised One, The Foretold Messiah, is born of the flesh, and is Our Living God, Our Supreme Savior and King of Eternal Life! And in this, we, your faithful followers, O Lord, do confess, acknowledge, and vow before heaven and earth, as the Absolute Written and Spoken Truth!

Amen …

Chapter and verse that inspired prayer:

Matthew 10:32    Whosoever therefore shall confess me before men, him will I confess also before my Father which is in heaven.

# February Twenty-Two: "Lord, Bless The Family"

(As inspired from Ephesians 3:14-15)

Lord Jesus, hear our prayer ...

Blessed is the family of faith, Lord Jesus, for a family that exactly follows and believes in your Holy Gospel of Love is verily surrounded by the Compassionate Guardianship of your Spiritual Care! Our Hallowed Lord Christ, we believe in the sanctity and the unity of Christian family values; for a house divided is a house defeated! Lord Jesus Christ, through the Incredible Wisdom of Your Holy Word, we pray that your Protective Love and Sacred Name will forever reside within the hearts of all families in whom all souls of heaven and earth are named and claimed by our Heavenly Father!

We know that there will always be times of uncertainty and difficulty within any family, but we are also assured that complete faith in you, Our Lord and Radiant Redeemer of Lives, will also help every family member to rise above and overcome all personal problems that they may have! Therefore, in your Stupendous Name, O Prince of Peace, purify, unify, and strengthen all the families of the world to discover inner harmony and tranquility within their lives, as you direct all hearts to seek and find and serve the One and Only God of the universe, You, The Savior of All Families, Our Lord Jesus Christ, He, by whom all Christians are named!

Lord of All Generations, we pray that you will always be in the midst of every family that truly honors your Blessed Word; because, you have told us, that whenever two or more are gathered in your Name, you are there! And whenever people come together to worship you, they become as true members in your Faithful Family of Heavenly Saints and Angels! Jesus Our Lord, we beg of you: Bless the family, bless this family, and bless all families in your Righteous Name!

Amen ...

Chapter and verse that inspired prayer:

Ephesians 3:14-15    For this cause I bow my knees unto the Father of our Lord Jesus Christ, (15) Of whom the whole family in heaven is named ...

# February Twenty-Three: "All Things Are Possible"

(As inspired from Luke 17:19)

Lord Jesus, hear our prayer …

O Lord, throughout the New Testament, you have taught us that inconsistent faith is incompatible with your Ministry! Lord Jesus, we pray for all people who lack total belief in your Commanding Truth; for there are individuals who profess to love and adore you, yet, they dishonor their neighbor; and others, declare love for their neighbor, but take your name in vain. We ask in your Name, Lord Christ, to make clear your Heavenly Vision in the minds and souls of every person who is in contradiction of their faith and belief as a Christian; for all earthly and spiritual dreams come from the heart, and their fulfillment comes from the Purity of Trust in you, Our Lord! And if our dreams become lost or shattered, Lord Jesus Christ, we have faith to know that you will be there and you will restore our visions and make us whole again; because, all manner of amends and restitution exist within the Holy Realm of Heavenly Faith and Spiritual Forgiveness!

Our Good Lord, no person can show greater faith than by accepting belief in you, and through Absolute Faith in you, Lord Jesus, everything in life is possible! Lord of All Spiritual Happiness, you are the Abundant Faith and Direction of the world and the Eternal Blessing for all who are faithful to your Sacred and Blessed Word of Truth that directs and governs the very essence of life, of our lives, of everything that exists!

We proudly proclaim to all the inhabitants of this Living Creation and to the Heavens beyond our complete confidence in the Divine Wisdom of your Supreme Judgment and in the Exalted Power of your Compassionate Glory, Our Lord of Souls! And we can show no greater loyalty, as a Christian, than to confess our consummate belief in you, Lord Jesus Christ, to the world, therefore: May your Will be done on earth as it is in the Celestial Heavens above! Bless the children of your name, Lord Christ our Savior and Personal Redeemer!

Amen …

Chapter and verse that inspired prayer:

Luke 17:19    And he said unto him, Arise, go thy way: thy faith hath made thee whole.

# February Twenty-Four: "Lord, We Are As One Voice"

(As inspired from 2 Chronicles 5:13)

Lord Jesus, hear our prayer …

O Lord, we openly profess to be individuals who are positive, beyond a flicker of disbelief, that your Loving Presence is the Core of Existence in all life, in all souls, and in all things seen and unseen! And we thank you every day, Our Most Precious Lord, for as Christians, we experience the wonderful knowledge of your Infinite Influence in our daily lives: The wind whispers your Glorious Name, the sun reflects the Purity of your Radiance, and the entire universe is filled with your Luminous Love; Dear Lord, we are as one voice, honoring and thanking you for the wonders of life! You are the Song in Our Souls, Lord Jesus Christ, you are the Constant Melody that beats in our hearts, you are the Chorus of Compassion that endures forever in a Blest Melody that is sung throughout the whole of your Living and Loving Creation!

The House of The Lord is wherever you exist, Lord Jesus, and your Holy Word, Our Infallible Lord, exists everywhere! And for this reason, when we are by ourselves, or when we have gathered together in your Majestic Name, we speak to you, Lord God, as if your were standing right next to us, simply, because you really are! Our Lord of Everlasting Existence, you are the Center of Our Love, the Focus of Our Lives, the Heartbeat of Our Universe! Wherever we are, Lord Jesus, you bless us with your Holy Presence. If we are alone, you are there! If we are on a crowded street, you are there! If we are gathered with family or friends, you are there! Glory be to you, Lord Jesus Christ Our Most Compassionate King, for your Ever Present Spirit protects us forever, and forever will we give praise and thanks to you!

Amen …

Chapter and verse that inspired prayer:

2 Chronicles 5:13    It came even to pass, as the trumpeters and singers were as one, to make one sound to be heard in praising the LORD; and when they lifted up their voice with the trumpeters and cymbals and instruments of music, and praised the LORD, saying, For he is good; for his mercy endureth for ever: that then the house was filled with a cloud, even the house of the LORD.

# February Twenty-Five: "How Quickly You Answer"

(As inspired from Acts of the Apostles 2:25-26)

Lord Jesus, hear our prayer …

O Lord, our hearts rejoice in you, our words exalt you night and day, and our souls gladden in the wonderful knowledge that you forever dwell within our lives: Bless us with Peace and Spiritual Prosperity, Our Sovereign King, that we will one day be able to journey home to you and exist forever in your Heavenly Kingdom of Love and Kindness!

And so, all journeys begin with a first step, but when you began your journey on earth, Lord Jesus, and ended your Sacred Mission for us, it was actually our first step towards Spiritual Salvation and the beginning of our true destiny as Christians! The sweet blessings of your Inner Passion are always before us, Lord Christ, and our hearts revel in happiness knowing that our souls are forever saved through the Marvelous Miracle of your Divine Promise of Deliverance! Day and night, night and day, King of Glory, you are forever in our thoughts and prayers! When we are happy, we celebrate in your name. When we are sad, we call upon your name; and how quickly you answer! Morning or evening, dusk to dawn, your Compassionate Spirit moves through our souls and through our lives, Our Lord, and becomes the source and the reason for our Spiritual Hope! Doubt makes us question, but prayer gives us the answer; and only you, Lord Jesus Christ, are deserving of all honor and acclaim, for you answer all prayers according to personal need, and you are continually with us each and every promising and protecting way! Pray for us now, Our Lord of Salvation, that we may remain strong and fixed in our Christian goals and ambitions in life; let our futures remain bright and filled with happiness, and may your Hallowed Countenance forever guide our individual souls in our personal journeys through life!

Amen …

Chapter and verse that inspired prayer:

Acts of the Apostles 2:25-26   For David speaketh concerning him, I foresaw the Lord always before my face, for he is on my right hand, that I should not be moved: (26) Therefore did my heart rejoice, and my tongue was glad; moreover also my flesh shall rest in hope:

# February Twenty-Six: "Lord, Help Us To Become Worthy"

### (As inspired from Psalms 18:3, 6)

Lord Jesus, hear our prayer …

We call upon you, Lord Jesus, and we are delivered from the shadows that hide from your Resplendent Light of Goodness! And whenever the deluge of strife rains down upon us, O Lord, the only Healing Refuge from all sorrow is found in you! Through you, Lord Jesus, we find a safe haven against the snares of life's many entrapments. Even during times of distress, Dear Lord, we will always venerate the Sacred Sanctity of your Authority over darkness to protect us, lauding the Matchless Power of your Innocent Purity, which is known throughout the whole of creation! And throughout our lives, Our Prince of Peace, we will always call upon you to shelter us, because you alone have The Exalted Power and Majesty to conquer all adversity that comes along in life; and so, Our Great Lord, help us to become worthy of your many blessings, by blessing all who follow the Path of Righteousness!

Because you are so special in our hearts, O Lord, we openly display our physical and spiritual obedience to you, Our Deserving and Compassionate King, He, who deserves everyone's respect! We also give Total Adoration to you from the deepest reaches of our inner most feelings, praising you intently from the sincerity of our souls! Lord Jesus, we give to you, completely of our hearts, for you alone are worthy of Pure Love! Please, Christ Our Lord, help us to understand what it is to become good Christians, deserving of your Unceasing Love and the many blessings that are found in your Divine Mercy and Protection! And lastly, to the world, we loudly and proudly proclaim: Only through you, Lord Jesus Christ of Infinite Power, will anyone ever find their True Redemption and their True Worth in life! Praise be your Name unto all nations of the world and into the heart of every person that lives and breathes under the protection of your Glorious Sun!

Amen …

Chapter and verse that inspired prayer:

Psalms 18:3, 6   I will call upon the LORD, who is worthy to be praised: so shall I be saved from mine enemies. (6) In my distress I called upon the LORD, and my cry came unto my God: he heard my voice out of his temple, and my cry came before him, even into his ears.

# February Twenty-Seven: "Darkness Lost To The Light"
### (As inspired from 2 Timothy 4:6-7)

Lord Jesus, hear our prayer ...

Our hearts are opened to the Sacred and Holy Spirit of Our Lord Jesus Christ; into your hands, Our Anointed Savior, do we individually deliver our personal affirmation and solemn testimony of belief and obedience to your every Word of Truth! We pray that we are worthy!

God the Spirit, through the lives of the Apostles, you have inspired us to realize that life is not about our earthly life, but Eternal Life! If, during our lifetimes, we attain great wealth, power, and material gain but lose sight of your Heavenly Radiance, we will have filled our souls with nothing but empty shadows; therefore, whether with family, friends, or by ourselves, in all matters of the world, in all compassionate concerns, and in all things holy or temporal, Lord God, we promise that our Christian faith shall endure; and in our spiritual growth, we will continually fight to keep our hearts pure and our spirits uplifted to you! Lord Jesus, please know that we love and cherish the Tender Spirit of your Ever Forgiving Mercy, and that we will never turn aside from the Holy Statutes of your Commanding Word! O Lord, that we may forever find favor in your eyes, may our prayers be honorable to your ears and may our love continually shine brightly before the Altar of your Merciful Judgment. And then, in the end, when we have finished our journeys in life, when our time has finally arrived, Dear Lord, we will be welcomed into your Heavenly Family by the Warm Embrace of your Loving Grace; and we will be able to proudly acclaim that we fought the good fight, that we kept our faith; and again, darkness lost to the Light!

Amen ...

Chapter and verse that inspired prayer:

2 Timothy 4:6-7    For I am now ready to be offered, and the time of my departure is at hand. (7) I have fought a good fight, I have kept the faith:

# February Twenty-Eight: "Lord, All We Really Need Is You"

(As inspired from Revelation 19:5-7)

Lord Jesus, hear our prayer …

There, before us, is Victory in the Lord! And it is obtainable by everyone! And all we ever have to do to achieve it, is stay on the Path of Righteousness, and never lose sight of your Great Blessing, Eternal Life!

Alleluia to you, Lord God, whose Sacred Sovereignty reigns over this world and throughout your Heavenly Kingdom above! The many voices of your faithful multitudes thunder through the heavens, O Lord, as we rejoice and exult in your Victory on Earth! May all who follow you, Lord Jesus Christ, become true reflections of your Omnipresent Love, now and throughout all eternity! Our Most Hallowed Lord, we praise you and we thank you for attending to our spiritual and physical needs. Let all people, great or small, give their continual heartfelt adulation to you, Lord God Almighty, and realize that your Love and Mercy will forever Command Supreme in the hearts of all who sincerely worship you!

When we thirst, water will quench our desire. When we hunger, food will fulfill our need. When we are cold, clothing will cover and give warmth. But when our hearts are heavy and our spirits are empty, no amount of material gain, popularity, or earthly wealth will ever fill the void in our souls, nothing, that is, except you, Lord Jesus Christ; for of all the things that we really need in life, Lord, all we really need is you! Hallelujah! Hallelujah! All praise and glory to you, Our Lamb of God! And now, through the Apostleship of Prayer, Almighty and Hallowed God, we, your faithful, do advocate the following great reform for the whole earth: With open hearts, praise Our Lord Jesus Christ, everyone, the powerful and the meek; the rich and the poor, the brilliant and the dull, rejoice in His Name, giving Him honor and love until the end of time!

Amen..

Chapter and verse that inspired prayer:

Revelation 19:5-7     And a voice came out of the throne, saying Praise our God, all ye servants, and ye that fear him, both small and great. (6) And I heard as it were the voice of a great multitude, and as the voice of many waters, and as the voice of mighty thunderings, saying, Alleluia: for the Lord God omnipotent reigneth. (7) Let us be glad and rejoice, and give honour to him: for the marriage of the Lamb is come, and his wife hath made herself ready.

# February Twenty-Nine: "Lord, Grant Us Many Days"

(As inspired from Ruth 1:16)

Lord Jesus, hear our prayer ...

O Lord, we give thanks to you for this extra day to give you praise! Lord God, from your Sermon on the Mount, when you fed thousands of people who were spiritually hungry, your message concerning life was simple: With love and charity and forgiveness in our hearts, we are to follow you and seek the Glorious Kingdom of God, and our reward will be Eternity in Heaven! Lord Jesus Christ, we humbly accept and willingly follow your Hallowed Passages of Truth! Bless us and keep us safe, Our Good Shepherd, all the days of our lives! And all the days of our lives, we will venerate and glorify your Blessed and Holy Name!

Thank you, Dear Lord, for this extra day to give thanks. Thank you for this additional time to reflect upon all that you have given to us. Lord Jesus, our hearts and spirits leap with joy, for truly, we cannot express in words alone, the feelings that we have and hold true in our daily praises of you! Infinite Lord, grant us many days and many years of fruitfulness that we may follow the True Spiritual Path to the Way of Eternal Life and Deliverance. O Cherished Lord, wherever your Love takes us, there, is where we want to be! And wherever you are, we long to be with you; for your Word of Peace. Lord Jesus Christ, shall be our Spoken Word, and your Hallowed Truth shall be our Personal Conduct! Bless us, Our Lord of The Alpha and Omega, in the name of The Father, The Son, and The Holy Spirit, that we may stand today, tomorrow, and forever righteous in your Beautiful Word of Life!

Amen ...

Chapter and verse that inspired prayer:

Ruth 1:16    And Ruth said, Entreat me not to leave thee, or to return from following after thee: for wither thou goest, I will go; and where thou lodgest, I will lodge: thy people shall be my people, and thy God my God:

For the leap year.

# March One: "A Creation That Was Created For All"
### (As inspired from Genesis 9:16-17)

Lord Jesus, hear our prayer …

Today, we triumphantly march forward in your Resplendent Glory: O Lord, when the sun comes out, after a gentle rain, the multitude of colors in the rainbow remind us of your Everlasting Love and how this loving creation is your Eternal Promise to all creatures, great and small, and to everything that has the breath of life! Lord Jesus, we pray for all who may cause harm to the environment through the blindness of their actions. We also ask of you, Lord God, to open their eyes that they may see the harm of their destruction and the folly of their ignorance. Enlighten their hearts, O Merciful Lord, to understand that earth is the only planet upon which our physical lives exist!

Our Wonderful Lord, your faithful are a people that are blessed in your bounty and who love and respect this world. We beseech you, Lord Jesus, to humble those who are self-serving and misguided in their gainful intentions. Instill in them, Lord Christ, a sincere love and respect for this life giving creation, your creation, a creation that was created for all!

For the sanctity of all life, we pray to you Lord Jesus: Impart your compassion into the hearts of everyone! Deliver your faithful from the wrath of those who cause harm to the waters, to the land, and to the air through personal arrogance and ignorance! Bless all life, Lord Jesus Christ, that it may forever flourish and remain! And command your love to continually pour out upon this wondrous planet called earth and upon all who are faithful to your Unblemished Word and to the Commandment and Agreement of your Covenant between heaven and earth!

Amen …

Chapter and verse that inspired prayer:

Genesis 9:16-17    And the bow shall be in the cloud; and I will look upon it, that I may remember the everlasting covenant between God and every living creature of all flesh that is upon the earth. (17) And God said unto Noah, This is the token of the covenant, which I have established between me and all flesh that is upon the earth.

# March Two: "Sheaves Of Faithful Souls"

(As inspired from Isaiah 58:8-9)

Lord Jesus, hear our prayer …

Here we are, Lord of the Visible and Invisible, gathered together to offer our most gracious praise of adoration to your existence: Thank you, Lord God, for protecting our spirits and our hearts through the cold season of short days and long nights. And through your Loving and Guiding Light, Lord Jesus, we know that we will be able to courageously step into the unknown of life's many seasons. For with the security of your Infinite Mercy and Forgiveness, Lord Christ, we will be guided through any period of trial and tribulation; when you enter the heart, O Lord, the snows of winter begin to melt and the pure waters of spring begin to flow and nourish the soul! And when your Holy Spirit enters our lives, Our Victorious Lord, the long shadows of doubt and ignorance end and the Radiance of your Pure Love shines down upon us to produce sheaves of faithful souls for your Glory; and your Heavenly Glory, Lord Jesus Christ, is our reward!

Our Heavenly King, we ask of you: Please, remove from the midst of the world all contempt, and replace it with your Compassionate Affection! Lord Jesus, allow the season of light and growth to quickly spring forth and remain forever within the hearts and souls of every person on earth! May everyone's Christian faith continue to abundantly grow in your Spirit, Lord Christ Our Namesake, that we may all become a bountiful harvest of your Glorious Love! And through a constant vigil of our spiritual development, we will achieve a bounteous yield of world faith for you, Lord God Creator of All Life!

Amen …

Chapter and verse that inspired prayer:

Isaiah 58:8-9    Then shall thy light break forth as the morning, and thine health shall spring forth speedily: and thy righteousness shall go before thee; the glory of the LORD shall be thy rereward. (9) Then shalt thou call, and the LORD shall answer; thou shalt cry, and he shall say, Here I am. If thou take away from the midst of thee the yoke, the putting forth of the finger, and speaking vanity;

# March Three: "A Heavenly Home Of Glory"

### (As inspired from 1 Samuel 2:8 and John 14:2)

Lord Jesus, hear our prayer …

You have taught us through Scripture, Our Lord of Fulfillment, that every human soul is cherished by our Heavenly Father who desires each of His living creations to be happy and to one day return home! From out of the dust of spiritual despair, Lord God, you have lifted our souls and created for us a new life of hope! As the sun brightly rises to meet the new day, we too, Lord Christ, awaken with lifted spirits to gloriously acclaim this day for you! We worship you. Lord Jesus, and with each waking day, we give our complete love to you! And through your Love, Lord Jesus Our Christ and Savior, we have become pillars of faith who will one day inherit a Heavenly Home of Eternal Glory in the many mansions throughout your Glorious Kingdom of Merciful Salvation!

With each waking day, Lord of Light, you give us spiritual security that continually nourishes our Christian faith! For only through your Grace and Goodness, Lord Jesus, are we able to live in harmony and peace all the days of our lives. O Lord, we thank you for this glorious day! And we greatly thank you for the wonderful blessing of our Christian faith and for strengthening our spirits and for giving our lives direction and purpose! Establish our place in the Holy Estate of your Heavenly Love, Lord Jesus Christ, by sealing our souls with the Sacred Signet of your Divine Majesty!

Amen …

Chapter and verse that inspired prayer:

1 Samuel 2:8   He raiseth up the poor out of the dust, and lifteth up the beggar from the dunghill, to set them among princes, and to make them inherit the throne of glory: for the pillars of the earth are the LORD's, and he hath set the world upon them.

John 14:2   In my Father's house are many mansions: if it were not so, I would have told you. I go to prepare a place for you.

# March Four: "Teach The Truth"

(As inspired from 2 John 4)

Lord Jesus, hear our prayer ...

You have shown us, O Lord, through the Gospels and through the lives of the apostles that our Christian faith is not reserved solely for the adults; thus, we proudly proclaim and pray in the Hallowed Name of our Lord Jesus Christ, that all parents, for the future of Goodness, will raise up their children in the eyes of God; and then, the eyes of God will always be upon them!

We are all but Children of Our Lord Father God Almighty; and we learned from those who taught us. Lord Jesus, from generation to generation, we pray that you will instill into the tender hearts of your faithful youth an earnest desire to be honest and to build upon their Christian faith. Inspire in us now, O Lord, to individually seek the proper knowledge and advice that our children must learn to become good and faithful Christians of their faith; and let us never hesitate to teach the truth and to always speak the truth to our everyone, young or old, no matter how innocent or small or cleavor the deception may appear to be; for you have taught us that even the smallest of blemishes will boldly stand out in your eyes, Our Lord and God!

We have fled from the spiritual shadows and ignorance of our innocent youth, Lord Jesus, and as adults, we have charged into the Light of your Truth and Wisdom! Help us, Lord of the World, that we may offer New Generations in Christ, the mettle to face all indecisions and to complete all tasks that are placed before them. We also ask of you, Our Good Shepherd, to establish in all children the courage to meet every challenge in life and to stand firm against the deceivers and dissenters of your Word. And in doing so, Lord of Forbearance, permit all young people, everywhere, to grow profusely in their understanding of Christianity and in your Spirit of Truth, Lord Jesus Christ! We pray to you, O Lord: Bless the children; for they are the true blessings of life, of our lives, and of all life yet to come into existence!

Amen ...

Chapter and verse that inspired prayer:

2 John 4    I rejoiced greatly that I found of thy children walking in truth, as we have received a commandment from the Father.

# March Five: "Your Wondrous Creation Of Love"

(As inspired from Philippians 3:20)

Lord Jesus, hear our prayer …

All praise to you, Our Heavenly Host, for every person who begins life, begins as a blank slate, an innocent soul, and through the blessed teachings of your Hallowed Scriptures, is one day converted into a heavenly soul of love and compassion who patiently awaits your Holy Reunion on earth, Lord Jesus Christ Our Savior and Redeemer! And, Lord Jesus, we pray that your return will be soon!

It is our heartfelt prayer, Lord Christ, that all your faithful followers will be of one mind, one heart, and one belief; because you are the Gate through which everyone must pass through to receive the Kingdom of Heaven! Lord God, when there is a convergence of Christian belief, there is a unity of faith, an agreement of souls, and a dialogue that expounds our understanding of your Benevolent Generosity on earth; therefore, Lord Christ, we extol the wonders and signs of your Great Love; for you are the Spirit of Hope, Our Lord and Savior, Our God of All That Is! Lord Jesus, we are humbled, for the proof of your Holy Spirit abounds everywhere!

Whatever our eyes see, our hearts greatly rejoice in you, Our Lord of Perfection! And wherever we stand, we look around and see your Holy and Unflawed Reflection as it encircles the whole of earth and all of the life that exists within it! Lord Christ, everyday we express our gratitude and joy for you, and as every new day begins, our voices celebrate your Glorious Works! Continuously, throughout the day, Lord Jesus Christ, our spirits take delight in all the miracles of life that abound in your creation! And when evening comes, our prayers and thoughts reflect the thanks we feel towards you, Our Lord of Abundance, that we are a part of life, and that we have lived another glorious day in your Wondrous Creation of Love!

Amen …

Chapter and verse that inspired prayer:

Philippians 3:20   For our conversation is in heaven; from whence also we look for the Saviour, the Lord Jesus Christ:

# March Six: "The Gift Of Life"

### (As inspired from Ecclesiastes 5:18)

Lord Jesus, hear our prayer ...

What other creature on earth has the ability to ponder a sun set, to lovingly smile at a newborn, or to contemplate and truly comprehend the creation and its Creator! As humans, we thank you, Lord Jesus, for we are separate from all other creatures and life forms. Almighty God, you gave us the ability to think, to reason, to know where we came from, and to fully understand that you, Our Heavenly Father, created us in your image! In all of creation, the greatest gift that you have ever given us, Lord Christ, is this gift of life; and miraculous and marvelous is this heavenly knowledge that we possess! Pray for us, Our Lord Jesus Christ, that we will never abuse our most precious gift, that we will never take it for granted, and that we will continually strive to improve on our spiritual and physical lives! Encourage us, Prince of Life, to live this great and wonderful blessing to its fullest and to the best of our abilities! And we also ask of you, Dear Lord, that you will inspire us to be forever thankful for the portion of life that you have bestowed upon us as individuals!

If we believe and righteously build upon this wondrous gift from you, Lord Christ, then you are righteously glorified! But if we harm or ignore or destroy this sacred blessing, then we will have defiled it. Therefore, Our Lord of All Life, through a conscious and considerate awareness, we will honor our incredible gift of life by believing in and by maintaining the virtue of your Goodness throughout our Christian lives! All glory and all grandeur go to you, Lord Jesus Christ! May we forever protect this Most Heavenly and Blest Gift, our gift of life.

Amen ...

Chapter and verse that inspired prayer:

Ecclesiastes 5:18   Behold that which I have seen: it is good and comely for one to eat and to drink, and to enjoy the good of all his labour that he taketh under the sun all the days of his life, which God giveth him: for it is his portion.

# March Seven: "All Are Welcomed"

(As inspired from Matthew 13:23, 37)

Lord Jesus, hear our prayer ...

From the foundation of creation, your Holy Word, Our Lord of Bounty, is the Good Seed of Life from which all Unblemished Love and Virtue have grown; and the loving soul of every person has been invited to share in your Most Bountiful Harvest. Lord Jesus, as the good earth receives a seed to nourish and to properly grow, so too, do we long for your Spiritual Nourishment that we may grow righteously in your sight and become a part of the abundant harvest that shares in your Perfect Word, which will endure forever and ever into Everlasting Glory and Eternal Life! O Lord, we are truly overwhelmed with happiness and joy, to know that all are welcomed, by your opened arms and Tender Grace, to partake in Goodness! And to your Spirit of Compassion, we offer up our personal praises to the Profound Magnitude of your Generosity: Blessed are the people and the nation who honor and obey your Commandments of Love and Peace!

Lord Jesus, just as the good soil receives the rain, and the blossoming flowers gather the light, and the loving parent warmly honors their own child, we know that every God-fearing person on this planet is welcomed into your Faithful Family of Love; for your Heavenly Family is but a single Creation of Compassion and Forgiveness! And we pray to you, Lord Jesus Christ, that our lives will always be filled with the fruits of love and virtue, so that one day we too will truly be accepted and welcomed into your Bountiful Beautiful Kingdom of Love; for then, and only then, will we truly inherit our glorious fulfillment from the Sower of the Good Seed of Life, The Son of Man, Our Lord and God for All Eternity!

Amen ...

Chapter and verse that inspired prayer:

Matthew 13:23, 37   But he that received seed into the good ground is he that heareth the word, and understandeth it; which also beareth fruit, and bringeth forth, some an hundredfold, some sixty, some thirty. (37) He answered and said unto them, He that soweth the good seed is the Son of man;

# March Eight: "Lord, We Gloriously Belong To You"

### (As inspired from Matthew 5:28 and Hebrews 11:9-10)

Lord Jesus, hear our prayer ...

Lord, we humbly ask of you to forgive us our misdeeds and transgressions against your Commandments that we may have committed through our actions, our words, or even our thoughts. For you have taught us in Scripture that when a person merely thinks of an affront against the Will of God, they have already committed the offense against His Will; but also, we are taught to immediately ask forgiveness, and it shall be given! Praise be to you, Lord Jesus, for our Spiritual Salvation and Deliverance from everything that opposes The Trinity of Love and Holiness!

We confess to the world and to all who exist that the Sovereign Architect and Supreme Engineer of our earth, our universe, and even our souls, is God Almighty! Therefore, all of creation has become the Land of Promise; and we praise you, Lord God, for you are the maker and builder of mountains, valleys, rivers, deserts, and Oceans! You, Our Great Lord, till the good earth, sow the seeds that grow the wild flowers, the grasses of the prairies, and the woodlands of the forests and jungles! You, Lord Jesus, tend to all the creatures in the world, to the fowl of the air, and to the fishes under the sea. You, Our Holy Spirit of Love, bring the gentle rains, the warm breezes, and the life giving light from the sun! Praise be to you, The Essence of Our Total Existence! Lord, we gloriously belong to you, Christ Jesus Our Savior, Creator of nations, of peoples, of love, of everything, and of everyone that ever was, is, or will ever be! Blest are you, Lord, forever into eternity; for we are the heirs in your Promise of Salvation! Blessed are all who faithfully believe in you and follow you, Our Lord Jesus!

Amen ...

Chapter and verse that inspired prayer:

Matthew 5:28     But I say unto you, That whosoever looketh on a woman to lust after her hath committed adultery with her already in his heart.

Hebrews 11:9-10     By faith he sojourned in the land of promise, as in a strange country, dwelling in tabernacles with Isaac and Jacob, the heirs with him of the same promise: (10) For he looked for a city which hath foundations, whose builder and maker Is God.

# March Nine: "Through Daily Devotions, We Will Grow"

(As inspired from 1 Kings 8:38-39)

Lord Jesus, hear our prayer …

Through daily devotions, we will grow as individuals, as a nation, and as a world captivated in the Holy Spirit of Our Living Loving God who reigns on earth and in the heavens above: Bless us, O Lord, and anoint us with your Good Graces! Lord God, you know every heart of every person who truly loves and worships you. Please, Lord Jesus, know that our hearts are pure when we pray to you; for we understand and we know that prayer is as important to the immortal soul as breathing is to physical life! And through daily personal prayers, every faithful person in the world has the ability to grow stronger in their belief and spirit! Lord Christ, we pray for one another: Forgive us our weaknesses and strengthen our spiritual faith that bonds us to your Heavenly Love and Mercy! Bless us, Lord Jesus Christ, in our daily endeavors throughout our individual Christian lives!

Dear Lord, our daily prayers to you should be as natural as a heartbeat; for the answer to all prayers is only obtained through an impassioned faith in you, Lord Jesus! Therefore, on a daily basis, throughout the day, throughout the year, and throughout our lives, Our Lord of Forgiveness, we will keep you in our hearts, in our thoughts, and in our individual lives, with an intense and undaunted belief, now and forever! Thank you, Lord God, for all of our prayers that you answer and resolve through soulful and sincere supplication! And thank you again, for reaching out from your Heavenly Throne and touching us with a Blessing of Hope!

Amen …

Chapter and verse that inspired prayer …

1 Kings 8:38-39    What prayer and supplication soever be made by any man, or by all thy people Israel, which shall know every man the plague of his own heart, and spread forth his hand toward this house: (39) Then hear thou in heaven thy dwelling place, and forgive, and do, and give to every man according to his ways, whose heart thou knowest; (for thou, even thou only, knowest the hearts of all the children of men;)

# March Ten: "We Belong To You, Lord"

### (As inspired from Psalms 34:3-4)

Lord Jesus, hear our prayer …

Dear Lord, we know that all who honestly seek you as their Personal Savior against the uncertainties of this world, will most definitely and joyously find you in the midst of their lives! Lord Jesus, we magnify your Loving Presence within our souls, in our hearts, and throughout every waking moment of life by proudly proclaiming our Christian belief and testimony in you: O Lord Most Glorious and Radiant, we truly honor you everyday in word, thought, and personal actions! We ask that you will comfort our souls and deliver us from our personal fears and doubts: Into your hands, Lord Jesus, do we place all of our concerns and confidently celebrate our victory through exaltations of you! Our spiritual and physical jubilance for you is but a small reflection of the great love and the great happiness that we have found in your Victorious Truth and Absolute Existence! We worship you, Lord Jesus Christ, with a joyous laudability in our hearts as we esteem you in prayer and duly proclaim your Beautiful and Majestic Name to the world! Blessed is Our Comforter of Life!

To you, Lord Jesus Christ, belongs the highest of acclaim! To you alone, Lord Jesus, is given the greatest of glory! And only to you, Lord Christ, do we owe our endless and unceasing obedience! We exist solely for you, Our Prince of Peace, because your love unites the world in a Divine Fellowship of Compassion! From our hearts, from our minds, and from our mouths do we magnify you in renowned praises of truth: To you, God of Life, belongs all existence and every individual soul who magnifies your Magnificent Name everyday of their life, and we, your loving faithful, belong only to you, Our Beloved and Honored Lord of Heaven and Earth!

Amen …

Chapter and verse that inspired prayer:

Psalms 34:3-4   O magnify the LORD with me, and let us exalt his name together. (4) I sought the LORD, and he heard me, and delivered me from all my fears.

# March Eleven: "We Have Become Pillars Of Faith"

(As inspired from Mark 8:36)

Lord Jesus, hear our prayer ...

Lord God, our temporal dreams are but sand dunes in the wind; and oh, how quickly our visions are scattered by the winds of doubt. For if we follow the false allurements of the world, Lord Jesus, we cannot possibly profit in our heart's desire. But if we faithfully serve you, Lord Jesus Christ, we will build an establishment of spiritual existence upon the bedrock of true Christian faith, by which all dreams are fulfilled! And because all things are possible through you, Lord Jesus, it is for this reason that we confidently pray to you: That our future goals, directions, and ambitions will be within accomplishment, bless us and award us determination and the necessary skills to achieve our individual heart's desires!

We pray to you, O Lord, that we will be able to continually withstand the worldly temptations of pride and arrogance, and that we will never extol ourselves above others; but that we will always bestow all honor and glory upon you alone, Lord Jesus Our Heavenly King, who awards all victory!

Look into our hearts, Lord of Judgment, and look into our spirits. We have become pillars of faith in your name! And through our deepest and most spiritual love that we have for you, Lord Jesus, it is our heart's desire to serve you with only the greatest of acclaim for the heavenly wonders of your Divine Guidance and Greatness! Lord of Heaven and Earth, you alone are worthy to be called The Exalted Eminence by all who faithfully follow the Holy Precepts of your Hallowed Word! In your name, Lord Jesus Christ, bless us and protect us, and empower our souls to prosper greatly through our Christian faith!

Amen ...

Chapter and verse that inspired prayer:

Mark 8:36   For what shall it profit a man, if he shall gain the whole world, and lose his own soul?

# Mark Twelve: "Send Your Guiding Light, Lord"

(As inspired from Jeremiah 29:13)

Lord Jesus, hear our prayer …

Our Lord and Personal Savior, that we may find the Essence of Heaven's Light, sanction your cleansing fires to purge the shadows of all darkness: Please, O Lord, forgive and bless and heal our souls that we may sincerely ask for and receive of your Redeeming Mercy and Safekeeping! Help us, Lord Jesus, in our soulful search to be non-judgmental, accepting, and morally good in all that we do and say. Lord Jesus Christ, we seek the faithful, correct path to your Immaculate Heart! And in our prayers, we ask for your Spiritual Direction and Counseling. Lead us, Lord of All True Forgiveness, to your Loving Presence, to the wisdom of your Endless Grace and Endearing Salvation! All praise to you, Almighty God, for we have willingly submersed our souls into your Hallowed Existence through the Wonderful Baptism of The Holy Spirit of Love! Triumphant and Forever Victorious is your All-conquering Spirit! Amen!

Our Lord of Infinite Domain, no one needs to search the world, nor research volumes of literature, or even ponder your whereabouts, all anyone ever has to do to find you, is simply, to look within their own loving heart. Send your Guiding Light, Lord Christ, that we will be able to safely pass through all the many shadows of this world. Help us, Lord Jesus, to perceive and accept the only Truth of this World, Your Truth! And in our search, Lord Jesus Christ, if you find us worthy, please, receive and embrace our spirits with the Loving Radiance of your Total Perfection! And when you look into our individual hearts, Lord Christ Our Savior of Souls, you will discover that our personal faith is a Heavenly Reflection of your Most Blessed and Sacred Heart of Holiness!

Amen …

Chapter and verse that inspired prayer:

Jeremiah 29:13   And ye shall seek me, and find me, when ye shall search for me with all your heart.

## March Thirteen: "We Pray, Lord, That We Will Never Falter"
### (As inspired from Jonah 4:2)

Lord Jesus, her our prayer ...

We pray for every person in every religion, belief, and creed around the world that their faith will one day lead them to the Absolute Truth, to you, Lord Jesus Christ, in Whom is the Final Judgment and Reward for all nations and all peoples!

O Lord, throughout the ages and throughout Scripture, you have taught your faithful that you are The Truth of Life, The Kingdom of Heaven, The Only Way! And that no one may reach our Heavenly Father, except through you! Blessed are you, Our Most Gracious Lord, benevolent in all forgiveness and compassion; our immortal souls gather close to you! Lord Jesus, everyday, life's trials and ordeals temper our spirits and test our individual faith. The winds of indecision continually try to erode away spiritual visions. But when dark clouds gather and threaten our light, we stand fast, secure in our beliefs, ensured in our knowledge that you, Our Lord Jesus, are always there to help us, to comfort us, to stand with us, now and forevermore! We pray to you, Lord God, that we will never falter in our Christian faith. Keep us strong in our individual beliefs, Dear Lord, from this time forward! And from now and until the end of all time we will follow you, Lord Christ, as obedient Christians, by the Commandments of the One and Only Absolute Faith for Personal Salvation, Christianity! Lord Jesus Christ, you are Merciful, Compassionate, and Slow to Anger; and through your Great Kindness, Love and Mercy shall follow us in this world all the days of our lives, until that blessed day when we are embraced and reunited in the Loving Arms of The Father, The Son, and The Holy Spirit, in Whom All Are One!

Amen ...

Chapter and verse that inspired prayer:

Jonah 4:2    And he prayed unto the LORD, and said, I pray thee, O LORD, was not this my saying, when I was yet in my country? Therefore I fled before unto Tarshish: for I knew that thou art a gracious God, and merciful, slow to anger, and of great kindness, and repentest thee of the evil.

# March Fourteen: "We Give Thanks For This Day"

(As inspired from Ester 9:19)

Lord Jesus, hear our prayer …

Anoint your faithful, O Lord, with lasting happiness! Destroy in us, any and all negative thoughts that we may dwell upon; instead, instruct our spirits and our minds to ponder on anticipating the best possible outcome from any unwary situation that might take place in our lives; inspire us to always turn to you, Lord God, to resolve the many problems that we are faced with during our lifetimes! Teach us to Pray Correctly!

Through the peace and tranquility that abounds from your Never Ending Love and Holy Spirit, we give thanks for this day and for every day of gladness that you share with us! Our Lord Jesus, no matter how dark the night is or how overcast the day seems or how difficult the odds are, we are, at all times, comforted in our hearts through your Invincible Spirit! Permit us, Lord Christ, to discover within ourselves an inner energy for positive living and for assured thinking as you have so portioned out to each of us according to the measure of our individual faith and need! And how inspiring it is to know that the Conquering Power of your Healing Love flows outward to help everyone, everywhere, who calls upon your Precious Name to overcome their individual problems and difficulties! And with complete confidence in your Spirit and Strength, Lord Jesus Christ, we will make every day a day of heartfelt gladness through uplifted thinking, spiritual living, and through a genuine love for one another, as we triumph over any and all adversity, through the Power of your Divine Kindness!

Amen …

Chapter and verse that inspired prayer:

Esther 9:19    Therefore the Jews of the villages, that dwelt in the unwalled towns, made the fourteenth day of the month Adar a day of gladness and feasting, and a good day, and of sending portions one to another.

# March Fifteen: "Your Law Of Love"

(As inspired from 2 John 5-6)

Lord Jesus, hear our prayer …

Dear Lord, your wonderful Commandments are the constant and correct laws that govern the heart, the mind, the spirit and all of creation; and your laws, Lord Jesus, are not only made for the innocent and for the healthy, but also for the ill, for the confused and disobedient, and even for the lawless. Through your love, Lord Jesus Christ, we ask that all people will be released from their fears, from their failures, and from their frustrations in life by uniting under one flawless doctrine, your Mandate of Love; which is to love one another as we love ourselves and you, Lord God!

Lord Jesus, each and every one of us walks upon the same good earth, breathes in the same air, and stands in the same light! People are as similar as blades of grass, and yet, as different as night and day. By individually sharing our Christian faith with others, and by uniting our feelings in a true compassion of understanding for one another, the world will find a oneness, Our Great Lord, through the perfection and protection of your Life Giving Tenet of Love!

In this world, we have many religions, varied beliefs, and individual convictions, but in your Heavenly Kingdom, there is only One Truth, You, Lord Jesus! O Lord, we know that every soul in existence belongs to the same family through your Heavenly Love of Creation, and we pray that everyone on earth will ask to be released from their own personal prejudices and desires to be united under your Celestial Commandment of Compassion; the Universal Truth that governs the whole universe and all that exists, which is, of course, your Law of Love that is written and sanctioned for everyone!

Amen …

Chapter and verse that inspired prayer:

2 John 5-6   And now I beseech thee, lady, not as though I wrote a new commandment unto thee, but that which we had from the beginning, that we love one another. (6) And this is love, that we walk after his commandments. This is the commandment, That, as ye have heard from the beginning, ye shall walk in it.

# March Sixteen: "The Light Of The World"

(As inspired from John 3:16)

Lord Jesus, hear our prayer …

We praise, we exalt, and we marvel at your compassion for us, Lord God, that you would have sent your Perfect Light into our world of darkness and doubt. No Father ever loved their children more than the Father that could give Eternal Life through the Everlasting Love of Total Redemption! We are truly humbled, for we are in utter awe and reverence of your Merciful and Sacred Heart, Lord Jesus! And from every human heart that beats and from every Christian soul that exists on this good earth, we do commit our immortal souls to you, and vow, at all times, to worship only you. Lord Jesus Christ, who was born of flesh, was falsely accused, was tortured and crucified, died, and yet, on the third day, rose again from the darkness of death, and is now and forevermore, The Light of the World, and in whose Word the Laws of heaven and earth do exist!

All life is drawn to the Light, and all life that proceeds into the Light will overcome any captivity and be forever released from the earthly bonds of this temporal world that can suppress and subdue the spiritual heart and soul. Lord Jesus, our lives have been greatly blessed through the Glory of your Pure and Innocent Love! And through your Crucified Innocence, our very souls have been saved for all eternity! All thanks, all praise, and all Glory to you God, Our Savior, Our Spirit of Absolute Holiness; blessed is the creation, our creation, from which the Trinity of Love was established before time began!

Amen …

Chapter and verse that inspired prayer:

John 3:16    For God so loved the world, that he gave his only begotten Son, that whosoever believeth in him should not perish, but have everlasting life.

# March Seventeen: "Become True Reflections"

(As inspired from 1 Samuel 12:24)

Lord Jesus, hear our prayer …

Lord All Powerful, throughout the Old and New Testaments, you have shown us that fear is a form of great respect, and as Christians, we should fear only the power that destroys the immortal soul, but not the temporal body! Lord, for the great things that you have bestowed upon us, we give to you our deepest thanks and solemn promise to forever serve you with loving respect, total obedience, and an honest heart. For as the infinite universe is an embodiment of your continual compassion for us, Lord Jesus, we pray that all of us will also become true reflections of your Loving and Giving Spirit of Kindness!

O Lord Jesus, please accept the integrity of our love as we outwardly profess our Christian faith of obedience and devotion to you: Our sole passion in life is to spiritually and physically serve you, Lord Jesus Christ Our Holy Hallowed Host! For just as the sun, the moon, and this world all bear witness to the ultimate perfection of your holy creations, we ask of you, Lord God: Please, encourage us to also become living testimonies of goodness in our own lifetimes, here on earth! And to you, and only you, Our Most Sacred and Holy Spirit of Love, we serve you with truth, through sincerity of the heart: That we may praise you with words of worthiness, baptize us in the Purity of Your Perfection!

Our Heavenly King, as all nature and life mirrors the grandeur and beauty of your love for us, we too shall become constant reflections of our love that we may always stand confidently in your sight by spiritually accepting and thoughtfully doing your Commandment of Love, Lord Jesus Christ: To do for others as we would do for ourselves!

Amen …
Chapter and verse that inspired prayer:

1 Samuel 12:24    Only fear the LORD, and serve him in truth with all your heart: for consider how great things he hath done for you.

# March Eighteen: "Lord, We Pray For A Vision"

(As inspired from 2 Thessalonians 2:16-17)

Lord Jesus, hear our prayer …

For those who truly love and trust in you, Our Hallowed God of Love, the Infinite Source of all Living Waters begins at the summit of your Undeniable Compassion and Understanding of us! Dear Lord Jesus, we pray that you will forever intervene in our lives when life seems to be at its darkest and loneliest, when our visions are empty and shallow, when our world is clouded by fear and doubt, overshadowed by lost hope and eclipsed by broken dreams; because, Our Lord Jesus Christ, in this darkened world, you are the only Ray of Hope that we, as Christians, may grasp onto and dearly hold true to ourselves! We pray that you will hear us, Our Gentle Prince of Peace, for your Everlasting Mercy is, without a shadow of spiritual doubt, the Salvation of Our Eternal Hope Through Grace, in which we so dearly search for and cling to in life!

You comfort our thoughts, Lord God, and permanently institute in our hearts, an Undeniable Assurance in ourselves! Dear Lord, through faith, we pray for a vision of Truth, for a lighted candle to show the way, and for our souls to follow a Sanctified Destination. And, Lord Jesus, you are the Unparalleled Destination in life that every person must follow and that anyone ever needs to pursue! Warrant us, Our Lord of Total Grace, to find complete fulfillment in our lives. Instill in us, as faithful Christians, the desire to continually believe, to forever accept, and in every instance, to always trust in your Merciful Compassion, Lord Jesus Christ, now and throughout the passing of all time, and, until the end of all time!

Amen …

Chapter and verse that inspired prayer:

2 Thessalonians 2:16-17   Now our Lord Jesus Christ himself, and God, even our Father, which hath loved us, and hath given us everlasting consolation and good hope through grace, (17) Comfort your hearts, and stablish you in every good word and work.

# March Nineteen: "Begin The Resolution Of World Strife"

### (As inspired from 2 Peter 1:2-3)

Lord Jesus, hear our prayer …

Because we have completely accepted you, Lord Jesus Christ, into our hearts, Grace and Peace will forever be magnified and multiplied in our souls and in the souls of all people who do the same; blessed is your Perfect Name throughout all creation! Lord Jesus, we realize that when our hearts embrace your Most Infinite Wisdom, your Truth will guide and direct our spirits towards your unequaled compassion. And when we personally receive you, Lord Christ, into our lives, we are partaking in your All-encompassing Power of Love that teaches us how to live our lives correctly in this world. Lord Jesus Christ, through your Divine Calling, all people will find their personal sanctuary of peace in your Faultless Wisdom of Truth and Excellence!

O Lord, what are the words that may be written or spoken that would end all war or rumors of war; peace is not an illusion, for we are not destined to forever follow the precepts of Cain, but the teachings of Christ! Lord Jesus, if all people of all nations would truly receive and accept your wisdom, it would allow the Power of True Love, the Power of Absolute Faith, and the Power of your Perfect Word to guide and direct the earth to become a planet of peace, in complete harmony with the Holy Spirit of Compassion! Therefore, through our own personal and individual acceptance of your Holy Word, Lord Jesus Christ, here and now, we can individually begin the resolution of world strife! Lord Jesus, empower the minds of all peoples and of all nations on earth to open their hearts and fill their spirits to capacity with the Unerring Truth of your Limitless Love and All-knowing Judgment!

Amen …

Chapter and verse that inspired prayer:

2 Peter 1:2-3    Grace and peace be multiplied unto you through the knowledge of God, and of Jesus our Lord, (3) According as his divine power hath given unto us all things that pertain unto life and godliness, through the knowledge of him that hath called us to glory and virtue:

# March Twenty: "A Visible Force Of Spiritual Energy"
### (As inspired from Ezra 3:11)

Lord Jesus, hear our prayer ...

O Heavenly Father, our spirits are lifted high as we sing out our praises of thanks to you; for you are so good to us and your Endearing Mercies endure forever! We pray that your Perfect Love, Lord Jesus, will become the solid foundation for everyone's faith in the world! And as we truthfully and sincerely take care of our own faith, we know that you will also take care of us! Therefore, we ask of you, O Lord: Concur with all who seek to establish a life of religious goodness! Let all people in their spiritual journey, begin with a solid foundation of your love; this, in turn, will then grant to all who try, everywhere, a wonderful chance to grow into a visual viable force of Christian faith in your Glorious Name!

We pray for all the lost souls of the world who have no idea how greatly improved their individual lives could become, if only they had you, Lord Jesus Christ, in their lives to help guide them towards a life of fulfillment and complete happiness: Let all eyes see you and all hearts accept you!

Lord Jesus, you have shown us that a warm summer breeze is comfortable, but nothing will slow nor halter the winds of a raging storm! Or that a gentle hill may slopes upwards above the horizon, but the enormity of a snow capped mountain can even stop the clouds of the sky! And a quiet, shallow stream can flow for miles, but the deep torrent of a rapidly moving river has the ability to actually cut through stone! Lord Christ, we pray, instill in us a zeal of faith that will be like a raging storm, an enormous mountain, and a turbulent river that will condone nothing to stand in the way of our spiritual progression of faith that we have in you, Christ Jesus Our Lord! We pray for all people: Increase the world's knowledge of you, Lord of All Nations, of All Peoples, and of All Souls, into a visible force of Spiritual Energy!

Amen ...

Chapter and verse that inspired prayer:

Ezra 3:11    And they sang together by course in praising and giving thanks unto the LORD; because he is good, for his mercy endureth for ever toward Israel. And all the people shouted with a great shout, when they praised the LORD, because the foundation of the house of the LORD was laid.

# March Twenty-One: "Promise Of Eternal Life"

(As inspired from Ezekiel 34:26-27)

Lord Jesus, hear our prayer …

Blessed are you, Lord God, for you have delivered us from our spiritual bondage through the power of your Redeeming Grace! We give you great thanks, Lord Jesus Christ, for the first day of a new life, for the first days of rebirth, for these, the first days of spring! You cause the gentle rains to fall that nourish the good seeds in the soil, which will mature into strong plants and produce many of its own kind. And we pray to you, Lord of the Resurrection, that we too may become the good seeds of your Never Ending Mercy and grow righteously in your sight, so that one day, we will also be able to yield an abundant harvest of faithful souls from the many unbounded blessings that we receive, which are found throughout the Majestic Showering of your Supreme Compassion!

Never, will we forget whom we serve in body and soul; from you, Lord of the Universe, shall our Heavenly Increase on earth be remembered, for you are The Hallowed Presence in our lives and in the lives of every person who as ever been or is yet to be! O Lord, we give you all acclaim and thanks for this season of promise and rebirth; for it symbolizes the constant continuation of your Forever Creation, founded by the Healing Waters of the Eternal and Holy Spirit! We are very delighted and pleased, Lord Jesus, for these first days of life's resurgence; but most of all, we are continually grateful to you for being a part of your Promise of Eternal Life, which begins here, this day, on this fertile soil through a Confession of Truth, that you, Lord Jesus Christ, are the Only Son of the Living God in heaven!

Amen …

Chapter and verse that inspired prayer:

Ezekiel 34:26-27  And I will make them and the places round about my hill a blessing; and I will cause the shower to come down in his season; there shall be showers of blessing. (27) And the tree of the field shall yield her fruit, and the earth shall yield her increase, and they shall be safe in their land, and shall know that I am the LORD, when I have broken the bands of their yoke, and delivered them out of the hand of those that served themselves

# March Twenty-Two: "May We Stand Perfect And Whole"

### (As inspired from James 2:5)

Lord Jesus, hear our prayer …

Every life is touched, somehow, by the actions and reactions of others. Always, life is a constant work in progress, an ever changing series of temptation and trial, success and failure, guarded and guided only by the strength of our own individual Christian faith in you, Dear Lord! And in our hearts, we love you and we cherish you, Lord Jesus Our Heavenly King; and in our spirits, we treasure the Consummate Power of your Great Holiness! O Lord, we extol and take pride in your Spiritual Might, for it is bounded by no realm, no dominion, nor by any being, or entity! Thank you for being our Lord and God: Our hearts resound with great jubilation, knowing that we are heirs in your Kingdom of Heaven, which you promised to all who love you and who follow your Great Commandments!

And it is such a wonderful gift and a personal blessing to know and to accept, Lord Christ, that only the purest of faith in you will fill a dark void within the loneliness of one's own life. And only the truest of faith in you, Lord Jesus, will move minds, peoples, and entire nations! But only the most absolute of faith in you, Our Lord Jesus Christ, will restore life and give reason to an empty existence! Lord God, you are the True Faith, the Only Faith, the Absolute Faith of this earth and in the heavens above! And that all the faithful souls in the world may one day inherit your Vast Kingdom of Love, Our Great Lord, we pray for your Spirit of Holiness to engulf our total being: May we stand perfect and tall, one and all, before the Holy Throne of your Immaculate Heart! And may you bless everyone, everywhere. Dear Lord, so that all people may also share in our Christian Understanding and Blessings of Faith that we have received from you, Our Good Lord Jesus Christ and Personal Savior!

Amen …

Chapter and verse that inspired prayer:

James 2:5    Hearken, my beloved brethren, Hath not God chosen the poor of the world rich in faith, and heirs of the kingdom which he hath promised to them that love him?

# March Twenty-Three: "We Lift Our Praises To You, Lord"

### (As inspired from Psalms 34:1-2)

Lord Jesus, hear our prayer …

With you in the world. Lord Jesus, earth and its inhabitants are free to choose Light over darkness, to embrace mercy rather than adversity, and to select the path of The Way, instead of a wayward path of self-destruction! You are the Anointed One, Lord Jesus, and blessed are the many gifts of love that you confer upon us! There is not a day, nor an hour, or even a second that passes when we are not blessed by your Benevolent Compassion! From the very air we breathe, to the soil we stand upon, to the warmth of the sun, we are continually surrounded by the Generous Graces of your Loving Miracles, and we are humbled. Lord of Spiritual Purity, we praise the greatness of your Compassion and Mercy that you hold for us! Forever, Lord Christ, we will glorify, exalt, and magnify your name from the center of our spiritual and physical essence! Blessed is your Holy Name! Hallowed are your many blessings! And blest are you, Lord Jesus Christ!

We worship, we adore, and we acclaim you as God Most High, Our Lord of Heaven and Earth; and from the sincerity of our hearts, we lift our praises to you, Lord God: May the heavens above continually hear our adoration for you; may the earth below forever acclaim your Goodness; and everywhere, Lord Jesus, throughout the entire universe, may all of creation give witness and glory to the loving splendors of your Never Ending Love! Pray for us, Our Lord Christ, that we will endure and achieve our Christian goals and aspirations that we have individually set for ourselves; guide our destinies and safeguard our directions! And through your Exceeding Generosity, our personal ambitions will be clarified and reached!

Amen …

Chapter and verse that inspired prayer:

Psalms 34:1-2    I will bless the LORD at all times: his praise shall continually be in my mouth. (2) My soul shall make her boast in the LORD: the humble shall hear thereof, and be glad.

# March Twenty-Four: "Lord, Let Us Mirror Your Image Of Love"

### (As inspired from Colossians 3:8-10)

Lord Jesus, hear our prayer …

We pray to you, O Lord, let us mirror your image of Love and Compassion! Lord Jesus, when this day comes to an end, help us to put away any and all grievous feelings and emotions that we may have caused or received through thoughtless actions. Clear our minds of resentment and heal our hearts of malice, Lord God, as you fill our individual lives with a genuine compassion for other people, which will also encourage us to outwardly radiate your Faultless Spirit of Kindness. Our Beloved Christ, we pray for the inward strength that will empower us to reflect a true image of Christian love that is spiritually immersed in your Heavenly Vision of Goodness!

Lord Jesus, before the new day begins, soften our hearts so that we will forgive any transgressions that we may have committed or were committed against us. Lord Christ, give us the spiritual strength to humble ourselves in order to seek forgiveness from anyone that we might have injured. And, Lord, teach us to accept and be truly thankful for our blessings of family and friend; and to never hesitate to share or to evangelize our wonderful Christian faith with others!

Lord Jesus Christ, throughout this day and every day that we live, you enlighten our spirits, renew our hearts, and give reason for our individual lives to become a living banner for peace and goodwill towards others, all the days of our lives! And now, Our Lord and God. Spiritually direct us to leave behind the person we were, and authorize the birthright of a New Life, so that we may become a New Soul, reborn through your Holiness, Christ Jesus Our Personal Savior. Lord of Heaven and Earth, to serve you and our fellow Citizens in God!

Amen …

Chapter and verse that inspired prayer:

Colossians 3:8-10    But now ye also put all these; anger, wrath, malice, blasphemy, filthy communication out of your mouth. (9) Lie not one to another, seeing that ye have put off the old man with his deeds; (10) And have put on the new man, which is renewed in knowledge after the image of him that created him:

# March Twenty-Five: "We Are Never Too Lost To Be Found"

(As inspired from John 8:31-32)

Lord Jesus, hear our prayer …

Dear Lord, whether we are gathered in company or stand alone, as Christians who acclaim your Beautiful Presence in our lives, we are forever thankful to you because of your Long-suffering Patience for our return to the Bountiful Resplendence of your Enlightenment! As humans, we so do desire to think and to act accordingly to your teachings and Commandments, Lord Jesus Our Christ and Deliverer! And it is our intent and our purpose in life to follow, without failure, your Most Precious Illuminating Word of Hope and Spiritual Salvation! Pray for us, Good Lord, that we will be strong in our direction and in our individual resolutions of faith!

When we pray to you, Lord, we profess and believe that you already know the sincerity of our wants and the truth of our needs, even before we ask; for you, Lord Jesus, are all knowing and all seeing! Our Precious Lord, we will always believe and we will always follow your Way as the Only Way in Life; for then, we shall become Righteous Disciples of your Perfect Word! Lord of Redemption, we proudly submit our heartfelt confession of faith to the world, to all nations, and to every person: That you are The Way and The Path to All Virtue on earth and in heaven above, for your Truth has truly set us free!

O Praiseworthy Lord, you always know that we are never too lost to be found, that we are never too great to be humbled, and that we are never too wrong to Be righted! For you, Lord Jesus Christ, are the All Knowing and the All Forgiving! And with absolute faith in our hearts, we know this to be absolutely true throughout the whole of creation!

Amen …

Chapter and verse that inspired prayer:

John 8:31-32    Then said Jesus to those Jews which believed on him, If ye continue in my word, then are ye my disciples indeed; (32) And ye shall know the truth, and the truth shall make you free.

# March Twenty-Six: "We Do Not Have To Look Very Far"

### (As inspired from Isaiah 45:6)

Lord Jesus, hear our prayer …

When we rise with the morning sun, Lord Jesus, we feel and see the genuine warmth in your loving touch of life upon the whole of creation; for you alone are Lord Supreme, God and Creator of Heaven and Earth, and there is no one else beside you! Therefore, we ask in your name, to bless and protect this living planet, Our Eternal Blessedness, for the whole world itself, and all of its inhabitants, is your Church of Love, and all life that exists upon it, worships you!

When we breathe in a breath of air, Lord Jesus, or feel a gentle breeze moving with us, we know that it is your Beautiful Spirit upon the earth that allows it to be. And when there is a spring stirring, a rebirth of nature, all of life's creatures are singing out your name, Lord Jesus; through the natural beauty of their many songs, we clearly hear their innocent praises of your Glorious Word! Lord Jesus Christ, we do not have to look very far nor search very long to find true testimony of your existence; for surely, your blessed witnesses are everywhere!

We thank you, O Lord of Promise, for this day and for every day that you spend among us! And wherever we are, we will always be able to witness the Undeniable Truth of your Hallowed Presence through the wonderful sounds of creation, worshiping you, Lord Jesus, in their innocent songs of life! From the birds of the sky, to the babbling brooks, or a thunderous rain storm, and even the innocent chirping of small insects, all sound is a reflective praise of your Magnitude and Goodness, Heavenly Father, that is found within every creature and creation on earth and throughout the entire universe!

Amen …

Chapter and verse that inspired prayer:

Isaiah 45:6    That they may know from the rising of the sun, and from the west, that there is none beside me. I am the LORD, and there is none else.

# March Twenty-Seven: "The Lord Of All Creation"

(As inspired from Psalms 100:4-5)

Lord Jesus, hear our prayer ...

On earth, as well as in heaven above, there is always a host of heavenly voices, a chorus of angels and saints singing praises of adulation and devotion to their Glorious King and Savior, to you, Lord Jesus Christ! And throughout all the generations of time, Blessed is the Word of the Lord; for your Holy Truth abides from one generation onto the next and into your Kingdom above! Therefore, with complete wonderment in our hearts, we gaze upon life's creations and give all acclaim and glory to Our Lord and God of Salvation! Receive us, Lord Everlasting, as we humbly offer to you, our complete love, our total faith, and our constant prayers of devotion and thankfulness: Through the Gates of Heaven, our individual praises and personal appeals pass straightforward to your Blessed Attention, Our Heavenly Lord, because you listen to those who love and adore you with every fiber of existence; thank you for hearing us!

Lord, you created all the animals and plants and all things that compose this beautiful world: Stone, water, fire, and air, are all incredible creations of your Masterful Design, and we, Lord Jesus, born of flesh and spirit, are creations of your Divine Design! And from the moment that we are born, we are set adrift in life. Happy are we to have you in our lives, O Lord, for without your guidance, our course through life would be aimless, uncertain, and with no destination. But just as the sun, the earth, and all the seasons have been set in motion with purpose and direction, we too will find our purpose and direction in life through obedience to your Word, through trusting in your Holy Spirit, and through a heartfelt love for you, The Lord of All Creation! Glory to your Immaculate Birth, your Life of Triumph, and your Miraculous Resurrection!

Amen ...

Chapter and verse that inspired prayer:

Psalms 100:4-5    Enter into his gates with thanksgiving, and into his courts with praise: be thankful unto him, and bless his name. (5) For the LORD is good; his mercy is everlasting; and his truth endureth to all generations.

# March Twenty-Eight: "May They Be Humbled"

### (As inspired from 3 John 11)

Lord Jesus, hear our prayer ...

We are creations of your Great Love, and greatly, do we love you: Blessed are all who do good in your eyes, Lord God, and blest are all who see your Heavenly Goodness throughout the creation and are thankful to you for their life and their well-being!

O Lord, in our lives, there are countless things that are beyond our understanding and our control: The vastness of the universe, the infinite soul, how a tiny seed can produce a mighty tree, chance and destiny, and life itself; but for these and other mysteries of life, Lord Jesus, you have blessed us with the faith to accept and follow the Great Knowledge of your Wisdom. For when we follow the wrong paths in life, we become separated from your Holy Light and become lost in the shadows of darkness, always in doubt, always in fear. Pray for us, Lord Jesus, that we will forever follow the Way of your Wonderful Wisdom; for it is your Exalted Enlightenment that goes before us, showing the correct path to you, Our Lord of Radiant Truth!

Our Lord and God, you are alive in the past, you exist in the ever-flowing present, and you wait for us in the future! Blessed is your Great Understanding of all things! Lord Jesus, please know that we marvel at and accept the very mysteries of life as a sign of your Divine Power and Presence in our lives! And when we are ready to reap fruits of your wisdom, we know that you will so bless us with the knowledge, as the you have done in the past so many times. But for anyone that so professes to be great, wise, and knowledgeable in all things, may they be humbled by the mystifying majesty of a single drop of rain that you created from nothing!

Amen ...

3 John 11     Beloved, follow not that which is evil, but that which is good. He that doeth good is of God: but he that doeth evil hath not seen God.

# March Twenty-Nine: "Please, Remember Our Supplications"

### (As inspired from 2 Kings 20:3)

Lord Jesus, hear our prayer …

A prayer for Spiritual Unity: We are most grateful, Dear Lord, that you are Long-suffering in your Compassion for everyone to find you and return to your Heavenly Fold. Lord of All Nations, we beseech you: Continue to shepherd the world in your direction! Even though there are many Christian churches around the world that are separated by different doctrines and countless miles, all of us, as faithful followers in our Christian fellowship, are bound by our common faith, belief, adoration, and love for you, Lord Jesus Christ! Therefore, please, remember our supplications and how much you are truly loved by everyone on earth and how much joy there is when we all get along and do well in your sight!

And when we, your faithful, pray to you, O Lord, from this land or from distant foreign lands, we reflect upon our incredible blessings in life that every person in the world shares together; we remember the gracious and glorious things in nature that naturally occur throughout the year and throughout all nations: The gentle rains of the first days of spring, the tender warmth of a midsummer's breeze, the beautiful colors of autumn, and our spirits being lifted with winter's first fragile falling of snowflakes. These are the many miraculous memories in life that are freely given to us by you, Lord Jesus, for our own spiritual inspiration and fulfillment. Our Lord and Christ, you have forever filled our lives with blessed memories of joy, and we will never forget where all good memories come from; from this bountiful beautiful creation that you have given to everyone through your Sacred Love, Lord Jesus Christ! Remember your faithful in all nations who grace the lands of this good planet earth, we pray for unity. Amen!

Amen …

Chapter and verse that inspired prayer:

2 Kings 20:3   I beseech thee, O LORD, remember now how I have walked before thee in truth and with a perfect heart, and have done that which is good in thy sight. And Aezekiah wept sore.

# March Thirty: "Through The Lessons Of Life"

### (As inspired from Revelation 2:2-3)

Lord Jesus, hear our prayer …

Through the many chronicles that are shared with us throughout the Scriptures, Heavenly Father, you have shown us that there is a reason and a purpose for everything in life; and blessed is this Knowledge!

Our Light of the World, we truly pray to you for direction in life: By following the Wisdom of your Ways, we willingly accept and patiently endure the many lessons that lie ahead; and there are countless lessons that must be learned. Bless you, Lord Jesus, for you know the truth that abides in every heart! And in our hearts, through sincere confession and contrition, we seek your Divine Absolution for our transgressions. Our Merciful Lord, we continually ask forgiveness for casting any shadows of misdoing or misdeed; because, we cannot bear the darkness of your absence, for we always seek the Protection of your Loving Radiance! And in accordance with the Holy Precepts of your Heavenly Inspiration, guide us, Lord Jesus Christ, in our pursuit of moral virtue.

Through our lessons in life, Dear Lord, you have taught us to recognize and to perceive that which is good; and you are the only one worthy of being called Good. Through the lessons of life, Lord Jesus, you have shown us which paths to follow; because your paths are always true and correct. And if we correctly follow your teachings, Lord Jesus, from all the lessons learned in life, we will gain great knowledge for the salvation of our immortal souls! Lord Jesus, that we shall forever follow a righteous path in life, open our eyes to your Truth, our minds to your Wisdom, and our hearts to your Perfect Guidance! Bless you, Lord Jesus Christ, for you know the sincerity and direction of every heart!

Amen …

Chapter and verse that inspired prayer:

Revelation 2:2-3    I know thy works, and thy labour, and thy patience, and how thou canst not bear them which are evil: and thou hast tried them which say they are apostles, and not, and hast found them liars: (3) And hast borne, and hast patience, and for my name's sake hast laboured, and hast not fainted.

# March Thirty-One: "For All Bonded Souls"

(As inspired from Isaiah 61:1

Lord Jesus, hear our prayer …

Centuries ago, Our Lord and Messiah, when you walked among us and instructed your disciples and taught the masses, your beautiful message on earth was simple, Lord Christ, for it is one of love and forgiveness. We must love one another, and we must forgive one another; because it is impossible for even the slightest shadow to exist in the Heavenly Light of your Purity! Therefore, Our Precious Lord Jesus, we pray for all souls who are being held in spiritual, mental, or physical bondage, whether they are innocent of their actions or guilty of their infractions, we pray deeply for their spiritual enlightenment and physical release! Break the chains of injustice, Lord God, and open the doors of Salvation for all who truly desire to walk in the Radiant Light of your Holiness, Our Lord Jesus Christ, Savior of the world!

Our Good Lord, we pray for all bonded souls to be enlightened with a deepened Spiritual Knowledge to understand that even though a person may commit an offense against God's Commandments or society's laws, and then pay their debt to society, if they have not fully repented in their heart of their transgression, they still must, one day, answer to the Highest of Authority, to you, Lord of Heaven and Earth! Therefore, let us confess in our hearts, before the world and the Kingdom of Heaven, that Our Lord and Christ died and Resurrected for our transgressions, and forgives all who are sincerely sorry for their personal offense against the Will of God! Bless us and forgive us, Our Lord Jesus Christ Who Reigns Supreme in Heaven and Earth! Free the spiritually impoverished life from the anxieties of any self-imposed imprisonment, Lord God; because, you are The Only Way that a soul may gain freedom from all earthly entrapments and bondage!

Amen …

Chapter and verse that inspired prayer:

Isaiah 61:1    The Spirit of the Lord God is upon me; because the Lord hath anointed me to preach good tidings unto the meek; he hath sent me to build up the brokenhearted, to proclaim liberty to captives, and the opening of the prison to them that are bound;

# April One: "Your Creation Is A Sculptured Work Of Art"

(As inspired from Genesis 1:27, 31)

Lord Jesus, hear our prayer …

Praise to you, Our Heavenly Creator, Our Lord and God, You, Who formed us in your Hallowed Likeness and bequeathed upon us a living soul with freewill that we may choose between right and wrong! Through everlasting acclaim, we, your faithful, will forever be thankful to you for the Miracle of Our Existence!

Our Heavenly Father, we will never cease to venerate this blessed world and all the life forms that you created on it as perfect and good! Your creation is a sculptured work of art, a masterpiece throughout the ages, for all ages! All life was formed by your hands, Lord God, for you are the True Sculptor of this beautiful planet, and nothing nor anyone could ever match the crowning majesty of your living loving work of art! Blue skies, white clouds, red sunsets, and all of life in its myriad of colors, prove that there are no greater works of art than those that exist and arise from your Loving Hands, Our Lord Jesus Christ! Eternal glory and perpetual praise to your Magnificent Wisdom! And how great your Understanding is, Lord, not to have made only one variety of tree, or one type of flower, or one species of any living creature; for no creation on earth nor any life that exists is greater than itself but merely distinguished as unique from one another! All life is a Blessed Miracle! And we pray to you, Lord God: Open the eyes and the hearts of every human to no longer see or envision a one-sidedness of life but to see and appreciate the truly Resplendent Decision of your Divine Diversity of All Life; because, in your Divine Image, we were created, Lord of Creation, and your Holy Image is Blest and Consecrated!

Amen …

Chapter and verse that inspired prayer:

Genesis 1:27, 31    So God created man in his own image, in the image of God created he him; male and female created he them. (31) And God saw every thing that he had made, and, behold, it was very good. And the evening and morning were the sixth day.

# April Two: "A Treasure From Heaven"

(As inspired from Romans 8:27-28)

Lord Jesus, hear our prayer ...

Every innocent soul that is sent to earth, O Lord, is a treasure from heaven. And each and every person that is born has been given an unique gift; it is a blessing from the Holy Spirit of Your Love! Lord Jesus, help us to attain our dreams and to fully develop our personal talents and goals, but not as we see them, as you created them! Dear Lord, we have searched our hearts, and it is our spiritual resolution to follow your Unerring Will throughout all the days of our lives! We earnestly entreat you, Lord God, and soulfully ask you for your Divine Intercession into our lives, from which the true fulfillment of our lifelong purpose and calling will be done on earth as it was designed and intended in heaven!

Our spirits are restless, but we know that all who serve your Infallible Will, Lord Jesus, will share in the blessed bounty of your Unfailing Love! And all who pray to you in resolute faith, receive of your Wonderful Blessings! Joyous are we, Lord Jesus Christ, for you receive all who come to you! And with unremitting obedience in our spirits, we will gladly serve your Matchless Will and Intended Purpose that you created for our lives on earth, Most Precious Lord! And with total humility in out hearts, we joyfully accept your Plan of Perfection that you have chosen for us! And now, our souls are completely at rest, Lord God, knowing that our mission and goal in life will be thoroughly met through the spiritual resolution that we have individually made, and that is to follow you, Lord Jesus, at all times; because, all else in life and in this world is inconsequential to the achievement of Eternal Life in your Kingdom of Heaven!

Amen ...

Chapter and verse that inspired prayer:

Romans 8:27-28   And that he searcheth the hearts knoweth what is the mind of the Spirit, because he maketh intercession for the saints according to the will of God. (28) And we know that all things work together for good to them that love God, to them who are called according to his purpose.

# April Three: "You Are The Light Of The World"
### (As inspired from John 8:12)

Lord Jesus, hear our prayer …

Lord of Radiance, with spring in the air, all of life and nature is being resurrected from its long winter's sleep; and once again, Lord God, your cycle of love is made manifest! Blessed is the continuation and fulfillment of Scripture; which, is a world without end. And within everyone, exists the power to become a complete person, and, Lord God, you are that Divine Power Within! We pray for those in life who live with an emptiness and a constant void in their soul; because, without you, Lord Jesus, futures and destinies are incomplete, filled only with a glimmer of how it could be! And for those who seriously seek the Radiance of your Compassion, we accept, we believe, and we know, through our Christian faith, that they will surely find you, Lord Jesus Christ; for you are the Light of the World!

Our Lord and God, you fill the world and all lives with a happiness that cannot be explained by words alone, for a person must personally experience your Deep Spiritual Love through an acceptance of your Most Holy Spirit to fully understand and appreciate the wonderment of it all! And then, they will actually feel the Miracle of Heavenly Joy within their hearts and within their lives! For without you in one's life, Lord Jesus, there is an emptiness, a void of infinite dimension that cannot be filled by temporal promises or by anything else! And for a person to wander and waste their lifetime in darkness, is sadly, a wanting life, filled only with a haunting hollow existence! But for those who desire to leave the shadows of their discontent, we pray for them that they may see the Resplendence of your Compassionate Mercy, Our Light of Life; for only by you, Lord Jesus Most Merciful, is the human spirit made whole again, and only through you, O Lord, does all life blossom and flourish!

Amen …

Chapter and verse that inspired prayer:

John 8:12     Then spake Jesus again unto them, saying, I am the light of the World: he that followeth me shall not walk in darkness, but shall have the light of life.

# April Four: "Lord, We Pray For Your Perfect Blessing"
### (As inspired from Titus 3:7)

Lord Jesus, hear our prayer …

Throughout the millenniums of time, we have come to realize, that it is impossible for us, the human race, to find total world harmony by ourselves, and it is for this reason why we urgently petition you, Our King and Savior, to inspire our nations, our leaders, and every person in every country to establish an individual resolution of personal peace!

Lord God, we pray that your Merciful Gifts upon the whole world, and upon everyone who abides within, will continue from one generation unto the next, forever into eternity! And for that to happen, we knowingly ask for a blessing of worldwide morality! May everyone on the face of this good planet, be justified in their love of virtuous conduct, Lord Christ; simply, because it is spiritually good and morally right to do so!

Through the Grace of your Endless Salvation, Lord Jesus, you have given your faithful the right to become heirs of an Eternal Life in your Heavenly Family. Christ Our Lord, we pray for your Perfect Blessing of Love: Sanction the Mercy of your Immaculate Heart to continually be with us, so that one day we will inherit the Promise of your Heavenly Kingdom! Lord Jesus, we individually attest that we will diligently strive to live a just life, morally right, principled, and doing good works in all things that we do, through faith in your Never Ending Love! But most of all, Lord Jesus Christ, we will endlessly Glorify your Presence in our hearts, with our lips, and in our spirits, now and forevermore, on earth as it is done in heaven!

Amen …

Chapter and verse that inspired prayer:

Titus 3:7   That being justified by his grace, we should be made heirs according to the hope of eternal life.

# April Five: "We Will Forever Worship"

(As inspired from Obadiah 15)

Lord Jesus, hear our prayer ...

In your Heavenly Kingdom of Heavenly Hosts, Dear Lord, your mansion has many rooms, great and small. And as we live, love, worship, and serve your will on earth, we will one day merit and receive what we truly valued in our individual lives on earth! Lord Jesus, it is our prayer and hope that we will have truly valued love and goodwill towards all throughout our entire lives! Bestow upon us now, O Lord, an inspiration to always be aware of our spiritual goal in life, and that is to one day return to your Loving Embrace in your Heavenly Kingdom; for the ultimate gift of spiritual love on earth is a complete surrender of all that one possesses; including life itself! And from you, Our Lord and God, who freely sacrificed the ultimate, that others may live, we humbly pay homage to the Hallowed Greatness in your Gift of Eternal Existence, which you have bestowed upon us; blessed are you, you, Lord Jesus Christ

Today, as everyday, through the Good Graces of God, we are individually given another chance, another opportunity to resolve our personal conflicts; blessed are you, Our Prince of Peace, for we have learned a great spiritual lesson: As we live our lives, so shall we reap our rewards. And that we may live forever in your Heavenly Mansion of Love, we will forever be true to ourselves and to one another, as we continually and truthfully worship and extol praises upon you, Lord Jesus; for with you beside us, our reward is always with us; and our Eternal Life is a gift more blessed than anything this world could ever offer!

Amen ...

Chapter and verse that inspired prayer:

Obadiah 15   For the day of the LORD is near upon all the heathen: as thou hast done, it shall be done unto thee: thy reward shall return upon thine own head.

# April Six: "Lord, Your Gifts Are Perfect And True"

(As inspired from Zephaniah 3:17)

Lord Jesus, hear our prayer …

A Heavenly Gift from your Holy Spirit is more than a present, more than material goods, for your gifts are everlasting, permanent, and cannot be destroyed nor lost! Lord Jesus, your Love is the Flowing Essence within our hearts, the Living Spirit of our lives, and your Beautiful Image will forever remain in our thoughts! We have patterned our lives after your Bountiful Goodness; and your Goodness, Lord God, from generation to generation, is reflected dearly in your willingness to give freely of your Abundant Love! And the Redeeming Power of your Precious Love, Lord Jesus Christ, is so mighty and unequaled that we rejoice endlessly in spirited song and praise! O Lord, you have created nations, defeated foes, healed the downtrodden, saved the innocent, and increased our knowledge for the betterment of all humanity! Truly, Lord Christ, your gifts are Perfect and True; and all who declare absolute belief in you, will one day be received fully into your Sacred Gift of Eternity!

There is a continuous melody of joy within the hearts of all people who honor and love through your name, Our Divine Lord Jesus! And throughout our individual lives, we pray that our own personal deeds and thoughts will always be true reflections of your Infinite Compassion; because, we must all learn to share, serve, and give willingly of ourselves, as you have so inspired us, Lord Christ, through the soul saving Scriptural Teachings of your Wonderful Ministry and Life on earth; for freely you have given of your gifts, Our Most Perfect Lord, and freely we will give thanks and praise to you all the days of our lives!

Amen …

Chapter and verse that inspired prayer:

Zephaniah 3:17    The LORD thy God in the midst of thee is mighty; he will save, he will rejoice over thee with joy, he will rest in his love, he will joy over thee with singing.

# April Seven: "Our Bond Is Sealed"
### (As inspired from Haggai 1:13, 2:4, 2:23)

Lord Jesus, hear our prayer …

Dear Lord, from the beginning of time, and throughout the ages of time, all of time knows the Purity of your words that are written in the Holy Bible; and we greatly honor you, Lord Jesus, with righteous words of honest praise! From ancient days to the present, Lord God, your Glorious Voice travels through all the generations of time into the hearts and minds and souls of all who are willing to receive and accept your Words of Truth! And to all who remain faithful to your Hallowed Word, O Lord, you have bestowed a wonderful message of Love and Promise: A Sacred Oath of Assurance to be with us, that you are always with us, and that our bond is sealed; for you have lovingly chosen us, Lord Jesus, and we, as faithful followers have definitely heard your voice and Message of Love!

Hear our united voices, Lord, for they are clear and sincere! Please, listen to our words of praise, because they are soulful and innocent! Lord Jesus, our prayers and devotions come to you from a deep love that is found within each and every one of us! And with the purest of intentions in our words, we truthfully vow to only and always follow you, Lord Jesus Christ; for it is right and natural to follow the Word and Way of Goodness, now, and through all the time in eternity! And as Christians, we proudly promise, with all of our hearts and souls, to be strong and to firmly trust in the faith that we have in you at all times, Lord God: Blessed is your Absolute Presence within our individual lives, and Blest is everyone that prays for your Immaculate Heart to exist within their souls!

Amen …

Chapter and verse that inspired prayer:

Haggai 1:13, 2:4, 2:23    Then spake Haggai the LORD's messenger in the LORD's message unto the people, saying, I am with you, saith the LORD. (2:4) Yet now be strong, O Zerubbabel, saith the LORD; and be strong, O Joshua, son of Josedech, the high priest; and be strong, all ye people of the land, saith the LORD, and work: for I am with you, saith the LORD of hosts: (2:23) In that day, saith the Lord of hosts, will I take thee, O Zerubbabel, my servant, the son of Shealtiel, saith the LORD, and will make thee as a signet: for I have chosen thee, saith the LORD of hosts.

# April Eight: "Allow Your Wisdom, Lord, To Govern"
### (As inspired from Colossians 1:9-10)

Lord Jesus, hear our prayer …

All things that live or exist are relevant to your Divine Plan, O Lord! And it is our prayer, Lord God, that all people, throughout this world, will be filled with the Visionary Inspirations of your Infallible Will! Please, allow your wisdom, Lord, to govern our discernment of your Deep Compassion for us, which was created for one and all! Instill into the hearts of everyone, Lord Jesus, the ability to accept your Compassionate Judgment and the ambition to increase their own personal understanding of your Divine Love. And through a worldwide acceptance of your Spiritual Enlightenment, all civilizations, everywhere, will be guided to see and perceive that all harmony originates from you! Lord Jesus Prince of Peace, we pray that the earth will be filled with the wonderful knowledge of your Loving Spirit, and that the world will warmly welcome and cherish your Authority of Love! And then, Lord Jesus Christ, there, in every single human heart and soul, shall you abide within our midst, forever and ever!

Pray for us, Lord Jesus, that your faithful followers will lead the world in your direction by using proper examples in word, behavior, and a genuine fellowship of Christian faith through a profound practice of your Wonderful Teachings and Exalted Commandments of Love! Inspire us, Dear Lord, to be worthy as we walk in your Redemptive Light and to be fruitful in everything good that we do on earth! And lastly, Our Invincible Lord, we ask of you through exalted prayer: Expand the world's Spiritual Awareness that everyone, everywhere, may actually see and perceive the Great Power that may be achieved in life by using Goodness and Kindness as their directing force!

Amen …

Chapter and verse that inspired prayer:

Colossians 1:9-10  For this cause we also, since the day we heard it, do not cease to pray for you, and to desire that ye might be filled with the knowledge of his will in all wisdom and Spiritual understanding; (10) That ye might walk worthy of the Lord unto all pleasing, being fruitful in every good work, and increasing in the knowledge of God;

# April Nine: "Your Love Is The Power Of Life"
### (As inspired from Philemon 5-7)

Lord Jesus, hear our prayer …

Our Lord of Perpetual Faith, we totally and completely believe in the physical, mental, and spiritual healing empowerment of your Holy Compassion, for your Love is the Power of Life! Lord Jesus, you give rest to the weary, you mend our wounds and dry every tear, and you conquer all malevolence! Wherefore, our deep Christian faith remains obedient to none other, Lord Christ, for your Unblemished Spirit is the Holy Manifest in all life! And only through your Tender Care, Lord Jesus Christ, does our total being flourish in your Sacred Love that is eternally with us forevermore! Dear Lord, we pray to you for world conversion: Permit everyone on this good planet to receive and enjoy the Nurturing Benevolence of your Conquering Love; speak to our souls in the universal language of love, by encouraging the hearts of all nations to seek peace!

Our Lord of Infinite Glory, as proud followers of our beautiful faith, you have inspired us to see that darkness of the heart is a place where nothing radiant is possible; and we have willingly stepped forward from our shadows of doubt into your Glorious Light of Understanding where all things are possible! Lord Jesus, we stand before you as faithful Christians, asking that you will hear our prayers and knowing that you will answer them; for we passionately believe and trust in your Flawless and Infinite Love! O Lord, we pray, lead the world to your All-encompassing Holiness; refresh the daunted spirit within us, and bring forth the Living Energy of Goodness that exists in everyone!

Amen …

Chapter and verse that inspired prayer:

Philemon 5-7   Hearing of thy love and faith, which thou hast toward the Lord Jesus, and toward all saints; (6) That the communication of thy faith may become effectual by the acknowledging of every good thing which is in you in Christ Jesus. (7) For we have great joy and consolation in thy love, because the bowels of the saints are refreshed by thee, brother.

# April Ten: "Teach Us How To Forgive And Forget"

## (As inspired from Daniel 9:9)

Lord Jesus, hear our prayer ...

Forgive us, Lord God, for our rebellious nature, turn us away from all malice of thought. We pray for your Spirit of Accord, O Lord, to enter into all lives and soothe the ill winds of unrest and confusion in the world; for even in the slightest of breezes, a steady flame will flicker, a still leaf will sway, and a calm water ripple. We pray to you, Lord Jesus, Creator of All Mercy and Forgiveness, that we may gently move through our days and years with a forgiving heart, a peaceful mind, and a spirit in harmony with all life. Into your Redeeming Hands, Lord Christ, do we entrust, surrender, and renounce the memories of all misgivings! Glory to you, Lord God, for our hearts are joyous and content!

Pray for us, Our Lord of Mercies, that we, as Christians, will not allow any negative thoughts and feelings to harbor within our individual lives! Because, to permit and ignore destructive emotions to continue, rather than to be solved and resolved, is an affront to you, O Lord, and a deception within ourselves; which is also contrary to your Commandment of Love and Forgiveness!

Merciful Lord, for those who have offended our hearts and our spirits, even the slightest, we seek to forgive and remove all hurtful memories; for it is not the action that haunts the soul but the memory thereof. And any shadow of anger that is allowed to linger, will grow and blur the vision of those who yearn to walk in your Light; therefore, Lord Jesus, as you have forgiven us so many times, teach us how to forgive and forget all the wrongful and haunting memories that may bother us. Inspire us, Lord Jesus Christ, that we may forever walk peacefully in your Redemptive Salvation as a True Christian of Peace and Forgiveness!

Amen ...

Chapter and verse that inspired prayer:

Daniel 9:9    To the LORD our God belong mercies and forgivenesses, though we have rebelled against him;

# April Eleven: "The Family Is Truly Blessed"

(As inspired from Luke 15:32)

Lord Jesus, hear our prayer …

We ask of you, Our Heavenly Father, to bless every member of our family and all the families of the world! Every individual in a family is an integral part of the whole; and no whole is complete when even the smallest part is missing. Lord Jesus, it is a happy, happy reunion when one of your lost returns to your Sacred Heart, to your Loving Embrace, to your Spirit of Hope, and proudly glorifies your Name and attests to your Goodness! And when all members of a family are united in their belief of your Glorious Love, the family is truly blessed! O Lord, hear the prayers of those who are faithful Christians to the Sanctity of your Name! See the joy in our hearts! Feel the love in our spirits! We are rejuvenated by the Radiance of your Unrivaled Compassion! And daily, Lord Jesus Christ, now and forever, may every member of your family on earth and in heaven above, be a constant witness and testify to the Glory of your Great Love for the family!

The ocean is a global body of water, composed of single drops of rain; the dessert is a vast area of land, made up of tiny grains of sand; and our atmosphere encircles the entire earth with countless molecules of life giving oxygen. These Incredible Blessings are joined together to create and sustain life, our lives, all human lives in a worldwide union of Divine Creatures whose duty and mission on earth is to love you, Lord Jesus, and to love one another with equal compassion! Therefore, we ask of you to pray for us, Our Lord and God, that our Spiritual Vision for world peace will first begin within the family: Lord of Purity, we, on earth, are all joyous brothers and sisters who are united by your Holy Word, and that you will forever dwell in our lives and in our hearts, Lord Jesus Christ, we bow and submit to your Majestic Glory and Love; for whosoever follows you, is also a cherished member of your worldwide Christian family, and we are completely of one accord in this world and with heaven above by your Marvelous and Miraculous Name, by which all your faithful followers call themselves!

Amen …

Chapter and verse that inspired prayer:

Luke 15:32    It was meet that we should make merry, and be glad: for this thy brother was dead, and is alive again; and was lost, and is found.

# April Twelve: "We Call Upon You, Lord"

(As inspired from 1 Kings 18:24, 37-39)

Lord Jesus, hear our prayer …

Lord God, hear our prayer: We are all but spiritual fugitives, cast upon the dubious shores of fear and doubt, a hapless generation in a world of temptation and allurement; but through you, we are rescued and saved from all moral denouncement! Therefore, we call upon your Merciful Name, Lord Jesus, to deliver us from ourselves, we call upon your Forever Forgiveness to save our souls, and we call upon your Redeeming Justice, and you are there, O Lord! We will always call upon you, Lord Jesus, because, you have the Sole Authority to remove the darkness, to fill the emptiness, and to move the unmovable. For only we, as humans, will intentionally hurt one another physically, mentally, or spiritually; but it is only you, The Good Nazarene, Our Lord and Christ, who can mend, heal, and make us whole again! Jesus Our Savior, we ask of you to soften all hearts that are hardened against your Glorious Compassion and release the Heavenly Love that is locked up within everyone's spirit; because every person alive is truly an innocent child of your Beautiful Creation, which, Dear Lord, makes us all brothers and sisters!

We call upon you, Lord, You, who turned the eternal blackness into Light, who created the heavens and the earth, who carved out mountains, oceans, and valleys, who gives love, peace, and salvation to the whole world, we call upon the Enlightenment of your Holiness! Consume all doubt and deceit with the Fires of your Compassion, and allow everyone in the world to know the Greatness of your Goodness! And then, all people, everywhere, will rightfully sing out to you: Our Prophesied Messiah and Christ, you are the True God, the Lord of Heaven and Earth, and Holy is your name, Jesus of Nazareth!

Amen …

Chapter and verse that inspired prayer:

| 1 Kings 18:24, 37-39 | And call ye on the name of your gods; and I will call on the name of the LORD: and the God that answereth by fire, let him be God. And all the people answered and said, It is well spoken. (37) Hear me, O LORD, hear me, that this people may know that thou art the LORD God, and that thou hast turned their heart back again. (38) Then the fire of the LORD fell, and consumed the burnt sacrifice, and the wood, and the stoned, and the dust, and licked up the water that was in the trench. (39) And when all people saw it, they fell on their faces: and they said, The LORD, he is the God; the LORD, he is the God. |
| --- | --- |

# April Thirteen: "The Daily Miracles Of Life"

### (As inspired from Hebrews 2:4)

Lord Jesus, hear our prayer …

Dear Lord, we pray: Instill into the hearts and minds of all people, the ability to realize the significance and the importance of their own individual existence within this wonderful world! Our Lord and Merciful God, we acknowledge the soothing caress of your Tender Spirit whenever we encounter and embrace the Living Miracles of your Resplendent Love throughout this Grand Creation! And we thank you, Lord Jesus, for the daily wonders of life that encompass our lives! When the light breaks through the dawning darkness, when a cool and refreshing morning dew forms, when the sun crests high in the sky to warm this good earth, when a soothing rain falls to nourish the rich soils, when two fall in love, marry, and new life is created; we venerate and welcome all the miracles of your Grand Creation, which is living proof of your Triumphant and Conquering Love that you bestow upon us daily through the Holy Spirit! Blessed and Pure is the Spectacular Wonderment of Life on earth; the world from which we are created and sustained! Thank you, Lord Jesus Christ!

O Lord, pray for us that we will never take for granted the everyday miracles that quietly take place around us: The movement of the tides, the air we breathe, the moisture laden clouds, the sunlight, the countless creatures of and in the earth, the green plants, trees, and a multitude of other life forms and normal occurrences that make life and living on this planet possible; for this, we give to you our greatest thanks, Lord Jesus, our complete obedience, and our constant love, which you make possible through the Abundance of your Immaculate Heart!

Amen …

Chapter and verse that inspired prayer:

Hebrews 2:4    God also bearing them witness, both with signs and wonders, and with divers miracles, and gifts of the Holy Ghost, according to his own will?

# April Fourteen: "We Are Servants To Your Glorious Word"
### (As inspired from 1 Corinthians 7:22, 24)

Lord Jesus, hear our prayer …

Centuries ago, Lord, you came to earth as a Servant of The Heavenly Father and of all humankind, and through your innocent death, when you gave your life as ransom for many, you became the King of All Nations and of All Peoples! Proudly and freely do we bond our souls to your Holy Spirit of Love, Lord Christ, that we too will be called True Servants who abide within their Living God! Glory to you, Lord Christ Our Magnificent King!

Dear Lord, we would be lost without you; wandering through an empty existence, hand-in-hand with fear and betrayal. But now that you are in our lives forever, Lord Christ, forever we will follow you! Lord, our hearts have heard your calling, and gladly, we answer! Proudly, Lord Jesus, our spirits long to serve your Heavenly Will! And willingly, we are servants to your Glorious Word! Hear our praises, Lord Jesus Christ, as we joyfully surrender to your Benevolent Grace and Goodness!

O Lord, you have bestowed upon us a wonderful blessing of Faith and Obedience, and how marvelous this blessing is! And whenever we testify and witness to our faith in you, Lord Jesus, please strengthen us to always be proud of our personal actions and responsibilities as true Christians: Our Lord and God, we ask that you will continually guide each and every one of us to reach total spiritual fulfillment through a direction in life that you have so intended for our individual lives!

Amen …

Chapter and verse that inspired prayer:

1 Corinthians 7:22, 24   For he that is called in the Lord, being a servant, is the Lord's freeman: likewise also he that is called, being free, is Christ's servant. (24) Brethren, let every man, wherein he is called, therein abide with God.

# April Fifteen: "Your Power Is Absolute"

(As inspired from Zechariah 10:12)

Lord Jesus, hear our prayer …

Our Great and Wondrous Lord, you have enlivened our spirits to realize that nothing happens by itself, that all things in this world are dependent upon something else for its existence; and all things exist because of you, Our Heavenly Father! The wind generates its force from the earth. Gentle rains come from the oceans. The lightning finds its energy in the clouds. The world is warmed by the sun. All faith is obtained from an inner source of trusting in you, Lord God! And we receive our strength from your Love and Glory, Lord Jesus! Great and Holy is the Authority of your Love, Lord of All Compassion and Mercy, for through your Loving Grace, you have made the impossible possible, the inconceivable conceivable, and the unattainable attainable!

As individuals, we are powerless, but with you in our lives, Lord Jesus, we become a spiritual force that is limitless! And through deep compassionate faith, there is more power in one act of kindness than all of the combined energy of a raging storm! Through you, Lord Christ, the ability to love and the grace to forgive, creates the core and strength of faith, our faith, which is more commanding than all the natural forces on earth! And through your Sublime Compassion, Lord Jesus Christ, the bitter storms of rage and anger cannot possibly survive in the Unbounded Passion of your Loving Mercy! All glory and authority to you, Lord, forevermore, for your Power is Absolute and Unconquerable! And all the days of our lives, we will proudly carry and proclaim our Christian name! Strengthen us, Lord Christ, as individuals, and empower our personal faith with a Divine Sanction to resist all that is against your Righteous Will for this planet and for our personal lives!

Amen …

Chapter and verse that inspired prayer:

Zechariah 10:12    And I will strengthen them in the LORD; and they shall walk up and down in his name, saith the LORD.

# April Sixteen: "The Lord Of All Glory And Wisdom"
### (As inspired from 1 Corinthians 2:5, 7)

Lord Jesus, hear our prayer …

We believe and we profess that there is not a single word in the Christian Bible that is false or misleading! And through deep and soulful prayer, Our Heavenly Father, every person alive has the ability to obtain understanding and discernment of your Holy Word! Your wisdom, Lord Jesus, far exceeds our perception and our knowledge of creation and all of its intricate mysteries of life. But through an unyielding faith and trust in you, Lord Christ, the mysteries of cause and effect are soon revealed. We pray for your Divine Guidance, O Lord, that our spiritual and individual faith should never abide within the interpretations of a secular world, but only through your Heartfelt Inspirations that are found in Scripture, Our Lord Jesus Christ, He, Who is the Word made Flesh in All Glory and Wisdom!

Our Lord and God, through a deep faith in you, the unknown becomes known, the uncertain becomes clear, and the confined becomes unlimited! Through you, Lord Jesus, all knowledge is made known. And for that reason, through our personal faith, we remove all worries and burdens from our shoulders and place them into your Loving Care and Understanding. Thank you, Lord, for resolving our personal conflicts and giving us, individually, peaceful hearts. Please hear our prayer request: Dear Lord, for those who are troubled and bewildered for unknown reasons, sanction their lives with the Golden Understanding of your Peaceful Love, in a Deep Compassion so compelling, that every problem anyone has, is immediately resolved through trust and faith in you, Lord Jesus Our Christ and Savior!

Amen …

Chapter and verse that inspired prayer:

1 Corinthians 2:5, 7    That your faith should not stand in the wisdom of men, but in the power of God. (7) But we speak the wisdom of God in a mystery, even the hidden wisdom, which God ordained before the world unto our glory:

# April Seventeen: "We Exalt And Acclaim Your Excellence"

(As inspired from 1 Samuel 2:1)

Lord Jesus, hear our prayer …

We are immovable, transfixed in our Christian faith, that you, Our King and Christ, will defeat and overcome all worldly and spiritual problems that arise every day in our individual lives! There is nothing that cannot be resolved through prayer! Lord God, you are the foundation of our faith, there is no one Holier than You! Please hear us, Lord Jesus, as our spirits are raised into a single voice of praise! And we will shout it on the mountain, we will shout it in the valley, we will shout it throughout this land, Lord Jesus Christ, that we love you and that we greatly rejoice in our hearts for your Unending Redemption of our souls! Therefore, let our exaltations ring out and echo throughout the day, to every soul in all the world and through the heavens above that: Jesus Lives! Jesus Is! Jesus Loves! Jesus Conquers! Jesus Forgives! Hear, believe, and be saved!

Encourage us to adorn our lives with your compassion, Lord Christ, that all people, Christian and non-Christian alike, may clearly see the visible force of your Resolute Love that you have for us! Allow goodwill and forbearance to abound in our hearts as a true witness to the world of our Miraculous Salvation through your Unlimited Grace and Mercifulness! Lord Jesus, we exalt and acclaim your excellence to one and all; for there is no other heart more praiseworthy, more perfect, nor more pure than your heart! Lord Jesus Christ, you are the foundation and the cornerstone of this world and of all lives! Hear our united voices, Lord God, above all others: Let your enemies fall by the wayside as we boldly proclaim our Divine Reclamation from the world through your Never-ending Love for all humanity!

Amen …

Chapter and verse that inspired prayer:

1 Samuel 2:1     And Hannah prayed, and said, My heart rejoiceth in the LORD, mine horn is exalted in the LORD: my mouth is enlarged over mine enemies; because I rejoice in thy salvation.

# April Eighteen: "Your Word Of Life"

### (As inspired from 1 John 1:1-2)

Lord Jesus, hear our prayer …

All the forces of nature are humbled before you, Our Heavenly Lord and God! Even the infinite universe is dwarfed by the Presence of your Holy Spirit! Mighty and All Powerful are you, Lord, and yet, the Tenderness of your Gentle Compassion is forever around us.

O Lord, you are the True Word of Life, and through a deep and sincere love, you created the universe, the earth, the oceans, the dry land, and the heavens above for every human soul! And as we gaze upon your miraculous work, our hearts cry out in unison: Precious and Great are you, Lord Jesus Christ! Therefore, we will never forget to praise you daily, Lord, knowing that your faithful are never forgotten! Everyday, we will gaze upon our gifts of love, Lord Christ, and give thanks, because we know, Lord Jesus, that your faithful are forever blessed by you! And forever, we will remain grateful as we will continually bear witness to your glorious gifts of compassion; for we too were created by your Word of Life, Lord Jesus!

We believe that all the Christian faithful on earth are united in one belief, in one allegiance, in one baptism of rebirth, that you, Christ Jesus, are The Lord of All Salvation! And we pray to you, Our Glorious King, that all Christians around the world, will forever be united in your Commandment of Love and Goodwill Towards All People! Lord God, we will forevermore be thankful to you! Even if the mountains fall away, and the oceans dry up, and the stars fade from the heavens above, we will still sing praises of love and glory to you, Lord Jesus, now and through all of eternity; for wherever you are, life is made manifest!

Amen …

Chapter and verse that inspired prayer:

1 John 1:1-2   That which was from the beginning, which we have heard, which we have seen with our eyes, which we have looked upon, and our hands have handled, of the Word of life; (2) (For the life was manifested, and we have seen it, and bear witness, and shew unto you that eternal life, which was with the Father, and was manifested unto us;)

# April Nineteen: "You Understand"

(As inspired from James 2:23)

Lord Jesus, hear our prayer …

Our Almighty Lord and God of Creation, you are The Prime Force of Life, the Single Reason for our existence, and through your Most Hallowed and Reverent Regard, our lives are sustained and numbered forever!

No greater friend may be found in the world, then One who willingly lays down their own life that others may be forgiven and attain Eternal Life! We pray for your blessing of true friendship in this world, O Lord, for we know that you listen, that you care, and that you understand all problems and obstacles in life. How wonderful it is for us, Lord Jesus, to know and to realize that all solutions to all of our worldly problems rest in your Unfailing Understanding of every situation! Lord God and Christ, there is no greater friend in the world than you! And whenever we need someone to trust, someone to walk with, someone to talk to, or even someone to confide in, we know that you are always there for us! Lord Jesus Christ, we have no greater friend in the world than you!

We pray for all good souls who truly seek a genuine fellowship with others: Lord God, to all in need of compassion and companionship in their lives, we earnestly pray that they will find you, for your Unequaled Love offers the world a constant blessing of harmony and spiritual fellowship. Lord Jesus, may your Unbounded Love be accepted into the lives of all people who are in need of faith and friendship! For when you, Lord Jesus, called certain individuals your friend, Scripture was truly fulfilled, even as Our Father Abraham believed in you, and was called Friend by Almighty God!

Amen …

Chapter and verse that inspired prayer:

James 2:23   And the scripture was fulfilled which saith, Abraham believed God, and it was imputed unto him for righteousness: and he was called the Friend of God.

# April Twenty: "You Seek Those Who Are Lost"

## (As inspired from Ezekiel 34:15-16)

Lord Jesus, hear our prayer ...

Through you, Our Lord of Perfect Judgment, the lives of all people will surely find a Calming Peace that is unequaled in the universe! And in your Wonderful Name, we ask: Let friendship and accord abound throughout and between all the nations of the world!

Our Lord and God, bless this residence and all who gather here in peace! In times of doubt and darkness, when we feel empty and weak, you raise us up to your Healing Light, Lord, and give rest to our wearisome spirits. Blessed are you, Our Good Shepherd, for you seek those who are lost and bring them home again. You mend the broken spirit and you strengthen the weakened heart. Lord Jesus, we lift our thoughts and our voices heavenward to you and give acclaim and thanksgiving for your Limitless Patience and Eternal Wisdom! Please, Lord Christ, accept our profound praises that we offer to your Magnificence: You have given our souls new life, you have removed the darkness of doubt from our lives, and you have showered down upon us blessings of happiness and jubilance!

Your Justice, O Lord, is Swift and Exact and Accorded Correctly, your Love is Precise, Unsurpassed is your Mercy, and Noble is your Judgment; for all who receive it, receive justly! Lord Jesus Christ, shepherd us with peace, protect us against worldly adversity, bring home all souls who are lost and wander without course and bearing, and strengthen all who are spiritually ill and lack direction in their lives; this we ask through your Impervious Will, as Our Lord and God! Dear Lord, we, who love and honor you, ask that you will bless us and keep us safe within the Protective Circle of your Infinite Love!

Amen ...

Chapter and verse that inspired prayer:

Ezekiel 34:15-16    I will feed my flock, and I will cause them to lie down, saith the Lord God. (16) I will seek that which was lost, and bring again that which was driven away, and will bind up that which was broken, and will strengthen that which was sick: but I will destroy the fat and the strong; I will feed them with judgment.

# April Twenty-One: "A Oneness With All Life"

(As inspired from Galatians 3:28)

Lord Jesus, hear our prayer …

Lord of the Universe, you have blessed all of creation with an Incredible Miracle, in that there is a oneness with all life: The solid earth is as one, all the waters are one, we breathe in one atmosphere, there is but one sky, and we have but One God, who loves each and every one of us! And through your eyes, Almighty God, there is neither race, nor color, nor gender, nor great or small, we are all simply one in your sight. And, Lord, you have blessed us with a wonderful insight, to which there is a natural unification with all life. And when our hearts truly believe in the unity of love, we then become in agreement with you, Lord Jesus, and merge as one into a true blessing of life's harmony.

When we unite in our Christian faith with others, we know that we are part of a loving fellowship through a special bonding and belief in you. Lord God! And when we begin to completely rely on our faith in you, Lord Jesus, there is a union of peace, a profound joining of love and understanding for all life! And when we find that true faith is possible, and within the grasp of our own hearts, our souls find a oneness with the creation, O Lord, in a deep spiritual awareness that all life and all love comes from One Source, and it is you, Lord Jesus Christ, who is the origin of all that is good! Therefore, we realize that the strength of Christianity does not lie within the male or female, or through the rich or poor, nor by the great or meek, but within each person who individually proclaims that their Personal Savior is Lord Jesus Christ, King and Redeemer of Souls!

Amen …

Chapter and verse that inspired prayer:

Galatians 3:28    There is neither Jew nor Greek, there is neither bond nor free, there is neither male nor female: for ye are all one in Christ Jesus.

# April Twenty-Two: "We Will Follow Your Infinite Wisdom"

(As inspired from Matthew 19:26)

Lord Jesus, hear our prayer ...

We praise you greatly, Lord, for inspiring responsible people that serve our community in which they represent. We thank you for our leaders who lead wisely, and we pray for those whose decisions are clouded by self-serving pride and arrogance.

From the beginning of time, Lord God, throughout all time, and into all future time, all the kingdoms and powers on earth cannot measure up to a single moment of your Heavenly Command and Authority! Lord Jesus, no earthly sovereign has ever equaled nor could ever match a single second of your Divine Influence upon humankind! And for this reason, Our Lord and Christ, we pray for our leaders on earth: Guide their difficult decisions, fill their lives with compassion, and allow your love to influence their thoughts and judgments for the physical and spiritual betterment of everyone! Soften the hearts of our leaders to solve and resolve problems for all citizens; and strengthen our law makers in their determination to always govern justly!

O Lord, we also pray for personal guidance: That our individual judgments will be just and sound, inspire us to make correct decisions. Lord Jesus, throughout the day, throughout lifetimes, impossibilities arise and often become stumbling blocks for our personal goals in life. But through the Matchless Power of your Divine Supremacy, Lord Jesus Christ, you make all things possible in life, because, nothing is impossible for you, and everything is possible with you! Lord God, we will follow your Infinite Wisdom and trust in the covenant of your Holy Authority, as so ordained from a time before all time. And by your Holy Will, we, as Christians, accept our own spiritual responsibility to embrace peace and forgiveness in our homes and in our hearts!

Amen ...

Chapter and verse that inspired prayer:

Matthew 19:26    But Jesus beheld them, and said unto them, With men this is impossible; but with God all things are possible.

# April Twenty-Three: "We Enter This World With Nothing"

(As inspired from Hebrews 3:14)

Lord Jesus, hear our prayer …

We forever acknowledge, Lord of This World, that everything given or received on this good earth is a blessing from you! A tree does not own the soil that it grows in, a fish does not lay claim to the stream that it swims in, and a bird does not possess the tree that it nests in; and neither do we have permanent title nor infinite ownership over any part of the creation. All of our possessions are blessings from you, Lord Jesus, that are given to us for our use and for our safekeeping. And from the beginning of our lives and until the end of our lives, we thank you, Lord, for allowing us the Sacred Entrustment of your creation and to be partakers in all the wonderful blessings that you have surrounded us with!

All that we have and all that we own belong to you, Lord God; we neither possess nor really own anything! All materiality is nothing more than a loan. We are merely the occupants, the tenants of earth, in partnership with the creation! We enter this world with nothing, and we will leave with nothing; except for all the Glorious Love that we find in you, Lord Jesus Christ, and the spiritual goodness that was created in our souls during our lifetime on earth!

O Lord, your voice reaches through the generations of time, for you speak to us from the Gospels as you spoke to the multitudes in your Sermon on the Mount: For those that are poor in spirit, who mourn, and for all who hunger, and are merciful, and are pure of heart, the peacemakers, anyone who is persecuted because of Righteousness, and all that are falsely accused because of their personal convictions and belief in Christianity! Please, let your Light, Dear Lord, Shine Brightly upon your Promise to all people that You, The Anointed Son, Our Heavenly Father, and The Holy Spirit of All Creation are One and The Same! And in this we firmly attest and believe!

Amen …

Chapter and verse that inspired prayer:

Hebrews 3:14    For we are made partakers of Christ, if we hold the beginning of our confidence stedfast unto the end;

# April Twenty-Four: "We Seek Your Truth, Lord"

(As inspired from Job 36:4-5)

Lord Jesus, hear our prayer ...

We pray that your blessings of common sense and good judgment, Lord, will fill the world and motivate every heart to develop a deep and personal knowledge of your Holy and Precious Spirit! We pray, Lord Jesus, that you will command insight and discernment to become a natural part of everyone's awareness. And then, through truthful thoughts and honest actions, every individual on earth will become a positive reflection of your Goodness! Thereby, the words and ways of this planet will never be false reflections, Lord God, because your Hallowed Word only reflects Perfect Wisdom and Strength, and your Judgment is always with us!

Hear our praise of adoration for you, O Lord: Behold, our Lord Jesus Christ, He is Wise, He is Merciful to all, He is our God and Personal Savior, Amen! We pray, Lord Jesus, that you will inspire us to never blame, condemn, accuse, judge, nor wrongfully punish one another under false pretense. Lord Christ, please, forever guide us in our spiritual search for your Truth and Wisdom. Strengthen our thoughts and deeds to become a constant beacon for our Christian lives. Fortify our inner faith that it will go before us as a guiding light. And as we seek your Truth, Lord Jesus Christ, may we never chastise those who remain in the shadows of doubt, but simply be there for them when they too desire to come forth, seeking the Enlightenment of your Good and Perfect Knowledge! And for those who have yet to find you, Our Savior of Souls, we beseech you: Become the Beaconning Fire of their Spiritual Salvation, brightly burning on the darkened shores of their discontent!

Amen ...

Chapter and verse that inspired prayer:

Job 36:4-5   For truly my words shall not be false: he that is perfect in knowledge is with thee. (5) Behold, God is mighty, and despiseth not any: he is mighty in strength and wisdom.

# April Twenty-Five: "You Are The Perfect Wisdom"
### (As inspired from Proverbs 14:5-9)

Lord Jesus, hear our prayer …

Thank you, O Lord, for the Prudent Knowledge that is found within the pages of the Bible: Lesson after lesson, not only teaches us virtue, but also why we should leave the shadows and live in the Light!

According to the Holy Scriptures, Dear Lord, you have given to the world all the possible things that are needed to live a good and devout life! You are the Wisdom of the World, Lord Jesus, and through the glory and virtue of your Divine Word, we have individually been given a most remarkable blessing of freewill; the ability to choose: To love, to comfort, to help, to be wise, to be charitable, to know right from wrong, to perceive and understand the power and presence of our Lord and God on earth! Please, hear our personal creed, Lord Jesus Christ, as we attest to your Undeniable Presence: We place all of our faith in your Profound Judgment, we avow to trust only in your love, and we profess to pray only to you, O Lord, for there are no false promises, there are no false hopes, and there are no false witnesses in you! Christ Jesus Our Lord, within your Glory there can only be Absolute Truth. And within your Heavenly Protection, there can only be Faith of Unconditional Purity! And through your Holy Spirit of Love, Lord Jesus Christ, Grace and Peace are magnified within our spirits! Therefore, from the earth below, to the heavens above, we confess with heart and soul, Lord Jesus, that you are the True Embodiment of All Righteousness and that you are the Perfect Wisdom for all people and for all times! Bless us with your favor, Lord God, for we keep your Blessed Commandments deep within our Christian faith through a personal and willing obedience to your Holy Word!

Amen …

Chapter and verse that inspired prayer:

Proverbs 14:5-9    A faithful witness will not lie: but a false witness will utter lies. (6) A scorner seeketh wisdom, and findeth it not: but knowledge is easy unto him that understandeth. (7) Go from the presence of a foolish man, when thou perceivest not in him the lips of knowledge. (8) The wisdom of the prudent is to understand his way: but the folly of fools is deceit. (9) Fools make mock at sin: but among the righteous there is favour.

# April Twenty-Six: "Lord, Help Us To Understand"

(As inspired from Acts of the Apostles 2:21)

Lord Jesus, hear our prayer …

Lord God, you give all things to all people according to their needs. You also gave us this beautiful day and the good faith to know that tomorrow will come; for where we have been, we will reflect and remember; for where we are, we will give thanks; and for where we are going, we will pray to you, Lord of Heaven and Earth, and call upon your Sacred Name for guidance, mercy, and spiritual strength: By your stripes, through the shedding of your Innocent Blood, and in your Glorious Name, Lord Jesus Christ, we are truly healed of all spiritual and physical maladies!

Lord of Forgiveness, we call upon your Merciful Name and ask for salvation: Help us to understand that the past is in the past, that all memories, good or bad, are simply stepping stones for today, and that our regrets and our own personal disappointments are merely lessons of faith for a better tomorrow! Lord Jesus, inspire us that we may go forward with our lives and ambitions. Permit us, Our Lord of Hope, to release any pain from the past that may hinder our future direction. Entitle each and every one of us to accomplish our own destiny and true purpose in this lifetime, Lord God, by allowing us to fully appreciate every moment of life and by using this time to plan for a better tomorrow! And through your Infinite Guidance and Divine Salvation, Lord Jesus Christ, our spirits will always be comforted in the wonderful knowledge that you created us for a Divine Reason, and that reason is simple and pure: To find you and to love you with all of our heart, mind, and soul! Praise be to our Lord and God, for we have truly found your Hallowed Presence within our lives!

Amen …

Chapter and verse that inspired prayer:

Acts of the Apostles 2:21  And it shall come to pass, that whosoever shall call on the name of the Lord shall be saved.

# April Twenty-Seven: "You Are The Eternal Flame"

(As inspired from 2 Corinthians 4:18)

Lord Jesus, hear our prayer …

On earth, infinity is a concept that our human minds cannot fully appreciate nor comprehend; and only through sincere faith in your Hallowed Word, do we accept the Promise of an Eternal Life in heaven; Blest are you, Lord Christ, and Blessed be your Everlasting Name, Our King and Savior, Our Christ Jesus!

All worldly goods are temporal and are limited by time; and it is only you, Lord Jesus, that is infinite. All worldly promises are uncertain; only you, Lord Christ, are the foundation for all truth. And all worldly happiness is but a fleeting moment in time; therefore, the only real and Never-ending Happiness in life is found through you, Lord Jesus Christ Our Savior!

We have no one else before us, and there is no one else but you in our lives, Lord Jesus, for you are God, our only God! You are the True Light that surrounds and protects the world from all darkness! You are the Eternal Flame that forever burns within the hearts and souls of those who truly believe in you! You are the Perpetual Truth in the Spirit of All Life! Please, Lord Jesus, believe in us and accept our words as sincere; for as Christians, we are completely devoted to you! And now, we pray: Bless and protect our immortal souls that we may exist and live forever in your sight! Praise be your Sacred Name, Lord Jesus Christ, in the dawning of the day's awareness, through the morning light, after the hours of midday, and during the darkness in the evening, even into the Infinite and Unseen Existence of the Holy Spirit, Who exists throughout the ever flowing of all time, even unto eternity!

Amen …

Chapter and verse that inspired prayer:

2 Corinthians 4:18    While we look not at the things which are seen, but at the things which are not seen: for the things which are seen are temporal; but the things which are not seen are eternal.

# April Twenty-Eight: "Open Their Eyes"

(As inspired from Amos 5:8)

Lord Jesus, hear our prayer …

Bless us, Our Flawless Lord, with an ability to comprehend the mystery of Immortality; but also, inspire us to accept all that we do not readily understand, through the power of faith in you! And when we are ready, as a human race, to receive all answers, you alone, Our Lord and God, will lead us to the resolution and revelation of all Truth!

The star filled sky after dusk is a heavenly blessing for spiritual inspiration! To actually gaze upon the countless stars and see deeply into the infinite depths of outer space is to truly perceive your Boundless Spirit, Our Lord and God, who has always existed and will always be, forever, without end! The vastness of the universe, O Lord, is indisputable evidence of your Endless Glory and Eminent Presence: The morning sun displays your Radiant Love, the countless stars reflect the Unlimited Abundance of your Ceaseless Compassion, and the multitude of life that exists is unbounded proof of your Ever Flowing Benevolence! Lord Jesus Christ, your Immaculate Image is always before us; how can anyone open their eyes and not see you!

Lord God, your Unparalleled Love is revealed to us everyday and in so many ways: The towering mountains, the rolling dunes, the winding rivers, the sloping valleys, the green forests, the billowing clouds, the blue skies above, and all the wild flowers of the field as they unfurl their colors to declare your Majesty each and every morning! Dear Lord, in all truth, you are revealed to us throughout the creation, this day and everyday that we live to witness your Beautiful and Holy Existence in our lives, Lord Jesus Christ Our God Eternal!

Amen …

Chapter and verse that inspired prayer:

Amos 5:8   Seek him that maketh the seven stars and Orion, and turneth the shadow of death into the morning, and maketh the day dark with night: that calleth for the waters of the sea, and poureth them out upon the face of the earth: The LORD is his name.-

# April Twenty-Nine: "Where There Is Truth, There You Are, Lord"

## (As inspired from Exodus 34:6)

Lord Jesus, hear our prayer ...

Our Merciful God, we, your faithful, humbly beseech you: Allow your Spirit to pass before us and proclaim our souls in your Gracious Name, that we belong to you, Our Heavenly Lord and Christ, and only to you!

O Lord, we begin each day with an individual confession of personal faith. Through daily prayer and forgiveness, this day, as everyday, will begin with a blessing of love and a spiritual cleansing: Thank you, Lord God, for this moment in time. Please, forgive us our transgressions, Lord Jesus, for we so desire that your Kingdom will one day be our Forever Home! Our souls on earth are in heavenly exile, and everyday, we pray that we are deserving of your Hallowed Love and Care! Lord Jesus, your Ever Healing Mercy is abundant and longsuffering, your Sacred Heart is Most Gracious and filled with Pure Goodness, and when we pray to you with purity of spirit and complete devotion in our words, we know that you will receive us. When we rejoice with heartfelt sincerity, Lord Christ, we know that you will hear us. And when we respect others, with genuine compassion and heartfelt commitment, Lord God, we know that you will regard us with Spiritual Love; for where there is love, there is truth, and truth is the essence of a Christian life! Therefore, today, and everyday that we live our lives, Our Merciful Lord, we will direct our hearts to be true to ourselves, to be honest with one another, and to be forever faithful to your Holy Word, Lord Jesus! For where there is truth, there you are, Lord Jesus Christ!

Amen ...

Chapter and verse that inspired prayer:

Exodus 34:6    And the LORD passed by before him, and proclaimed, The LORD, The LORD God, merciful and gracious, Longsuffering, and abundant in goodness and truth.

# April Thirty: "Lord, Remain With Us"

### (As inspired from Revelation 22:1)

Lord Jesus, hear our prayer ...

Through Divine Revelation, as so related through chapter and verse of the Gospels, Lord Jesus Christ, you have Promised to your faithful, an Everlasting Kingdom of Peace and Love! Blessed are all who keep your Commandments on earth, for they will have Your Heavenly Promise to the Tree of Life and will be permitted to enter through the Holy Gates of Eternity!

Thank you, Lord God, thank you so very much for resolving every problem that we have! Through you, there is not a single situation that cannot be solved! All afflictions and all diseases are conquered and eliminated through Pristine Prayer and Soulful Offerings of repentance and obedience to you! Lord, your Love is Unflawed, as clear as crystal, as pure as the River of Life that continuously flows to nourish, to cleanse, and to quench the spirits of all who thirst so desperately to drink from the Fountains of your Living Waters! Lord Jesus, fill our lives with the Holy Compassion of your Immaculate Heart that our souls will forever be immersed in your Ever Flowing Love! Lord, remain with us, forgive us, and accept us as faithful Christians, Our Lamb of God, who are devoted only to your Most Holy Name, to the Throne of God in the Kingdom of Heaven!

We pray, O Lord, that your Holy Spirit will abide within us and nourish the souls of your faithful to an Unequaled and Magnificent Fulfillment! Permit your Healing Love to flow continuously through us that our immortal spirits will never again thirst! Fill our hearts to capacity, Lord Jesus, that we may never become a desert of spiritual loneliness! Cleanse our thoughts of all adversity and instill in us the Wisdom of your Ever Flowing Forgiveness. This we ask in your Wonderful and Blessed Name, Lord Jesus Christ!

Amen ...

Chapter and verse that inspired prayer:

Revelation 22:1    And he shewed me a pure river of water of life, clear as crystal, proceeding out of the throne of God and of the Lamb.

# May One: "In The Beginning Of Time"

(As inspired from Genesis 1:24-25)

Lord Jesus, hear our prayer ...

Bless everyone, Lord God, with a blessing of Discernment; for there are times when it is beyond our understanding, but not our appreciation, as to why there are so many minute creatures in the world that seem of little importance, but actually play an enormous role in the wonderment of creation! In the beginning of time, O Lord, you brought forth all life and saw that it was good! You have filled the earth with a great diversity of life. And all the living creatures, large or small, from those that fly to those that crawl, forms the connecting framework of this living planet! Blessed is your Vision, Lord Jesus Christ, for whenever we see even a drop of dew resting on a blade of grass, or the springing forth of a budding leaf, or the miniature hatching of new life, we are reminded of the small, but no less important, blessings of life throughout this wondrous world!

And that everyone may share in your Wisdom for earth's creation, Lord Jesus, impart in us, and all people around the world, a sincere respect for the many different forms of life that exist, no matter how insignificant a life form may appear to us; for you created the air to breathe, the water to drink, the soil to nourish, and all the countless marvelous creatures therein to live and share in your bountiful blessings! Thank you, Lord Jesus, for all life; for everything in creation is a blessed and intricate part of your Divine Web of Life! And we honor you, Lord, and give you our heartfelt gratitude for all life and for allowing us to be a part of your life, Our Lord and God of Creation!

Amen ...

Chapter and verse that inspired prayer:

Genesis 1:24-25     And God said, Let the earth bring forth the living after his kind, cattle, and creeping thing, and the beast of the earth after his kind: and it was so. (25) And God made the beast of the earth after his kind, and every thing that creepeth upon the earth after his kind: and God saw that it was good.

# May Two: "Calm Our Passions And Open Our Eyes"

### (As inspired from Ephesians 3:16, 20)

Lord Jesus, hear our prayer ...

By your Holy Name, Lord God, we beg of you: Authorize the Power of Peace to rule abundantly in our hearts as we continually seek out Goodness in our Christian lives! Through the Divine Spirit of Holiness, we pray for a renewal of Spiritual Might! Help us, Lord Jesus, to develop our individual convictions that will be able to withstand any and all faithless promises and perversions of the truth. Open our eyes that we may clearly recognize the signs of destructive pride and false allurement; emotions that tend to cloud personal achievements in life. Also, remove from our thoughts any feelings of disappointment and frustration, for they only serve to weaken and repress the human spirit. Quell our undesirable emotions, Lord Christ, so that each and every one of us may fully understand the folly and disillusionment of jealousy and petty arguments, which serve no purpose for the betterment of humanity nor in one's own life!

We pray: Please, calm our passions and open our eyes, instill into your faithful an inner strength, forged by the fires of our faith in you, Lord Jesus Christ, that will give us the true mettle to subdue and control our emotions and actions during any trial or tribulation throughout our lives! Grant us the riches of personal assurance and confidence in all that we do, according to the blessings of the Holy Ghost that moves within the spirit of our Christian faith! And now, Our Heavenly Spirit of Love, we offer our heartfelt thanks through honest and sincere words of gratitude and adulation for all that you have done for us: All Glory is yours, all Victory is yours, and we, your faithful ones on earth, are yours, now and into the Far-reaches of time!

Amen ...

Chapter and verse that inspired prayer:

Ephesians 3:16, 20   That he would grant you, according to the riches of his glory, to be strengthened with might by his Spirit in the inner man; (20) Now unto him that is able to do exceeding abundantly above all that we ask or think, according to the power that worketh in us.

# May Three: "Let Us Never Lose Confidence"

(As inspired from Hebrews 10:35-36)

Lord Jesus, hear our prayer …

Our wonderful Christian faith has taught us that personal confidence is gained through belief in one's ability, and our individual faith is formed and strengthened through patience and acceptance of God's Will! Thank you, Lord of Heavenly Reward, for our personal triumphs and successes in our Christian faith and convictions!

We are in total Christian unity, Lord God, when we pray to you for all people, everywhere, to know and understand the Great Power that exists within everyone, the Power to Love; and what a wonderful blessing it is! O Lord, may we never direct the anger of heated emotions to pass from one day unto another. Help us, Lord Jesus, to resolve any bitterness in our hearts and dissolve any and all ill feelings that we may have towards family, friend, or even a stranger. Heavenly Father, help each one of us to achieve our individual best as a person in Christ! And bless us, Lord Jesus, and let us never lose confidence or be defeated by our emotions; but remain thankful, comforted by hope, and encouraged by your ageless lessons of Enduring Patience!

Throughout our individual lives, Lord Jesus, during times of joy and peace, during moments of confusion and turmoil, we know that you have always been there for us, and that you will always be there for us! And it is our solemn promise, Lord Jesus Christ, from sunrise to sunset to sunrise again, that we will never permit a single day to pass without you being in our individual thoughts and in our personal prayers! Grant the Power of Love to shine brightly in our countenance, Lord, as a reflection of our love for you, Our Lord and God Almighty!

Amen …

Chapter and verse that inspired prayer:

Hebrews 10:35-36    Cast not away therefore your confidence, which hath great recompense of reward. (36) For ye have need of patience, that, after ye have done the will of God, ye might receive the promise.

# May Four: "Our Lord Of Everlasting"

(As inspired from Amos 4:13)

Lord Jesus, hear our prayer …

Heavenly Father, we thank you for our world in which we live! In our solar system, earth is the only planet with such a great abundance of life! And there are countless blessings of which we, as humans, are totally unaware! O Lord, a special acknowledgment and thank you for the many invisible miracles that are unseen by the human eye; and we give praise for our Heavenly Gifts! Lord God, there are so many things and events on earth that benefit humanity, and yet, are never seen or known! But without these beneficial plants and animals and organisms and minerals and happenings that are imperceptible to human sight, life as we know it would not be able to exist! Thank you, Lord Jesus, for your Great Wisdom and Understanding!

Lord God, you created the infinite space that holds the universe and our planet earth! You constructed the massive mountains and the beautiful sky overhead. You caused to exist the drifting clouds and the early morning mist. And with a mere thought, you conceived of every living creature in nature. Lord Jesus, you are the Creation and the Creator of all that subsists; for everything that ever was, that is, or that will ever be, is a True Blessing of your Love for us! And truly, you have blessed us, Lord Christ, for you have given to us the ability to reason, to think, and to be thankful for our blessings! No other living creature has the ability to thank and celebrate their Creator! You have set us above all other creatures that we may worship and extol praises of joy upon you, Our Lord Jesus Christ, Our Savior, Our Lord of Everlasting! Therefore, we extol great adulation and tribute to you, Our God of Hosts, for the Miracle of Pure Existence!

Amen …

Chapter and verse that inspired prayer:

Amos 4:13   For, lo, he that formeth the mountains, and createth the wind, and declareth unto man what is his thought, that maketh the morning darkness, and treadeth upon the high places of the earth, The LORD, The God of hosts, is his name.

# May Five: "The Wisdom Of The Ages"
### (As inspired from James 3:17)

Lord Jesus, hear our prayer …

O Supreme and Glorious Lord, as faithful Christian followers of your Spiritual Holiness, we ask of you: Bless all of us with insight, good sense, and wise judgment in all that we think, say, and do! Because, without a doubt, from you, Lord Christ, comes all the Wisdom of the Ages! From you, Lord Jesus, comes an Unceasing Outpouring of Salvation. And from you, Lord of Total Mercy, comes the direction of life, the definition of faith, and the purpose of love! We pray: May the entire world find your Path of Righteousness, Our Lord Jesus Christ, for it is the True Way, the Right Way, and the Only Way to a life that is Everlasting, filled with the Gentle Peace of your Magnificent Sanctification of Souls!

That the world may resolve its problems in a peaceful and an honorable way, Lord God, we seek your Intervention. That all families, everywhere, will resolve their differences, we plead for your Intercession, Lord Jesus. And that each and every individual person resolves their own personal conflicts through a deep Spiritual Understanding, we ask for your Guidance and Judgment: Lord Jesus Christ, we pray that all deceiving appearances and false assumptions of virtue will be removed from the face of the earth, allowing only your Holy and Divine Godliness to prevail in our lives! And like a lightning bolt from the heavens above, O Lord, we pray that you will soon return from your Hallowed Kingdom with Great Power and Great Glory to gather your flock and shepherd your faithful to lie down beside peaceful waters; and never again will we war or do wrong or cause harm to one another!

Amen …

Chapter and verse that inspired prayer:

James 3:17   But the wisdom that is from above first pure, then peaceable, gentle, and easy to be entreated, full of mercy and good fruits, without partiality, and without hypocrisy.

# May Six: "Blessed By Your Unbounded Holiness"
### (As inspired from Deuteronomy 7:9)

Lord Jesus, hear our prayer ...

Bless us and preserve us, Lord God, for we confess our true belief in your Most Precious Word of Life. Lord Jesus, your Glorious Truth has survived the annals and passages of time. From a distant and remote village, to a present worldwide faith, Christianity has survived genocide, war, famine, pestilence, despotic rule, ignorance, doubt, and all manners of stumbling blocks and will continue to grow from generation to generation until the passing of all time! And throughout the world, whenever rightful believers gather together in your Name to give thanks, it is our sincere prayer, Lord Jesus, that we may be counted among the faithful in your Glorious Name! Please hear and accept our testimony of true faith: Lord Jesus Christ, we profess to be loyal and truthful disciples of your teachings and Commandments of Life. And that we may forever abound in your Merciful Blessings, Lord, we offer praise and thanks to you for making right our lives through the comforting and Sacred Words of the Old and New Testament! Blest is the Bible, Wondrous is your Word of Love!

Generations have been and will continue to be blessed by your Unbounded Holiness, Lord. Therefore, we have searched heart and soul, and we can say unconditionally that we believe and that we firmly stand by your Word of Wisdom; for you are the True and Faithful Lord of Generations yet to be! And that everyone may remain honorable and faithful witnesses to your Perfect Glory, Lord Jesus, we pray that you will continually preserve and bless us throughout all the ages of time! Bless Christianity and bless those who are true and honorable followers of your Precious and Holy Spirit!

Amen ...

Chapter and verse that inspired prayer:

Deuteronomy 7:9    Know therefore that the LORD thy God, he is God, the faithful God, which keepeth covenant and mercy with them that love him and keep his commandments to a thousand generations;

# May Seven: "May Every Soul Be Delivered"

(As inspired from Titus 3:5)

Lord Jesus, hear our prayer ...

Lord God, we are all but Heavenly Pilgrims in a journey on earth, in search of answers, and we know that only you are the solution for every problem and situation that may arise in our lifetimes! Hear our prayer of spiritual gratitude: Blessed are your Glorious Works, O Lord, which are done for the Restoration of All Souls by the Hallowed Glory of God Almighty, Our Triumphant King! And now, receive our prayer request, Lord Jesus: Through a Total Spiritual Immersion of Mercy, renew our souls and lives in the Regenerative Powers of The Holy Spirit!

We want to thank you, Lord Christ, for all the joy, for all the love, and for all the wonders of life that you have given to each one of us, we, the tenants and keepers of our beautiful Christian faith! But we especially want to thank you, Lord Jesus, for the Miraculous Blessing of Birth! For truly, life is a Hallowed Miracle! Our Lord, we cherish and we celebrate the birth of a child as a Sacred Innocence! May every new life that is born into this beautiful world have the wonderful opportunity to be Spiritually Immersed into the Living Waters of the Holy Ghost! Inspire all parents to teach their children to learn the virtue of love, the value of good works, and the sound doctrine of obedience to your Hallowed and Noble Word; and please, Spiritually instruct each child to grow and develop into adulthood, Lord Jesus Christ, according to and guided by the laws of your Infinite Goodness! And then, at life's appointed time, may every beautiful soul be delivered into your Loving Hands and be received into your Never Ending Kingdom of Perfect and Divine Love that exists for all, for all eternity!

Amen ...

Chapter and verse that inspired prayer:

Titus 3:5   Not by works of righteousness which we have done, but according to his mercy he saved us, by the washing of regeneration, and renewing of the Holy Ghost;

# May Eight: "The Holy Spirit wilt Intercede"

(As inspired from Romans 8:24-26)

Lord Jesus, hear our prayer ...

Heavenly Father, pardon us and deliver us from our individual transgressions! Our Lord and God, your obedient faithful are saved by the strength of their faith In you! Through the abundance of your Immense Compassion, bless us, Lord Jesus, and fill our lives with Continuous Hope and the knowledge of anticipated fulfillment of prayer, through our deep trust and belief in you! Silently we pray.

The trials and tribulations of this world come and go, but your Love and Mercy, Lord Christ, are Forever Enduring! And through the perseverance of our prayers, Lord Jesus, we know that you will protect your faithful from all malice, misfortune, and misdeed. For we know, Lord Jesus Christ, that the Holy Spirit will forever intercede into the lives of those who are patiently faithful. O Lord, may we, your faithful disciples on earth, forever praise and herald the Good News of your Great and Godly Goodness! Through Deep Reverence, we are humbled.

Please hear our words of heartfelt celebration in gratitude to you, Lord, for all of our needs have been answered! And we rejoice in knowing that you count us among your faithful; for we continuously pray for your Divine Intercession! And through the proven patience of prayer, we have absolute confidence and faith, Lord Jesus, that you will intervene into the lives of those who follow your every Commandment of Love, and that your Holy Spirit will shield and deliver us from the afflictions of this world! Lord God, may your Abundant Love and Mercy shower down upon us evermore! With Gladdened Hearts, We Celebrate!

Amen ...

Chapter and verse that inspired prayer:

Romans 8:24-26    For we are saved by hope: but hope that is seen is not hope: for what a man seeth, why doth he yet hope for? (25) But if we hope for that we see not, then do we with patience wait for it. (26) Likewise the Spirit also helpeth our infirmities: for we know not what we should pray for as we ought: but the Spirit itself maketh intercession for us with groanings which cannot be uttered.

# May Nine: "Our Faith Is Always In You, Lord"

### (As inspired from 2 Thessalonians 3:2-3)

Lord Jesus, hear our prayer …

Centuries ago, in the beginning of our Christian faith, there was only One Following, One Belief in you, Our Messiah Lord Jesus! And we pray: Return us now, Our Savior of Souls, to a time of Simplicity, to an era of Unity and Strength, to an Understanding of Oneness! Lord of All That Is Holy, you have shown us, through your Unswerving Love, that our individual faith is the spiritual fiber in life that keeps a family together, established in truth, and united by a Oneness of Belief; we thank you, Lord Jesus, for your Bonding Love that holds our Christian families together. Bless us, O Lord, and deliver every member in the family from the evils of this world! Bestow upon us your blessings of Love and encourage the faith in our individual families to blossom forth, Lord Christ, into a Radiant Glory of your Pure and Manifest Goodness. Lord Jesus Christ, we pray for everyone in this world: Establish and place your Flawless Truth into all hearts and deliver all inhabitants of earth into the Light of your Supreme Love and Protection!

We give thanks, Lord God, for all the love that is interwoven into the faithful and loving family. And everyday that we step out into the world, we know that we will never walk alone. Our faith is always in you, Lord Christ, for you will fortify and safeguard our journeys throughout life! Lord Jesus, bless us and oversee our troubles and any avenues of difficulty that we may encounter; keep us safe from all harm and watch over us now and until the completion of our individual earthly journeys in time. Bless the Unity of our belief, Lord, and strengthen our personal determination of Christian Oneness with you, Our Personal Savior and Lord of Heaven and Earth!

Amen …

Chapter and verse that inspired prayer:

2 Thessalonians 3:2-3    And that we may be delivered from unreasonable and wicked men: for all men have not faith. (3) But the Lord is faithful, who shall stablish you, and keep you from evil.

# May Ten: "You Are Our Refuge, Lord"

(As inspire from 2 Samuel 22:2-3)

Lord Jesus, hear our prayer …

Lord God, only you have the right to determine all destinies on earth, and we, who believe in your Power, have the right to pray for your Divine Guidance: Deliver all who pray to you with a forthright and devout heart, wash away any problems that engulf the spirit, soothe the troubled mind, and make clear the clouded vision that so desires to see their Way to The Path of your Infinite Righteousness!

The known universe is a creation of immense proportion; wherein, its center is unknown, but through faith, it is clearly understood to be engulfed by your Holy and Gentle Spirit of Love! Hear us, Lord God, as we give acclaim for our lives: As the sun is the center of our solar system, as the soul is the internal measure of our true existence, your Holy Spirit, Dear Lord, clearly becomes the focus of all life. And as your Spirit flows within us, Lord Jesus, your Love becomes the True Essence of our being! You are the foundation of our Christian faith! You are our refuge from all chaos. You are the Mountain that shelters us from the storms Of life. And in your Forbearing Salvation, Our Lord and God, we place all our trust and hope. Please, Lord Christ, grant your Wonderful Wisdom to guide and shield us as we build our lives around you. Become our Fortress against the adversaries of Truth and Goodness! And through the protection of your Holy Spirit of Grace, we will always find a True Sanctuary in our lives! O Lord, hear our prayer of gratitude: For as the heart is the center of the body, and the soul is the core of existence, your Immaculate Spirit Lord Jesus Christ, is the body and soul of the world, of our lives, and of all Love Eternal!

Amen …

Chapter and verse that inspired prayer:

2 Samuel 22:2-3    And he said, The LORD is my rock, and my fortress, and my deliverer; (3) The God of my rock; in him will I trust: he is my shield, and the horn of my salvation, my high tower, and my refuge, my savior; thou savest me from violence.

# May Eleven: "Forever Abide Within Our Lives"

(As inspired from 2 Peter 1:19, 21)

Lord Jesus, hear our prayer ...

Our Lord in Heaven, move every heart on earth to understand the impact of love upon this planet, and how great our lives will be when everyone puts aside their biases and truly loves their neighbor as they love themselves! Lord, your love is the brilliant morning star for all to follow through their travels in a darkened and troubled world. And all who pursue and keep your Spiritual Ways, Lord Jesus, will indeed find peace in their hearts, fulfillment in their souls, and new lives of existence through the Dawning Awareness of your Great Compassion! Thank you, Lord Christ, for bringing love to our planet earth! Thank you for sending your Holy Spirit to comfort, to redeem, and to bring peace into the world! Thank you, Lord Jesus Christ, for making our spirits whole and our lives meaningful. And thank you, Our Anointed Messiah, for fulfilling the Scriptures of the Old Testament, and for being the Final and Greatest Prophet of them all!

Your Holy Spirit brings the Word of Truth into the depths of all souls, Lord, and we pray that your loving Spirit will forever abide within our lives, within our hearts, and within the total realization of all people on earth; for truly, Lord Jesus Christ, only through the Radiant Acceptance of your Spiritual Truth, will Hallowed Love turn a darkened and troubled world towards the Light of Truth and the Spiritual Salvation of Personal Redemption!

Amen ...

Chapter and verse that inspired prayer:

2 Peter 1:19, 21    We have also a more sure word of prophecy; whereunto ye do well that ye take heed, as unto a light that shineth in a dark place, until the day dawn, and the day star arise in your hearts: (21) For the prophecy came not in old time by the will of man: but holy men of God spake as they were moved by the Holy Ghost.

# May Twelve: "We Are Endlessly Grateful To You"

### (As inspired from Romans 8:32)

Lord Jesus, hear our prayer …

Heavenly Father, you gave to the world your only Son to be sacrificed in a Ransom of Innocent Blood, so that all humans may gain Eternal Life; let the whole world remember, Lord God Almighty, just how much you love us: Impart into the hearts of all people on earth, Christ Our King, the Celestial and Angelic Knowledge of your Undeniable Presence!

Blessed is your Spirit of Abundance, Lord Jesus, for you have freely given to us, all the things of your Sacred Heart! Through your Towering Generosity, which extends throughout the creation and throughout all of existence, you have shown us the absolute meaning of Benevolent Compassion for those that you cherish: One seed will become an enormous tree that produces countless offspring; a single cloud will become an outpouring that falls and fills a vast reservoir; and your Innocent Soul, Lord Jesus, filled with Love and Wisdom, was born without sin and was hailed, Lord Emmanuel, by angels, grew into a mighty Christian Nation of faithful and fruitful followers who worship you to this very day and call you, God!

Your Goodness, Our Lord and God, is a Glorious Sea of Generosity, and we are endlessly grateful to you for your profusion of love into our lives. And in all truth, and in all respect, and in all admiration, we exalt you, Our Good Prince of Peace, above all, and above everything on earth and in life! Indeed, we are blessed to receive your Never-ending Grace and Benevolence; and how fortunate we are to be called Christians who follow and honor your Perfect Name, Our Lord Jesus Christ!

Amen …

Chapter and verse that inspired prayer:

Romans 8:32    He that spared not his own son, but delivered him up for all, how shall he not with him also freely give us all things?

# May Thirteen: "A Life In Harmony With Itself"

(As inspired from Colossians 1:14)

Lord Jesus, hear our prayer …

Through the shedding of your Innocent Blood, Our Sacred Savior, all is forgiven, all are healed, and redemption of the immortal soul begins! Please, Christ Our King, hear our prayerful pleas.

Dear Lord, when we feel the uncertainty of doubt, caused by the shadows of misdeed or thought, without a doubt, there is no where to turn but into the Light of Mercies; and, Lord Jesus Christ, you are the Light of Pure Forgiveness! Wherefore, we humbly beseech you, O Lord, and ask you for Spiritual Help and Redemption! Please, absolve us of any and all offenses, transgressions, or wrongdoings that we may have incurred; for whatever we have done to others or to your Word, we have also done wrongfully to ourselves and our souls. Therefore, Lord of Compassion, heal our eyes of blind ambition and fill our hearts with a real Christian understanding of doing what is right, simply, because it is the right thing to do!

Our Lord and God, that we may emulate your Grace and Goodness throughout our lives, reveal to our hearts a life in harmony with itself. Help us, Lord Jesus, to never become complaisant with inferior values of morality in mind, spirit, or body. Lord Christ, we pray for a continual renewal of our Christian faith through your Divine Intervention into our lives and into the lives of all who honestly seek the Heavenly Guidance of your Glowing Salvation of Life! Find us worthy, Lord Jesus Christ, by instructing our souls to be obedient to your every Loving Commandment and to serve your Holy Spirit through love and humility!

Amen …

Chapter and verse that inspired prayer:

Colossians 1:14   In whom we have redemption through his blood, even the forgiveness of sins:

# May Fourteen: "Your Word, Lord, Is Love"

(As inspired from 1 John 4:7-8)

Lord Jesus, hear our prayer …

As devout Christians, we affirm, we know, and we believe that our Heavenly Father is Pure Love, that our Lord Jesus Christ is Pure Love, and that our Holy Spirit is Pure Love, for love is The Beginning.

Every new morning is a blessing, because, we are given another day to worship and extol our praise of happiness upon our Creator, upon you, Our Lord and God! Lord Christ, whenever we stand in the Sun's Light and marvel at the sight of this beautiful planet and all that unfolds before us, we are transfixed and transformed into beings of Spiritual Love! Lord Jesus, you are the Author of Life, and within each chapter of existence, there resides the indisputable proof of your Divine and Precious Word, and your Word, Lord, is Love, the Purest Love that could ever exist or be imagined!

Lord God, you are the Master Planner of All Creation! No one else could have ever designed and built the majesty of snow capped mountains and green valleys, or the calming beauty of blue oceans and painted deserts, nor the emerald splendor of rain forests and lush fields of wild flowers. No, nature did not come about by accident or coincidence, Lord of Creation, for only you are the True Composer of our infinite universe! From a small and gentle songbird to a deafening cascading waterfall, and all of life's loving sounds in between, there is most definitely a constant melody of praise and glory that is continually heard throughout the ageless and glorious composition of this wondrous creation as it sings out in unison: Blessed are you, Lord Jesus Christ, Lord of Existence, Lord of love, Lord of All that is! Holy! Holy! Holy is your Name!

Amen …

Chapter and verse that inspired prayer:

1 John 4:7-8    Beloved, let us love one another: for love is of God; and every one that loveth is born of God, and knoweth God. (8) He that loveth not knoweth not God; for God is love.

# May Fifteen: "Restore And Make Whole The Shattered"

### (As inspired from 3 John 2)

Lord Jesus, hear our prayer …

Those who wrongly persecuted you, Lord Christ, were humans deceived, our brothers and sisters of long ago, believers in the same God of Adam and Eve, Noah, Mosses, Abraham, and King David! Forgive us, Almighty JEHOVAH, for we knew not what we did: Our Precious Lord and Messiah, you were robed in scarlet, falsely accused, beaten, scourged, spit upon, and yet, you, The Lamb of God, willingly took our insults, our slaps, our mocking laughter, and still, you forgave us, and still, you love us! O Lord Jesus, you have saved us and redeemed our immortal souls through sacrifices of blood, life, and long-suffering!

Glory to you, Lord of Mercy, pure and absolute is the power of your love; for only you can bring together the scattered, and only you, can restore and make whole the shattered! But above all things, Our Lord and God, we know that you want us to prosper in our spiritual and physical well-being. And through our individual faith and your endless love, Lord Jesus Christ, we will receive a true healing of the mind, the body, and the soul, according to your Righteous and Illuminating Spirit of Love!

Glory be to you, Lord God, for the power of your love reaches deeply into the very fiber of our existence to heal and restore all spiritual and physical health! And through true faith in your Absolute Power, Lord Jesus, we will forever remain resolute in our Christian belief that you answer every prayer according to its need and according to your Magnificent Will! Pray for us to be strong and to have faith in your Holy Resolution: We believe and we accept that your will be done on earth as it is in heaven!

Amen …

Chapter and verse that inspired prayer:

3 John 2    Beloved, I wish above all things that thou mayest prosper and be in health, even as thy soul prospereth.

# May Sixteen: "A Constant Utterance Of Praise"

### (As inspired from Jude 24-25)

Lord Jesus, hear our prayer …

Pray for your faithful children on earth, Lord Jesus, strengthen and fortify our Christian values and our personal determination to fulfill and keep your every Commandment of Life! Please, help us to individually realize that we are responsible for our personal actions and decisions that may affect others and their decisions to follow the path of your Righteous Goodness!

Great is your Glory and Majesty! Forever is your Dominion and Power! O Lord, when you walked the earth, you humbly stood by all, serving the poor, the lame, the sick! Your Radiant Silhouette of Love was robed in mercy as you reached out to touch the infirm, the lost, the hopeless, the dead, and to heal all, with a loving smile of forgiveness! Lord Christ, you gave cause for exceeding joy, for all life, and for all living things to be thankful for their existence! And we, your faithful, also thank you, Lord Jesus Christ, for this day, for this hour, and for every moment in time that gives pause to reflect and proudly acclaim our blessings of love!

Whether we set a foot or afloat in our daily journeys in life, Lord God, we are completely confident; for our personal safety and well-being derives from you! Lord Jesus, you kindle our spirits to leap with jubilance, you inspire our hearts to deeply fill with love, and you cause our words to be a constant utterance of praise and adoration for your Unconquerable Majesty! And now and forever, Lord Jesus Christ, and into infinity, your Love and Glory will always be the origin of our overwhelming happiness, here, on earth! We pray to you, Our Sacred and Holy Christ, inspire the whole world to acclaim your Magnificent Presence on earth, in their hearts, in our hearts, and everywhere else in this Holy Creation!

Amen …

Chapter and verse that inspired prayer:

Jude 24-25    Now unto him that is able to keep you from falling, and to present you faultless before the presence of his glory with exceeding joy, (25) To the only wise God our Saviour, be glory and majesty, dominion and power, both now and ever. Amen.

# May Seventeen: "We Thank You, Lord, For Everything"

(As inspired from Deuteronomy 8:3 and Isaiah 43:3)

Lord Jesus, hear our prayer …

In the beginning was the Word, Our Lord and Savior, for you have created everything in the world and have given freely to all people of your Spiritual Generosity: A physical life for our immortal souls, the ability to give our Creator praise, a mind that can create good for all humanity, and a wonderful planet to live upon, abundantly filled with a multitude of life; for this, and so much more, Dear Lord, we give endless thanks and adulation!

In the beginning was the Word, and the Word is you, Lord God Almighty! Heavenly Father, blessed is your Life Giving, Soul Saving Words that are found in the Living Holy Truth of Love! From actual words spoken by our Creator and recorded by God-fearing prophets of old, we have learned, through chapter and verse, that only unblemished gifts of devout prayer, soulful words spoken in total honesty, will veritably reach your Kingdom on High. Lord Jesus; therefore, please, Lord Christ, hear the sincerity in the praise that we offer to you: We thank you, Lord, for everything! Each day, from within, we give true acknowledgment to you, Our Lord of Heaven and Earth, for everything that has been allotted to us in our lives! And for everything that we partake and receive from the harvests of the soils on this good earth, we are truly blessed by you, Lord Jesus, for our precious portions in life! And as food is the sustenance of our physical lives, so too are your Holy Words, Lord Jesus Christ, the sustenance of our immortal souls; for we do not live by food alone, but by every chapter and verse and word of your Heavenly Spirit of Love! Blest is the Spoken Word of the Lord and blessed is every person who hears and lives their life in accordance to your Holy Ordinance of Compassion!

Amen …

Chapter and verse that inspired prayer:

Deuteronomy 8:3    And he humbled thee, and suffered thee to hunger, and fed thee with manna, which thou knewest not, neither did thy fathers know; that he might make thee know that man doth not live by bread only, but by every word that proceedeth out of the mouth of the LORD doth man live.

Isaiah 43:3    For I am the Lord thy God, they Holy One of Israel, thy Savior:

# May Eighteen: "On A Mission From You, Lord"

(As inspired from Hebrews 13:1-2)

Lord Jesus, hear our prayer …

All the answers to all the mysteries and questions of the world, are known in heaven! Thank you, Lord All-knowing, for sharing this knowledge with us, for the reassurance that everything will one day be revealed and explained, and for our powerful faith that Christianity awards us!

O Lord, because we know that you care about us and that you pray for us to safely return from every journey that we take in life, hear our prayer request: During our absence from loved ones, we long to see a familiar face, a friendly smile, and to have personal confidence in any situation. Thank you, Dear Lord, for the blessing of fellowship that exists between people. For when we are far from home, in unfamiliar surroundings, as a stranger in another land, we reach out from our emotional feelings of insecurity, Lord Jesus, and call out to you for comfort and peace! And from our silent supplications, we find that moment of truth comes through you, Lord Christ, in our prayers as we ask for safety, self-confidence, and fellowship; and through your Unwavering Spiritual Strength, we receive our heavenly assurance from all harm and disarray. Lord God, allow your Spiritual Compassion to continually grow within our hearts; create in all of us, a deep sense of awareness that will inspire us to recognize the sincerity and needs of family, friends, strangers, and travelers that abide among us. Help us to develop a mindful knowledge that every person on earth is fully known by you, and that any heart we soulfully touch could be that of a Heavenly Traveler, sent on a mission from you, Lord Jesus Christ! Blessed are the angels of God, who serve you, Lord, night and day, and do always behold the face of the Holy Father!

Amen …

Chapter and verse that inspired prayer:

Hebrews 13:1-2    Let brotherly love continue. (2) Be not forgetful to entertain strangers: for thereby some have entertained angels unawares.

# May Nineteen: "With You, Nothing Is Impossible"

### (As inspired from Luke 1:36-38)

Lord Jesus, hear our prayer ...

Our Divine Lord and God, we honor you with love and spiritual obedience, for you have Promised the World that the day will come when everyone will be able to walk the earth in peace, will carry love within their hearts, and will feel compassion for friend and stranger alike; because, with God, nothing is impossible!

As Christians, we proudly attest to being servants of our Divine Savior, Lord Jesus Christ, the Only Begotten Son of God the Father; blessed are all who believe! Thank you, Lord, for your Heavenly Intercessions of love that exists within all who are loyal and faithful to your Word! Through your Spiritual Inspirations, we are guided in our paths of thought, conduct, and decision. Lord Jesus, enlighten our Spiritual Understanding of life that we may receive and perceive your Perfect Design as you have so created for our lives. Enable us to leave our shadows of doubt to forever sojourn in the Light of your Unconquerable Truth! And according to the Gift of your Blessed Word, O Lord, we pray to you for Spiritual Knowledge and Encouragement! From the soles of our feet to the crowns of our heads, we are obedient servants of your Divine Love. Lord Jesus, lift our spirits and inspire our hearts to fulfill our heavenly destinies that you have so accorded us from the beginning of time! Help us to eternally leave the darkened paths of incertitude and ignorance and proudly forge ahead in our Christian understanding, Dear Lord, that with you, nothing is impossible! And now, we earnestly beseech you, please, send your most powerful Guardian Angels, Lord God, to forever protect and watch over our destined paths; from the venues of which all will be judged by the Son of Man, in the Wonderful Days of His Second Coming!

Amen ...

Chapter and verse that inspired prayer:

Luke 1:36-38   And, behold, thy cousin Elisabeth, she hath also conceived a son in her old age: and this is the sixth month with her, who was called barren. (37) For with God nothing shall be impossible. (38) And Mary said, Behold the handmaid of the Lord; be it unto me according to thy word. And the angel departed from her.

# May Twenty: "We Search The Depths Of Our Emotions"

(As inspired from 1 Timothy 2:7-8)

Lord Jesus, hear our prayer ...

With lifted hands, repentant and unstained, we offer the purity of our prayers without anger and without doubt, knowing fully well that you, Lord God, answer all prayer requests that are offered in the sincerity of heartfelt appraisal! Therefore, during our prayers, Lord God, we search the depths of our emotions and yield to the Loving Mercy of your Holy Spirit to release any pent up anger and bitterness that we may find within ourselves. And in all verity, we are overcome with much joy and happiness, Lord Jesus, when we surrender to the Far Reaching Truth of your Immaculate Heart! For without any doubt in our convictions, we proclaim the Excellence and the Perfection of your Loving and Living Holy Spirit that continually grows within our lives and within our very souls!

Thank you, Our Lord God, for showing us, through Scripture, that all problems, natural disasters, catastrophes, worries, and the woes of the world can be avoided and are not the result of your wrath but the consequences of our own spiritual disobedience and denial of your Hallowed Protection that is constantly offered! And now, through devout prayer, we yield up our temporal wills to you, Lord, and gladly accept your Heavenly Will as our own! We acclaim and we believe in the Empowering Love of your Sanctifying Word as the source of our spiritual might and salvation! Into your hands, Our Dear Lord Jesus, do we place our faith, our hopes, and our lives; for only through you, Lord Jesus Christ, will our eternal spirits ever find a lasting peace and a real happiness in this life that you have ordained for us on earth!

Amen ...

Chapter and verse that inspired prayer:

1 Timothy 2:7-8    Whereunto I am ordained a preacher, and an apostle, (I speak the truth in Christ, and lie not;) a teacher of the Gentiles in faith and verity. (8) I will therefore that men pray every where, lifting up holy hands, without wrath and doubting.

# May Twenty-One: "We Shall Forever Maintain Our Faith"

(As inspired from Esther 10:1-2)

Lord Jesus, hear our prayer …

When we really believe that we are suffering in pain, and can no longer go on, we must remind ourselves of the horrible pain and suffering that our Lord endured through His beatings, imprisonment, humiliation, whipping, hunger, thirst, mental anguish, being nailed to wooden beams, and yet, He asked the Father to forgive us, never once thinking of self-destruction.

The laws of humankind can be broken, manipulated, overruled, or sustained, but the Laws of God are perfect and permanent; and as faithful Christians, all we have to do to receive is believe! O Tender and Merciful Lord, as it is written throughout the prophecies of the Old Testament and the Glorious New Testament, nothing is able to stand in the way of your Exalted Will. When sadness enters the heart and inflicts the mind and the spirit, we know that your Great Love, Lord Jesus, will vanquish and triumph over the gloom; for your Love conquers all! When clouds of depression gather to eclipse the light, we know that the hollow shadows of fear will never prevail against the intensity of your Unwavering Laws, Lord Christ; for your Will Is All Commanding! And when the ill winds of doubt cut deeply through the soul, ignorance will be defeated by the Glory of your Magnificent Judgment, Lord; for nothing on earth or in the heavens above is able to resist you! Our Infinite and Precious Lord, we shall forever maintain our faith in you; for we know that you will forever protect and save your Chosen Faithful through all the physical, mental, and spiritual storms of earth! Peace and continuous protection flow outwardly from your Sacred Heart, Lord Jesus Christ, unto all the Christians in all the great lands and seaways of the world! Glory and praise to the Presence of your Uncompromising Power of Goodness, as it is written, so it is declared!

Amen …

Chapter and verse that inspired prayer:

Esther 10:1-2    And the king Ahasuerus laid a tribute upon the land, and upon the isles of the sea. (2) And all the acts of his power and might, and the declaration of the greatness of Mordecai, whereunto the king advanced him, are they not written in the book of the chronicles of the kings of Media and Persia?

# May Twenty-Two: "Proven In Every Place"

### (As inspired from 2 Corinthians 2:14)

Lord Jesus, hear our prayer …

Daily, Lord Jesus, our souls triumph in your Victory on the Cross! Because of your Resurrection, we have peace in our hearts, assurance of Eternal Life, and a Spiritual Calming that causes our physical lives to find your Infinite Love in every moment of our existence!

We accept and partake in our Heavenly Father's Bounty of love and Salvation! Lord, the vine of life is a Christian fellowship that you created, which joins the heart, the mind, and the soul of family and friends into a special eternal bond of trust and love! Thank you, Lord Christ, for the glory and the splendor of life's moment! We thank you for this beautiful and lovely day that was created and designed from your Abundant and Manifest Love! How alive all life seems when we are able to witness and experience your Love, Lord Jesus, with family and friends, as it is mirrored throughout this incredible planet: Earth's clean fragrance after a gentle spring rain, the luminous brilliance of a midday sun, the vibrant sounds of nature coming to life, the soft petals of a red red rose, the crisp sweet freshness found in the fruits of a valley orchard, or even the brilliant blossoms of a mountain vineyard. O Lord, we pray that everyone, everywhere, will be able to see and perceive the reflective miracles of your Magnificent Love and Spiritual Doctrine; for it is proven in every place, throughout this good earth, that your Perfect Design is created for all life! And wherever there is life, Our Lord of Creation, there exists the True Reflection of your Glorious and Triumphant Compassion for the whole world! Blessed is your Bountiful Protection, Lord Jesus Christ, and blest is the special bond of Christian fellowship that you have given to all who faithfully believe and follow every Word of your testimony that was given on earth so many centuries ago! Amen!

Amen …

Chapter and verse that inspired prayer:

2 Corinthians 2:14    Now thanks be unto God, which always causeth us to triumph in Christ, and maketh manifest the savour of his knowledge by us in every place.

# May Twenty-Three: "Life Is A Blessed Gift Of Love"

(As inspired from Isaiah 45:17-18)

Lord Jesus, hear our prayer …

We pray that every ear will hear, that every heart will accept, and that every soul will trust in the Undeniable Presence of your Living Existence in our world! Our Living God, we pray for all the nonbelievers who exist on your miraculous creation called earth, and yet, do not acknowledge its Creator: Forgive them their blindness and inspire their soul to see, to recognize, and to believe in you, Our True Embodiment of Divine Grace! Our Savior Jesus Christ of Nazareth!

Heavenly Father, in the heavens above or on the earth below, there is no Greater Love than One who gives their life for all that others may live; thank you, Lord Jesus, for your Innocent and Unselfish Sacrifice! Blessed are we to receive of your love, to live life through your guidance, and to be called Christians! Lord Christ, from the heart of your Heavenly Compassion, life is a Blessed Gift of Love, and we thank you for all of our blessings: As the seed produces the tree, the good tree produces its fruit, and a tree is always known by its fruit; thus, the compassionate cycle of God's creation continues. From one generation unto another, Lord Jesus Christ, your Circle of love is unbroken! Please, hear our most sincere praise of love, Our Dear Lord, when our souls cry out to you: Endless Salvation goes out to the world when Love and Mercy flow from your heart; for there is no human language that can fully express the spiritual joy of a new life that is born to your Namesake, Our Gentle Lord Christ! We will continually adore your Everlasting Gift of Perfect Love, O Lord, from one generation to another, now and forever, in a world that you created, a world without end!

Amen …

Chapter and verse that inspired prayer:

Isaiah 45:17-18    But Israel shall be saved in the LORD with an everlasting salvation: ye shall not be ashamed nor confounded world without end. (18) For thus saith the LORD that created the heavens; God himself that formed the earth and made it; he hath established it, he created it not in vain, he formed it to be inhabited: I am the LORD; and there is none else.

# May Twenty-Four: "Most Gracious Lord, Receive Us"

(As inspired from Hosea 14:2)

Lord Jesus, hear our prayer …

You have taught us through love, O Lord, that when a person genuinely cares about another, the love that is shown ripples outwardly to touch others! In your Holy Name, Lord God, we humbly ask that you bless this family and bless this home and forgive all transgressions that may abide within our hearts and upon our immortal souls. We pray to you, Lord Jesus, that you will receive us and take away our individual offenses so that all who live within this dwelling will always be worthy of your Merciful Blessings and Spiritual Protection! Dear Lord, inspire us to create a peaceful home, a home that harbors a family of love and respect in an atmosphere that reflects your Heavenly Concern for each and every family member. Look into the Christian hearts of all who gather in your Name, Lord Jesus Christ, see the sincerity of our compassion and devotion for one another that resides within us; and to you, Lord of Redemption, we render up innocent prayers and praises from the purity of our love and admiration that we have for you!

Truly, no words have ever been written that could actually express our heartfelt gratitude to you, Lord Jesus, for being present in our lives! So, we will simply bow our heads and offer a silent, personal prayer of thanks to your Holy Spirit from deep within our souls! Most Gracious Lord, receive us as you receive our spiritual words of exaltation: Blessed are you, Lord of Hosts, and with everlasting praise upon our lips, we will give continuous thanks to your Most Holy and Blessed Existence in our lives, even unto eternity! Thank you, Lord Jesus Christ, for hearing our individual prayers.

Amen …

Chapter and verse that inspired prayer:

Hosea 14:2   Take with you words, and turn to the LORD: say unto him, Take away all iniquity, and receive us graciously: so will we render the calves of our lips.

# May Twenty-Five: "You Do Great Things Everyday"

(As inspired from Joel 2:21, 26)

Lord Jesus, hear our prayer …

We pray everyday and experience God's Triumphant Conquest over darkness and over all the ills of the world! Praise to our Righteous King Lord Jesus Christ, to you, Our Conquering God, to the One who holds the keys to Life Everlasting, we celebrate and revel in your Valiant Name: Heaven be praised, for earth and its inhabitants are free!

At the dawning of each day, our spirits awaken and our hearts open to receive the Wondrous Radiance of your Love, O Lord. Through you, Lord Jesus, our hearts are glad and we rejoice greatly; for you do great things everyday for everyone and for everything that exists! At sunrise, each day, all life arises to receive a renewed life from the brilliance and purity of the Glorious Sun. Throughout the day, all life is consumed with the wonder of its creation. And at dusk, the world peacefully slumbers in the Miraculous Embrace of your Loving Care. Therefore, Lord God, we are clearly assured in our lives that you will always protect and watch over us, even if the skies are graying or the winds are howling or the storm clouds are gathering into rumbles of thunder, we will always feel safe and satisfied, filled with pride and respect for you, Our Divine Intercessor, as we proudly acclaim to the whole world that you are The Savior, Our Lord and Christ, Our God of Heaven and Earth, the earth that you created! Praised be your name, Lord Jesus Christ, in this world, in the heavens above, and throughout the distant parts of the universe! Hear us now, Lord, as we pray for all who are spiritually asleep, may they awaken to the resplendent beauty of a new day and of a new existence in your Holy Spirit of Love!

Amen …

Chapter and verse that inspired prayer:

Joel 2:21, 26  Fear not, O land; be glad and rejoice: for the LORD will do great things. (26) And ye shall eat in plenty, and be satisfied, and praise the name of the LORD your God, that hath dealt wondrously with you: and my people shall never be ashamed.

# May Twenty-Six: "Hear Our Words Of Praise"

(As inspired from Acts of the Apostles 17:27-28)

Lord Jesus, hear our prayer …

Our Heavenly Father, Our Princely King, Our Holy Spirit, we seek your Hallowed Presence at all times, and your Love continuously reaches out and embraces the very existence of our souls; for all who call out to you, God, will find an answer within!

Lord, your Divine Love is truly recognized when it reaches deeply into a person and touches the very fiber of their soul! The heart knows when true happiness lingers in the mind, for nothing can remove that longing, that beauty, or that passion to possess the compassion that beckons love to remain forever in its state of perfection; and, Lord, you are the Perfection of love! You are as close to us as a whisper, as a thought, as our very own flesh, and we beseech you to please hear our words of pure wonderment as we seek your Loving Influence in our lives, in our hearts, and in our spirits: Bless us, Lord Christ, with your Holy Spiritual Presence! Because, through you, Lord Jesus Christ, we will be able to live our lives as total and complete human beings, fulfilled by your Sacred Words of Redemption, borne by your Eternal Promise of Salvation, and saved by the ransom of your Innocent Life!

O Lord, we pray to you: Hear our words of praise, our Most Holy and Perfect Prince of Love! Only through you, are all lives made complete; only in you, does true faith have meaning; and only for you, is life worth living! Hear us, Lord Jesus Christ, in our daily devotions. Please, listen to our words of adoration! From out of love do we utter our words of intent and devotion: Glory be to you, Lord Jesus, Our God of Life and Absolute Salvation! We bow our heads and pray that our prayers will reach your Hallowed Throne in the Kingdom of Heaven: Keep this nation safe, protect our souls from all temptation, and deliver everyone from their personal transgressions! Amen!

Amen …

Chapter and verse that inspired prayer:

Acts of the Apostles 17:27-28      That they should seek the Lord, if haply they might feel after him, and find him, though he be not far from every one of us: (28) For in him we live, and move, and have our being; as certain also of your own poets have said, For we are also his offspring.

# May Twenty-Seven: "Love Conquers All"
### (As inspired from Hebrews 13:4 and Genesis 2:24)

Lord Jesus, hear our prayer …

There is no greater blessing of the heart than true love between a man and a woman, as so intended by you, Our Lord and God! You have taught us that reverent, honest, and genuine compassion for one another is truly our fulfillment of life! Pray for us, your faithful, Lord, that we will continue the Christian tradition of Holy Matrimony between husband and wife, of male and female, of mother and father, of children and the family!

From a time before time, today, and even into tomorrow, the wisdom and strength of one power has survived all and will continue to prevail beyond all time. In heaven or on earth, no power is greater than the power of your love, Lord Jesus; and we thank you for your Heavenly Blessing of Love. So powerful is this force that when the seeds of love spring forth between a man and a woman, two lives join, blend, and blossom into one flesh; for from their families, two must part, but in a solemn vow of love, they unite again as one. And from that Sacred Promise, taken before you, Lord Creator of Love, there begins a lifelong merging of devotion. Therefore, when two shall meet and fall in love, there lies deeply within them a natural emotion by Divine Design. And by light of day, or by dark of night, this blessing of true love reigns supreme throughout the universe and throughout all who live their lives according to the authority and sanctity of your Word, Lord Jesus Christ; and we thank you for bestowing your blessing of love upon earth! Blessed and honorable is a marriage of love; for truly, Lord, love conquers all!

Amen …

Chapter and verse that inspired prayer:

Hebrews 13:4   Marriage is honourable in all, and the bed undefiled: but whoremongers and adulterers God will judge.

Genesis 2:24   Therefore shall a man leave his father and his wife mother, and shall cleave unto his wife: and they shall be one flesh.

# May Twenty-Eight: "Deliver Us, Lord"

### (As inspired from Exodus 6:6)

Lord Jesus, hear our prayer …

Whether we leap through the air in joyful praise, Lord, or sit quietly, rejoicing in soulful silence, we know that our words of adoration will reach into heaven: Bless the children who follow the Radiance of your Holy Spirit, redeem every faithful soul who totally surrenders to your Never-ending Love, and fulfill the lives of all people who honestly seek the True Light of the World!

Bless the Redemptive Majesty of your Immaculate Heart, Lord God, for you are the True Redeemer of lost spirits, of broken hearts, and of shattered lives. We pray to you for Spiritual Deliverance, Lord Jesus: Bring us out from beneath the burden of any personal depression, and please, rid our spirits of any bondage to any undue trouble or stress in our lives! Reach into the core of our existence, Lord Christ, and restore our souls to the Loving Caress of your Unending Grace! Open our eyes to the Heavenly Strength of your Divine Might and heal our hearts through your Just and Exact Judgments. Please, fill our spirits with the Unblemished Love of your Great and Holy Spirit! And we ask this of you, Lord God, because, only through you will we ever know the actual meaning of Spiritual Redemption. And only through you, O Lord, will we ever find a physical and soulful healing of our worldly problems! Deliver us, Lord, from all unnecessary trials and tribulations that may arise within our lives! Turn aside the shadows of our unwarranted fears. Into your Loving Hands, Lord Jesus Christ, do we place our devoted love, our sincerest trust, and our final destinies in life! Reach out to us, Our Heavenly King, from the Majesty of your Hallowed Realm and reclaim and deliver your obedient servants!

Amen …

Chapter and verse that inspired prayer:

Exodus 6:6   Wherefore say unto the children of Israel, I am the LORD, and I will bring you out from under the burdens of the Egyptians, and I will rid you out of their bondage, and I will redeem you with a stretched out arm, and with great judgments:

# May Twenty-Nine: "Servants Of Your Gentleness"

(As inspired from 2 Timothy 2:19, 24)

Lord Jesus, hear our prayer ...

We urgently pray for our planet and all of its inhabitants! Our Prince of Peace, we earnestly entreat you: Please, place a Spiritual Blessing into the heart of every individual in every nation on earth, to develop a deep desire to work for the betterment of the world!

We, your steadfast and loving subjects, by following your Commandments of Love, become pillars of faith within our own communities and within our individual families! And that we may solidly stand upon the foundations of our wonderful Christian beliefs and become positive monuments to the Wondrous Glory of your Goodness, Lord God, we pray that you will help us to temper our lives with the patience of your Profound Judgment! Assist us, Our Lord Jesus, as we constantly endeavor to become loyal and faithful servants of your gentleness. Please, O Lord, encourage us, as individuals, to tower above any disparity that we may hold for others as we earnestly seek peace and resolution in our own lives! Provide each one of us with a Christian understanding for compassion and forgiveness, Lord Jesus Christ, that so endlessly prevails in your Word of Truth! And in doing so, we will learn to become patient with one another and become gentle with our emotions; and by example, teaching tolerance and love to others!

For all that you have done for us, Lord Christ, we are forever grateful. Permit us now to show our gratitude to you, Lord God, through our faith and love as we pray: Guide us in our pursuit to become steadfast towers of obedience to your Tender Word of Love, Lord Jesus; and through a simple showing of respect, forgiveness, and genuine fellowship towards one another, all of us will achieve our spiritual goals in life!

Amen ...

Chapter and verse that inspired prayer:

2 Timothy 2:19, 24    Nevertheless the foundation of God standeth sure, having this seal, The Lord knoweth them that are his. And, let every one that nameth the name of Christ depart from iniquity. (24) And the servant of the Lord must not strive; but be gentle unto all men, apt to teach, patient,

# May Thirty: "Remember Those Who Have Gone Before Us"
### (As inspired from 1 John 3:1, 14)

Lord Jesus, hear our prayer …

As we pray and give thanks for all that we have received as Christians, Lord, we are most thankful for the Blessing of love that you have bestowed upon our lives. And that we will always remain as a Christian family, faithful to your Holy Name, we will forever share in our Compassionate Blessing, Lord Jesus Christ, by loving one another as we love ourselves! And that we may forever keep our memories alive for one another, let us also remember those who have gone before us, our family and friends. Therefore, we dedicate this soulful prayer and this day to a spiritual testimony for those who touched our lives, but now, have journeyed home to their Heavenly Rest in Eternity, to be with you, Lord Jesus Our Christ, Our Lord Who Lives Forever and Ever: Bless their souls and keep them safe!

Please, O Lord, heal the sadness and the longing that we feel for those whom we miss so dearly. Their memories are forever with us, but their immortal souls are forever with you in Paradise, Lord Jesus, and their love will forever transcend all time! Help us to understand, what has to be, has to be; as all waters return to the oceans, as every leaf must fall to earth, all life must one day return to the world from whence it came; therefore. Our Lord of Resurrection and Life, we humbly pray to you: Prepare a heavenly place for us when we too shall one day return home to your Infinite Embrace of Compassion and be reunited with all the loving and wonderful souls of every family member and friend that we ever knew and loved on this good earth!

Amen …

Chapter and verse that inspired prayer:

1 John 3:1, 14   Behold, what manner of love the Father has bestowed upon us, that we should be called the sons of God: therefore the world knoweth us not, because it knew him not. (14) We know that we have passed from death unto life, because we love the brethren. He that loveth not his brother abideth in death.

# May Thirty-One: "Show Us The Way, Lord"

(As inspired from Revelation 22:16)

Lord Jesus, hear our prayer ...

Our souls sing out joyfully in loud exultation whenever we rejoice in the Great Glory of our God, in you, Lord Jesus Christ, descendent of a Heavenly Father and an earthly King! The Immaculate Birth of your Heavenly Soul, has given Salvation to all earthly souls! Thank you, Our King of Glory, for your Selfless and Liberating Love has delivered the world from its captivity!

The prophets of old spoke of you, the heavenly angels heralded your birth, and we worship you, Lord Jesus, Our Anointed One, The Root of David! Lord of the Eternal, send your Angel of Truth to the hearts and minds of all people on this planet, heralding the Good News of their Salvation through belief in you and through the forgiveness of all iniquity! Blest be your Holy Word Lord God, for truly, you are the bright morning star that removes all darkness and shadow in our lives, you are absolutely The Origin and Foundation of All Goodness in everyone's soul, and you are the Infinite Direction for Everlasting Life that we, as Christians, must always follow! Without you, Lord Christ, we are like lost children crying out from a desert of hopelessness. But through you, our despair is quickly lifted by your Radiant Spirit of Hope! Therefore, we pray for your Holy Guidance, Lord Jesus, because we know that your Love honors the pure heart, and all prayers spoken in truth and sincerity will radiate brightly before your eyes. And that we will not stumble or fall along our chosen path, Lord Jesus Christ, we ask you to show us The Way, Lord; inspire each and every one of us to follow the Heavenly Destiny of our Christian faith to the summit of your Unblemished Truth! And in doing so, we will individually achieve Spiritual Salvation and Eternal Life after this life! Praised be to you, Our King and Deliverer, instill into all people the True Knowledge that you exist and await our love and devotion!

Amen ...

Chapter and verse that inspired prayer:

Revelation 22:16    I Jesus have sent mine angel to testify unto you these things in the churches. I am the root and the offspring of David, and the bright and morning star.

# June One: "Your Promises Are Forever Kept"

### (As inspired from Genesis 9:12)

Lord Jesus, hear our prayer …

We revel in the knowledge that your Heavenly Kingdom, Lord Jesus Christ, is impervious to darkness, that the waters are Living and Pure, and that even the slightest shadow cannot exist in the Reigning Radiance of your Blessed Goodness! To Our Royal Sovereign in Heaven: We vow forever obedience to your Holy and Ruling Majesty over all life! By your care, Lord Jesus, and through your Supreme Love do we exist! And although we are not worthy of your Great and Wonderful Covenant, we humbly praise you: Lord, we stand in awe and take wonder in the harmony and the union of everything around us. The sun summons forth life from the darkness. The sky nourishes the good soil with moisture. The earth feeds all life. The winds move the air around the world so that all living things may breathe. And like a beautiful song that constantly flows from your lips, Lord Jesus, the creation is alive and living in accord with itself and with every living creature that exists within it! Glory to you, Lord Christ, for you are the Keeper of your Word; from generation to generation, and unto all eternity, your promises are forever kept; in a world without end! Inspire our personal convictions, Our Lord of Life, to continually preserve and conserve this world upon which we exist! Instill in our individual hearts the ability to perceive the natural balance and order of nature. Please, O Lord, encourage us to maintain the dignity and the preservation of all life as you have so maintained and protected the human race and our individual lives since the beginning of all time: Infallible are your Promises, Forever is your Sacred Word, Lord Jesus Christ Our Heavenly King!

Amen …

Chapter and verse that inspired prayer:

Genesis 9:12   And God said, This is the token of the covenant which I make between me and you and every living creature that is with you, for perpetual generations:

# June Two: "Lord, You Are The Rock Of Truth"

(As inspired from Deuteronomy 32:4)

Lord Jesus, hear our prayer …

Blessed are you, Lord God, for always being truthful in all that you say and do! Strengthen us, Lord, to be spiritually and morally upright in all that we say and do! Because, honesty is a Heavenly Blessing, a blessing of integrity, morality, and absolute straightforwardness, without disguise or pretense. Bless all virtue, for in life, Truth is the Only Way, and the only way to gain the Wisdom of Goodness is through you, Lord Jesus!

You are the Rock of Ages, and that your Spiritual Inspirations may continually prevail in our lives, Our Most Sacred Lord Christ, sanction our minds to choose and use only words of integrity. That we may continue our life's journey, guided by your Holy Design, Lord God, entreat us to never compromise our values! And that we may forever abide in your sight, O Lord, we will, at all times, exercise obedience to our Christian precepts of your Holy Teachings through Scripture! Dear Lord, you are the Rock of Truth from which the foundation of the world was formed. Iniquity and deception do not exist in you, you are The Absolute Perfection of the Lamb of God! Your Holy Word is Flawless, Correct, and Righteous in all ways. And that we may follow in your footsteps, night and day, now and forever, please, light the pathway to Righteousness and encourage our spirits to become Vestiges of Virtue! Lord Jesus Christ, guide our hearts to the Purity and to the Excellence in the Holy Spirit of Truth by all that we do, think, and say; and let it become natural for all people, everywhere, to do what is right, simply, because doing right, is right in the sight of the Lord!

Amen …

Chapter and verse that inspired prayer:

Deuteronomy 32:4    He is the Rock, his work is perfect: for all his ways are judgment: a God of truth and without iniquity, just and right is he.

# June Three: "You Are The Lord, Our God"

### (As inspired from Ezekiel 34:30-31)

Lord Jesus, hear our prayer ...

Lord, we gather as one Christian voice in our love for you, and as one people, we belong only to you. Lord Jesus, you are the Spiritual Shepherd of our Souls. Watch over us and protect us from the predators of the world; for you are the Lord, our God, and you are always with us! Great and merciful is your Holy Spirit, Lord Jesus Christ, All Powerful is your Heavenly Might!

Lord of Peace, hear us in our prayer of adoration, praising your Bountiful Love, for truly, Lord, your Beautiful Spirit is Glorious and Benevolent, and everything in life is possible through you: All chaos is calmed, all darkness becomes light, all prayer is answered, all hunger is fed, all thirst is quenched, all pain is removed, all need is met, all labor is rewarded, and all disdain becomes love! Glory be to you, Our Lord Most High, for we give our absolute faith, our complete obedience, and our entire trust into your Tender Care, now and throughout all the passing of eternity, Lord Jesus Christ Our Savior and King! Shepherd us, Good Lord, for we are the faithful flock of your Heavenly Fold, and we hear and know your voice as we safely pasture without fear or harm in your Forever Flowing Fields of Love!

And now, we pray for all people that are lost in life, who wander without cause, and lack spiritual direction: Enlighten their individual hearts and souls, Dear Lord, through Heavenly Insight, that they too may find their purpose for existence, which is you, Lord Jesus Christ!

Amen ...

Chapter and verse that inspired prayer:

Ezekiel 34:30-31   Thus shall they know that I the LORD their God am with them, and that they, even the house of Israel, are my people, saith the LORD God. (31) And ye are my flock, the flock of my pasture, are men, and I am your God, saith the Lord God.

# June Four: "The True Power Of Peace"

(As inspired from Exodus 15:2)

Lord Jesus, hear our prayer ...

You are the Rhythm within our Song of Life, the Internal Strength and Fortitude of our Christian faith, and we adorn our hearts with joy and celebration because you exist in our lives! Our Infinite Lord of Goodness, through diligent prayer, we, those who follow your Commandments, will make a dwelling place within our souls for your Holiness; a Spiritual Tabernacle of Love and Obedience!

Heavenly Father, we are your eternal children and we have no other authority or power before us! We see with our eyes and we believe with our hearts, but our souls know the real truth, for all truth is with you, Our Lord and God of Heaven And Earth! Thank you, Lord Christ, for our blessing of inner peace that is found within the acceptance of your Unremitting Salvation! Throughout the entire world and throughout all the ages of time, there exists a Sacred Spiritual Melody that brings harmony to all of nature. And, Lord Jesus, it is the pleasing sound of your Blessed Name to which all life is drawn! In your Name, Lord God, is the Celestial Song that quells a troubled soul and comforts a brokenhearted existence. You are the Eternal Music of Hope and of All Mercies! Lord Jesus, our hearts and our spirits are continually filled with the beautiful sound of your Hallowed Name! O Lord, you are adorned in the Glorious Song of love, the reason for all existence, and the true power of peace! And from our hearts, united as one voice and one mind, we continually exalt and give praise to the Holiness of your Everlasting Presence, Lord Jesus Christ, King of Kings, in whom resides Perpetual Power and Infinite Grace!

Amen ...

Chapter and verse that inspired prayer:

Exodus 15:2     The LORD is my strength and song, and he is become my salvation: he is my God, and I will prepare him an habitation; my father's God, and I will exalt him.

# June Five: "We Disavow The World And Avow Your Love"
### (As inspired from Titus 2:12-13)

Lord Jesus, hear our prayer ...

Lord God, when the passion of love overwhelms the soul, the two become as one and cannot be separated, for they are now intertwined in a singular body and form, forever Christian, until eternity! Our Good Father in Heaven, we pray for a joining of all earthly souls to your Love and Goodness: Allow all the love that is in the world to come forth and unite in a fellowship of trust and cooperation.

Through Scripture, we have learned that all life on earth begins and ends, that power is given and taken away, and that all physical wealth is one day lost. Lord Jesus, we pray for this present world that we are in, but through righteous living, we plan for the next world! Lord Christ, everything that we have and all that we own are merely temporary possessions; we, ourselves, own nothing. Lord Jesus, only through the benevolent sharing of your Blest Creation, with us, do we posses any material goods or things of value. The entire creation is here for everyone to use, to glorify, and to give thanks to you for its existence! Every physical and worldly thing belongs to and returns to the earth! And if we disavow the world and avow your love and your name, Lord Jesus Christ, then our hearts and our immortal souls will belong only to you! For it is our deepest prayer, Lord Jesus, that we will one day leave this world and return home to your Heavenly Embrace; therefore, we will give ceaseless thanks and endless exultation, knowing that all who love you are blessed and will one day reunite in your Divine Kingdom of Heavenly Hosts to live forever and ever!

Amen ...

Chapter and verse that inspired prayer:

Titus 2:12-13   Teaching us that, denying ungodliness and worldly lusts, we should live soberly, righteously, and godly, in this present world; (13) Looking for that blessed hope, and the glorious appearing of the great God and our Saviour Jesus Christ;

# June Six: "Please, Lord, Hear Our Endless Prayers"

(As inspired from 1 Thessalonians 5:17)

Lord Jesus, hear our prayer …

Through your Holy Spirit and Scriptural Enlightenment, Lord God, your Word has taught us the wondrous power of a sincere prayer! When all hope seems lost, a simple prayer of genuine belief will restore our vision and inspire our hearts to have complete trust in our Christian faith. And like the Crystal Clear Waters that never cease flowing from your Heavenly Throne, Lord, we solemnly promise to always pray to you for our every need, now and forevermore, without ceasing!

Our Lord of Patience, as you have shown us through countless miracles and blessings, prayers from the heart have the power to calm the winds of torment, to silence the sounds of anger, and to release the bonds of stress. Prayer is the life and the soulful nourishment of our very existence. And through the power of unremitting prayer, all of life's difficulties are resolved and its impossibilities are solved. Please, Lord, hear our endless prayers to you; for only you can fulfill the needs of the heart, of the mind, and of the spirit, and only in your name, Lord Jesus Christ Our King of Salvation and Mercy, do we pray and give eternal thanks! Lord God, hear the words of our prayer request: Forgive us our transgressions, heal our physical bodies, redeem our immortal souls, and authorize peace to reign supreme in our lives, now into the Everlasting!

And now, Our Lord and Prince, our very souls will sing out praise without ceasing: You and The Father are One, you are the Son of God, you are The Holy Spirit of Love, you are the Son of Man, you are The Everlasting, you are The Light of the World, you are the Crystal Clear Waters of Life, and through your Glorious Name, our bonds are broken! Glory to you in The Highest! Lord Jesus Christ Our Forever Salvation!

Amen …

Chapter and verse that inspired prayer:

1 Thessalonians 5:17    Pray without ceasing.

# June Seven: "Change The Direction Of All Nations"

(As inspired from Amos 5:14-15)

Lord Jesus, hear our prayer ...

All people who embrace the Word of God, pursue Peace and Goodness in their lives! God of Hosts, you Promised Grace and Deliverance to our kindred ancestors aeons ago and to all their future generations, from whom we have descended, and you kept your Magnificent Word! Blessed are you, Lord Jesus Christ!

O Lord, that all people, everywhere, may seek The Light instead of darkness, we offer a special prayer to change the course of all lives and souls on earth: Lord Jesus, we pray for an end to all wars, to all hatred, and to all fighting throughout the entire world! Allow the authority of your Magnificent Grace to move all people on earth to develop a true understanding of living peacefully with one another. Inspire everyone to realize that peace is not an impossibility; because all they need in their lives is the Sanctity of your Great and Never-Ending Love! Lord Jesus, bless all nations with an ambition to seek friendship and fellowship from their neighbors. Allow everyone to possess the wisdom of harmony and to understand what a terrible waste there is in fighting, in hating, and in warring against one another! Only you, Lord Jesus Christ, are the True Treaty of Peace that ends all pain and suffering in the world! Please, Lord God, establish your judgment in every heart that exists in every part of this world! Change the direction of all nations and move this planet from its ills of darkness towards a revival of your Love and Enlightenment; for your Consuming Compassion will conquer all who establish love in their hearts and seek your Goodness in their lives!

Amen ...

Chapter and verse that inspired prayer:

Amos 5:14-15   Seek good, and not evil, that ye may live: and so the LORD, the God of hosts, shall be with you, as ye have spoken. (15) Hate the evil, and love the good, establish judgment in the gate: it may be that the LORD God of hosts will be gracious unto the remnant of Joseph.

# June Eight: "Your Love, Lord, Is Always With Us"
### (As inspired from Nehemiah 1:5)

Lord Jesus, hear our prayer …

We beseech you, Our Invincible Lord of All Creation, whose Hallowed Powers are unlimited, please, hear our unified voice that asks for mercy, for you are the only one, Lord Jesus, who can bring everlasting peace to this planet: We pray to you for the end of all inhumanities around the world; may your Holy Commandments Rule Supreme; allow accord, not discord, to reign in every nation; sanction love to direct all hearts; and authorize compassion to become the driving force behind earth's future direction!

Lord God of Great Mercy and Judgment, we are faithful to your Unerring Commandments that protect our spiritual and physical lives from the enemies of peace! From day's radiant beginning, through day's darkest moments, your love, Lord, is always with us; and nothing can harm us while we remain under the Protective Regard of your Benevolent Love! Lord Jesus, King of Heaven and Earth, we beseech you, please, open the floodgates of your Hallowed Compassion to sojourn with us, now and forevermore! No other love is greater than yours, Lord Christ, and no other love has the profound intensity to enlighten entire nations, peoples, and all of the ageless passing of time! O Lord, we are forever bound in a Soulful Embrace of your Spiritual Tenderness and Mercy! We pray to you, Lord Jesus Christ, to keep us safe and well: Watch over us during the light of the day and throughout the dark of the night! Remove all shadows of fear and doubt from our lives and instill courage into our hearts. Therefore, as you so protect and keep us from the forces of darkness, Lord Christ, anoint us also to continually grow in the radiance of your Beautiful and Bountiful Holiness! Blessed are you, Our Lord of Peace!

Amen …

Chapter and verse that inspired prayer:

Nehemiah 1:5    And said, I beseech thee, O LORD God of heaven, the great and terrible God, that keepeth covenant and mercy for them that love him and observe his commandments:

# June Nine: "Lord, We Will Never Waver"

### (As inspired from Ephesians 3:8-9)

Lord Jesus, hear our prayer …

Every day of life is a humbling experience when we consider the many blessings afforded us: Another day to right all wrongs, another day to show loved ones how much we care about them, another day to give thanks to our Creator, another day to earn Eternal Life, and another day to simply appreciate, venture forth, and live Another Day!

Together, we offer up our prayers in a united Fellowship of Christianity, in one praise, in one belief, and in one spiritual voice that rings loudly throughout the creation that you, Lord God, are the Lord of Infinite Love! We pray to you, Lord Jesus, that your Precious Word may fill the lives of all people, everywhere, and throughout every tongue of every nation! And then, as a planet unified in your Word, Lord, we will never waver from our faith in your Infinite Power.

O Lord, we pray that everyone, all around the world, will ultimately come together in agreement through the Longsuffering and Infinite Majesty of your Holy Word of Life! Grant a worldwide miracle to occur, Lord Jesus, where all people will learn to build and maintain lives and communities that abide together in fellowship and friendship! Encourage neighborhoods to become safe havens for young families to live and to raise their children, so that all children of the world will grow up healthy and strong and wise in the Ways of your Righteousness, Lord Christ! And through your Infinite Guidance of Goodness, Lord Jesus Christ, all people, from every corner of the planet, will be assured that open arms and true friendship is the Only Way of life in the lives of all who embrace your Consummate Word of Joy!

Amen …

Chapter and verse that inspired prayer:

Ephesians 3:8-9    Unto me, who am less than the least of all saints, is this grace given, that I should preach among the Gentiles the unsearchable riches of Christ; (9) And to make all men see what the fellowship of the mystery, which from the beginning of the world hath been hid in God, who created all things by Jesus Christ:

# June Ten: "Faithfully Obedient To Your Word"

(As inspired from Daniel 7:27)

Lord Jesus, hear our prayer ...

Good Lord, our dreams become reality when you enter into our lives! You are the answer and the solution to all questions and problems, Lord Jesus! It is only through you, Lord Christ, that earth and all who live upon it are released from the far reaching effects of doubt and darkness. It is the Illumination of your Divine Mercy, Lord Protector, that takes away our shadows of dismay. It is the Radiance of your Salvation, Lord, that removes our web of fear. And it is the brilliance of your love, Lord Jesus Christ, that shines down upon all life, saving everyone from the snares and entanglements of all worldly troubles and stumbling blocks! Bless us, and keep us well, Lord God.

Through you, O Lord, our lives are blessed and our spirits are redeemed. Hear our individual praises, Lord Jesus, as we personally give thanks for all things living and for all things material, for all things great and for all things small, and for all things mighty and for all things meek! Lord Jesus Christ, your Holy Kingdom is in heaven, and you are the bridge between heaven and earth! And that one day we may cross over the Bridge Everlasting, we, as joyous Christians, do swear to serve your Unceasing Glory and Never Ending Salvation being faithfully obedient to your Word and Commandment of Love!

Our Lord and King, only you do we serve and obey, and it is with wonderful joy that we sing out our spiritual praise to you: Thank you for our earthly home, but greater is your Kingdom Most High, whose Heavenly Home is The Everlasting and awaits all who love you, Our Prince of Peace, with every fiber of our existence!

Amen ...

Chapter and verse that inspired prayer:

Daniel 7:27    And the kingdom and dominion, and the greatness of the kingdom under the whole heaven, shall be given to the people of the saints of the most High, whose kingdom is an everlasting kingdom, and all dominions shall serve and obey him.

# June Eleven: "The Footpaths Of Our Destinies"
(As inspired from Joel 2:8)

Lord Jesus, hear our prayer …

As devoted and devout followers of our Christian faith, we ask that our prayers will go before us, Lord God, to uproot any misfortune that may rise up around us! Bless you, O Lord, for directing the footpaths of our destinies. Indescribable is your Ageless wisdom, Lord Jesus! And because of our wondrous lessons that are found throughout the Bible, we have been shown that life is a winding road filled with many pitfalls and detours; and only you, Our Lord and King, are able to remove the hazards that lie before us, making our purpose and way in life clear. Please, Lord Christ, take away every obstacle and danger that may prevail against us on our pilgrimage through life; and help each one of us, Lord Jesus Christ, to safely arrive at our foreordained destinations!

Lord, we realize that the entrapments in life's journey are many and are often concealed from view. And that we may clearly see the Ways of your Divine Judgment, we thank you, Lord Jesus Christ, for helping us to remain on our personal paths of spiritual devotion and obedience. Lord God, pray for us that we will never veer from our chosen Christian course of living our lives strictly through the wonderful guidance of your Most Holy Spirit, who continually watches over us during times of darkness and light, unrest and calm, turmoil and peace, and we thank you greatly, Lord Jesus, through words of heartfelt praise: Lord God, you are the Stronghold of our eternal souls and we long await your Spiritual Salvation to redeem us from the troubles and ills of this world! Blest are you. Lord of Life!

Amen …

Chapter and verse that inspired prayer:

Joel 2:8    Neither shall one thrust another; they shall walk every one in his path: and when they fall upon the sword, they shall not be wounded.

# June Twelve: "We Aspire To Serve Your Will On Earth, Lord"
### (As inspired from Eza 9:8)

Lord Jesus, hear our prayer ...

The darkest night is always followed by the dawn; a raging storm succumbs to the calm; and chaos is forever consumed by peace: You are the Supreme Being, All-powerful, Wise in all that you do, and oh how merciful you are, Lord God, to never test your faithful beyond their endurance!

Like an innocent budding flower, Lord, in your Heavenly Garden of Paradise, life is a constant unfolding, where, every day becomes a new experience; and what ever must happen here on earth, simply happens, for true destiny always unfolds with heaven's exactness! And we, as Christians, must live our lives in the fullest of God's Grace by accepting the Will of our Lord and Savior, as that, which must happen. Therefore, in this world, we find refuge in your Mercy, Lord; for our hearts have become Hallowed Places by which our souls are truly filled with adoration for your Compassionate Love. And through faith, we will escape the bitter trials and tribulations of this world by finding a True Sanctuary in your Loving Peace! Lord Jesus, you enlighten our visions and give us insight and direction. To you, O Lord, we offer our constant love and our spiritual embraces. Look deeply into our hearts and into our souls, Lord Jesus Christ, that every transgression may be absolved. And may you always receive and accept our devotions. Our Heavenly Lord, as honest and sincere; for it is with absolute love and obedience that we aspire to serve your Will on earth, Lord of Hosts, as it is done in heaven!

Amen ...

Chapter and verse that inspired prayer:

Ezra 9:8   And now for a little space grace hath been showed from the LORD our God, to leave us a remnant to escape, and to give us a nail in his holy place, that our God may lighten our eyes, and give us a little reviving in our bondage.

# June Thirteen: "We Pray For Spiritual Charity"

(As inspired from Matthew 10:8)

Lord Jesus, hear our prayer …

Freewill is a beautiful gift from our Creator and is the Center and Core of our existence as humans; for no plant nor animal has the responsibility of choice between good and evil. Freely we give of our prayers and love, and freely, our Lord Jesus gives of His Pure Heart and Sincere Desire for our welfare and peace of mind.

Our Lord of Total Compassion, it is our sincerest prayer that Spiritual Charity will abound throughout this world, for our truest blessings in life are given to us without cost: Freely, the sun shines down its light upon everyone, the four winds blow, the gentle rains fall from above, there is love, friendship, warm smiles, all are given and received at will. And with great certainty in our praises, we thank you, and we worship you, Our Lord God, for our spirits have been exceedingly blessed! Lord Jesus, you have always given unconditionally of your Love and Forgiveness; and without hesitation, we have accepted the Mercies of your Great Compassion! Every blessing that we receive comes from your Reverent Goodness, Lord Christ! Therefore, throughout our lives, in honest and soulful testimonies, we will always share our abundance of faith with all others; for through the sharing of Christian faith, we give thanks and we give witness to the Greatness and Commanding Glory of Our Living God, you, Lord Jesus Christ! And to those who are weak and poor in spirit, we continually give of our prayers and spiritual encouragement! Lord, as members of your loving multitude, we pray for Life Changing Charity to abound in the hearts and prayers of everyone on earth; for freely, we have received in your Exalted Name, and freely, we will give in your Name, Lord Jesus Our Most Hallowed and Holy Christ of Heaven and Earth!

Amen …

Chapter and verse that inspired prayer:

Matthew 10:8    Heal the sick, cleanse the lepers, raise the dead, cast out devils: freely ye have received, freely give.

# June Fourteen: "Lord, We Have Chosen Your Way In Life"

### (As inspired from Isaiah 58:11)

Lord Jesus, hear our prayer ...

On earth, there always exists the unexpected, the unknown, chance and mishap! Only in heaven is there total security, and for this reason, Our Lord and God, we pray to you for your Heavenly Insight to be our guiding light during our darkest hours in this world. Blessed is your Divine Understanding of all generations and of all people in all lands!

Lord Jesus, as Christians, we joyfully profess our reverence for your Ageless and Infinite Magnificence; for all knowledge springs forth from one source, O Lord, and it is your Immaculate Heart that rivers all compassion on earth! Through your Merciful Care, our lives are enhanced and our souls are saved! And whenever we are faced with difficult decisions, we always pray to you, Lord of Glory, for your Flawless Inspiration and Guidance. Bless us now, and help us to individually make clear and correct choices in life. Only in you do we trust, Lord God, and only through your Shepherding Wisdom will we be continually directed to discern the truth in all that we do. For clearly we have chosen your True Way in life; and Your Way, Lord Jesus Christ, is clearly the only correct choice in life, for all lives, and for all lifetimes! We pray for all people in the world to make correct and viable decisions concerning their own lives and the lives of their loved ones: Put all anger away and permit forbearance to rule the day, and Our Lord will guide us forevermore on our paths to His Endearing and Fulfilling Love!

Amen ...

Chapter and verse that inspired prayer:

Isaiah 58:11    And the LORD shall guide thee continually, and satisfy thy soul in drought, and make fat thy bones: and thou shalt be like a watered garden, and like a spring of water, whose waters fail not.

# June Fifteen: "Love And Reverence Towards You, Lord"

### (As inspired from 2 Corinthians 5:1, 6, 7)

Lord Jesus, hear our prayer …

Every day, new journeys begin and old conquests end. All praise to you, Lord, for it is only through your Ceaseless Caring, Our Holy King, that we are able to individually reach our goals and safely conclude all journeys in life! Therefore, we offer this simple prayer, O Lord, for anyone and everyone who has left their home to begin a new life on their own: Please, Lord Jesus, fill their mind with Goodness, always be present within their heart, and permanently reside in their spirit. Allow all the lessons that they have learned in you, Lord God, to become a solid foundation for their new life. Inspire them to continually mirror a perfect adoration towards you, Lord Jesus, as they firmly establish themselves in their new vision and dwelling of hope. But in all things, teach them to live by respect and to always use sound judgment that will be a Christian Reflection of their love and reverence towards you, Lord Christ; for your Holy Word has taught us that we must completely trust in our faith in you and not by the things that are of this world, which can allure, deceive, and weaken even the strongest of spirits!

Lord God, for those who are about to establish their lives, we pray: May the Hallowed Foundation of their Faith be the framework that is used to spiritually build all lives and all dwellings that will continually reflect love, adoration, and a total obedience to your Holy Spirit of Love, Lord Jesus Christ, now and forevermore! And now and forevermore, may they have the wisdom and the courage to always walk proudly in the Spiritual convictions of their Christian faith; because only through deep faith is it possible to successively endure and soundly survive the temptations and judgments of this world!

Amen …

Chapter and verse that inspired prayer:

2 Corinthians 5:1, 6, 7    For we know that if our earthly house of this tabernacle were dissolved, we have a building of God, an house not made with hands, eternal in the heavens. (6) Therefore we are always confident, knowing that, whilst we are at home in the body, we are absent from the Lord: (7) (For we walk by faith, not by sight:)

# June Sixteen: "Lord, Shower The World"

(As inspired from Habakkuk 3:2, 18)

Lord Jesus, hear our prayer …

Lord Jesus Christ, you are the God of our Salvation, of our Redemption, of our Deliverance, and we ask, we plead, and we pray for your Great Mercy! Lord God, restore our lives to your Glorious Safekeeping: Allow love to vanquish fear, permit harmony to dispel chaos, and encourage everyone, everywhere, to respect one another through a worldwide Spiritual Fellowship that will engulf the entire planet and all who live upon it!

O Lord, shower the world with the gentle rains of your Ever Present Love! We pray: Strengthen our spirits that we may endure the storms and tribulations that may come our way. We fill our minds and our lives with an absolute devotion and total reliance for you, Lord Jesus, that we may clearly follow in the Ways of your Merciful Heart. Lord Jesus, inspire the roots of virtue to grow deeply into the very fiber of our souls and encourage our Christian values to become strong and vibrant in the Glory of your Righteousness! Lord God, you are the Spiritual and the Physical Strength of our total existence. Without you in our daily lives, there would be no blessings; but through you, Lord Jesus Christ, we walk tall and proud and we continually rejoice in your Merciful Salvation of love! Please, pour out upon our wonderful planet the gentle rains of your Most Perfect Kindness and permit all people to be Enlightened with the Heavenly Knowledge that every person alive has the right and the same opportunity to grow towards the Radiance of your Adoring Compassion; for the power of goodness and the power to do good is a force within the grasp of every human on earth! And blessed are the faithful who exercise their God Given Right to choose Light and Goodness over the shadows of malicious intent!

Amen …

Chapter and verse that inspired prayer:

Habakkuk 3:2, 18   O LORD, I have heard thy speech, and was afraid: O LORD, revive thy work in the midst of the years, in the midst of the years make known; in wrath remember mercy. (18) Yet I will rejoice in the LORD, I will joy in the God of my salvation.

# June Seventeen: "Lord, We Seek Yow Love And Protection"

(As inspired from 2 Chronicles 15:2)

Lord Jesus, hear our prayer …

Lord, you are the lifeblood of our total existence, physically, mentally, and spiritually! All Holiness flows from you, Lord Jesus, and all life is nourished by it! Your Holy Spirit moves through our lives and touches each and every person sworn to serve your Gentle and Merciful Heart. And as we individually seek you, Lord Christ, we will each find you in our own way, and we will each receive your grace in accordance to the strength of our individual faith; which protects us from the shadows of misdirection and misfortune. But if anyone, through their own freewill, personally forsakes your name, Lord Jesus, by removing their direction and faith in you, they risk losing the protection of your Heavenly Grace and will suffer the dark shadow of adversity to cross their path. Lord Jesus, we sincerely pray, wherever we may be in life, keep us from the misfortunes and misdirections of the day. Keep us in the Light, away from the gathering darkness; surround us and protect us, Lord Jesus Christ, through the Radiant Redemption in the Holy Spirit of your Love!

O Lord, we pray for your presence and guidance in our lives whenever we have a day of mishap, adversity, or hardship; for it is on such days when nothing seems to go right. It becomes a day that is overshadowed by incidents, accidents, and wrong decisions. And we realize, Our Lord Jesus, that any day, everyday, even today could shower disappointment and failure. But we also recognize, Lord God, that when you are with us, your Spiritual Strength and Inspiration protects and guides us through the shadows of all adversity! Endlessly, Lord, we seek your Love and Divine Protection, now and forever, through all times and places in this blessed creation!

Amen …

Chapter and verse that inspired prayer:

2 Chronicles 15:2    And he went out to meet Asa, and said unto him, Hear ye me, Asa, and all Judah and Benjamin; The LORD is with you, while ye be with him; and if ye seek him, he will be found of you; but if ye forsake him, he will forsake you.

# June Eighteen: "Grant Us Wisdom Of The Heart"
### (As inspired from Zechariah 8:16-17)

Lord Jesus, hear our prayer …

Your Great Love for us, Lord Jesus, is the cornerstone of our true feelings for family, friend, and even stranger! Please, accept our sincere confession of belief: O Prince of Peace, your message in life and our mission in life are the same, it is one of love, love for everyone! We pray that all people will learn to accept, with complete understanding, that there is no other way, than The True Way, Your Way, Lord Christ, of total and sincere acceptance of all people, through love, compassion, and forgiveness! Therefore, we ask of you, Lord God, to grant us wisdom of the heart, for it is our desire to execute sound judgments of truth and peace towards all people, throughout our lives! And with complete surety, Lord Jesus, we confess that you are the Light and the Gospel of the World! And in all certitude, Lord, we pray that you will remove all the doubt and insecurity that exists in our lives; scatter the shadows of gloom and doom so that they will never dwell within our memories ever again! Help us and redirect us, Lord Jesus Christ, that we will forever be worthy to stand in the Radiant Blessing of your Hallowed and Holy Spirit! Fill our hearts to capacity, Lord Christ, with the prescripts of your Infinite Wisdom that our precious souls may find Eternal Life as so promised by the Scriptures of your Holy Teachings! And we know, Lord of Judgment, that we also must do our part by carrying no ill feelings nor speaking wrongly of any family member, friend, or even stranger; because in doing so, we are fulfilling your Scriptural Message and Commandments of Love!

Amen …

Chapter and verse that inspired prayer:

Zechariah 8:16-17    These are the things that ye shall do; speak ye every man the truth to his neighbor; execute the judgment of truth and peace in your gates: (17) And let none of you imagine evil in your hearts against his neighbor; and love no false oath: for all these things that I hate, saith the LORD.

# June Nineteen: "We Humble Ourselves Before You, Lord"
### (As inspired from Isaiah 23:9)

Lord Jesus, hear our prayer …

As proud Christians of our faith, we lift our spirits up to you, Our Exalted King, and pray: We are totally submissive to the Immeasurable Splendor of your Most Holy Virtue, Our Lord and Creator; for the towering pride of a mountain will ultimately crumble away, the lofty brilliance of a star will eventually fade, and the arrogant might of a tall oak will one day tremble and fall! Lord Jesus, these natural erosions of downfalls that occur in nature, remind us of our own humility. All arrogant pride is but dust in the wind; for even a small turbulence of vanity will gather together fine particles and blind the vision of those who stand firmly within its vortex. And, Lord, as you have so stated in Scripture, even from the beginning of time, that all prideful honor is nothing more than empty lies and cannot exist in the Light of your Heavenly Glory! Therefore, we humble ourselves before you, Lord God, that vainglorious arrogance may never exalt us. And that the false promises of conceit and pride will never be our spiritual undoing in life, we forever promise to be obedient to you, Lord Jesus Christ, for only you deserve to receive the acclaim and the praise for all that is done in this incredible world without end!

O Lord, hear our fervent testimony of truth: We, your faithful living, have found you, and we pray for and encourage those who are lifeless in spirit to rise again and seek the Life Giving Force of your Almighty Love! Because, through you, Lord Jesus, there is Great Glory; for you, there is Wonderful Pride in our lives; and to you, we believe that all the Honor on earth is to be bestowed!

Amen …

Chapter and verse that inspired prayer:

Isaiah 23:9   The LORD of hosts hath proposed it, to stain the pride of all glory, And to bring into contempt all the honourable of the earth.

# June Twenty: "Your Triumphant Love"

(As inspired from Acts of the Apostles 15:11)

Lord Jesus, hear our prayer …

A special prayer of thanks, Lord: Blessed be Abraham, Father of All Nations, he, who feared God most, was willing to sacrifice his own son, his own flesh and blood, to you, Lord God Almighty, that all future generations may live and share in your Triumphant Love and your Magnificent Name, Lord Jesus Christ, Our Savior of the World!

It is our prayer, Lord, that you will bestow upon us an inner strength to resist and withstand the temptations of all conduct that is contrary to the Good Graces of your Holy Word. Lord Jesus, we know and we accept the soulful responsibilities that constitutes the true Christian Way, and that is to forgo many of life's worldly goods and temptations; as you so forwent forty days of physical and Spiritual temptations in the wilderness! And that we may continuously grow in our faith, Lord, we pray that you will grant us Spiritual and physical forbearance; for as a stagnant pool breeds contemptuous things, a moving stream purifies as it gains momentum, and so must our faith become in you, Lord Christ! Therefore, like a gently moving stream that becomes a rushing torrent, we too shall become a downpour, a deluge, a raging flood of unwavering faith as we rush towards the Glory and Goodness of your Triumvirate Love! Instill in us, Lord, a surge, a passion, an undeniable force that will carry us to the serenity and joy of your Glorious Compassion! Allow us, Lord Jesus Christ, to forever follow the course of your Perfect Path as we forever bathe in the Ever Flowing Grace of your Most Merciful Love!

Amen …

Chapter and verse that inspired prayer:

Acts of the Apostles 15:11    But we believe that through the grace of the Lord Jesus Christ we shall be saved, even as they.

# June Twenty-One: "The Season Of Fulfillment"

(As inspired from Luke 21:30-31)

Lord Jesus, hear our prayer …

We praise you immensely, O Lord, for the Kingdom of God is forever at hand, because, in your Loving Sacrifice of Life, you willingly placed yourself into the authority of those who did not believe that you were The Messiah, The Word Made Flesh, Our Living God! And now, the only way that we, as Christians, can thank you enough, is to show a deep reverence for you by loving one another as much as you love each one of us! Amen!

Your Kingdom, Our Heavenly Father, is an Immaculate World, adorned with a multitude of unblemished souls from countless generations of those who have faithfully followed your Commandments all the days of their lives. Lord, as we bathe in the Sun's Light, we reflect upon our intentions of faith: Dear Lord, we are loyal, obedient, and sincere to our Christian beliefs, which we have established in our hearts, for the bounty of your Infallible Love that protects us during all the seasons of the year! And of all the seasons, Lord, we warmly welcome the season of growth and maturity. It is the warmest of times, it is a time filled with vitality and promise, and it is a time of life when all the fruits of labor begin to ripen. It is the season of fulfillment, of happiness, and of boundless beauty. It is a time of tending and caring for all that is good and worthwhile. And if we have sowed and properly cared for the seeds of our youth and enlightenment, we will one day be in your Holy Kingdom, Lord Jesus Christ, summering our spirits in the Living Meadows of your Heavenly Love, forever and ever.

Amen …

Chapter and verse that inspired prayer:

Luke 21:30-31    When they now shoot forth, ye see and know of your own selves that summer is now nigh at hand. (31) So likewise ye, when ye see these things come to pass, know ye that the kingdom of God is nigh at hand.

# June Twenty-Two: "Your Great Love"

### (As inspired from Joshua 22:5)

Lord Jesus, hear our prayer …

Our Father of Heaven and Earth, we not only desire to follow and serve and accept every Sacred Commandment of your Living Word, but we also pray that the whole world will learn the Wonderful Knowledge of your Holy Presence within every soul on earth: For every human that is alive, Bless them, Lord Christ, with the Spiritual Acknowledgment of your Hallowed Existence and Truth!

We are thankful to you, Lord God, for everything that we have accomplished in life as Christians! And we will continually strive to be worthy of every blessing that you bestow upon us, Lord Jesus: The blessings of love, faith, confidence in ourselves, and the supreme joy that life, through your Generous Grace, Spiritually offers us! O Lord, in our heart of hearts, we desire fully to walk on the Radiant Path of your Hallowed Truth, to follow the Teachings of Your Great Love, and to also serve Your Perfect Will through a total commitment of mind and soul!

Lord, to obtain permanent happiness in one's life is to realize life's fulfillment as you have so intended. And through a personal acceptance of your Commanding and Holy Will, Lord Jesus, everyone will achieve everything that you have destined for them; for your Love and Compassion are truly abundant for all, Lord! And for all who desire to find peace and happiness in their lives, Lord God, their searching will end when they place You in their hearts! Lord, we pray that everyone on earth will understand and accept the following truth as your Reality of Life: To those who are willing to freely submit themselves to your Spiritual Generosity, Lord Jesus Christ, life's promised joy will surely be found; and it will be an Over-flowing and Never-ending Happiness!

Amen …

Chapter and verse that inspired prayer:

Joshua 22:5    But take diligent heed to do the commandment and the law, which Moses the servant of the LORD charged you, to love the LORD your God, and walk in his ways, and keep his commandments, and to cleave unto him, and to serve him with all your heart and soul.

# June Twenty-Three: "In Universal Peace And Harmony"
### (As inspired from Philemon 3, 12, 17)

Lord Jesus, hear our prayer …

During times of chaos, there is a struggle for calm. When there is stress, there is a desire for tranquility. And where there is malevolence, the Radiance of Compassion will quietly surface and dissolve the shadows of deceit. From deep within our spirits, through sincere prayers and heartfelt appeals, we ask of you, Lord, to vanquish the spawn of all hostility between peoples and nations, allow the Seed of Friendship to grow within the hearts of everyone on earth, in every family, and within every individual person on this planet! Let us learn to receive one another as we would receive a brother or a sister; and allow this Great Healing to begin today, through your Heavenly Direction and Holy Spirit!

Our Lord and Christ, may this day and every day bring blessings of unity for the world; for each day of peace is a day of triumph for you, Lord Jesus! And for each day of our earthly existence, we will pursue and proclaim your Victory in our lives! Thank you, O Lord, for your Long-suffering Accord that guides all life to its Rightful and Complete Fulfillment. And through the Loving Grace of your Divine Understanding, Lord Jesus Christ, we will all learn to greet and receive one another each day, anywhere, everywhere, in universal peace and harmony; blessed is the peaceful soul, and blessed is your Spirit of love, Our Prince of Peace, Our Messiah and Lord, whom we receive in our hearts with the deepest of love and respect!

Amen …

Chapter and verse that inspired prayer:

Philemon 3, 12, 17   Grace to you, and peace, from God our Father and the Lord Jesus Christ. (12) Whom I have sent again: thou therefore receive him, that is, mine own bowels: (17) If thou count me therefore a partner, receive him as myself.

# June Twenty-Four: "All Life, Everywhere, Gives Praise"
### (As inspired from Habakkuk 2:14)

Lord Jesus, hear our prayer …

When the Great Veil in the Temple tore in half, it signified, not only your separation from life, Lord Jesus, but also a division of belief, a new beginning, Christianity; and for all humankind, everywhere, forgiveness, eternal life, and spiritual salvation!

From a remote village, in a distant past, during a period of great tribulation, Lord God, you became the Son of Man and sacrificed your life that all may live, and your Glory and Authority grew and continues to grow and cover the world to this very day! How can we ever thank you or praise you enough, Lord! We raise up our hands and proudly exalt your name, Jesus Christ of Nazareth, above all others! Renown are the works of your Love and Mercy! And all who are enlightened with this knowledge will boldly profess and give witness to the miracles and to the wonders of your Great and Endless Compassion; for your Blessed Glory is Unending and Boundless and fills the earth as the waters fill the oceans! And everyone that is blessed, from sea to shore, from mountain top to rolling valley, from desert sands to forest green, from one end of the universe to the other end of infinity, all life, everywhere, gives praise and Constant Glory to your Magnificence, Our Savior and God, Lord Jesus Christ!

And now, O Lord, we pray for that special day of your Promised Return! A day when the entire world will witness your Miraculous Appearance and believe in One Supreme Being of Love and Perfection for all people, for all tongues, for all nations! Truly, your Sacred Arrival will be a Holy Phenomenon unprecedented by anything that has ever taken place on earth! O Lord of US All, we pray that today will be that day!

Amen …

Chapter and verse that inspired prayer:

Habakkuk 2:14     For the earth shall be filled with the knowledge of the glory of the LORD, as the waters cover the sea.

# June Twenty-Five: "The Child Is The Seed Of Hope"
(As inspired from Zechariah 8:12)

Lord Jesus, hear our prayer …

Everything you do, God, is perfect, you suffer no imperfections. The purity in a child is the Guiltless Perfection of your Heavenly Kingdom, which is reflected in their beautiful eyes, in their trusting smiles, and in their innocent souls! Dear Lord, a very personal prayer of parental thanks from all the ages of time: Of your infinite creations, Lord God, we especially thank you for the boundless energy and beautiful innocence of a newborn child; for the child is the Seed of Hope, the future of peace, and of all destinies, yet to follow. And that future generations of life may forever prosper and grow in your Wonderful Word of Life, Lord Jesus, we humbly ask you, Our Most Holy and Sacred God Protector, to please watch over all childhood purity that is born in the souls of our children; because, you have taught us through Scripture, Lord Jesus Christ, that forbidden knowledge does not exist in the young heart of an innocent child, and such is the Kingdom of Heaven!

From a small seed, a mighty tree will grow tall and strong. And from that tree, fruits will sprout and ripen to produce more seeds. And its descendants will spring forth, Lord, to produce a glorious orchard for your eyes to see. Lord Jesus, the seeds of life are abundant, and the fruits of labor are many; please, Lord Christ, as you shower down your love to cover us, inspire us also to nourish all offspring, protecting the fruits of life. And as the children grow towards maturity, may they always remain in the Light of your Goodness, Lord Jesus Christ, and become fruitful as they themselves mature in their spiritual and physical growth. Thank you, Lord God, for your Generous Abundance of life, of hope, of children to love, to cherish, and to protect!

Amen …

Chapter and verse that inspired prayer:

Zechariah 8:12    For the seed shall be prosperous; the vine shall give her fruit, and the ground shall give her increase, and the heavens shall give their dew; and I will cause the remnant of this people to possess all these things.

# June Twenty-Six: "Heal Us, Lord"

### (As inspired from Jeremiah 17:13-14)

Lord Jesus, hear our prayer ...

As true Christians, we do not hide from the Radiance of Happiness, only from the shadows of our own personal disparity. And through your Goodness and Direction, we are impassioned souls, Lord God, that search in the Light for that Delicate Thread of Life, that Crystal Clear Stream of Wonder and Understanding, which directs our course, our destiny, and our reason to exist! And it is only you, Lord Jesus Our God, who makes our lives meaningful! Please, allow us to touch the Universal Heart of Salvation and permit all who earnestly pray to be set free of their temporal and worldly temptations, to be Spiritually Delivered into your hands through the Power of your Hallowed Name!

Heavenly Father, from your Kingdom on High, you sent forth a Hallowed Force to cover the world in an Ever-flowing River of Pure Salvation! We thank you, Lord, for the Spiritual Waters that Sanctify and Satisfy all who thirst for Personal Deliverance. We pray, Lord Jesus, that you will direct us to the Crystal Clear Waters of your Living Spirit for which we spiritually thirst! O Lord, you are the Source and the Fountain of the Living Waters from which all life springs forth; and never shall we part from you! Without you in our lives, Lord, our hearts would slowly sink into a dark river of doubt that would silently form and flow within our spirits. We pray to you, Lord Christ, to hinder its shadowy course of deceit. Remove the river of fear and permit only the purity of your Eternal Love to flow within us! Heal us, Lord, and seal our hearts that we may always be whole. Save us. Lord God, that our spirits will remain free to praise and honor you! And return us, Lord Jesus Christ, to the Paradise of your Loving Peace, where we may forever bathe in the Living Waters of your Eternal Salvation!

Amen ...

Chapter and verse that inspired prayer:

Jeremiah 17:13-14    O LORD, the hope of Israel, all that forsake thee shall be ashamed, and they that depart from me shall be written in the earth, because they have forsaken the LORD, the foundation of living waters. (14) Heal me, O LORD, and I shall be healed; save me, and I shall be saved: for thou art my praise.

# June Twenty-Seven: "Your Spirit Is Continually With Us"
(As inspired from 2 Corinthians 3:16-17")

Lord Jesus, hear our prayer …

Our Lord and God, we pray for all people, for those without sight and for those who have sight but are blind to the enormous proof of your Divine Existence in their lives! O Lord, reveal to us your timeless love, lift the cloak of our earthly ignorance and bestow upon us the wisdom of your Heavenly Truth! Please, Lord Jesus, suffer no worry nor doubt to ever gain a stronghold in our lives; but to always remain far, far away from us in the unseen shadows of darkness where they are borne. Direct our spiritual happiness to outwardly reflect the person that We truly are. And from silent whispers of continual praise for you, Lord Christ, our emotions are free to fill the air with your Spirit of Love! For wherever your Heavenly Spirit dwells, Lord Jesus Christ, hearts are freed from the dreadful and exhausting bonds of all earthly anxiety and stress! Praised be your Holy Spirit of Love and Liberation!

In the stillness of the night or in the brightness of the day, we know, Lord Jesus, that your Presence is always near! Timeless and eternal, your Spirit is continually with us! And even if we are alone or with family or friend, Lord God, we know that you are there for us. Thank you, Lord Jesus Christ, for being with us in all that we say and do. Where the Spirit of Goodness prevails, there is total freedom from all the troubles of the world; and we are released from the taxing bonds of disdain, for we have gained immunity against the darkness of deception, as we proudly stand in the Liberation of your Eternal Light, Our Lord of Spiritual and Physical Liberty!

Amen …

Chapter and verse that inspired prayer:

2 Corinthians 3:16-17    Nevertheless when it shall turn to the Lord, the veil shall be taken away. (17) Now the Lord is that Spirit: and where the Spirit of the Lord is, there is liberty.

# June Twenty-Eight: "We Are Shepherded By Your Goodness"

(As inspired from Micah 7:7)

Lord Jesus, hear our prayer …

All people are Spiritually Connected, united by your Holy Spirit of Love. Lord, you have inspired us to realize that we are not islands, adrift in an ocean of loneliness. And that we must not only pray for ourselves everyday, but also for one another! Lord Jesus, you hear us when we sincerely speak to you. But when two or more are gathered together, praying in your Precious Name, a tumultuous voice of praise echoes throughout Heaven in joy! Therefore, in your name, Lord Jesus Christ, do we rejoice: Thank you, Lord of Heaven and Earth, for the well-being of our family, friends, and neighbors! Direct our lives to willingly follow in your Perfect Compassion!

Lord God, we come to you in all humility to perfect our destinies, and with eyes closed and heads bowed, we pray, Lord, that you will counsel our thoughts and turn our spiritual intentions towards the Way of your Purpose and Plan that you have so designed for us in life. Lead us away from our dubious visions of worldly gain that we may clearly see your traveled Path of Enlightenment, Lord Jesus! Help us to understand and to realize that every person is a living part of your Divine Plan and Purpose. And as we are Shepherded by your Goodness, direct and oversee our temporal ambitions, O Lord, that our works will always stem from the Heart of love in all that we profess and do. And in thought and in deed, we will celebrate each new day and glorify your Good Works as evidenced throughout this wondrous creation; for you alone are the God of True Salvation! Therefore, we will continually call upon your Atoning Name for our Blessings of love, and we give all the glory to you, LORD! Thanks be to you, Our Savior Lord Jesus Christ, for hearing our heartfelt praises of love and gratitude, and for inspiring our spiritual directions in life, and for perfecting our works of compassion towards one another.

Amen …

Chapter and verse that inspired prayer:

Micah 7:7    Therefore I will look unto the LORD; I will wait for the God of my salvation: my God will hear me.

# June Twenty-Nine: "Everything Occurs At Its Own Time"

(As inspired from Ecclesiastes 3:11)

Lord Jesus, hear our prayer …

O Lord, blessed are the cycles of life, for everything has its own private and unique timetable of occurrence! Like the rising of the sun or the movement of the tides or the changing of the seasons, everything occurs at its own time and in its own time; and for this, Lord Jesus, we give praise and thanks for all the great and miraculous wonders throughout the passing of time. And for this reason, Lord Jesus, we realize that whenever we are in a moment of life's loving caress, we must embrace it with all of our senses: Inhaling the sweetness of spring, feeling the warmth of summer, seeing the beauty of autumn, touching the first fragile frozen wonder of winter's snow, and then, and only then, will we have tasted the Majesty of Life, as you, God, have so intended for all humans!

A blade of grass grows green and tall and then withers in the fall. A fallen seed soon becomes a sapling and then a mighty tree, which then bears fruit of its own. An infant grows into a child, becomes a teenager, an adult, a senior, and then returns to your Heavenly Embrace. According to your Perfect and Wise Plan, Lord God, this is the way it is, this is the way it has to be, for this is the Way of Harmony! Praise be to your Great Wisdom, Lord Jesus Christ, for your Way is a promise for the continuation of your creation and for all future generations in your name!

And now, we ask of you, Almighty God, to render a Beautiful Blessing of Spiritual Forgiveness upon all who have gone before us, who lived their life by your Commandments, who loved you with all of their heart, and are now refreshed in your Never-ending Kingdom of Perpetual Love and Grace!

Amen …

Chapter and verse that inspired prayer:

Ecclesiastes 3:11    He hath made every thing beautiful in his time: also he hath set the world in their heart, so that no man can find out the work that God maketh from the beginning to the end.

# June Thirty: "You Continue Forever"

(As inspired from Revelation 1:8)

Lord Jesus, hear our prayer …

All knowledge is a blessing, for we are able to discern between right and wrong. And when we are Enlightened with your Wisdom, Lord God, we become a part of your Spiritual Understanding to do what is Righteous in life! Lord of Forever, your Love and Compassion encircles us, for you are the Beginning and the Ending to all that exists. You have always been and you will always be! You are all that ever was, you are all that is, and you are all that will ever be; undeniable is your Presence in the world, unquestionable is your Word of Holiness! Thank you for remembering us, Our Lord Jesus Christ!

If the rains cease to fall, and the rivers cease to flow, we know without a single doubt, O Lord, that you will continue to be. If the forests turn brown and the leaves and the fowl fall to the ground, we know absolutely, Lord Jesus, that you will remain. And if the tides are no more, and the earth becomes barren, we know with total certainty, Our Lord and God, that you will still exist, for you continue forever into the everlasting reaches of time and space!

Therefore, Lord Jesus, we know that it is everyone's obligation, each person's personal stewardship, and every human's complete responsibility to maintain and care for this creation, this planet of life; and this, we must accept willingly! For we must learn to love and care for this planet, our earth, our home, as you so love us, Lord Jesus Christ, as we love you, and as we love one another, now and forevermore, in a world filled with compassion and forgiveness, where time is without end!

Amen …

Chapter and verse that inspired prayer:

Revelation 1:8   I am Alpha and Omega, the beginning and the ending, saith the Lord, which is, and which was, and which is to come, the Almighty.

# July One: "Protect And Proclaim The Miracle Of Life"
### (As inspired from Genesis 9:2-3)

Lord Jesus, hear our prayer ...

Lord of Creation, forgive all people their lack of knowledge concerning pollution, contamination, and desecration of our living planet: Impart your Divine Understanding into every living being on earth, to see the destruction of defiling our natural resources for reasons of selfish gain and desire!

A special prayer offering, Lord God, that all people who populate this wonderful planet will individually safeguard its inherent beauty and life; therein, we graciously thank you, Lord, for entrusting us with the custody and the care of all the miraculous and bountiful creations that exist: The snowcapped mountains, the deep blue oceans, the vast deserts, the lush green jungles and forests, the rolling fields and shallow ponds, all the fresh flowing waters that spring forth and stream, the arch of the sky, and all the wonderful life that abides in this world! To you, Lord Jesus, we pray for your Heavenly Intervention to inspire a soulful concern, in every human throughout this world, to the safekeeping and perpetuation of all nature! Instill into the hearts and minds of those who govern and make rules for our natural resources, the knowledge and the truth of your Reverential Regard over this world that you love so dearly! Do not permit the clouded visions of greed and apathy to govern ambition, but allow everyone, everywhere, to protect and proclaim the Miracle of Life as you have so sanctified. And as we become true and honorable custodians in this house called earth, we will individually realize, Lord Jesus, your Heavenly Concern for all fauna and flora that live on and in this consecrated planet and throughout all the bodies of water and in the trees and in the firmament above! Therefore, through your Holy and Spiritual Inspirations, Lord Jesus Christ, we will all learn to share in and with this creation and retain its magnificence for a multitude of future millenniums yet to come!

Amen ...

Chapter and verse that inspired prayer:

Genesis 9:2-3    And the fear of you and the dread of you shall be upon every beast of the earth, and upon every fowl of the air, upon all that moveth upon the earth, and upon all the fishes of the sea; into your hands are they delivered. (3) Every moving thing that liveth shall be meat for you; even as the green herb have I given you all things.

# July Two: "The Fullness Of Our Faith"
### (As inspired from 2 John 8-9)

Lord Jesus, hear our prayer ...

Your Judgment, O Lord, is strict and demanding of our complete faith, because, Perfection exacts perfection! There is no one else before us, and there shall never be anyone nor anything else that could ever move or touch our hearts more than you! We have searched the deepest reaches of our souls and we ask forgiveness of all offenses! Amen!

Sometimes, Lord Jesus, the pressures of this world will tempt and challenge our very values and beliefs, and it is during these difficult times of personal trial, Lord, that we pray to you and call upon your Heavenly Authority and Strength: We confess to you, Almighty God, that you are the only God, the Living God, the Eternal God of Life. And to the world and to all who will listen, Lord Jesus, we avow your Word as the Absolute Spiritual Law of Heaven and Earth! You are the Light of the Universe and the Essence of All Love. Please, Lord Jesus, we ask of you to come into our midst and become the Living Energy of our spirits, The Pulse that beats within our hearts, and The Breath of Life that will sustain us from this day forward! And as every day ends and another begins, we will awaken each morning to a full reward in the fullness of our faith; for we abide by your Commandments, Lord Jesus Christ, and we completely accept the Sacred Scriptures as the Truth and the Only Doctrine of your Most Precious Word! Lord God, we beseech you, permit your Love to continually flow through the center of our Christian lives as your Holy Word becomes the lawful and rightful source of our total inner being, physically, mentally, and spiritually; for within us abides The Father, The Son, and The Holy Spirit!

Amen ...

Chapter and verse that inspired prayer:

2 John 8-9     Look to yourselves, that we lose not those things which we have wrought, but that we receive a full reward. (9) Whosoever transgresseth, and abideth not in the doctrine of Christ, hath not God. He that abideth in the doctrine of Christ, he hath both the Father and the Son.

# July Three: "There Is Love In The Whole Of The Universe"
### (As inspired from Deuteronomy 4:29-31)

Lord Jesus, hear our prayer …

Wherever there is love in the whole of the universe, O Lord, you are there! And now, united in a total commitment of heart and soul, we seek you, Lord Jesus, to offer a special prayer of appreciation: During any time of personal problems, you have always been the only one that has never forsaken nor abandoned us. You are as close to us as the very thoughts we think; and yet, we know that your Immaculate Heart encompasses the whole of the universe and all of infinity at the same time! Merciful God, we adore and we worship only you, and only you, Lord Jesus Christ, do we devote our complete love and obedience; for we value and esteem the Generous Apportionment of Life and Heavenly Blessings that you have given to us!

To those who shall be obedient to your Word, Our Lord of Heaven and Earth, of The Past, The Present, and The Future, you have given to all generations, The Promise of Mercy, Patient and Enduring Care, and an Eternal Life! Our Lord Jesus, through spiritual service to your Holy Word, our lives on earth will find complete fulfillment! Pray for us to remain faithful, to remain strong, to remain immersed in our Christian values! And with a total commitment of heart, mind, and soul, each person who abides in your Word will establish a personal covenant with you, Lord Jesus Christ Our Savior, which will then evangelize outward in a spiritual awakening of love for everyone! Praise be to you, Our Prince of Peace, for you are the Rising Sun, you are the Evening Sky, and you are Every Moment that we exist in the Universe of your Hallowed Love!

Amen …

Chapter and verse that inspired prayer:

Deuteronomy 4:29-31    But if from thence thou shalt seek the LORD thy God, thou shalt find him, if thou seek him with all thy heart and with all thy soul. (30) When thou art in tribulation, and all these things are come upon thee, even in the latter days, if thou turn to the LORD thy God, and shalt be obedient unto his voice; (31) (For the LORD thy God is a merciful God;) he will not forsake thee, neither destroy thee, nor forget the covenant of thy fathers which he sware unto them.

# July Four: "Willful Servants Of Your Supreme Will"

(As inspired from 1 Timothy 2:1-4)

Lord Jesus, hear our prayer …

Our Gracious Father of Heaven and earth, we offer a very special prayer for every man, woman, and child, that their lives will be lived in spiritual bondage to your Holiness: Lord Jesus, allow liberty and freedom to ring out in all corners of the world! Release all people from their bonds to transgression and fill their hearts with a True Understanding of Repentance! For all who are faithful to your Redeeming Word, Lord God, are saved by the Knowledge of your Exalted Truth; we pray that peace and honesty will be present in all lives, everywhere!

Here we are, Lord, willful servants of your Miraculous and Living Word! And as your will is done in heaven, Lord Jesus, so shall it be done on earth, in our minds, in our hearts, and in our spirits! Look upon us with favor, Lord Christ, as we pray to you for your Heavenly Intervention to direct our paths; for without you in our lives, O Lord, the seeds of aberration would take hold and begin to grow. And that we may always receive knowledge of your Truth, Lord God, may you always find our needs and supplications worthy of your Divine Intercession! Therefore, we are here, Lord Jesus, as willful servants of your Supreme Will, blessed by your Unflawed Love, and fulfilled through your Holy Spirit! And with only the highest of acclaim, do we revere your Compassionate and Sacred Word throughout the creation as Pure and Holy! Lord Jesus Christ, our Savior and God, please find us worthy of your blessings, for we are faithful followers, fully committed to the values and beliefs of Christianity! Into your Loving Embrace do we entrust our souls for all eternity, in whom we swear our Holy Allegiance and Alliance to your Sacred Throne in our Heavenly Kingdom on High!

Amen …

Chapter and verse that inspired prayer:

1 Timothy 2:1-4    I exhort therefore, that, first of all, supplications, prayers, intercessions, and giving of thanks, be made for all men; (2) For kings, and for all that are in authority; that we may lead a quiet and peaceable life in all godliness and honesty. (3) For this is good and acceptable in the sight of God our Saviour; (4) Who will have all men to be saved, and to come unto the knowledge of the truth.

# July Five: "Guide Our Intentions, Lord"

### (As inspired from Job 33:16-17")

Lord Jesus, hear our prayer ...

Our Anointed One, you have revealed to us through the Gospels, that whatever belongs to you cannot be consumed by the shadows, and only through our own personal and individual transgressions of freewill, can we relinquish your Spiritual Protection; O Lord of All Deliverance, we pray for Enlightenment: Lord Christ, you give purpose and direction to everyone's life. You are the beacon on a distant shore, the lighted candle in a darkened room, and the rainbow after a storm. Lord Jesus, you give reason and hope to all who are searching in life. Guide our intentions, Lord, and light the pathway for our Heavenly Salvation! Open our eyes and ears, Lord of All Knowledge, to the wonderful truth of living one's life through Righteous Values; for only in your Trusting Hands, Lord Jesus Christ, are we kept safe from the world's hidden dangers that silently cross our paths everyday in life.

Lord Jesus, we realize that no one can hide who they really are from you, for you have said so many times in Scripture that a tree is known by its fruit; and because only the heart of a sincere and humble Christian is able to truly understand your Expressed Word, blessed is the Revelation of your Spiritual knowledge, Lord God, that you impart to all who are faithful, obedient, and submissive to the Holy Commandments of Our Living God! Lord Jesus Christ, you are the Absolute Foundation of our Christian belief, you are the only reason that our faith endures, because you are the Revelation of True Love and Virtue. Blessed are you, Lord Christ, Our Messiah and King, and blessed are we for believing in you, accepting you, and having you in our lives from this moment forth into eternity! Pray for us, Our Lord Who Loves Us, that we will remain strong and determined in our Miraculous Christian Faith!

Amen ...

Chapter and verse that inspired prayer:

Job 33:16-17    Then he openeth the ears of men, and sealeth their instructions, (17) That he may withdraw man from his purpose, and hide pride from man.

# July Six: "Holy! Holy! Holy Are You, Lord!"
### (As inspired from Acts of the Apostles 4:24)

Lord Jesus, hear our prayer …

Of all the nations and leaders and territories of the world that proclaim power, Our Heavenly Father, you are the True and Only Superpower on earth, no other authority would have the right to their might, if it were not for you, Lord God Our Christ and King! Through you, Our Genesis of Life, all things are possible: To turn water into wine, to raise the dead, to calm a raging storm, to walk on water is to defy the natural laws of nature, which only you, Lord God, are able to do! And we offer our unremitting praises and thanks to you, Our Lord of the Universe, for you command the light to shine, and there is light; you command the seas to part, and they part; you command the forces of nature to do Your Will, and it is done! How incredible this is, and we give endless adoration and thanks to you, Lord Christ, Our God of Absolute Authority; He, who commands the rains to fall and oceans to form, the earth to shake and mountains to arise, and all life to awaken, and we were created! How can your existence be denied! We give our most humble praises and continuous thanks to your Indisputable Presence! For you, Our Living God, in the beginning, bid all life to come forth and every variety of seed to grow and produce more of its kind! May our total thankfulness to you, Lord Jesus Most Glorious, be forever everlasting, and may the whole world of creation and all life eternally sing out in one accord: Holy! Holy! Holy are you, Lord Jesus Christ, God and Creator of Heaven and Earth and of All that Exists!

Amen …

Chapter and verse that inspired prayer:

Acts of the Apostles 4:24    And when they heard that, they lifted up their voice to God with one accord, and said, Lord, thou art God, which hast made heaven, and earth, and the sea, and all that in them is:

# July Seven: "We Rejoice In Our Hearts"
### (As inspired from Mark 10:21-22)

Lord Jesus, hear our prayer …

Our greatest possession on earth, Almighty God, is the beautiful knowledge of your Infinite Love that you have for us! As a parent loves their child, so do you love us! Blest is the Enlightenment of Heavenly Compassion, for in its awareness is the Fulfillment of Life!

O Lord, we have taken up your cross in life and we follow no one but you; for whatever we have on earth, nothing will compare to our Treasures in Heaven! Great is your Understanding of us, Lord Jesus, because you know the truth in everyone's heart's desire! Lord God, give us the strength to endure whenever we are spiritually tested, as Christians, to correctly follow your Teachings and Tenets and Doctrines from which we base our belief and faith. Blessed is your Infallible Wisdom, Lord Christ, Wise and All Knowing are you! Kindle our understanding, Dear Lord, and help us to fully perceive that all worldly possessions and riches will never offer hope nor assurance for a future of love and happiness. And as we look around, Lord Jesus, we realize that everything we own as individuals, all of our earthly possessions, will one day fall to waste or be owned by someone else; but the love that emanates from our heart and soul has already been shared with others and is claimed by you! Lord Jesus Christ, your Immaculate Heart has inspired us to know that love is not a worldly possession but a Heavenly Gift, meant to be shared by all! Our spirits leap with joy, Lord God, knowing that your Love is freely given to everyone to have and to hold, eternally as their own, from this world into the next! And from this moment on, we rejoice in our hearts because of the Great Spiritual Possessions that come to us from your Divine Love and Concern!

Amen …

Chapter and verse that inspired prayer:

Mark 10:21-22    Then Jesus beholding him loved him, and said unto him, One thing thou lackest: go thy way, sell whatsoever thou hast, and give to the poor, and thou shalt have treasure in heaven: and come, take up the cross, and follow me. (22) And he was sad at that saying, and went away grieved: for he had great possessions.

# July Eight: "Forgive Us Our Weaknesses, Lord"

(As inspired from 1 Corinthians 2:5)

Lord Jesus, hear our prayer …

We know that your Holy Spirit is with us everyday, Lord. And whenever we feel an emptiness inside, or a loneliness in our souls, we pray that you will remove the void from our hearts and increase our spiritual faith. Please, Lord Jesus, take away the haunting hollowness from our emotions and fill our lives with your Meaning and Purpose. Forgive us our weaknesses, O Lord, and allow us to know and realize that our personal faith should never stand in the wisdom of any one human but only in the Authority of your Perfect Truth and Understanding. And through a personal acceptance in the Power of your Merciful Grace, Lord Jesus Christ, we will gain a full and complete awareness of your Sincere and Undeniable Inspirations; which will never leave a void of emptiness nor a shadow of doubt within our spirit and faith!

Lord God, from the beginning of our lives until the end, in darkness as well as in light, from our first breath until our last breath, we know that you are with us every moment of the day! Blessed is your Indisputable Love for us, Lord Christ, and blessed are we to receive it! O Lord, hear our profession of faith: All of the Strength and Might in heaven and on earth is from the Power of God, You, Lord God, who Reigns Supreme above all; and we, your faithful, absolutely believe this in heart, mind, body, and soul! Therefore, we ask you to bless us, to forgive us, and to receive us as passionate witnesses of your Affable Spirit of Kindness: We are a faithful nation of worldwide Christians, unconquerable is our God, you, Lord Jesus Christ, for we absolutely accept your Saving Grace as Unfailing and Constant!

Amen …

Chapter and verse that inspired prayer:

1 Corinthians 2:5    That your faith should not stand in the wisdom of men, but in the power of God.

# July Nine: "The Family Will Come Together"
### (As inspired from Ephesians 2:18-19)

Lord Jesus, hear our prayer …

Blessed is your Holy Name, Lord Jesus, for bringing all races, colors, languages, nationalities, genders, and ages together in one beautiful belief in you, as, Our Lord and God! Through devout faith in you, Lord Christ, and no one else, we have access to the Holy Father, and to our Heavenly Family of Saints and Angels and Members of the Household of God! And we are no longer considered gentile to faith, infidel to belief, a non-believer of Christianity, for now, we are of One Family, fellow citizens, united by the Glorious Throne of our Lord Jesus Christ who reigns in Heaven and on Earth, Forever and Ever!

O Lord, through your Never-ending Love and Mercy, the special bond that only family members share between one another will continue to survive and thrive. Through your constant faith in us, Lord Jesus, the family will remain united and Blessed. And through your Ever-present Compassion, the family will come together as one voice, bonded in an unwavering love for you, Lord Jesus Christ, and proclaim your Majesty and Greatness throughout the world and throughout their individual lives as true Christians! And as you so cherish the family, Lord God, your Eternal Compassion has also brought each family member together in a single praise that honors your love: Blessed is our Father of heaven and earth! And we pray, Lord Jesus, that one day, through your Redeeming Power and Glory, that every member of our family may be found worthy enough to unite with your Heavenly Family of Saints for All Eternity; for you alone, Lord Jesus Christ, are the Prevailing Strength and Brilliance within All Families united by The Father, The Son, and The Holy Spirit!

Amen …

Chapter and verse that inspired prayer:

Ephesians 2:18-19   For through him we both have access by one Spirit unto the Father. (19) Now therefore ye are no more strangers and foreigners, but fellowcitizens with the saints, and of the household of God;

# July Ten: "Calm Their Troubled Spirits"

### (As inspired from Luke 6:27-28)

Lord Jesus, hear our prayer …

Lord Jesus, you have taught us that love conquers all! And if someone is angry with us, then we, as true Christians, must not reciprocate the resentment, instead, we must pray for them to find inner peace and a release from their embittered emotions. Please, pray for us, Lord Christ, that we too will be strong enough in spirit and mind to heed your Wonderful Words of Forgiveness: Release us, Dear Lord, from our transgressions and misgivings towards others, and empower us with the Holy Spirit of Peace, that we will be inspired to seek understanding and fellowship with all whom we meet and greet in friendship, throughout our individual lifetimes!

Our Venerable Lord, we pray to you that our Christian values will prevail against all odds, against all doubt, and against all dissenters of peace and mercy! Deliver us, Lord God, from the causes of misfortune and from those who bring misfortune to us. Lord Jesus, we pray for all who easily anger, are quick to embitter emotions, and who openly display their hostilities towards others. Calm their troubled spirits, Lord, and fill their hearts with your forgiveness and compassion! Open their eyes, Lord Christ, that they may see the good in others as well as themselves. Free them from their terrible bonds of hostility and rage. Inspire them to release their stressed emotions through constructive means rather than being mean and destructive. We pray, O Lord, that you will implant within their souls the spiritual seeds of tolerance, of understanding, and of patience; but above all, Lord Jesus Christ, bless them and fill their lives to capacity with the Heavenly Wisdom of Personal Salvation, from which they too may receive and experience the Holy Spirit of your Love and Peace!

Amen …

Chapter and verse that inspired prayer:

Luke 6:27 -28    But I say unto you which hear, Love your enemies, do good to them which hate you, (28) Bless them that curse you, and pray for them which despitefully use you.

# July Eleven: "Our Lord Of Perfect Compassion"
### (As inspired from Mark 11:24)

Lord Jesus, hear our prayer ...

We greatly revere you, Lord God, for allowing us to awaken in another glorious day of life! How immeasurably marvelous it is to be a walking, breathing, living soul, formed by the Loving Hands of Our God Almighty! Hear us, Lord of Creation, as we proclaim our words of praise: We are truthful and genuine in our adoration of you, Dear Lord, and we thank you for everything in our lives that has come to pass! Gracious and blessed are you, Lord Jesus, for you know our needs before we ask! And whenever there is a special prayer of personal need, our Christian faith, in every instance, abides in you, Lord of Long Suffering; for we know that all wants are met according to your Loving and Forbearing Will! And accordingly, whatever we desire of the heart and soul, we know and believe that all prayers profoundly spoken from the spirit will be answered by you, Our Lord of Bounty!

Lord, your deep care and concern over our individual troubles and problems makes us blissful and happy; because, your love touches and fills the body and soul with Heavenly Solace. And as we are forever in need of your Spiritual Strength, we pray that you will continually nourish our souls with the Calming Powers of your Comforting Grace. And as we desire to always be of sound mind and body, we will always pray for perfect health in our physical, mental, and spiritual being. Therefore, keep us in your sight, Lord, and hear our words of truth: Enrapturing is your Benevolent Love that is constantly before us; and Absolute are you, Lord Jesus Christ, Our Lord of Perfect Compassion and Understanding!

Amen ...

Chapter and verse that inspired prayer:

Mark 11:24    Therefore I say unto you, what things soever ye desire, when ye pray, believe that ye receive them, and ye shall have them.

# July Twelve: "Watch Over The Innocence Of The Newborn"

(As inspired from Exodus 23:7)

Lord Jesus, hear our prayer ...

We praise you, O Lord, for the beautiful and innocent purity of the newborn infant; for such is the Kingdom of Heaven! Thank you so much for their trusting love and their heavenly virtue. Lord God, we pray for the physical, mental, and spiritual health of their young and magnificent lives to remain unblemished, forever! And as all children must grow into young adults and then into maturity, Our Lord Jesus, we beseech you: Allow the lessons that they learn in life to serve as meaningful enrichments that will properly temper and forge their hearts and spirits into becoming obedient and loyal followers of your Immaculate Heart. For whenever a person truly accepts you, Lord Jesus Christ, as their Personal and Divine Savior, they too become as an innocent newborn in their Christian faith, born again into a new world of Pure Love and Life Everlasting!

As true Christians, we are first born of flesh, and then born of the Holy Spirit when we personally find you, Our Savior, Our Lord and Christ! Dear Lord, hear our soulful prayer request for the newly born of flesh, and the newly born of the Spirit: We pray that your Christian faithful, all around the world, will be inspired by your Holiness, to remain far from all corruptible matters of the mind, the body, and the soul. We also pray for those who protect, guide, and watch over the innocence of the newborn: Inspire their hearts and their thoughts, at all times, to remain fully righteous and faithful to your Word as they nurture and care for the physical and spiritual needs of the child. Lord Jesus, enrich and bless the parents and the children of the world, keep them away from hurtful people and all harmful matters so that your Heavenly Family will be abundantly increased by the Righteous Souls of your Faithful and Fruitful Multitudes; by those who worship and believe in you with all of their heart, their mind, and their beautiful and loving soul!

Amen ...

Chapter and verse that inspired prayer:

Exodus 23:7    Keep thee far from a false matter; and the innocent and righteous slay thou not: for I will not justify the wicked.

# July Thirteen: "Wonderful Blessings Of Friendship"
## (As inspired from Proverbs 18:24)

Lord Jesus, hear our prayer …

Bless us, Heavenly Father, and receive us as we receive others in a warm embrace of Christian love! We thank you, Lord Jesus, in our fellowship with friends; for with their understanding and support, honest feelings of acceptance and trust fills the heart and the soul with wonderful blessings of friendship and accord! And through the blessings of peace and harmony that develops between people, a special union is created with one another in a spiritual bonding, as with a brother or a sister; and for this spiritual relationship of hospitality, we are most grateful to you, Lord Jesus Christ, for establishing the warmhearted closeness of brotherhood and sisterhood into our lives!

As you have taught us from Scripture, Lord Christ, the vine of life grows best from within a spiritual acknowledgment that joins the heart, the mind, and the soul of sincere friends into a lasting covenant, which is eternally entwined in honesty and love. And we thank you, O Lord, for inspiring your faithful to gather together through agreement in order to celebrate and honor your name as you have so intended, through peace and harmony. Lord Jesus, you have said, where two or more are gathered in your Name, you will be among us; therefore, please, continually bless this house and all who visit here in a genuine fellowship; for when friends gather together in peace, they are gathering together in your Holy and Reverent Name, which is Exalted and Greatly Magnified throughout the universe! And once again we say: Thank you, Lord God, for all close friends, because they become family, like brothers or sisters, during times of emotional and or spiritual need.

Amen …

Chapter and verse that inspired prayer:

Proverbs 18:24   A man that hath friends must show himself friendly: and there is a friend that sticketh closer than a brother.

# July Fourteen: "Love Abounds In Our Lives"

### (As inspired from Philippians 1:9)

Lord Jesus, hear our prayer …

That everyone may become stronger in their Christian faith, we ask of you, Lord, to increase our individual spiritual knowledge, make wise our personal judgments, especially in matters of the heart, and inspire all of us to be prudent in whatever we say to one another! Our spirits leap with joy as our eyes lift heavenward in complete admiration and adoration for you! Bless us, O Lord, and direct your True Compassion to guide our affections that we have for one another. Lord Jesus, when there are venerable praises upon our lips, we know that you will hear our words. When there is intense faith in our hearts, we know that your Holy Spirit is present! And when love abounds in our lives, we know that you are actually beside us! Blessed are you, Lord Jesus Christ, for there is never a need for anyone to feel sad or lonely when they fill their heart and soul with your Redeeming Love!

Lord, as the sunrise breaks the horizon and emanates its splendor, as a rainbow illuminates and glorifies the sky, and as a flower blossoms and displays its beauty to the world, so too must we radiate our faith as we outwardly show our love for you! Lord Jesus, your Tender and Merciful Heart gives Absolute Strength to our faith as our prayers are lifted upwards towards the Kingdom of God! Hear our exaltations of joy, Lord, as our spirits soar on the wings of wonderment! How jubilant we are, for all of creation has been placed before us, for us! Truly, as loyal and faithful followers of your Heavenly Love, we have been blessed beyond our expectations! Thank you! Thank you greatly! Thank you, Our Lord Jesus Christ, for everything!

Each and every Christian, Dear Lord, Loves you greatly with all of their Heart, with all of their Soul, with all of their Mind, with all of their Might, and with all that they Are, and with all that they are they give Praise to All That You Do, for All That You Have Done, and for Your Great Mercies Yet To Come!

Amen …

Chapter and verse that inspired prayer:

Philippians 1:9    And this I pray, that your love may abound yet more and more in knowledge and in all judgment;

# July Fifteen: "From Generation To Generation"

### (As inspired from Daniel 4:3)

Lord Jesus, hear our prayer …

Our Benevolent and Everlasting Father of Heaven and Earth, please, Lord God, hear the intensity of our prayerful petition as we offer a prayer for the world: May the Holy Ghost of Life come into our hearts and into our spirits and into the souls and lives of all people on earth! Bless our prayerful request, Lord God of Heaven and Earth and All That Exists, that it will truly become a reality in every nation and in every person around the world!

Thank you, Dear Lord, for this miraculous gift of human life! How wonderful it is to walk in your light, to breathe in your breath, and to live in your Spirit! How glorious it is to freely speak your name, Lord Jesus Christ, to praise your words, and to give you thanks for all that we have received through your bounty! And how fortunate we are to actually see the mighty wonders of your work, to hear the soul stirring sounds and songs of nature, and to feel the warmth of the sun or a soothing breeze upon our flesh. Everywhere, from generation to generation, we continually give witness to the great signs of your Endless Love that you have for us! But most of all, we are thankful, Lord Jesus Our Hallowed Christ, for the most precious gift in universe, the living and breathing life-form of a human being! For you, Lord, by creating this existence of flesh, this vessel of love for our immortal souls, gave us life that we may give physical witness and praise for our wonderful gifts of love! Glory be to you in the Highest, Our Lord God Eternal, whose Kingdom Is Everlasting and whose Power is Unlimited throughout heaven and throughout the great expanse of the infinite universe!

Amen …

Chapter and verse that inspired prayer:

Daniel 4:3    How great are his signs! And how mighty are his wonders! his kingdom is an everlasting kingdom, and his dominion is from generation to generation.

# July Sixteen: "Make Calm The Storms Of Frustration"

### (As inspired from Lamentations 3:21-22)

Lord Jesus, hear our prayer ...

Rich or poor, great or small, the powerful and the meek, the bright and the dull, all humans are subject to your Laws and Commandments; because, whatever we do on earth or in our lifetimes, is of little or no significance nor consequence, unless of course, it is done for the Will of God! And then, even a simple task of planting a single seed into good soil, if done for your Loving Will, Lord Jesus Christ, then becomes a special and reverent moment in your sight! Therefore, let us always give thanks and praise for everything, for everything we do, we do in your Most Holy Name, Lord God!

Dear Lord, you are The Comforter, The Savior, The Champion of Peace, and we pray to you for your Divine Mercy and Forgiveness! Lord Jesus, please, allow the foolishness of anger to subside in the hearts and minds of all people who are in personal turmoil! Make clear the emotions of world confusion and mistrust, and encourage all nations to see and understand the folly of their indignation towards peace! Quell the bitterness within the hardened heart, make calm the storms of frustration, and grant us the Mercies of your Tender Love, Lord God, to continually return to the hearts and souls of those who lead us; who make laws and decisions concerning the futures of those whom they govern. Through you, Our Prince of Peace, there is hope, and through prayer, we ask in your name, Lord Jesus Christ, for continued security and protection in our lives that may only be found by personally accepting your Divine Compassion for our individual souls, for the world, and for all people who live therein!

Amen ...

Chapter and verse that inspired prayer:

Lamentations 3:21-22    This I recall to my mind, therefore have hope (22) It is of the LORD's mercies that we are not consumed, because his compassions fail not.

# July Seventeen: "Shield Our Loved Ones"

(As inspired from Ephesians 6:15-16)

Lord Jesus, hear our prayer ...

Each morning, before we leave the sanctity of our homes to begin the day, we put on The Full Armor of The Lord, by asking you, Our Prince of Peace, to shore up and strengthen our individual faith that it will become our personal shield, protecting us against all injury and harm. Lord Jesus, you cannot be conquered nor subdued. All that exists in the heavens, the earth, and throughout infinity, is subject to your Hallowed Authority, for your Holy Power is Truly Undeniable! And how wonderful it is to be on the side of Righteousness; because, we are always confident of your Glorious Victories over all adversaries!

Your love, Lord, is an ever flowing Gospel of Heavenly Promise and Tranquility: A Spring of Pure Life that rivers forth in a barren desert to bring nourishment and fulfillment to the body and to the soul of our total being! Therefore, we are united in our thoughts and prayers, Lord Jesus, when we ask you to protect and shield our loved ones from the dilemmas of life. Secure and keep them close, Lord Christ, in your Fortress of your Eternal Peace. Do not allow the daily pressures of stress and tension to erode the confidence that emanates from the heart and soul of those for whom we pray. Guide their difficult decisions, help them to make good choices, wise choices, and bring them to the Spiritual Knowledge that you are always present in their lives, Lord God. And give them the ability to safely release their anxieties by allowing the peaceful calm of your Gentle Compassion to fill their hearts. And then, Lord Jesus Christ, like Crystal Clear Streams of Love flowing from your Heavenly Throne, their spirits will surge outwardly to become an ocean of faith and love for you!

Amen ...

Chapter and verse that inspired prayer:

Ephesians 6:15-16   And your feet shod with the preparation of the gospel of peace; (16) Above all, taking the shield of faith, wherewith ye shall be able to quench all the fiery darts of the wicked.

# July Eighteen: "Lord, We Rejoice In Your Righteous Authority"
### (As inspired from Leviticus 26:3-4, 9)

Lord Jesus, hear our prayer ...

In a world of uncertainties, we, your faithful Christian following, do not accept the shadows of doubt and fear, but place our total faith into the Conquering Love of your Great Commandments, from which we live our lives, and have established our spiritual beliefs! All Knowing and All Powerful is your Holiness! Thank you, Lord God, for your blessings are many! And through the power and consent of your Holy Word, we live our lives accordingly, in a just and true manner. And through the influence of your Holy Spirit, we properly conduct ourselves daily to become responsible and productive members of our Christian faith and the society in which we live; Jesus Our Lord, we rejoice in your Righteous Authority and Divinity, for you have multiplied our blessings greatly and greatly are we blessed!

Lord God, we hold your Sacred Commandments close to our hearts and duly follow your Heavenly Laws for Spiritual Survival. And it is our prayer that all individuals around the world will have the same opportunity and freedom to become respected and fruitful members of our wonderful Christian faith; therefore, Our Lord Jesus Christ, authorize the Miracle of Your Commanding Love to reach out and touch everyone, everywhere, throughout this magnificent world! And for those with little or no faith, Lord, we pray that they will find Spiritual examples that would best exemplify and reflect your Abundant Love for them! Lord, we also pray that every member of your faithful family will always accept, embrace, and inspire any and all people who seek you; may they find your Just and Merciful Spirit in a Beautiful Covenant of Compassion and Peace!

Amen ...

Chapter and verse that inspired prayer:

Leviticus 26:3-4, 9    If ye walk in my statutes, and keep my commandments, and do them; (4) Then I will give you rain in due season, and the land shall yield her increase, and the trees of the field shall yield their fruit. (9) For I will have respect unto you, and make you fruitful, and multiply you, and establish my covenant with you.

# July Nineteen: "Within Our Spiritual Lives"

### (As inspired from Romans 6:23)

Lord Jesus, hear our prayer …

Through scriptural inspiration, Lord Jesus, we have come to understand, as Christians, the true meaning of being personally and faithfully devoted to your every Commandment: For any act committed against your Perfect Word of Knowledge, results in a spiritual compensation of withdrawal from your Heavenly Light and Protection! And, Lord Jesus Christ, like the sun and stars, we know that your Blessed Holiness is always there, and it is the individual who withdraws, not you, Lord God, from the Sheltering Glow of your Magnificent Radiance! But through a genuine feeling of heartfelt repentance, we move ourselves back into your Heavenly Light of Protection! Blessed are you, Our Lord of Peace, and Blest is your Merciful Love and Forgiveness!

Increase our faith, O Lord, within our spiritual lives, to help us truly think as Christians, to genuinely love as Christians, and to actually act as Christians, by living our lives morally correct! Help us, Lord Christ, to see that a True Believer does not harbor anger nor revenge in their heart towards anyone, but instead, is forgiving and understanding. Please, Lord Jesus, create within us, a place of Spiritual Knowledge that will hold fast to our Scriptural Beliefs and Convictions, by allowing each and every faithful soul the ability to increase their own personal faith with the assured knowledge that your Merciful Love is obtainable by all who sincerely ask for it! Therefore, we ask of you, Our Lord and Savior, to forgive us for our errors in judgment and common sense. Hear us, Lord Christ, as we pray for spiritual strength and understanding. For it is during times of individual discontent, doubt, and disappointment that we generate in our own lives the chances for further adversity and conflict; but through personal atonement and constant obedience to your Eternal Word, Lord Jesus Christ, we will receive the Incredible Reward of Eternal Existence! And, we are forever grateful to you, Lord God; for your Infinite Wisdom shows us the Way to a Never-ending Life. Blessed is your Holy and Spiritual Light of Beckoning Love and Deliverance, for it is ever present in your Beautiful Word of Life!

Amen …

Chapter and verse that inspired prayer:

Romans 6:23    For the wages of sin is death; but the gift of God is eternal life through Jesus Christ our Lord.

# July Twenty: "There Are No Shadows In The True Light"

(As inspired from John 1:4-5)

Lord Jesus, hear our prayer …

We pray for all nations and for all people who know your Name, Lord Jesus, and yet, do not comprehend the Majesty and the Miraculous Power of your Divine Name as the Bearer of All Purity and Innocent Holiness. Lord God, in you is the Timeless Illumination of Honor and Dignity, which may be achieved within our own lives, but only be accepting you, Lord Jesus Christ, as our Individual Way to Personal Salvation within this temporal world! Blessed are you, Lord, The Son of Man!

The Sun is not reserved for some but for all, and for all who stand in the Light, freely receive of the Sun's Illustrious Radiance! Your Compassion for us, Lord Jesus, is an Endless Universe of Forever Love! We lift up our hearts and proudly attest our devotion to you, Lord of Heaven and Earth, by professing that you are the True Light of all Life. And proudly, our spirits raise heavenward as we bear witness to this truth, Lord Jesus, that there are no shadows in the True Light; for darkness cannot exist in the Purity of Your Glowing Goodness. And like the evening stars that shine so brightly above, Pure Love and Pure Faith are visible forces that will exist forever and ever! Lord Jesus Christ, we pray that you will direct the Brilliance of Your Light to become the Sole Source of Divine Energy in everyone's life throughout the world; for the True Light that shines on us, Lord, comes from you, The Holy and Eternal Son of Goodness! Blest is The Father, The Son, and The Holy Spirit of Resplendent Salvation, which is Gloriously Poured Out to all humankind, forever and ever!

Amen …

Chapter and verse that inspired prayer:

John 1:4-5  In him was life; and the life was the light of men. (5) And the light shineth in darkness; and the darkness comprehended not.

# July Twenty-One: "Your Spirit Touches Our Lives"
### (As inspired from Malachi 4:2)

Lord Jesus, hear our prayer ...

Please accept our earnest plea for all nations and all people around the world: O Lord, we fear for the souls of those who do not believe in your Hallowed Name; because, all truth stems from you, Lord Jesus Christ! And without your Divine Protection, the body and spirit are subject to the ills of the world. Only in your Sacred Name, Our Loving God, is there safety and assurance, and for this reason, we ask you to hear our soulful prayer request for everyone who needs you in their life: We call upon the Son of Righteousness to fill the emptiness in the lives and souls of those who are in want of Spiritual Redemption!

Lord God, you are instrumental in all that we are and in all that we do. And no matter where we journey and no matter where we sojourn in life, Lord Jesus, we do not have to venture very far to see the stirring power of your Majestic Love that constantly surrounds us! In your name, Lord God, rests the Holy Power of all that is unto eternity; because, your Spirit touches our lives daily. You heal us with a thought and soothe our troubled souls with a whisper; and your Tender Love quells and quiets all inner chaos. Gentle Lord, you inspire all life, everywhere! Just as the coolness of morning dew reaches out to refresh every living creature, so do you, Lord Christ, reach out to touch the essence of all creation! As the sun inspires a seed to grow, so do you, Lord Jesus, inspire all faith to prosper! And just as the gentle rains nourish the good earth that brings forth life, so do you, Our Lord and God Eternal, nourish our spirits with a Gentle Kindness that brings forth love from an empty heart! Thank you, Lord Jesus Christ, our Protector and Savior, for all that you have created in us, around us, and for us.

Amen ...

Chapter and verse that inspired prayer:

Malachi 4:2    But unto you that fear my name shall the Sun of righteousness arise with healing in his wings; and ye shall go forth, and grow up as calves of the stall.

# July Twenty-Two: "The Absolute Fulfillment Of Joy"

### (As inspired from Philippians 2:1-3)

Lord Jesus, hear our prayer …

Thank you for showing us that all confusion, disarray, arguments, dissension, and disobedience stem from a simple lack of total trust in your Holy Word, O Lord; whose Authority conquers all adversity, merely, through absolute faith and belief in you, Lord God!

Pray for us, Our Heavenly Father, that our individual actions and deeds will never be driven by anger nor pride, but in humility and high regard for others; because, in harmony, there is accord, and in disobedience, there is chaos. O Lord, we realize that we cannot always have what we want in life, but we also know that you will grant us what we truly need; for our true needs are always beyond our temporal comprehension, but our spiritual trust and understanding will always remain with you, Lord Christ; because in your Loving Mercies, there resides the Perfect Pathway to Peace! And through your Holy Scriptures of Wisdom and Love, we find the Absolute Fulfillment of Joy when we live our lives through your Compassionate Concern. Lord Jesus, we pray for those who recklessly run through life; for their spiritual paths are confused and their personal faith is in discord. Fill the division in their lives. Our Prince of Peace, and end their conflict within as you return them to the Ways of Righteous Living; grant the serenity and the tranquility that is found in your Immaculate Heart to be found throughout this world and throughout everyone's life! And that everyone on earth may live in perfect harmony, we thank you, Lord Jesus Christ, for giving us a True Language of Understanding in the Fellowship of your Holy Spirit! Hear us now, Our Lord and God, as our hearts loudly proclaim the Majesty of your Holy Spirit: All Glory and Power abounds within the Commanding Authority of your Supreme Love, which is immeasurable and irrefutable!

Amen …

Chapter and verse that inspired prayer:

Philippians 2:1-3   If there be therefore any consolation in Christ, if any comfort of love, if any fellowship of the Spirit, if any bowels and mercies, (2) Fulfil ye my joy, that ye be likeminded, having the same love, being of one accord, of one mind. (3) Let nothing be done through strife or vainglory; but in lowliness of mind let each esteem other better than themselves.

# July Twenty-Three: "Living In Your Words Of Peace"

(As inspired from Numbers 6:24-26)

Lord Jesus, hear our prayer …

The Sun rises from the east, a gentle dew quenches life's thirst, and all life awakens to the rays of a newly formed day! Our Heavenly Lord, your Everyday Blessings are Pure and Unblemished, beyond description, and we seek your Divine Encouragement in all that we do. Bless us and keep us safe, Lord Christ. Sanction the Beauty of your Glorious Love to constantly shine down upon our lives. Lift up our spirits towards your Heavenly Kingdom, Lord Jesus, that our hearts may forever dwell in the Kindness of your Merciful grace, in a Blessing of Eternal Salvation; because, living by your Words of Peace is our spiritual goal and true destination in life!

In you, Blessed Lord, we rejoice and give entirely of ourselves, both spiritually and physically. And through complete faith in your Infallible Blessings, O Lord, we offer this personal praise that reflects our complete belief in your Most Compassionate Love and Generosity: All acclaim and honor go to you, Our Good Prince of Peace, Our Savior and Redeemer of Life, Lord Jesus Christ, the Lamb of God, who lives forever and ever, Glory unto you in the Highest!

Almighty and Supreme God, our words are total reflections of our personal feelings for you, but human words alone cannot express or commend the spiritual praises that are worthy of you. And for that reason, we will outwardly adorn our hearts, our souls, and our lives with complete admiration for you, Lord Jesus Christ, by sincerely living your Words of Peace, today, tomorrow, and for the rest of our lives; thank you for this day and for all the days of our lives!

Amen …

Chapter and verse that inspired prayer:

Numbers 6:24-26    The LORD bless thee, and keep thee: (25) The LORD make his face shine upon thee, and be gracious unto thee: (26) The LORD lift up his countenance upon thee, and give thee peace.

# July Twenty-Four: "We Pray To You, Lord, Our Souls To Keep"

(As inspired from 1 Corinthians 4:4, 7)

Lord Jesus, hear our prayer …

Through parables, Lord Christ, you taught the masses many insightful lessons regarding life, and your teachings continue to enlighten all people to understand: That we have no control over the rising sun, we have no authority over the coming darkness, and every day begins and ends of its own volition. All that happens in between dawn and dusk is guided by the Hand of Heaven! You, Lord Jesus Christ, have Sole Power over every hour and minute of life; because, it is your voice that all creation hears, abides in, and obeys! Receive our words of praise, O Lord, as our spirits loudly proclaim the Wonder of your Judgment: Great is your Discernment of our individual hearts, Lord Jesus! Unbounded is your All-knowing knowledge of our lives! There is nothing that can be hidden from you; everything is seen and known! How wonderful it is to know that lies and deceit cannot possibly surpass your Invincible Wisdom! Thank you, Our Lord of Hosts, for being Absolutely Perfect!

Heavenly Father, through your eyes, we see that we are no less than and no more than what you created us to be, and you love us individually, no less than, and no more than, any other. We also appreciate that every human creation is beautiful, essential, and with purpose. And although the full meaning of all existence may be hidden from our earthly reasoning, Lord Christ, we know that all life has your Divine Right to Exist. For we do not really create nor give life, we, as humans, are merely the custodians and keepers of life; only you, Lord Jesus Christ, are the True Giver of Life! And we pray to you, Lord God, our souls to keep, in this world and in heaven above when we righteously return to your Kingdom on High! Therefore, Our King of Kings, for as long as we live upon this planet, please, continually bestow upon us blessings of health, wisdom, and understanding in all that we are, do, and discern. Thank you, Lord Jesus, for you are everyone's Light of the World and Staff of Life!

Amen …

Chapter and verse that inspired prayer:

1 Corinthians 4:4, 7   For I know nothing by myself; yet am I not hereby justified: but he that judgeth me is the Lord. (7) For who maketh thee to differ from another? and what hast thou that thou didst not receive? now if thou didst receive it, why dost thou glory, as if thou hadst not received it?

# July Twenty-Five: "Born Again"

(As inspired from John 3:3)

Lord Jesus, hear our prayer …

Our hearts rejoice and our spirits are uplifted with every new beginning; because, each wonderful morning offers your Faithful Following an opportunity to begin anew! It becomes a time to start over, to try again, and to gain further strength in our mission in life, which is to daily celebrate our existence in you, Lord Jesus Christ, He, who brings the Joy of Eternity into our lives!

Please hear us, Our Lord and God, for in all humility we sincerely ask that you will revive our souls in a reawakening of Christian values and moral excellence! From the heart and spirit, we pray to you, Lord, a special prayer for insight and direction: Lord Jesus, may all people, everywhere, in every corner of the world, find and understand the Great Wisdom of your Everlasting Love! For when a lost soul is saved by receiving you, Lord Christ, as their Personal Savior, they are born again as a new person! A redeemed soul that is borne of your Holy Spirit, Lord; and like a newborn child, their spiritual knowledge and life really begins! For there is a new and beautiful language to learn, and it is one of love and forgiveness; also, there awaits a new family, a Worldwide Christian family, one of trust and acceptance, whose Father resides in heaven and where every family member's heart accepts the Son of God as their very own Anointed Redeemer! Thus, a new life begins when someone is born again, a Spiritual Life of faith and compassion through you, in you, and for you, Lord Jesus Christ Our Savior!

Lord Jesus, we now silently and individually vow, in our heart of hearts, that we will lead the rest of our lives fully committed to you, Our Righteous One, and that you are The Way, The Truth, and The Life; because, no soul may enter into the Kingdom of God The Father, except through you, Lord Jesus Christ, The Son of Man!

Amen …

Chapter and verse that inspired prayer:

John 3:3   Jesus answered and said unto him, Verily, verily, I say unto thee, Except a man be born again, he cannot see the kingdom of God.

# July Twenty-Six: "The Perfect And True Destination"
### (As inspired from 1 Peter 3:10-12)

Lord Jesus, hear our prayer …

By our faith, O Lord, we are sure, through action and word, that we have the power to call down upon ourselves, the Goodness of Light or the shadows of adversity; for it is our personal freewill, sanctified by your Sacred Spiritual Wisdom, to do that which is right or to do that which is wrong! And it is our choice, furthermore, and forevermore, to do good, to speak of peace, and to live our lives according to your Word, as faithful Christians, dedicated to your Benevolent and Righteous Love! Lord Jesus, bless us and keep us close to your Ever Present Compassion, which burns brightly within this incredible world and within our immortal souls!

Life's journey is often filled with trials and tribulations and unpredictable events. But you, Lord God, are caring and giving and will harbor all who ask of you as they voyage through life; and knowing that your eyes are always upon your faithful, and your ears are always open to our prayerful words, we exalt your Profound Wisdom! Please, Lord Jesus, hear and accept our words of praise as pure and from the heart; for you are compassionate in all that you do. And in all humility, Lord Christ, we ask you to fill our days with lessons of your Divine Tenderness. Open our hearts and our lives to become Ports of Goodwill to one and all. Empower us with your Holy Spirit, Our Lord and God, that we may never carry ill feelings towards anyone but to always have feelings of compassion for those whose travels through life are marked with inadvertent misfortune. And throughout our life's journey, we will remain steadfast on our Christian course and in our sole conviction that you, Lord Jesus Christ, are the Perfect and True Destination for the whole world and for every soul that lives and breathes upon this good earth!

Amen …

Chapter and verse that inspired prayer …

1 Peter 3:10-12     For he that will love life, and see good days, let him refrain his tongue from evil, and his lips that they speak no guile: (11) Let him eschew evil, and do good; let him seek peace, and ensue it. (12) For the eyes of the Lord are over the righteous, and his ears are open unto their prayers: but the face of the Lord is against them that do evil.

# July Twenty-Seven: "The Whispers Of Innocent Praises"

(As inspired from Ephesians 1:33, 11)

Lord Jesus, hear our prayer …

Blessed is The Father, The Son, and The Holy Spirit, from which all life began! Our Living World is our inheritance, a gift that is to be passed down to future generations, yet to be born; and this, we cannot deny! Please, Lord God, give consideration to our prayer request and let it become your Loving Will on Earth: Empower every soul that is born, to find your Hallowed Presence within their lives and to spiritually embrace and nurture their love for this wonderful creation that we call earth! Thank you, Lord Jesus Christ, for your welcomed Intervention and Heavenly Concern!

You have blessed us, O Lord, with a world of wonderment! And forever blessed are those, Lord Jesus, who sincerely hear and see the wonderful counsel of your Glorious Will! Each day of our earthly inheritance inspires us to be aware of all the marvelous blessings that you have bestowed upon us. And we believe, when we hear the sounds of life, that we are listening to the Hallowed Pulse of Creation! Thank you, Lord Christ, for all the innocence of nature that fills our lives and our souls. From a brilliant blossom to a soaring wing over cascading waters, whenever we witness the pristine purity that is found in living things, we are Spiritually sensing the whispers of innocent praises for you, Our Good Shepherd, whose Glorious Love exists throughout this good and grand creation! Continually, and unto forever, Lord Jesus Christ, we will express our never-ending thanks for the many Spiritual and physical blessings that we daily receive from our Heavenly Heritage of love here on earth, in a world without end!

Amen …

Chapter and verse that inspired prayer:

Ephesians 1:3, 11 Blessed be God and Father of our Lord Jesus Christ, who hath blessed us with all spiritual blessings in heavenly places in Christ: (11) In whom also we have obtained an inheritance, being predestined according to the purpose of him who worketh all things after the counsel of his will:

# July Twenty-Eight: "We Will Find Your Voice Within"

(As inspired from 2 Kings 22:19)

Lord Jesus, hear our prayer ...

Lord God, we pray that you will continually hear our heartfelt praises and consider our spiritual and temporal needs. Through the teachings of the Apostles, through the Gospels, we have come to know that you will listen to a soul that is pure and reprieved of all transgression. Most Merciful Lord, please, accept our petition of soulful reparation: We will always believe in you. Lord Jesus, we will forever love our neighbor as we love ourselves, and we will continuously commit our lives to Goodness on earth as it is done in heaven; but most of all. Our Merciful Lord, we ask that you forgive us our individual trespasses and offenses that we have each personally committed!

It is never too late to humble one's spirit and to ask for forgiveness! Lord God, there are so many paths in life, but only one True Path will lead us home. And how blessed are we to be shown the Only Way that leads to an Eternal Life! Whether in the still of the night, during the clamor of a storm, alone, or on a crowded street, when we offer a profound and sincere prayer from the spiritual center of the heart, we will find your Ever-present love, Lord Jesus; for your Power is Ever-great, and your voice is always there, guiding us, deep within the innocence of every individual soul. And when we seriously listen to that Silent Holy Intuition, we will find your voice within! And it may rear up and roar like a lion or be as quiet and gentle as a whisper, but if it truly comes from the heart, we know, Dear Lord, that it rightfully comes from you! Therefore, during times of prayer or private devotion, we will listen to our hearts, to the purity of that voice within, and we will hear your Radiant Truth and trust in our Christian faith, for all truth emanates from you, Lord Jesus Christ, Savior and Redeemer of All Souls and of All Nations!

Amen ...

Chapter and verse that inspired prayer:

2 Kings 22:19    Because thine heart was tender, and thou hast humbled thyself before the LORD, when thou heardest what I spake against this place, and against the inhabitants thereof, that they should become a desolation and a curse, and hast rent thy clothes, and wept before me; I also have heard thee, said the LORD.

# July Twenty-Nine: "We Have Completely Turned To You, Lord"
### (As inspired from Jonah 3:10)

Lord Jesus, hear our prayer …

Nothing in this world nor on this planet could ever equal or compare to a moment of your Infinite Compassion that you freely offer to all who will believe in you, accept you as their Personal Savior, and love you into eternity! Dear Lord, look into our souls! Please, witness the spiritual determination and courage that we offer to you for our own Eternal Lives that must survive this world and its temptations! To you, Lord Jesus, we vow the following: We forgo and disavow all earthly pleasures in lieu of all that is Righteous! No wealth nor material gain could ever separate us from your Holy Presence that occupies our soul!

The longing for truth and virtue in our lives, Lord Jesus, comes from the depths of our immortal souls. We deeply pray, Lord Christ, that you will inspire us to turn away from all that is wrong in this world and to faithfully pursue all that is right in life! Spiritually encourage us to surrender and follow the faultless design and purpose that you have created for us. Oh, Lord God, how happy you have made us! Your Merciful Spirit has captured our love, and our obedience has brought us to a new Spiritual Awareness: Darkness has turned into light, turmoil has turned into peace, disdain has turned into love, and we have completely turned to you, O Lord! You bring happiness to a saddened spirit, fulfillment to an empty life, and love to a broken heart! In our minds and in our souls, we resolve, Lord Jesus Christ, to always be worthy of your Endless Love and Forgiveness! Bless us, Our Lord and King, and deliver us from our transgressions as we forgive all others who have transgressed against us!

Amen …

Chapter and verse that inspired prayer:

Jonah 3:10   And God saw their works, and they turned from their evil way; and God repented of the evil, that he had said that he would do unto them; and he did it not.

# July Thirty: "Help The World To Understand"

(As inspired from Deuteronomy 30:15-16)

Lord Jesus, hear our prayer …

Heavenly Father, daily, you set before each one of us, the choices of life and doing good, and the choices of darkness and doing wrong! All praise to you, Our Lord of the Commandments, because we have chosen virtue over adversity! O Lord, a special prayer of intention for earth, for all the nations, and for all the individuals that inhabit this planet: Lord God, remove the veil of deceit from our eyes and permit everyone, everywhere, to wisely use the wisdom and intelligence that you have given us! Shepherd the very thoughts of every person in this world to be creative rather than destructive. Guide us, Lord Christ, to set common sense above greed as you inspire the entire world to build a better way to live its existence in fellowship rather than hardship!

Dear Lord, impart to everyone the knowledge of how to use your Laws of Truth and Justice for the natural order of all life. Help us to engineer and to construct our lives, our way of living, our nations, peoples, and dwellings so that they are safe and harmonious with nature. Lord Jesus Christ, as Scripture has taught us, the very essence of life lies within the very fiber of all love! Therefore, we ask of you, Lord Immanuel, help the world to understand and help all people to receive your beautiful truth, which protects and preserves that delicate thread of love that holds these living soils and our existence together. We pray: Bless this land and its people, we, who praise and give thanks in your Glorious Name, Lord God!

Lord Jesus, protect all who are faithful to your Commandments of Life! Bless all who profess their faith and love for you. And consecrate all souls to an Eternal Life who firmly believe that you, Lord Jesus, is the Christ and is born of God!

Amen …

Chapter and verse that inspired prayer:

Deuteronomy 30:15-16    See, I have set before thee this day life and good, and death and evil; (16) In that I command thee this day to love the LORD thy God, to walk in his ways, and to keep his commandments and his statutes and his judgments, that thou mayest live and multiply: and the LORD thy God shall bless thee in the land wither thou goest to possess it.

# July Thirty-One: "Through Zealous Love"
### (As inspired from Revelation 3:16, 19)

Lord Jesus, hear our prayer …

Our love and our belief in you cannot be tepid nor morally feeble. We either believe in you and your Spoken Word one hundred percent, or we have selected reservations, which, in turn, means that we are not fully privileged to the blessings of your Heavenly Throne! Protect and save us, Lord God, from the folly of our misdirection. Direct and guide us to the Perfect Path of your Righteousness.

Blessed is your Glorious Compassion for us, Lord Redeemer, for we have been ransomed from darkness through the Ultimate Sacrifice of your Never Ending Love for us! And if we have offended you in any way, Lord Jesus Christ, in what we have done or have failed to do, we ask for forgiveness. For we belong completely and only to you, Lord Christ, in mind, in body, and in spirit! And that we may never become tepid nor lukewarm in our faith, we will continually pray to you for an Ardent and Never-ending Fulfillment of your Radiant Love, Our Lord and Christ!

There is no passion in moderate faith; therefore, during prayer, we will pray that our very words of adoration will spiritually leap upwards from every faithful heart and ascend to you, Lord Christ! During prayer, we will pray that the unbounded elation of our individual souls may be lifted towards heaven for you to see! And through our waking hours, we will pray that our actions and deeds will always bring happiness and jubilance to your eyes, Lord! For whatever we do, we do for you, Lord Jesus Christ, through zealous love and willful obedience!

Amen …

Chapter and verse that inspired prayer:

Revelation 3:16, 19    So then because thou art lukewarm, and neither cold nor hot, I will spue thee out of my mouth. (19) As many as I love, I rebuke and chasten: be zealous therefore, and repent.

# August One: "Guided By Your Glowing Radiance"
### (As inspired from Genesis 49:18)

Lord Jesus, hear our prayer …

Please, O Lord, send us blessings of Knowledge and Understanding, in order that we, as Christians, may perceive the cause and effect of our personal actions upon others and upon your Heavenly Judgment. As faithful followers of your Holy Design, we desire to never offend nor affront the sanctity of your faith in us! Disappointment in one another should never be an option in word, in thought, or in individual behavior, towards the fundamental beliefs of Ethics and Goodness!

We pray for a blessing of guidance in all that we do and say. When we stand upon the darkened shores of indecision, when doubt rules the hour, or when we have lost our way, we pray to you, Lord Jesus: Redirect our lives towards a firm renewal of faith, towards a cove of spiritual hope, towards the brilliant splendor of your unequaled love! For only your love, Lord Christ, is the true beacon of personal salvation that brightly shines through the darkest storms of life, guiding all who will follow your Radiance of Righteousness to the calm water's edge of Spiritual Tranquility.

Lord God, when we profess our love for you, we move towards your Holy Spirit of Enlightenment and away from the temporal entrapments of doubt and indecision. And that we may forever be guided by your Glowing Radiance of Love, Lord Jesus, empower our faith to continually follow a course in the direction of your Unerring Righteousness! Blessed are you, Lord Jesus, Rightful and Pure is your Unparalleled Mercy and Forgiveness that we may swiftly seize the sanctified Salvation of your Glorious Word!

Amen …

Chapter and verse that inspired prayer:

Genesis 49:18    I have waited for thy salvation, O LORD.

# August Two: "Bless This Simple Temple Of Faith"
### (As inspired from 2 Corinthians 6:16)

Lord Jesus, hear our prayer …

As Christians, we celebrate the human spirit through the joy of living; for we are truly the Living Temples of God! Blessed is our creation and sanctified are our lives! Lord God, there is not a single person born, who cannot inherit and achieve what is rightfully theirs, the Kingdom of Heaven! And all we have to do, is to live according to the Commandments and Judgments of Heaven, and accept you, Lord Jesus Christ, as Our Lord and Personal Savior from all darkness and adversity of this world!

O Lord, bless this simple temple of faith that loves you, that worships you, that adores you! And from the center of our spiritual knowledge and truth, Lord Jesus, we knowingly confess that there is no lonelier road than a road that leads away from you; there is no emptier life than a life without you; and there is no darker world than a world without the Radiance of your Unblemished Love! Bless us and have mercy on us, Our Lord of the Light, and from this moment forward, night and day, remove the shadows of discontent from our lives and grant us your Heavenly Glory that it may Radiate Brightly throughout our existence on earth! Our Lord and God, we offer this simple prayer request from the depths of our Christian faith: Fill our lives with the Undeniable Presence of your Divine Love and sanction our souls with your Reigning Holiness, Dear Lord, that we may proudly proclaim to the world that our Redeemer, Jesus Christ the Promised Messiah, is our God and we are His people, and you, The Father, The Son, and The Holy Spirit abide within us, always and always, forever and ever!

Amen …

Chapter and verse that inspired prayer:

2 Corinthians 6:16    And what agreement has the temple of God with idols? For ye are the temple of the living God; as God hath said, I will be their God, and they shall be my people.

# August Three: "The Creation Of Love"
### (As inspired from Galatians 5:22-23)

Lord Jesus, hear our prayer ...

Before your Sacred Throne, there is Perpetual Love, Joy, Peace, Kindness, and the Immaculate Purity of Goodness! We bow before your Sovereign Power of Authority, Our Precious Lord, and give praise: All Perfection in our world is momentary, a fleeting whisper that quickly fades; only in your Kingdom of Heaven, Almighty God, is Perfection Everlasting! Glory be to you forever!

Throughout the world, peace loving people continually gather together, O Lord, in your name, praying to you and asking for Spiritual Consecrations in their lives, and there is but one blessing that absolutely fulfills the need in every person; and, Lord Jesus, we completely acknowledge and thank you for your Sublime Gifts of Love: Unequaled is your Gift of Forgiveness, for it is filled with joy, tranquility, mercy, and a Host of Great Wonderment and Salvation! How can we ever thank you, Lord God, for the Creation of Love and for all that exists in this world because of your Great and Holy Compassion: We thank you, Lord Christ, for the joy in our lives, for the peace in our hearts, for our Christian faith, for all gentle spirits, for temperate and meek souls, for your Longsuffering Patience, and for every person that is blessed by the Impeccable Holiness of your Loving Spirit! Without any doubt, Lord Jesus Christ, only you are deserving of all exultation and admiration throughout the entire creation; for every thing we receive on earth is a Hallowed Gift from the Immaculate Divinity of Our Blessed Trinity! Dear Lord, it is our soulful prayer request that we will be numbered among those who faithfully gather in your name to praise you, to worship you, to honor you, and to proclaim our never ending love for you! All Glory unto you, Lord of the Highest, He, Our Perfect God, who lives and reigns in His Kingdom of Heavenly Souls that also live forever and ever in Loving Grace!

Amen ...

Chapter and verse that inspired prayer:

Galatians 5:22-23    But the fruit of the Spirit is love, joy, peace, longsuffering, gentleness, faith, (23) Meekness, temperance: against such there is no law.

# August Four: "One Table, Together In One Common Faith"

### (As inspired from 1 Corinthians 10:21)

Lord Jesus, hear our prayer …

Blessed is the Sacred Mystery of the Triumvirate Nature of The Father, The Son, and The Holy Ghost! Hear our words of agreement, Lord, as we give honor to your Divine Existence as One: Exalted is your Infinite Wisdom in all things, Lord God; for the leaves and the branches on the Tree of Knowledge receive the Radiance of the Sun, and are all upheld by its Mighty Trunk, which is supported and nourished by the many roots of its Faithful Foundation, and even though The Branches, The Trunk, and The Roots are all separate and equal unto themselves, they are all united into One, as you are, Our Tree of Life!

All the world is united by your wisdom, O Lord! Even though separated by land, all the oceans of earth belong to one planet. And high above the mountains, the deserts, and the waterways, your heavenly firmament separates no people nor any country. And even though governments and lives are divided by rivers and seas, beneath every single body of water, the solid land remains as one, as The Father, The Son, and The Holy Spirit are One! Lord Jesus Christ, we pray for the Day of Miracles, when all citizens, of all tongues, everywhere, in every nation, all around the world, will unite at one table, together in one common faith, free from the boundaries and limitations of individual antipathy and hostility, unified in one belief that your Holy Spirit remains forever in the hearts of all who are faithful to your Love and Word! Lord Jesus Christ Our Prince of Peace, please, count us among the true followers of your Most Hallowed Love, faithful in all that we do, unified by your boundless Spirit of Forbearance. We pray to you, Lord Christ, let all the Partakers of Peace come together in one voice of Grand Praise: Lord God, unite all the people of this planet into One Glorious Family, devoted only to your Will and Holy Name; and in a Unification of Your Love, we, as one people in Christ, will conquer all transgression and build a mighty nation of God Fearing People!

Amen …

Chapter and verse that inspired prayer:

1 Corinthians 10:21    Ye cannot drink the cup of the Lord, and the cup of devils: ye cannot be partakers of the Lord's table, and of the table of devils.

# August Five: "We Believe In Faith"
### (As inspired from Galatians 3:22 and Matthew 17:20)

Lord Jesus, hear our prayer …

Inspire us, Lord, to see the folly of arguing religious tenets and doctrines; for what one person accepts as their personal truth, is their own individual preference. As Christians, we never have to defend our belief in you, Lord Jesus Christ, simply, because we know that you exist! And to change or alter another person's mind, life, or persuasion, a sudden and personal striking understanding must take place! Therefore, our Lord and God, we pray for all people who do not accept your Hallowed Presence in the world nor in their individual lives: May a Great Epiphany occur in the hearts and souls of all doubters, and may they come to an inner realization of your Most Redeeming Love and Saving Grace!

Our Dearest Lord, we trust in you, we believe in faith, and we are assured by the Promise of your Sanctified Word! And as you have so taught us through Scripture and inspiration, faith is the acceptance of that which is unknown, but will be known. And that we may grow spiritually, physically, and mentally in your eyes, Lord Jesus, we pray for a total and complete wholeness of our inner belief. For we acknowledge, O Lord, that through pure faith, all concerns of the heart are made known; through sincere faith, all physical difficulties will be resolved; and through absolute faith, all thoughts and emotions will be enlightened by your Truth! Lord God, help each one of us to be loyal and dedicated to all that we know is true, to all that we are, and to all that we can be. Please, Lord Jesus Christ, authorize our spirits and our minds to fully comprehend that nothing is impossible through Total Spiritual Acceptance; a miracle of belief that is given freely to every Christian from the depths of your Merciful and Immaculate Heart!

Amen …

Chapter and verse that inspired prayer:

Galations 3:22   But the scripture hath concluded all under sin, that the promise by faith of Jesus Christ might be given to them that believe.

Matthew 17:20   And Jesus said unto them, Because of your unbelief: for verily I say unto you, If you have faith as a mustard seed, ye shall say unto this mountain, Remove hence to yonder place; and it shall remove; and nothing shall be impossible unto you.

# August Six: "Your Sheltering Arms"

(As inspired from John 11:25-26)

Lord Jesus, hear our prayer …

The Meaning of Life is within each one us, it is not a secret, and it is not locked up nor hidden away, it is you, Lord Jesus Our Meaning of Life, whom resides within all of us!

Heavenly Father, it is our soulful understanding that all the problems of this world cannot be solved nor resolved without the sincere acceptance of your Divine Spirit within the hearts of all humankind! We pray that you will send to earth a blessing of Heavenly Prosperity, Lord God, that everyone may become rich in the fulness of the Holy Ghost! Please, hear our prayer: Lord Jesus, you are The Beginning and The Ending, you are The Circle of Life, The Final Judgment, The Deliverer of Our Souls, and to the world, we proudly proclaim our belief in you that we may not parish, but exist in Eternal Life!

We, who love you, who worship you, and who believe in you, Lord God, are most grateful for your Loving Presence in our lives; because, spiritual existence would be impossible without you! O Lord, you are the Light and the Hope for All Souls! And even when we spiritually stand upon the distant shores of doubt, surrounded by the depths of darkness, and discomforted by the storms of dissension, it is you, Lord Jesus, that hears the sounds of our faraway cries. In you, Lord God, is our true faith and our solemn belief! Oh, Lord, although we may be on earth, far from your sheltering arms, it is the Radiance of your Love that guides us and will return us to the green pastures of your Heavenly Fold! Have mercy on us, Lord Jesus Christ, that we may one day come back to the Spiritual Home of your Everlasting Embrace and live eternally, forever renewed in your Loving Spirit of Grace: In this we attest and believe with total heart and soul

Amen …

Chapter and verse that inspired prayer:

John 11:25-26   Jesus said unto her, I am the resurrection, and the life: he that believeth in me, though he were dead, yet shall he live: (26) And whosoever liveth and believeth in me shall never die. Believest thou this?

# August Seven: "There Is No Greater Authority"

### (As inspired from Nehemiah 9:5 and Exodus 20:7)

Lord Jesus, hear our prayer …

All who are faithful to your Word, Lord God, stand together and praise your Sacred Name; and never will we use your name in vain! From you, we receive Spiritual Radiance. Through you, we are given sanctuary from all harm and discord. And in you, there is Absolute Spiritual Power! Throughout the storms of life, Dear Lord, we know that you will always shelter us from all conflict; for there is no Greater Authority, nor any presence more powerful, than you, Our Most Holy and Sacred Lord Jesus Christ! We seek and receive refuge in you during times of trouble and confusion; nothing is able to overcome nor destroy the Holy and Divine Protection that your Name accords! Therefore, through your Beautiful Presence in our lives, and through your Ordained Will, whatever is commanded to be on earth, as it is in heaven, will be! This we believe in with total confidence and in all certitude!

Where there is a will, there most definitely is a way! And through your All Knowing Holy Spirit, Lord Christ, our souls will always know the Precise Way to go; because it is your Way and your Will, Lord Jesus, that we live for! Blessed and Holy is your Exalted Name, Lord Jesus Christ, now and forevermore: For You and The Father are one! You are The Son of God! You are The Son of Man! You are the Everlasting! You are The Word Made Flesh! You are The Crystal Clear Waters of Life! And through your name, our bonds are forever broken! O Lord, our lives find jubilation in this extraordinary knowledge of Spiritual Understanding: All wonder and thanksgiving to you for sharing this Heavenly Discernment with your faithful! Amen!

Amen …

Chapter and verse that inspired prayer:

Nehemiah 9:5    Then the Levites, Jeshua, and Kadmiel, Bani, Hashabiah, Sherebiah. Hodijah, Shebaniah, and Pethahiah, said, Stand up and bless the LORD your God for ever and ever: and blessed be thy glorious name, which is exalted above all blessing and praise.

Exodus 20:7    Thou shalt not take the name of the LORD thy God in vain; for the LORD will not hold him guiltless that taketh his name in vain.

# August Eight: "Towers of Compassion"
### (As inspired from Luke 20:17)

Lord Jesus, hear our prayer …

There is a Timeless and Sacred Truth beyond all doubt, that your Holy Spirit resides within the confines of the forgiven soul, and all we have to do to obtain your Mercy, Lord Jesus, is to simply ask for forgiveness! Hear our confessions of love and our personal desires to be free of all temporal bondage as we ask for Spiritual Purification: Cleanse our souls, Lord Jesus, that you will hear our prayer requests, for you are The Tree of Life and The Lord of All Spiritual Knowledge, and your Love has set us free from our earthly confines of superstition, unreasonable fear of the unknown, and belief in idols and objects of passionate devotion! We confide only in you, Lord Jesus Christ, who is the Spiritual Object of our soulful affection!

We thank you for the shelter over our heads. We praise you for the food that feeds and nourishes our bodies. But most of all, we honor you for being so Loving and so Merciful! Lord God, you have given us this day and our daily needs, you are the Foundation of the World, the Embodiment of Love, and the Cornerstone of Our Existence on Earth! Lord Jesus Christ, it is our total desire to build our Christian lives around your Eternal Message of Truth! Day after day, as if placing stone upon stone, in a labor of love, our individual souls are building and becoming towers of compassion, built upon the Impeccable Foundation of Your Word! Lord of Life, receive our humble confession of truth: We will never reject you in word, in thought, or in spirit! Inspire us, Christ Our King, and protect us from all failure in life as we boldly shape and face our destinies towards the Celestial Direction of your Heavenly Spirit and Kingdom!

Amen …

Chapter and verse that inspired prayer:

Luke 20:17    And he beheld them, and said. What is this then that is written, The corner stone which the builders rejected, the same is become the head of the corner?

# August Nine: "Everyday Miracles"

(As inspired from Deuteronomy 29:2-6)

Lord Jesus, hear our prayer …

We are thankful to you, Lord of Heaven and Earth and All That Exists, for our blessing of faith: Because with faith, we truly understand and accept what a a miracle is and why they are possible! And during every part of our human existence, throughout all time and generations, through great signs and great trials, you have led your chosen people, Lord God, and you have given miraculous blessings of everyday miracles: An immortal soul that is touched by your Holy Spirit, a tender heart to perceive your Word of Mercy, clear eyes to comprehend and see your many works, and a sense of hearing that we, through the Gospels, may learn about the Revelations and Wonders of your Hallowed Existence! And in all that you have done for your faithful followers, for this world, for everyone, everywhere, permit us now to individually celebrate your Life Giving Bounty of Love! Lord Jesus, through personal praise and thanks, we exalt your Infinite and Unceasing Abundance of Divine Wisdom; for we are forever surrounded by your Many Works of Love! And whenever thoughts of uncertainty begin to gather upon the emotional realms of our individual lives, we will keep them far from us, Lord Christ, by increasing our personal Christian faith through the Power of Perfect Prayer: Lord Jesus Christ, we ask in your Sacred Name, let the might of your Eternal Holiness bring the calm of peace into our lives, silence the winds of indecision, and permit the Perfect Light of your Protective Radiance to shine down upon us and gather together all who love you and believe in your Majestic Name, and this we ask before the Purity of your Guiltless and Holy Throne of Justice!

Amen …

Chapter and verse that inspired prayer:

Deuteronomy 29:2-6    And Moses called unto all Israel, and said unto them, Ye have seen all that the LORD did before your eyes in the land of Egypt unto Pharaoh, and unto all his servants, and unto all his land; (3) The great temptations which thine eyes have seen, the signs, and those great miracles: (4) Yet the LORD hath not given you an heart to perceive, and eyes to see, and ears to hear, unto this day. (5) And I have led you forty years in the wilderness: your clothes are not waxen old upon you, and thy shoe is not waxen old upon thy foot. (6) Ye have not eaten bread, neither have ye drunk wine or strong drink: that ye might know that I am the LORD your God.

# August Ten: "Children Of Faith"
### (As inspired from 2 John 1-3)

Lord Jesus, hear our prayer …

Lord God, we pray that the entire world will one day realize the importance for every child to retain their spiritual, mental, and physical innocence throughout their developing years into adulthood. For it is during this time, that reason, compassion, and understanding shape their adult lives!

Lord, we pray for the physical, mental, and spiritual welfare of all children on earth: Bless the children of the world! And on behalf of every child, Lord Jesus, we pray that everyone, everywhere, who touches the heart and soul of a young person, may enlighten that child's faith in the knowledge of virtue and allow their innocence to continually grow in the direction of your Just Judgments; because children of faith become the future of their faith! And through Peace, Mercy, and Grace, Lord God, we pray that everyone, everyday, will remember in their own prayers, to pray for all the sons and daughters of this world; for everyone truly deserves assurance and encouragement in their life! And in all truth, and in all love, may the Grace of your Glorious Compassion, Lord of Peace, be found in all adults that have a family to raise; may the Sanctity of your Mercy, Lord of Compassion, shield all children from the perils of this world. And please, allow the Blissful Joy of your Harmony, Lord of Life, to be with them and to direct them, now and forevermore! We pray for a world, where all young people are prospering in their spiritual well-being, Our Lord Jesus Christ, which will create a promising future for all Christian generations yet to come into the Light; and let it begin today, now, in the name of Our Heavenly Father of Mercy, The Son of Truth, and The Holy Spirit of Love!

Amen …

Chapter and verse that inspired prayer:

2 John 1-3    The elder unto the elect lady and her children, whom I love in truth; and not I only, but also all they that have known the truth; (2) For the truth's sake, which dwelleth in us, and shall be with us for ever. (3) Grace be with you, mercy, and peace, from God the Father, and from the Lord Jesus Christ, the Son of the Father, in truth and love.

# August Eleven: "Your Love, Lord, Remains Constant"
### (As inspired from Micah 6:8)

Lord Jesus, hear our prayer …

Through your Immaculate Conception and Birth, Lord Jesus Christ, every true Christian believes that the Heavenly Father, Our God and Creator, was made manifest on earth; and through the out pouring of your Holy Spirit upon the world, your faithful have achieved Forgiveness and Redemption! We are followers of your Incorruptible Love, Lord God! And according to the Scriptures of your Magnificent Word, you have shown us what you require of your faithful: To worship and serve God with all of our might, to love one another, to be just, to show mercy, to forgive, to be without boastful pride, to stand in the Light of Goodness, and to always be faithful to your Every Word! Pray for us, Lord Jesus, that we may remain constant and strong in our amazing and wondrous Christian faith!

Your Compassion, Lord of Life, is the Sacred Fire that brightly burns in the darkness of the world. And like the stars at night, and the sun during the day, your Tender Love, Our Lord and God, remains constant! And if we should ever wander from your Beautiful Radiance, Lord Jesus, we know that your Light will constantly remain with us as a beacon, beckoning our return to your Loving Grace and Forgiveness!

Lord of Heaven and Earth, you hear our prayers when we stand in the light or when we stumble in the night. Strengthen us now, Lord Jesus, and inspire us that we may never stray from your Hallowed Existence, that we may forever remain firm in our Christian belief, and that we may always walk in the Splendor of your Perpetual Love. Fill our hearts and spirits with genuine humility, Lord Jesus Christ, that our love for you will boldly radiate throughout the whole of the universe, now and into the Eternal Realm of Mercy!

Amen …

Chapter and verse that inspired prayer:

Micah 6:8   He hath shewed thee, O man, what is good; and what doth the LORD require of thee, but to do justly, and to love mercy, and to walk humbly with thy God?

# August Twelve: "We Declare The Glory Of Your Compassion"
### (As inspired from Judges 5:31)

Lord Jesus, hear our prayer …

Today, as everyday, let us begin anew! May the enemies of love and goodness be turned from their ways, Lord God; accord all people to awaken in a renewed vision of hope and promise. Lord Jesus, permit everyone in the world see the glory and the beauty of life as you have so intended. Inspire everybody, Lord Christ, to envision a world that is filled with the warmth of your Great Love and your Great Goodness! Lord Jesus Christ, lead us away from all temptation and deliver us from the powers of darkness; for the Authority of your Love is More Commanding than anything on earth or anything that exists in the universe! Please, hear our plea for all people in all nations: Sanction every mind to understand that the woes of this world are not with you, Lord God, but with all humankind! Permit every soul to perceive the folly of transgression, and to know that it is us, as humans, who withdraw from the Light through our personal actions and resolutions; because, the Light will never withdraw from us!

Today, as everyday, O Lord, we proclaim the excellence of every blessing that you have bestowed upon us! And through your Love Blessings, our visions for the future are clear and our courses are set. Lord Jesus Christ, as we declare the Glory of your Compassion, allow us to continually walk forthright, free from all that is dishonest or done in the shadows of secrecy and deceit! And from our deepest desires for world accord, we ask with heart and soul, to please, direct all the enemies of peace to turn from their troubled ways and gain a new sense of living life through Harmony and Contentment, satisfied fully by the Tenderness of your Spiritual Kindness!

Amen …

Chapter and verse that inspired prayer:

Judges 5:31   So let all thine enemies perish, O LORD: but let them that love him be as the sun when he goeth forth in his might. And the land had rest forty years.

# August Thirteen: "Fill The Void In Their Hearts"

(As inspired from Acts of the Apostles 26:18 and John 13:34)

Lord Jesus, hear our prayer …

The Gospels are sincere and real; and all that you say is Clearly the Truth! Dear Lord, we pray that you will return us to the Purity of Christianity through the total elimination of all division from the New Commandment that you gave to us: That we should love one another as you loved us and as we love one another; and by this shall the world know that all Christians are one, sanctified in the unity of their belief in you! Lord God, bless us and increase the faith of Christianity throughout the known world: We pray for your blessing of Everlasting Forgiveness, O Lord, as we also pray for those who have yet to find you. Allow your Salvation to flow into the souls of all who are unaware of your Beautiful Presence in their lives. We pray for those who have never experienced the Truth of your Word; and we plead to you, Lord Jesus, to intervene into their lives. We pray for those who have never seen the Glory and the Righteousness of your Radiant Light of Hope; for they have eyes but are unable to see through their darkness. We pray for those who have never heard the Innocence of your Living Spirit throughout the world; for they have ears but cannot hear the Immaculate Harmony in your creation! And we pray for those who have never felt your True Compassion in life; for they have hearts that beat without purpose or passion. Lord Jesus Christ, hear our urgent prayers for all who are spiritually barren: Fill the void in their hearts, make known your Loving Spirit that exists in their lives, give them the wisdom to believe in you, and compel their souls to be complete through the Holy and Spiritual Presence of your Wondrous Love! Thank you, Lord God, for hearing our soulful and impassioned prayers!

Amen …

Chapter and verse that inspired prayer:

Acts of the Apostles 26:18    To open their eyes, and to turn them from darkness to light, and from the power of Satan unto God, that they may receive forgiveness of sins, and inheritance among them which are sanctified by faith that is in me.

John 13:34                    A new commandment I give unto you, That ye love one another; as I have loved you, that ye also love one another

# August Fourteen: "Uncertainties Will Cast Shadows"
(As inspired from Luke 11:17)

Lord Jesus, hear our prayer ...

When family and friends and even strangers unite in a single purpose, the power behind their faith intensifies and challenges all opposition and diversity; and it is for this reason that we entreat you in prayer, Lord Jesus: Baptize and unite all Christians throughout the world, Our Lamb of God, in the Beautiful Living Waters that continually flow from your Great and Sacred Throne of Life! Sanction our eternal souls to resist all transgression and deliver our spirits into the Loving Embrace of your Heavenly Fold! Lord, you always know what is in our hearts and in our thoughts. May our soulful intentions forever be unified with your Desired Purpose and Design that you established for us in this world. We pray that you will Fortify and Strengthen the Spiritual Goals of Everyone, everywhere, allowing all people to come together in friendship and fellowship, unified in faith, that we may be of One Purpose and of One Mind when serving your Will, Lord Jesus Our Christ! Please, command us to individually realize that a house divided cannot stand, that a family in turmoil cannot survive, that fractured love must be mended or will fragment even further, and that individual uncertainties will cast shadows of personal doubt upon oneself. Lord of Hope, encourage all the people in the world to become unified in one direction, with one peaceful objective, for a common presence of heart and soul, and that is to serve your Divine Purpose and Design, which was created solely for us even before time began; Lord God, we pray for Universal Resolution: Please, Lord Jesus, bless this planet and all its inhabitants with Everlasting Peace and Resolution!

Amen ...

Chapter and verse that inspired prayer:

Luke 11:17     But he, knowing their thoughts, said unto them, Every kingdom divided against itself is brought to desolation; and a house divided against a house falleth.

# August Fifteen: "We Follow No Other"

(As inspired from Luke 4:8)

Lord Jesus, hear our prayer …

In the evening, whenever we look up at the stars and gaze into the infinite depths of space, we are thankful to you, O Lord, for our world! For in the universe, there are barren moons and planets, void of anything alive: No flowers or trees, no oceans or rains, no spirit of presence, only plains of loneliness and shadows of desolation. But, the earth is a planet of life! Bless you greatly, Lord Jesus, for this miraculous creation and our physical existence!

Every innocent soul holds in their heart a heavenly vision of life, and its earthly attainment is possible, simply, through a sincere acceptance of you, Lord Jesus, through faith! For there is only One God in the universe, and, Lord Jesus Christ, you are The One, He, who sacrificed His life that all may obtain Eternal Life after this world! And we offer our deepest and most spiritual of adoration to the Glory and Fulfillment of your selfless Mission on earth! Praised be you unto eternity, Our Lord and God Jesus Christ!

We live and exist only for you, Lord Jesus. No promise of fortune or fame or glory could make us unfaithful to you! Not for all the wealth of this world would we turn aside from you, Lord Christ! Not for all the knowledge in the world would we forget you! And not for all the power that exists would we serve any other but you, Lord Jesus Christ. For you are the Way, and we follow no other way but the Perfect Way, the Way of Truth, the Way of Love, the Way of your Absolute Will! Lord, may your Peace and Forgiveness abound throughout the nations of the world and throughout the hearts of all peoples in every nation of the world! Bless us all, Lord God, and sanctify us through our faith in you; and there you shall abide within our midst, now and forevermore, until all eternity passes away!

Amen …

Chapter and verse that inspired prayer:

Luke 4:8    And Jesus answered and said unto him, Get thee behind me, Satan: for it is written, Thou shalt worship the Lord thy God, and him only shalt thou serve.

# August Sixteen: "Greet One Another With Peace"

### (As inspired from 1 Peter 5:14)

Lord Jesus, hear our prayer …

Through warm and genuine greetings of peace, strangers become friends, and friends become as family! Friendship is a Gift from you, Lord God, that we, as humans, may share with one another: Our emotions, our passions, our dreams and visions, our problems, our resolutions, our goals and achievements, and our personal space on earth as allotted by you, Our Lord Jesus Christ! Bless you for all the harmony in our lives and all the good days that we experience in life!

Our dreams are achieved only through a deep faith in our Christian convictions, and we pray to you, Lord Christ, to sanction our individual lives, according to the depth of our personal belief, with the Overpowering Presence of your Undeniable Love; and proof of your Love for us, Lord God, is monumental! And wherever we stand, we witness the evidence of your Heavenly Compassion: Whether on a crowded street or in an empty room of life, the echoes of the past remain constant and pure, reminders of who we are as Christians and where we are in time. Alone, or together with others, we are all bound to a Great and Eternal Love of Forgiveness and Compassion for one another! Everywhere we look, Lord Jesus, there exists Numerous Manifestations of your Unmistakable Love: Your Love is greater than all the treasures of the world, more radiant than all the stars of the universe, and more vast than infinity! Lord Jesus, permit us, as faithful Christians, to prove our love for you through personal praise and through a sincere showing of love for one another. For as you have taught the world through the teachings of your Holy Scripture, there is no greater testimony of love for you, Lord Jesus Christ, than a true showing of love for one another. And through a humble act of love and kindness, let us always greet one another with peace in our hearts and a warm and loving smile on our faces.

Amen …

Chapter and verse that inspired prayer:

1 Peter 5: 14    Greet ye one another with a kiss of charity. Peace be with you all that are in Christ Jesus. Amen.

# August Seventeen: "You Will Always Provide"

### (As inspired from Luke 18:27)

Lord Jesus, hear our prayer …

When our pathways seem darkest, when life's storms appear on the horizon, when we have used up every resource and there is no way out, Lord, we have found, through every adversity, that you will always provide! For only you, Lord Christ, can calm the ravaging seas, heal the sick, and even raise the dead! You, Lord Jesus, Purvey and Work Miracles of love that gives strength to every human need! Therefore, with our deepest assurance of faith in you, Lord Jesus Christ, we know that you have been and will always be there for us, yesterday, today, and even into tomorrow! Lord, give us the unbridled stamina to meet and to conquer our limitations. Prepare us mentally, Lord God, to face up to and to resolve the challenges of daily life. And grant us, Lord of Truth, the ability to understand that nothing on earth is impossible when you are with us!

Where we are, and whatever we are doing, grant us, Lord, the physical, mental, and spiritual determination to overcome our weaknesses. Lift our spirits to endure and prevail over the daily trials and tribulations of life. But most of all, Lord Jesus Christ, we are very thankful that you are with us, that you abide within our lives, and that you will remain with us forever; for all that is known to be impossible for us, Lord God, is possible with you! Therefore, Our Good Lord and Protector, we worship, pray, and give all praise to your Splendor and Wonder and Awe: Because of your Triumphant Victory, Our Lord Jesus, there is not a single existing soul that ever needs to be trapped within the dark reaches of doubt and fear, because our pathways to Eternal Happiness have been cleared!

Amen …

Chapter and verse that inspired prayer:

Luke 18:27    And he said, The things which are impossible with men are possible with God.

# August Eighteen: "Our Purpose On Earth"

### (As inspired from Romans 9:17)

Lord Jesus, hear our prayer …

Through Great Wisdom, our Lord raises up those to rule and those to be ruled. We pray to you, Lord God, sanctify the decisions of those who govern us, and bless us with the ability too always discriminate between right and wrong. Pray for us, Our Good Lord, that we will not blindly follow the actions and precepts of others; rather, let us always evaluate our personal conduct as Christians, according to your every Commandment!

Through you, Lord Jesus, every question has an answer; for every mystery, there is resolution; for every problem there is solution; and in this, there is no small doubt. A single blade of grass or a tall oak tree or a gentle moving stream all have reason and purpose for existing on earth. Please, Our Lord Christ, encourage us to serve you and to fulfill our true purpose on earth as you have so graciously intended for us, O Lord, and grant us the intuitive capability to understand and to accept our rightful significance in your creation. Help us to achieve whatever we are meant to accomplish in our lifetimes as Christians and empower us to fully appreciate any and all of our personal responsibilities and commitments that are within our control to a complete and satisfactory conclusion; for it is our desire to find our individual worth and meaning in life! Therefore, inspire us, Lord Jesus, to accomplish all that you have designed for us, in this we pray! But most of all, we ask, how best may we serve you, Our Lord Jesus Christ! For it is our utmost prayer and deepest desire to work for the spiritual betterment of all humanity throughout this wonderful world! Lord Creator, allow all who cherish this good earth, this creation of love, to work together in your Glorious Name for a Planet of Perfect Peace, through your Holiness and our mission and purpose on earth!

Amen …

Chapter and verse that inspired prayer:

Romans 9:17    For the scripture saith unto Pharaoh, Even for this same purpose have I raised thee up, that I might show my power in thee, and that my name might be declared throughout all the earth.

# August Nineteen: "We Are Faithful And True Believers"

(As inspired from Joshua 24:14)

Lord Jesus, hear our prayer …

Lord Jesus Christ, you are the Word of God, the Spirit Made Flesh, and the True Redemption for all humanity! How fortunate we are, Our Anointed One, to know that all who follow you are your Chosen People, and we, as loyal Christians, who believe in you, are forever faithful to your Immaculate Word of Love! Therefore, according to the First Commandment, we are not to have any false gods before us; because, all belief and worship in foreign entities and idols is an abomination to your Most Hallowed Glory! Blessed are you, Lord God, for you are the Only One we worship!

Our love for you, Lord God, is deeply rooted in the depths of our heartfelt trust that we have in you. And we pray to you, Our Lord Jesus, that every person of sincere and committed faith will forever remain in the direction of your Loving Spirit, no matter which way the ill winds of life's uncertainties and adversities may blow. Lord Christ, we pray that every human soul will always have the spiritual fortitude to withstand and defeat the challenges of inner doubt and personal uncertainties; for our reliance is totally in you, Lord of Forgiveness, and is forged from our continual confidence in your Most Holy Statutes and Judgments! O Lord, we are united in determination and certainty, and we proclaim that your Holy Spirit continually protects and guides all faithful believers of your Merciful and Infinite Love. All praises to you, Lord Jesus Christ, for we are faithful and true believers in you, in your Word, and in your Divine Power of Love; and it is only you, Lord God, who Reigns Supreme in Heaven and on Earth, whom, we wish to serve in body, mind, and spirit!

Amen …

Chapter and verse that inspired prayer:

Joshua 24:14    Now therefore fear the LORD, and serve him in sincerity and in truth: and put away the gods which your fathers served on the other side of the flood, and in Egypt; and serve ye the LORD.

# August Twenty: "Your Divine Words Fulfill"
### (As inspired from 1 Thessalonians 2:12-13)

Lord Jesus, hear our prayer …

Your Sacred Heart, Lord Christ, is the center of our universe! Your Holy Spirit is the Essence of our Existence! And your Hallowed Word is our reason for Living! Believe us, Lord Jesus, as we profess our never ending desire to remain within the gracious blessings of your Immaculate Protection: Lord God, we have been Spiritually Inspired to call upon your Heavenly Kingdom and Glory; praise be to you, O Lord, because, your faithful shall walk in The Light for all eternity!

Bless those, Lord God, who freely believe and freely receive of your Holy Spirit! Lord Jesus, our thoughts fill with grateful acknowledgment as we reflect upon our countless blessings; how fortunate we are to be in the Good Graces of your All Inspiring Love. Lord Christ, our hearts fill with happiness as we give thanks to you for the food that feeds and fulfills our physical needs. Lord Jesus Christ, our spirits leap with joy as we give praise to you for the Heavenly Words that feed and fulfill our spiritual needs on earth; how blessed we are to receive your Sacred Word of Life! And that we may continue to be worthy of your blessings, Our Living Lord, it is our prayer that all people of all nations will gladly and joyfully receive of your Spiritual Nourishment! May your Blessed Words of Faith and Hope be shared by all who hunger for the Spirit of Truth; because, your Divine Words fulfill and answer the needs of every man, woman, and child that globally exist on this most incredible planet and who continually pray to you for Guidance and for the Unconquerable Protection of Heaven! And into all eternity, we shall forevermore remain diligent in our Christian efforts to walk worthy in your sight, Our King of Glory!

Amen …

Chapter and verse that inspired prayer:

1 Thessalonians 2:12-13   That ye would walk worthy of God, who hath called you unto his kingdom and glory. (13) For this cause also thank we God without ceasing, because, when ye received it not as the word of men, but as it is in truth, the word of God, which effectually worketh also in you that believe.

# August Twenty-One: "All Time Is Of Your Design"

(As inspired from Psalms 119:108-109)

Lord Jesus, hear our prayer …

Our Heavenly King, your Most Precious Lessons are found throughout chapter and verse in the Glorious Gospels of your Magnificent Life, as spoken in Gethsemane, when you prayed to the Holy Father, " …let this cup pass from me, nevertheless not my will but as thou wilt," has taught us that our freewill is not necessarily the Will of God, but our own personal choice. It is a will that you freely gave to us, from which we may individually prove our love for you, Lord Jesus, by correctly choosing the direction of right and goodness over all that is wrong and adverse! Therefore, we pray that our decisions in life will always follow the Divine Will of The Father, The Son, and The Holy Spirit!

No angel in heaven nor any other living creature on earth has been blessed with freedom of choice! Thank you, Dear Lord, for our Heavenly Gift of Freewill and for our ability to choose our own direction and course in life. It is truly a blessing, Lord Jesus, that any person may change their own destiny, simply by changing their convictions in life. And as individual Christians, we have each personally chosen to follow your Unparalleled Path throughout our lives, which you have so divinely planned for every loving spirit, Lord Christ. And from the beginning of time until the end of time, all time is of your design! Our lives and destinies are completely in your Glorious Power, Lord Jesus Christ, and whatever you determine for our future, we will faithfully accept your judgment as flawless and certain. Into your Merciful Hands, Lord of Life, do we place the salvation of our souls and our lives and our futurities!

Amen …

Chapter and verse that inspired prayer:

Psalms 119:108-109   Accept, I beseech thee, the freewill offerings of my mouth, O LORD, and teach me thy judgments. (109) My soul is continually in my hand: yet do I not forget thy law.

# August Twenty-Two: "The Rewards Of Trust"

(As inspired from Ruth 2:12)

Lord Jesus, hear our prayer …

A misconception about the Old Testament, of which many people are unaware, is that its message does not live in the past, but is alive and well in the present! All the mistakes that nations and peoples generated Thousands of Years Ago, are still being made, and made against the Lord's Commandments; it is a pity that we do not listen to and Remember Our History and God's Will. May our Lord Jesus Christ strengthen our Spiritual Understanding, to hold firmly in our hearts, the Beautiful Judeo-Christian stories given to us in the Old and New Testaments.

Lord God, we hope and we pray that we started this day in the favor of your Holy Way! Your Hallowed Purpose is the singular reason for our existence in this world! And everyday that we awaken from the darkness into the Light of your Redemption, we offer thanks and praise for our salvation; for a sincere prayer spoken in the still of the night is more powerful than the dark and hollow stillness of the night. And throughout all the ages of time, through Scripture, through your Blessed Words, Lord Jesus, you have shown us that the power of faith is a simple act of belief. And through this innocent and humble action, the rewards of trust will fill a lonely and saddened heart with happiness; for truly, faith is the foundation of unfailing hope and the full reward of your Noble and Sacred Word!

Take us under your Protective Wings, O Lord, and watch over us all the days of our lives: Today and everyday, Lord, we will have complete faith and total reliance in you! From the beginning until the end, all that we are, we owe to you! And all that we can be, we pray to you! For all that we need, we receive through a trusting faith in your Beautiful Words of Truth as found throughout the Bible; because only you, Lord Jesus Christ, can restore and give Spiritual Restitution to an empty life; blessed are you, Lord God, and blessed are all who willingly and lovingly follow you each and every day of their life, even to the end of days!

Amen …

Chapter and verse that inspired prayer:

Ruth 2:12    The LORD recompense thy work, and a full reward be given of the LORD God of Israel, under whose wings thou art come to trust.

# August Twenty-Three: "An Edifice Of Goodness"

(As inspired from Hebrews 11:32-34)

Lord Jesus, hear our prayer …

From kings to shepherds, bond or free, men and women, children or seniors, all races, creeds, and languages, your Promise of Victory is a conflict already won; because, throughout all the ages, Our Lord and God, you have protected those whose deep faith in you was unmovable! All Praise and Glory to you, Our Heavenly King!

Bless us and inspire us, O Lord, to proudly stand up for what we morally and spiritually believe in! Wrought and shaped through the Holy and Spiritual influences of prayer and patience, we continually aspire to become living symbols of our Christian faith, Lord Christ! And just as a massive mountain casts its shadow, as a towering oak withstands a storm, or a mighty river carves out its path, we too desire to become vigorous and spirited symbols of our wonderful faith! Please hear us, Lord Jesus, for we each deeply seek to become an Edifice of Goodness, of spiritual strength, and of total obedience to your Word! And like the prophets of old, Lord God, we pray that our faith will overshadow all adversity, that our personal confidence will tower over the doubting mind, and that our moral convictions will carve out an unswerving path of devotion that will never alter or divert from its intended course and purpose; which is to serve our Lord and God, night and day! And Blest are you, Lord Jesus Christ, for you have always been the Intended Course and Purpose throughout all the endless ages of time; as it was in the beginning, is now, and forever shall be, you, Lord God, are the Path of Pure Righteousness!

Amen …

Chapter and verse that inspired prayer:

Hebrews 11:32-34  And what shall I more say? For the time would fail to tell of Gedeon, and of Barak, and of Samson, and of Jephthae; of David also, and Samuel, and of the prophets: (33) Who through faith subdued kingdoms, wrought righteousness, obtained promises, stopped the mouths of lions, (34) Quenched the violence of fire, escaped the edge of the sword, out of weakness were made strong, waxed valiant in fight, turned to flight the armies of the aliens.

# August Twenty-Four: "True Blessings Of Mercy"
### (As inspired from Acts of the Apostles 8:22")

Lord Jesus, hear our prayer …

Forgiveness is perhaps the singular most important Faithbased Blessing that a Soul may give or receive in their lifetime. Imagine in our own lives, never obtaining Mercy through any Trespass, given or prayed for. We Thank You, Lord Jesus, for Your Perfect Redemption in our daily lives.

Our Lord and Protector Jesus Christ, forgive us our transgressions this day, tomorrow, and throughout all the days of our lives! Thank you, Lord, for the blessing of Spiritual Deliverance; for your Redemptive Power will always release us from our own personal bondage. If we have wronged you in any way, Lord Jesus, forgive us; for it was done out of ignorance. If we have wronged someone else, we pray to you, Lord Christ, that they will forgive us; for what we did was unjustly done to another. And as individuals, loyal Christians, if we have wronged ourselves, we pray to you, Lord Jesus Christ, that we may be able to forgive ourselves; for we will have actually betrayed our own heart and faith.

Everyday, we transgress because we are human, and everyday, we must ask for your forgiveness because you are our Lord and God, He, who died for our transgressions that we may have Spiritual Grace! Therefore, only through your Never-ending Forgiveness and True Blessings of Mercy, Lord Jesus, will we ever become whole. Nothing on earth can give us Perfect Fulfillment, and no one else can make us Totally Complete except you, Lord of Mercy! We pray for, we accept, and we believe in your Gifts of Clemency, Lord Jesus Christ, for only through you will anyone ever receive Heartfelt Compassion, Unwavering Forgiveness, and a True Understanding of your Presence as it is meant to be within the heart, the mind, and the immortal soul! We thank you, Lord, for everything, but most of all, for your Love, which is the Essence in your Compelling Call to Salvation!

Amen …

Chapter and verse that inspired prayer:

Acts of the Apostles 8:22  Repent therefore of this thy wickedness, and pray God, if perhaps the thought of thine heart may be forgiven thee.

# August Twenty-Five: "You Are The Lord Of love"

### (As inspired from Ezekiel 11:19-20)

Lord Jesus, hear our prayer …

Lord God, through sincere belief in you, all people in the world have the same opportunity to receive a new spirit of life, a heart that beats with compassion, and a confident destiny to follow! Blessed are you, Our Savior Lord Jesus! For you are the Lord of love, and whenever we pray to you, Lord Jesus, we know that only the Purest of Love Emanates from your Sacred Heart! We know that only the Deepest of Forgiveness is given by your Holy Spirit! And we also know that only the Greatest of Compassion is shown by your Mercy, Lord Christ! And for all of these wonderful reasons, we are truly humbled whenever we pray to you, Lord of Life; for we know that we must pray to you with a pure heart, a cleansed soul, and a deep spiritual conviction, giving to you, Lord God, only the highest and greatest of praises that our souls may bestow! And as we individually pray to you, Lord of Mercies, we also ask that every individual throughout the known world may be permitted to learn of your Beautiful Truth and Hallowed Purity! We also pray that every person on earth will learn to trust in your Absolute Word of Perfection! Lord Jesus Christ, concur your Heavenly Wisdom to always be passed on from one Christian generation unto another generation through all the passing of time, throughout all nations, and throughout all the different tongues that exist on this planet, until the end of time; and then, everyone, everywhere, will come to know that they are, without any doubt, your people and that you are their Lord, The Lord of All Souls, The Lord and God of All People, Lord Jesus Christ Our Great and Compassionate King!

Amen …

Chapter and verse that inspired prayer:

Ezekiel 11:19-20   And I will give them one heart, and I will put a new spirit within you; and I will take the stony heart out of their flesh, and will give them an heart of mine ordinances, and do them: and they shall be my people, and I will be their God.

# August Twenty-Six: "Never Render Empty Promises"

(As inspired from James 5:12)

Lord Jesus, hear our prayer …

All throughout the Gospels, Our Heavenly Lord, you have shown us countless times that a person's word is their personal signature of truth! And for this reason, we praise your Signature of Truth, because it is never broken! Lord Jesus, help us, as Christians, to understand the importance of fulfilling one's word when it is given to others; bless us with a conscious reasoning to see that the fulfillment of positive intention has always been your Unfailing Way!

We turn to you, O Lord, whenever we need to acquire an intense faith that is so strong, it will enable us, as faithful followers of our deep belief in you, to conquer our own personal problems and overwhelm all the difficulties of this world! Our Lord and God, your Word is a Vow Never Broken! And we pray, Lord Jesus, whenever we give our word to one another, that we will be able to assure our intentions of good faith. Inspire us, Lord Christ, to remain faithful to our words of committal, to the best of our ability, so that we may never fall into disfavor or dishonor with others. Lord of All Truth, help us to honor our personal commitments in life. Guide us to wisely choose our responsibilities and obligations. And may our word of honor never render empty promises nor foolishly obligate us to an unreasonable or impractical oath, but let us always support our efforts to a successful fulfillment of our word. And when there is an uncertainty or doubt in our lives, may we learn to put aside our foolish pride and seek the advice and assurance of those who love and understand us. Thank you, Lord Jesus Christ, for your Love, for your Understanding, and for your Long-suffering Patience.

Amen …

Chapter and verse that inspired prayer:

James 5:12   But above all things, my brethren, swear not, neither by heaven, neither by earth, neither by any other oath: but let your yea be yea; and your nay, nay; lest ye fall into condemnation.

# August Twenty-Seven: "We Have Direction And Promise"

(As inspired from Acts of the Apostles 27:23-24, 44)

Lord Jesus, hear our prayer ...

Our True Messiah and only Savior Lord Jesus Christ, you are the Promised and Expected Deliverer of your people, and we pray to you for Spiritual Encouragement: Please, increase our personal knowledge of life's purpose! Help us, as Christians, as individuals, everywhere, to see and understand the mystery of living one's life through the Good Graces of Virtue! Instill into our hearts and souls the meaning of your Great Message on earth that everyone is truly their brother's and sister's keeper!

Glory unto you, Lord, you, who take away our fears, our shadows, and all of our doubts! Hear our praises, Lord God, from the heart, from the soul, and from all the faithful saints and angels who serve you night and day!

O Lord, like a warm gentle breeze, lift our spirits heavenward that our praises may soar with the angels above! By whom all things are granted and known, and for the happiness that you desire us to have, Lord Jesus, we call upon your Divine Spirit that we may confidently pursue our futures with clarity and faith! Lord of Heaven and Earth, we pray for fair winds and blue skies to gently caress our course in life. Through your Guidance, we have Direction and Promise, but without you, Lord God, we drift aimlessly with no true destination. Therefore, command the turmoil of our fears to crest and subside into the calm waters of your Blest Peace. And that we may escape all the hidden hazzards of life's unexpected ventures, we pray to you, Lord Jesus Christ, to turn back the angry winds of uncertainty and doubt and guide us along our chosen paths that we may safely avoid the perils of life, under your Loving and Spiritual protection!

Amen ...

Chapter and verse that inspired prayer:

Acts of the Apostles 27:23-24, 44    For there stood by me this night the angel of God, whose I am, and whom I serve, (24) Saying, Fear not, Paul; thou must be brought before Caesar: and, lo, God hath given thee all them that sail with thee. (44) And the rest, some on boards, and some on broken pieces of the ship. And so it came to pass, that they escaped all safe to land.

# August Twenty-Eight: "We Greatly Praise You"
### (As inspired from 1 Corinthians 10:13)

Lord Jesus, hear our prayer …

Whenever we are individually faced with personal trials and tribulations of this world, situations that must be resolved, there is no where to turn but into your direction, Lord Jesus, for we would be totally dismayed and utterly lost without your Divine Protection and Guidance through The Holy Spirit! No other force in the universe is capable of solving and resolving all problems, only you, Lord Christ, can perfect life's imperfections! O Faithful and Merciful Jesus, no matter how narrow the path is or how difficult the course is, with you directing our destinies, we are always assured of a safe arrival, by the Will of God!

Throughout our individual lives on earth, no night is a given, no dawn is a certain, and no sun sets with a promise to rise again for any one person. Each day that we live, our lives may contain various encounters that could beset our very souls; and we realize that the weight of emotional stress can only be lifted through faith in you, Our Most Glorious Lord! No temptation nor any grief is greater than your Love and Mercy, Lord Christ! For all too often, life becomes a crucible filled with worry and concern, and the sole manner by which the dark curtain of anxiety may be lifted, is through an intense trust in our Christian faith and a deep spiritual love for you, Lord Jesus Christ; and then, and only then, will we be able to bear the burden of our ordeal! And we greatly praise you, Lord of Salvation, for delivering us from the severity of trials and from the tribulations of temptation by allowing us to only bear what we are able to tolerate. Thank you, Our Lord of Compassion, for your Unyielding Grace, for your Longsuffering, and for your Endless Love, which are all Heavenly Blessings that are bestowed abundantly upon your faithful!

Amen …

Chapter and verse that inspired prayer:

1 Corinthians 10:13   There hath no temptation taken you but such as is common to man: but God is faithful, who but will with the temptation also make a way to escape, that ye may be able to bear it.

# August Twenty-Nine: "Your Word Will Endure Forever"
### (As inspired from 1 Peter 1:24-25)

Lord Jesus, hear our prayer …

O Lord, Forever Holy are the Scriptures, unending is your Heavenly Word; but in this world, we are limited by earth and sky, by land and sea, and by night and day. Our lives are bounded by deceit and pretense, by ignorance and doubt, and by adversity and disobedience. All temporal glories will eventually wither and fall; nothing material will remain or continue forever, what ever belongs to the world returns to the world! But you, Lord Jesus Christ, have no limitations, no boundaries, no borders! Your Truth is Boundless, your Perfect Love is Infinite, and your Word Will Endure Forever; for Pure Love is Endless, and The Utter Truth cannot be confined!

Thank you, Lord, for our world in which we exist, because, like your Incorruptible Word, it too will continue into the far reaches of time and space! Praise be to you, Lord Jesus, for you are Never Wrong, Infallible to error, and The Unquestioned Authority in Heaven and earth: and we are all blessed to know this! Lord God, you are the Entire Fulfillment of all dreams, of all wishes, and of all that we want and actually need in life! You are the beginning and the ending of our souls and destinies; no worldly gain could ever replace your Wonderful Presence in our temporal lives, Lord Christ! And no earthly knowledge could ever sustain our faith, more than our complete and total acceptance of your Absolute Existence in heaven, on earth, and within our lives! Blessed are the Gospels of Compassion, forever and ever will your Hallowed Word be heard, believed, and accepted by true followers of peace and love! Please, Our Glorious King, know that we, as Christians, are The True Followers of Peace and Love!

Amen …

Chapter and verse that inspired prayer:

1 Peter 1:24-25   For all flesh is as grass, and all the glory of man as the flower of grass. The grass withereth, and the flower thereof falleth away: (25) But the word of the Lord endureth for ever. And this is the word which by the gospel is preached unto you.

# August Thirty: "Lord, We Thank You For Everything"
### (As inspired from Hebrews 13:15)

Lord Jesus, hear our prayer …

Everyday, we are grateful to you, O Lord, for the nourishment that has been grown and set before us. Lord Jesus, we are very thankful for the nurturing hands that planted and tended the fields, the farms, and the gardens that grew all the vital sustenance that we enjoy. And, Lord, we also give you thanks for the care, the sunlight, and for the moisture that fell to nourish all that has been grown for us! And from our lips, Lord Jesus Christ, we praise you greatly through worship and sincere adoration: Dear Lord, we thank you for everything, for we absolutely know in our heart and soul, that it is you who provides all! Blessed is the Bounty of your Love that is found throughout the whole of creation!

Lord God, we pray that you will continually nurture and nourish the souls of your faithful and that your Mercy and Compassion will sustain and properly grow all the nations, the families, and the individuals of the world through your Loving and Nurturing Care! Please, Lord Jesus, forever empower your Holy Word to fill the hearts of everyone, throughout earth, so that everyone's life will be entirely fulfilled; blessed is Our Lord of Bounty! Blessed is the Word of God, and blessed are all who hear your Spiritual Inspiration and embrace it whole heartedly, in mind, in body, and in soul!

And, for all people who feel an emptiness within, that something is missing in their lives, who are starving for your Spiritual Nourishment, Lord of Judgment, we soulfully offer this prayer to you: Turn their eyes and their hearts to see and to accept you, Lord Jesus Christ, into their lives; wherefore, their hunger will subside and be no more.

Amen …

Chapter and verse that inspired prayer:

Hebrews 13:15   By him therefore let us offer the sacrifice of praise to God continually, that is, the fruit of our lips giving thanks to his name.

# August Thirty-One: "Victory Is Yours, Lord"

(As inspired from Revelation 6:2)

Lord Jesus, hear our prayer …

We hail you, Our Deliverer, in your Infinite Glory and Goodness! You are the Chosen One, He, who ascended with All Conquest and the Glorious Crown of Victory over all the enemies of Love and Peace! May our praises ring out forever! Our Lord and God, you are the Valiant King of Heaven and Earth, you defeated death, fulfilled the Scriptures, and began the True Faith for all to follow and to be Saved! All obstacles, all struggles, and all conflicts are overwhelmed by your Triumphant Compassion! Nothing and no one can stand in the way of your Great Power, Lord Jesus! Victory is yours, Lord, for you have conquered the world with your Radiant and Beautiful Love! And with the Brilliance of your Holy Spirit, Lord Christ, you encircle our lives in Lasting Happiness; for the Circle of Light is the Crown of Glory that cannot be defeated! And within this Glowing Circle of Eternal Life, we are forever protected from the shadows of darkness. Please, Lord of Unequaled Purity, sanction our lives and our souls to always remain within the Glorious Sphere of your Immaculate Heart! And let it be known to one and all who struggle daily for real happiness in their life, Lord Jesus Christ, that your Holy Spirit is within the reach of everyone; for all triumph is found within the Crowning Glory of your Perfect Word and in the Absolute Belief of your Conquering Love! We bow deeply to you, Our Resolute King of Divinity, and give spiritual thanks for our wonderful Christian faith, which conquers the heart through Heavenly Compassion!

Amen …

Chapter and verse that inspired prayer:

Revelation 6:2    And I saw, and behold a white horse: and he sat on him had a bow; and a crown was given unto him: and he went forth conquering, and to conquer.

# September One: "The Power Of Your Word"

### (As inspired from Genesis 24:26-27)

Lord Jesus, hear our prayer …

Today, as everyday, with words from the heart, we bow our heads in Adoring Reverence to Our Lord and God in Heaven, and worship Your Very Existence, we, the children of God, are those who believe in you, Lord Jesus, who obey your Commandments of Love, and who fully live a virtuous life; for we know that there is no transgression that may be hidden from you, Lord Christ, all that is adverse in one's heart, is known by you; and all souls that are wronged will be righted, and all people who injustly suffer will be atoned through your Healing Compassion! We surrender our hearts only to you, O Lord, by asking in solemn prayer that you will lead us away from all temptation and inspire us to live our lives according to the Blessed Word of your Merciful Truth! Our Lord Jesus, give us the inner strength and determination to combat the shadows of all deception. And that we may acquire the respect and trust of others, we pray: Help us in every instance to never speak falsely with one another! Spiritually encourage us, Our Blessed Christ, to never abide in the foolishness of personal pride but to affirm that the Knowledge of Truth will forever be spoken from our lips! Permit the Power of your Word, Lord Jesus Christ, to reach into the hearts and souls of all peoples, in all nations, everywhere, so that this world will permanently establish a Holy Covenant of Honesty as a Way of Life; and then, through you, Lord of All Mercy, the whole world will acquire the Sacred Spirit of Pure Innocence, which, through your Unblemished Truth, Lord God, will become Our Word of Love and The Essence of All Life on earth! Blessed is the Almighty Power of Great Goodness!

Amen …

Chapter and verse that inspired prayer:

Genesis 24:26-27   And the man bowed down his head, and worshiped the LORD. (27) And he said, Blessed be the LORD God of my master Abraham, who hath not left destitute my master of his mercy and his truth: I being in the way, the LORD led me to the house of my master's brethren.

# September Two: "The True Path Of Life"

### (As inspired from Proverbs 4:11, 18)

Lord Jesus, hear our prayer …

Daily, in Glorious Spiritual Celebration, Lord God, you kindle our souls to emanate all that is good and all that is right! Through the Divine Words of your Holy Scriptures, Lord Immanuel, written in timeless passages of chapter and verse, our hearts are overjoyed and our spirits are uplifted by the Beautiful Inspirations of your Holy Spirit! Lord Jesus, you have taught us the wisdom to all happiness is to pursue but One Way in this world; and we are ready to follow you, Lord Christ, The True Path of Life! Receive our words, Lord Jesus Christ, as we give veritable acclaim to you for giving us the right to travel in your Radiant Footsteps of Virtue, guided in life by your Never-ending Passages of Love!

The closer we get to you, O Lord, the brighter our days become. We pray for the day when all people in the world will walk in the Majestic Resplendence of your Glorious and Commanding Light, exalting their love and belief in you! Lord Jesus, we understand that words alone cannot guide the faithful spirit along your Righteous Path, and that the only way to our Heavenly Father is through you! And the only way to you is through a sincere and complete acceptance and belief in you, Lord Christ! Therefore, please accept our words as genuine and honest, stemming from the essence of our Christian faith, as we proudly proclaim to the world that: We accept, we believe, and we completely surrender our souls to you, Lord Jesus Our Good Christ and King! Please remember us, Lord Emmanuel, to our Heavenly Father in His Hallowed Kingdom of Saints and Angels!

Amen …

Chapter and verse that inspired prayer …

Proverbs 4:11, 18     I have taught thee in the way of wisdom; I have led thee in right paths. (18) But the path of the just is as the shining light, that shineth more and more unto the perfect day.

# September Three: "Lord, There Is Much To Marvel"

(As inspired from Mark 10:6-8)

Lord Jesus, hear our prayer …

At the dawn of creation, you brought us into existence, Lord God, male and female, in your image, and you blessed us and gave us dominion over every plant, animal, and creature that moved upon earth! Into our own hands did you give us the responsibility and care of this wondrous world of life! Please, Lord Jesus, bless us and impart upon every individual human, the Knowledge to Conserve and Preserve our planet from personal ignorance and waste. Instill in our hearts, an innate desire to do good and to safeguard the rights of nature in all concerns and causes for our creation's future prosperity and existence!

O Lord, there is much to marvel at in life! Praise be to you, forever and ever! In the beginning and from the beginning, you have created a multitude of existence, and all the remarkable differences between each creation of life, and after its own does each life create! A seed will reproduce the parent plant from whence it came. A living creature will reproduce its likeness. And, Lord God, you created us in your image to be children of God, and you brought forth in each one of us, a natural affection for one another. And through true love, two souls will unite, male and female, into one flesh, one spirit, one faith, one family, and in one devotion for your Perfect Wisdom and Judgment! Yes, Lord Jesus Christ, there is so much to marvel at in life and give witness to; because, we, your faithful followers, stand in awe, and we are humbled, simply, to be a living part of your Loving and Wondrous Creation!

Amen …

Chapter and verse that inspired prayer:

Mark 10:6-8    But from the beginning of the creation God made them male and female. (7) For this cause shall a man leave his father and mother, and cleave to his wife; (8) And they twain shall be one flesh: so then they are no more twain, but one flesh.

# September Four: "All Power Is Given"

(As inspired from Romans 13:1)

Lord Jesus, hear our prayer ...

On earth, all power is given from above, and we pray for all who have the responsibility and the commission to govern others. Blest is the command that is given to them by you, Lord God; for all the Kings and Queens and rulers and overlords and presidents and governing officials that be, throughout the nations of the world, are subject to you! We, as individuals, can authorize no genuine control nor possess any real domain except that which is given from above by the Divine Authority of your Great Judgment, Lord Jesus! Therefore, we pray that you will continually bless and direct the leaders of this world: We pray for your Spiritual Love, Lord Christ, to be in the hearts and minds of those who govern and rule. For there is no greater authority that rules, than the power that rules through love; and the world is humbled, Lord Jesus Christ, for we know that everyone is loved by you!

Through the Strength and the Holiness of your Complete Love, Lord Jesus, we learn patience, tolerance, and a sincere understanding for one another. And we pray for your Heavenly Influence, Lord Christ, to encourage all earthly powers that govern others, to guide and delegate their authority with a humble understanding of your Great and Sovereign Love in their souls; Lord Jesus Christ, inspire the aspirations in their ambitions to always be administered with liberty, justice, and a Spiritual Compassion for All! Lord God, allow all persecution of innocence to fade into the dark shadows from whence they came, and Sanction only the Radiance of your Purity to Reign Forever on earth!

Amen ...

Chapter and verse that inspired prayer:

Romans 13:1    Let every soul be subject unto the higher powers. For there is no power but of God: the powers that be are ordained of God.

# September Five: "You, Lord, Are Eternity"

### (As inspired from 1 Corinthians 15:52)

Lord Jesus, hear our prayer …

O Heavenly Father of All That Is, our world was formed in the palms of your hands, created through the Miracle of Love, how can we, as humans, ever express our true gratitude and praise, except through perfect obedience to your Hallowed Existence: As children of the Living God, we proudly profess our never-ending love for you, Lord Jesus!

We voice our acclaim and give spiritual tribute to you, O Lord, for all the centuries of time that have passed. And through the passing of seasons, eras, histories, and all the epochs of time, nations have risen and fallen, cities have come and gone, and rulers have judged and been judged. Nevertheless, in all the millenniums that have passed, your Beautiful Word, your Great Love, your Unflawed Truth, your Glorious Spirit, and all that you have spoken and declared, Lord Jesus, has triumphed and remained throughout the passing of all time! What more proof does the world need as a testimony to your existence, The Holy Power of All Love! Lord Jesus Christ, we give ceaseless praise, sincere worship, and all of our obedience unto you, eternally, from this time forth, and into all time yet to come. For in the twinkling of an eye, Our God of Great Compassion, you can create a universe of love or remove a lifetime of hurt. And for a brief moment in eternity, our temporal time will be and will pass, but you, Lord, are Eternity! And just as the enormity of the universe extends forever into the far reaches of infinity, your Grand and Radiant Presence overshadows the magnificence of the creation! Simply because, no work of art is greater than its Creator, than you, Our Lord and Savior!

Amen …

Chapter and verse that inspired prayer:

1 Corinthians 15:52   In a moment, in the twinkling of an eye, at the last trump: for the trumpet shall sound, and the dead shall be raised incorruptible, and we shall be changed.

# September Six: "Bless Our Young People"

### (As inspired from Leviticus 10:10-11)

Lord Jesus, hear our prayer …

With every birth, the newborn child begins their life as an empty slate of pure holiness, waiting for direction, support, and love. And, Lord, we know and accept that it is the moral accountability of every human alive to direct and encourage all children to understand and to believe in the Loving Goodness of God, of you, Our Lord Jesus Christ! Pray for us in this world, Lord God, to see and recognize our responsibility as our brother's and sister's keeper. And in the end, you, Lord Almighty, will be Blessed with Infinite Souls of Kindness for your Kingdom in Heaven!

Through moral lessons and examples, we have learned the spiritual difference between the light and the dark, between right and wrong, and between holy and unholy! Lord, for the spiritual growth and gain in all children, we pray for your Divine Intervention into their lives. And through your Heavenly Inspirations, Lord Jesus Christ, the children of the world will learn to accept and understand that your words and statutes are Unflawed and Perfect; and then, everywhere, nations will rise up and become faithful followers of One Belief and of one Christian faith in your Hallowed and Infinite Goodness!

Bless our young people, Lord, and fill their spirits with the will and the desire to develop strong and healthy minds, bodies, and souls. Build determination and courage into their hearts that they may become symbols of unblemished character. Put strength and purpose into their spirits that they may present themselves as Emissaries of Goodwill. Also, Lord Jesus, provide our youth with the common sense and wisdom that is needed to survive in the world today, that they may become examples of Moral Excellence and Fortitude, and one day, lead the Way for other future Christian generations that are yet to be born!

Amen …

Chapter and verse that inspired prayer:

Leviticus 10:10-11     And that ye may put difference between holy and unholy, and between unclean and clean; (11) And that ye may teach the children of Israel all the statutes which the LORD hath spoken unto them by the hand of Moses.

# September Seven: "Honor And Receive Others"

(As inspired from Galatians 5:14 and Matthew 5:44)

Lord Jesus, hear our prayer …

All perfect resolutions are through Grace, and all answers are found in the Purity of you, Lord Jesus Christ! We bear our souls, Lord, and ask of you to please vanquish all feelings of resentment that we may have within our individual hearts! Permit us, instead, Lord God, to release all feelings of injustice as we gain in our Heavenly Knowledge of your Loving Forgiveness!

Receive us, O Lord, into the fulness of your Everlasting Love. And just as the soil accepts the rain, as an ocean accepts a river, and as all life accepts the radiance of the sun, we too, as humans, must learn to accept one another in a Heavenly Embrace of Peace. Instill into our hearts, Lord Jesus, a Spiritual inspiration to care for each other with an unconditional love, just as you, Lord God, Unconditionally Love us. And just as you receive and accept us, Our Lord and Christ, we too must learn to honor and receive others through trust and kindness. Lord of Forgiveness, through your Infinite and Patient Understanding, we pray that you will bless us with the Spiritual Knowledge to welcome and believe in others as we would want to be received and esteemed by you! Because, you have taught us, Lord Jesus Christ, that we must love one another as we love ourselves; that we must pray for and encompass our enemies with harmony rather than hate; and that we must all learn to accept the offender but reject the offense. Pray for us, Our God of Great Compassion, as we sincerely pray for one another in a true supplication of Christian forgiveness!

Amen …

Chapter and verse that inspired prayer:

Galatians 5:14    For all the law is fulfilled in one word, even in this; Thou shalt love thy neighbor as thyself.

Matthew 5:44    But I say unto you, Love your enemies, bless them that curse you, do good to them that hate you, and pray for them which despitefully use you, and persecute you;

# September Eight: "Delights Of Mercy"

(As inspired from Ephesians 4:31)

Lord Jesus, hear our prayer:

All lives were emancipated from the bondage of darkness, Lord Jesus, when you liberated our souls through the Ransom of your Innocent Blood! And it is in our sincerest supplications, Lord God, that we beg of you, please, release the world from the snares of malicious intent and instill into the hearts of all people the Delights of Mercy. Forgive us, Lord Christ, when we create turmoil in our lives, rage in our souls, and malice in our minds. Quell the stirring bitterness of all who anger; for in chaos, there is no calm. We pray that you will elevate everyone's Spiritual Awareness to a New Horizon of Hope and Peace; because in your Blessed Clarity, Lord Jesus Christ, obscurity cannot be found! And we, your faithful followers, are weary of malevolence in the world, strife in our personal lives, and do earnestly seek Spiritual Tranquility and world peace in our lifetimes: Bring to an end, Lord Jesus, all physical wrath, all thoughts of anger, and all spiritual wickedness on earth! Amen!

Forgive us and bless us, Lord of Heaven and Earth, when we create and accept stress and unrest into our lives; for whosoever resides in you, O Lord, will find their bitterness turns to sweet and their darkness turns to light! Lord Jesus Christ, illuminate everyone's personal shadows in the Dawning Radiance of your Eternal Hope and Salvation! Remove the wrath that resides within the hearts of those who cannot find the Quiet and the Calm of your Forgiveness and Compassion. Lord God, fill their spirits with the Wonderful Resplendence of your Peace and Love, and in your name, Our Triumphant God and King, we ask that you will sanctify our lives as peacemakers and intercessors of our Christian faith!

Amen …

Chapter and verse that inspired prayer:

Ephesians 4:31    Let all bitterness, and wrath, and anger, and clamour, and evil speaking, be put away from you, with all malice:

# September Nine: "You, Lord, Are Holy"

(As inspired from 1 Peter 1:16)

Lord Jesus, hear our prayer …

You are the Holy of Holies, Our Lord and God, the innermost part of our souls, Our Righteous and Sacred Place where we may speak to you in words of Great Reverence. Every single word in the Bible is a testament of your Truth, Lord God! And how Illustrious and Wonderful your Wisdom is, Lord! Because, through a natural calling and order in life, all of creation individually accepts and truly welcomes your Caring and Comforting Caress into its Blessing of Existence: See the boldness in a blossoming flower, inhale its beautiful fragrance, hear the songbird's continuous praise, touch the softness of a newborn's life, and taste the sweetness of a honeybee's labor! Lord Christ, we too confess and commend that you are the Hallowed Reason for Our Being, and only the highest and purest of acclaim and love do we give to you; for you, Lord, are All Holy, and you are the cause of all that exists! Lord Jesus, you are The Earth and The Sky, The Moon and The Stars, The Sun and The Rain, The Mountain and The Valley, The Question and The Answer, you are The Supplication and The True Acknowledgment, The Beginning and The End. You are The Natural Source of All Life and The First Origin of All that is! There is no one nor anything before you! Lord of Perfection, your Heavenly Powers extend beyond the universe, beyond the reaches of all darkness, and beyond all infinity; and yet, you are as close to us as the very air that touches our flesh and gives us life! Blest are you, Lord of True Goodness! Hallowed are you, Lord Jesus Christ, and Endless is your Glorious Spirit of Love, forever and ever, in everything that is, was, or ever will be, your Holy Spirit is foremost important for our survival in this world, in the next, and in our Christian lives!

Amen …

Chapter and verse that inspired prayer:

1 Peter 1:16    Because it is written, Be ye holy; for I am Holy.

# September Ten: "We Shall Reap What We Sow"

(As inspired from Galatians 6:7)

Lord Jesus, hear our prayer …

Our Lord Faithful and True, there are times when the mistakes we make in life become the bitter sweet lessons not to be repeated; and to regret the same error over and over, is a sign of personal weakness. Therefore, we pray to you, Lord God, for your Forgiveness, Strength, and Direction. Please hear our prayer: We praise you, Dear Lord, and give heartfelt thanks to you for the many fruits of our labor; for you have taught us that we shall reap what we sow in life! And if our labors are great, Lord Jesus, we know that our harvests will be greater! Bless us, Lord Christ, with a Spiritual Conviction of Righteousness in all that we do, in all that we say, and in all that we hold true as Christians!

As we work and live in this world, Dear Lord, we pray that our spirits will endure and our faith will prevail against all the storms and troubles that appear in life! We ask that you will bless us, so that our lives will overfill with the good fruits of honest labor. And may you, Lord God, continually watch over each and every one of us as we pursue our individual callings and destinies in life!

In your name, Lord Jesus Christ, we will forever seek refuge from the elements of darkness and adversity. And we pray to you, Lord of Salvation, that when the time comes for you to gather your faithful from among the Harvests of your Love, we will be counted among the faithfully gathered! May God bless this generation and all generations yet to come into the Marvelous Knowledge and Acceptance of your Hallowed Presence on earth as it is in heaven above!

Amen …

Chapter and verse that inspired prayer:

Galatians 6:7  Be not deceived; God is not mocked: for whatsoever a man soweth, that shall he also reap.

# September Eleven: "Love Dwells Within Love"

### (As inspired from 1 Chronicles 16:8)

Lord Jesus, hear our prayer …

Your countless Divine Deeds and Great Mercies, Lord God, are known throughout the world and throughout the hearts of your faithful: Adam and Eve, Noah's Covenant, the test of Abraham's faith, Moses the Law Giver, Ruth's virtue, King David's faith, Solomon's wisdom, the beautiful Psalms and Proverbs, Christ's birth, the Messiah's healing of the sick, the Death and Resurrection of Jesus Christ! Blessed are you, Our Lord and God, for light radiates from within light, truth resides within truth, love dwells within love, and all that is good comes from you! Lord Jesus, through continuous faith, adoration, and obedience to your Word, we know that your Mercy will remain with us and within us. And through continuous devotion, prayer, and praise, we know that your Endless Love, Lord Jesus Christ, will continually grow inside and around us to serve as a True Banner for our personal and individual Christian hearts!

The Gospels have given us clear exhortation of what is righteous and what is not; and through the comfort and strength of your Infallible Will, we will remain faithfully vigilant in our Christian belief, staying watchful and alert for the temporal trappings of this world!

Our King of Kings, who on earth or in heaven cannot read the Scriptures and behold the Many Miracles that were witnessed by the peoples and prophets of old! O Lord, you are Adorned in Glory and you are Glorified through praise and thankfulness. When we give praise to you, Lord Christ, we glorify our faith in you! And when we give thanks to you, Lord Jesus Christ, we know that we are truly blessed by you! Please, Lord Jesus, allow your Love to remain with us and within us throughout our lives and throughout our existence into eternity!

Amen …

Chapter and verse that inspired prayer:

1 Chronicles 16:8    Give thanks unto the LORD, call upon his name, make known his deeds among the people.

# September Twelve: "You Stand Alone In Greatness"

(As inspired from 1 Chronicles 17:19-20)

Lord Jesus, hear our prayer …

All prayerful words that are spoken from the purity of the heart, echo loudly throughout the Kingdom of Heaven! Lord of The Final Judgment, we pray that you will judge us worthy: In the twinkling of an eye, you heal our shattered lives, our broken hearts, our wandering spirits, and give us new destinations! Blessed are you, Lord God, for with a mere thought, you caused all things to be! The creation of your Bountiful Love is Vast and Wondrous! And we rejoice, we revel, and we exult only in you, Lord Jesus! The earth is noble, the stars are abundant, the universe is infinite, but all are overshadowed by the Power of your Glory, Lord Christ! How can the design be more divine than the designer! There is no one, there is nothing else that exists, absolutely nothing that possess your Hallowed Grandeur, Lord Jesus Christ; for you stand alone in Greatness! Blessed is the Holy Magnitude in the Unconquerable Might of Your Righteousness on earth as it is in heaven; and now, today, tomorrow, and forevermore will we witness to all that you have done for us and for the world!

Our Living God, we profess your Undeniable Majesty to the world: Remarkable is your Creation of Life! Immeasurable is your Perfect Truth! Forever is your Never-ending Mercy! Glorious is your Infinite Love! And Spiritually Blessed are those who confess and testify to the Towering Abundance of your Supreme Greatness! Hear us, Lord Jesus Christ, for you are The Alpha and The Omega, The Beginning and The Ending, He who Transcends All Time, Our Righteous Redeemer, and we, your faithful servants, are humbled by the very mention of your Beautiful Name!

Amen …

Chapter and verse that inspired prayer:

1 Chronicles 17:19-20  O LORD, for thy servant's sake, and according to thine own heart, hast thou done all this greatness, in making known all these great things. (20) O LORD, there is none like thee, neither is there any God beside thee, according to all we have heard with our ears.

# September Thirteen: "The Wisdom Of Scripture"

(As inspired from 2 Samuel 7:28-29)

Lord Jesus, hear our prayer ...

We ask of you, O Lord, to bless the dwellings of your faithful! Lord God, you are the Bright and Morning Star, and we pray to you for all the nonbelievers and the non-Christians around the world, that you will touch their hearts and allow them to understand that the Fulfillment of Life is Eternity, which can only be attained through you, Lord Jesus! In life, as Christians, our blessings are many: Fellowship, friendship, male and female falling in love, marriage, the birth of children, the family; which, in turn, are followed by new generations growing spiritually in their Christian faith. These are the forever moments in life that are cherished blessings from the Bounty of your Love, Lord Jesus; and we thank you for every precious moment of life! And gladly, without hesitation, Lord of All Who Live, we have become willing servants to the Goodness of your Sacred Words as written by the saints and prophets that were inspired by the Holy Words of your Divine Spirit; thank you, Lord Christ, for the Wisdom of Scripture brings hope, promise, and direction to our lives; your Words are True and Infallible, and we pray to you that our lives will continually reflect the lessons that we gain and learn through the Spiritual Knowledge of the Holy Spirit! All blessings in life come from you, Lord Jesus; therefore, we give heartfelt thanks to you for every single blessing, great or small, that we receive. And we pray: Our Lord Jesus Christ, please, bless every family and every person who rejoices and gives thanks to you for their individual and personal discernment of your Holy Word, as found throughout chapter and verse of The Greatest Book Ever Written, our Holy Bible of Godly Works, Formed in Truth, Promise, and Eternal Goodness!

Amen ...

Chapter and verse that inspired prayer:

2 Samuel 7:28-29    And now, O Lord God, thou art that God, and thy words be true, and thou hast promised this goodness unto thy servant: (29) Therefore now let it please thee to bless the house of thy servant, that it may continue for ever before thee: for thou, O Lord God, hast spoken it: and with thy blessing let the house of thy servant be blessed for ever.

# September Fourteen: "True Love Offers True Forgiveness"

(As inspired from Matthew 6:14)

Lord Jesus, hear our prayer …

The answer to all of life's complex problems is simple: When angry, pray for peace; when threatened, pray for your enemy; when in doubt, pray to God! For when any situation arises, we will pray to the Only One who can do something about our issues, we will pray to you, Lord Jesus Christ! And as true Christians, if we possess the faith to believe that our needs will be answered, then our needs will be answered!

In prayer, we ask of you, Lord God, to forgive us our transgressions; and just as you have forgiven us our trespasses, we must also learn to sincerely forgive others that trespass against us! Enliven in us, Our Lord Christ, the tenets to eagerly forgive and forget the misdeeds of others that we will not seek revenge nor retribution against them. Instill into our hearts the ability to perceive and understand the perfection of your Spiritual Benevolence; create within us, Lord Jesus, the strength to forgive. Allow the Divine Influence of your Never Ending Salvation of Love, Lord Jesus Christ, to soften the hearts and enlighten the spirits of all people, Christian and non-Christian, everywhere in the world, to gain the True Knowledge of Benevolent Compassion for the Spiritual Gain of One and All!

According to individual need, we ask that you will bless us with a Spiritual Healing: Lord God, defeat and consume the vindictive heart that may reside within us. Temper our spirits and illuminate our personal understandings to know that True Love offers True Forgiveness; for only you, Lord Christ, are the essence of True Love and True Forgiveness throughout the heavens and the earth! Blessed is your Merciful Heart!

Amen …

Chapter and verse that inspired prayer:

Matthew 6:14   For if ye forgive men their trespasses, your heavenly Father will also forgive you.

# September Fifteen: "The Lessons Of Your Love"

(As inspired from 2 Thessalonians 2:13)

Lord Jesus, hear our prayer …

Through a Spiritual Sanctification of the Holy Ghost, we, your faithful, have been chosen and bonded, from the beginning of time, to witness and praise the Great Works on earth of The Father, The Son, and The Holy Spirit!

Our Beloved Lord, because you love us, and because all that you say and do is Unflawed in Every Way, we are bound through love, to always give thanks to you, our Lord and God! From birth, our innocent beginnings, until our unknowing ends, our individual lives will hold many lessons; and all who receive mercy and salvation throughout life are sanctified by their faith in you, Lord Jesus! And as we go through our many stages and phases of existence on earth, we ask you to encourage us and guide us in all directions, Lord Christ, and to become our Spiritual Mentor! For we must sincerely learn to completely trust in you, Lord of Wisdom; and to always thank you for all the Spiritual knowledge that we acquire, for all the experiences that we gain, and for all the lessons that we learn through trials of the heart and spirit. And beyond any doubt, the lessons of the world can be false and cruel, but the lessons of your Great Love, Lord Jesus Christ, are Perfect and True; sanctify our souls, Lord, that we may have Life Eternal! And as Christians, we are aware of how easy it is to wander from one's chosen course, and this is why we pray to you, Lord God: Guide our steps and protect us, Our Precious Lord, along the narrow footpath of life.

Amen …

Chapter and verse that inspired prayer:

2 Thessalonians 2:13   But we are bound to give thanks alway to God for you, brethren beloved of the Lord, because God hath from the beginning chosen you to salvation through sanctification of the Spirit and belief of the truth:

# September Sixteen: "Gifts From The Holy Spirit"

### (As inspired from 1 Corinthians 12:1, 3)

Lord Jesus, hear our prayer …

All matters in heaven and on earth are possible through you, Our Chosen One! Lord of All Inspiration, you have given us the insight to know that when there is a positive will, and where there is strong faith, there is most definitely a way! According to the powers of our Christian faith, O Lord, as found in your Mercy, in your Love, and in your Unerring Will, everything that we need in life is a blessing within reach! Praiseworthy are you, Lord Jesus, and praised be your blessings; for we proclaim life's consecrations as wondrous gifts from the Holy Spirit! Lord God, your Gifts of Love bring peace and harmony into our lives. Your Gifts of Faith bring hope and assurance into our lives. And for the rest of our lives, Lord Jesus Christ, we will forever promise to protect, care for, and nurture your Most Sacred Blessing, your Gift of Eternal Life!

God the Father, we rejoice in your gifts as we pray for and celebrate all the faith and happiness of those around us; but we also pray for those who do not share in Spiritual Insight; may your Blessing of Mercy forgive all transgression: Please, forgive those who constantly use your name in vain, Lord Jesus Christ, for their curse is empty and meaningless and their spirit is filled with false knowledge. Lord God, we pray to you, Enlighten the heart, the mind, and the soul of all who are unenlightened!

By the Grace of the Holy Spirit, grant us your Blessing of Wisdom and give each one of us a clear discernment to always know the right direction to follow in life, by sanctioning your Constant Love to continuously shield us from the onslaught of life's discontent and sorrow! Thank you, Our Heavenly Lord, for your Spiritual Concern!

Amen …

Chapter and verse that inspired prayer:

1 Corinthians 12:1, 3    Now concerning spiritual gifts, brethren, I would not have you ignorant. (3) Wherefore I give you to understand, that no man speaking by the Spirit of God calleth Jesus accursed: and that no man can say that Jesus is the Lord, but by the Holy Ghost.

# September Seventeen: "Purify Our Hearts"

(As inspired from 2 Chronicles 29:18)

Lord Jesus, hear our prayer …

We are as holy vessels, formed by your Word of Love, and before we present our prayer petitions to you, Lord God, we must be spiritually cleansed. During prayer, we will put aside any emotional indignation and come to you in sincere innocence, Lord Jesus. Furthermore, we will resolve all ill feelings, conflicts, and personal turmoil, and purify our hearts in your Loving Forgiveness; for when we greet you in prayer, Lord Christ, we must greet you in a pure spirit that is cleansed by your Love and Peace! We praise you, Lord Jesus Christ, for blessing and absolving our souls, for this is our offering of love that we proudly present to you: Your Spirit of Compassion moves through the souls of those who walk in peace and proudly carry your name upon their lips and in our hearts; bless all of us, Our Lord of Heaven and Earth, and accept our truest offering of love and obedience!

We greet you, Our Lord, with clear minds, open hearts, and uplifted joy! And just as the Holy Ghost is Perfect and Pure, Lord God, so must our hearts, our spirits, and our minds be when we offer our soulful requests to you; because, we know that all prayer offered in innocence is received and answered by the Holiness and Purity of your Love and Mercy! Bless us and cleanse us, Lord Jesus Christ, in the Radiant Purification of your Unremitting Grace and Salvation! We ask to be in your Favor, Our Lamb of God; therefore, remove from our souls all blemish that offends you and fortify our convictions to remain loyal and true to our Christian values! And by doing so, we will be closer to Eternal Life, free from the binding forces of this temporal world!

Amen …

Chapter and verse that inspired prayer:

2 Chronicles 29:18    Then they went in to Hezekiah the king, and said, We have cleansed all the house of the LORD, and the altar of burnt offering, with all the vessels thereof, and the showbread table, with all the vessels thereof.

# September Eighteen: "In Their Innocence"

(As inspired from Isaiah 11:6)

Lord Jesus, hear our prayer ...

We ask in your Name, Our Lord and God: Bring to an end all hostility and all revenge that exists in the hearts and minds of humankind, turn animosity into a genuine concern for the destinies of all people around the world! And now, a special prayer request, O Lord, for the futures of all children of all races and of all nationalities throughout every civilization on this planet: Lord Jesus Christ, we pray that every child, in every country on earth, will grow up to be wise and strong and follow in the ways of your Truth and Wisdom. For when your Word was made Flesh, King of Kings, through the Immaculate Birth of a child king, and it was from that moment on that the world was led away from its darkness and into the Radiant Purity of your Saving Grace! Thank you, Lord Jesus Our Deliverer, for saving the souls of countless multitudes through your Innocent Death and Glorious Resurrection; which, praise the Lord, Spiritually has given the whole world and all of its people, everywhere, Salvation and Direction towards a New Life of heartfelt compassion!

And now, we pray that all young people of all races will learn to praise your name and Glorify your Greatness: Lord God, allow no false beliefs nor false witnesses to stain the innocence of children nor hamper their ability to seek and find the Absolute Truth of your Magnificent Word! And that all children, everywhere, may have the same opportunity to grow in your Hallowed Graces, we ask that you will help us and guide us, Lord Jesus, in our thoughts and in our deeds. Give us the courage and determination, Lord Christ, to set good examples and to be good examples for every child around us; because, the innocence in the children of the world belong to you, Lord Jesus Christ, and their futures belong to the betterment of the world!

Amen ...

Chapter and verse that inspired prayer:

Isaiah 11:6    The wolf also shall dwell with the lamb, and the leopard shall lie down with the kid; and the calf and the young lion and the fatling together; and a little child shall lead them.

# September Nineteen: "Hosanna In The Highest"

(As inspired from Luke 19:40)

Lord Jesus, hear our prayer …

Time and time again, Lord Jesus, you have given your faithful so many reasons to accept and to believe in your Loving, Living Existence! The Splendor of your Divine Holiness outshines the most radiant star! The Beauty of your Inviolable Goodness is matchless in nature! And the Towering Magnificence of your Ever Present Compassion overshadows the magnitude of any mountain range in our universe! But as great as the creation may be, nothing in the creation is greater than its Creator; is greater than you, Lord God, Creator of Heaven and Earth and all that exists! And now, we deeply and personally profess our intense faith in you, Our Triumphant King and All-powerful God: From the center of our souls, we have gathered together all the love there is within, and offer it to you for all eternity!

Hear our praise that acknowledges your All-knowing Wisdom, Lord, which rules the natural order and balance of nature: We give thanks for the sun and the stars that remain constant, for the earth upon which we exist, for the perfect cycles of the moon and tides, for the good rains that fall to nourish the soil, for the day, for the night, for your Eternal Love and our spiritual salvation! Lord Jesus, because of the order and harmony that is found in our lives, in this world, in the universe, and in your Divine Design, we give continuous exaltation and adoration to you from a heartfelt song that continuously sings out from the center of our souls! And if all the mountains and valleys and rivers and trees could also sing, there would be a deafening melodious melody of praise forever sung, night and day! And if all life could rise up simultaneously and adore you in song, Lord Jesus Christ, there would be a mighty and joyous song continuously sung throughout the infinite universe, as it is in heaven, singing: Praise! Praise! Praise to you, Lord God! Hosanna in the Highest!

Amen

Chapter and verse that inspired prayer:

Luke 19:40    And he answered and said unto them, I tell you that, if these should hold their peace, the stones would immediately cry out.

# September Twenty: "The Season Of Maturity"

(As inspired from Acts of the Apostles 14:17)

Lord Jesus, hear our prayer …

Our Lord and Rock of Ages, we gratefully thank you for Spiritually Guiding us safely through the passing of time; for autumn signifies not only the decline of a season, but also directs us to a new interim of discovery and celebration in our lives! O Lord, now that summer has almost passed, we await and welcome with great anticipation the season of maturity! For when the fall approaches, it becomes a time when all life shows its true colors; and it also becomes a time when all life reaps the fruits of its labors. Blessed are you, Lord Jesus, for filling our hearts with Spiritual food and gladness! And for what was tilled, planted, and cared for, we pray, Lord Jesus Christ, that everyone will be fulfilled in the harvest of your Bountiful Love and Blessedness! And through your Healing Blessings, your Perfect Faith will leave no soul in darkness; will dispel all spiritual hunger; and will fulfill every individual need in those who believe!

On this day, Our Victorious King, we individually witness to the world, through personal praise, all that you did on earth was for us, and was Righteous and Good! From sunrise to sunset, from month to month, from season to season, in wisdom and reason, your Abundant Generosity is poured out to the world. Lord God, entitle your faithful to reap the fruits of their labors, and shepherd everyone, everywhere, to become a storehouse of love, filled with your Unblemished Virtue! And we, as impassioned Christians, pray that you will inspire us and guide us, Our Lord Jesus Christ, to embellish our souls with a passion for goodness that would become an outward display of love and mercy; for truly, a tree is known by its fruit and a soul by its reflecting goodness!

Amen …

Chapter and verse that inspired prayer:

Acts of the Apostles 14:17 Nevertheless he left not himself without witness, in that he did good, and gave us rain from heaven, and fruitful seasons, filling our hearts with food and gladness.

# September Twenty-One: "Comfort Us With Your Compassion"

### (As inspired from Psalms 27:8-9)

Lord Jesus, hear our prayer …

Wherever we are, we earnestly seek your Divine Intervention into our lives! Lead us and protect us, Lord God, whenever we are removed from the care and security of our loved ones. And when we are far from home, Lord Christ, we know that you will be in our midst. When we are lonely and alone, we know that your Love will fill the void in our hearts. And when we are removed from family and friends, we know that you will comfort us with your Compassion and surround us with your Spiritual Salvation. Lord Jesus Christ, our Good Shepherd, we seek the continual comfort of your Merciful Embrace as we pray to you: Forever guide us in our pursuit of happiness and Spiritual Fulfillment; through your Hallowed Authority, confer upon your faithful followers, Almighty God, a blessing of Christian determination in all that we do and wherever we go!

O Lord, we pray for those who are alone and far from their home: May the days of their separation be few and safe from all harm and danger. And secured by their Christian faith, please help all who travel to be shepherded once again to the warm delights of those who love them; encourage them, Lord Jesus Christ, to continually find personal security and redemption in their lives by following the Unparalleled Path to the Sacred Care of your Comforting Love. Therefore, with you in our lives, Lord of Pure Mercy, we know for sure that we are never really lost, never alone, and never very far from our Heavenly Home!

Amen …

Chapter and verse that inspired prayer:

Psalms 27:8-9    When thou saidst, Seek ye my face; my heart said unto thee, Thy face, LORD, will I seek. (9) Hide not thy face far from me; put not thy servant away in anger: thou hast been my help; leave me not, neither forsake me, O God of my salvation.

# September Twenty-Two: "Your Path Of Righteousness"
### (As inspired from 2 Samuel 22:2 and Revelation 3:12)

Lord Jesus, hear our prayer …

Lord Jesus, you are The True Deliverer, He, Who cannot be Defeated! From the beginning of time, Lord Christ, your Almighty Power and Grace have delivered people out of darkness, out of foreign lands, out of bondage, and out of harm's way! And worthy are those who follow your Path of Righteousness, Lord Jesus Christ, for you will sanctify their chosen course in life and deliver them to the Spiritual Salvation of your inner peace that resides in the Fortified Fortress of Forgiveness and Heavenly Love! Strengthen us, Our Beloved Lord, and establish our abilities to discern and fully perceive the Spiritual meaning of Forgiveness; for as Christians, to truly understand sincere mercy is to know and to accept that whenever there is bitterness in one's life, it can be resolved through True Forgiveness, and then, it will no longer exist in the heart, in the mind, and in the soul!

Our Lord and God, we pray for the day when every eye in the world will gaze upon and witness your return from heaven in all your Glorious Love and Judgment, adorned in White Raiment, wearing a Holy Crown of Victory and your New Name for every nation and tongue on earth to worship and adore as One People in Your Name!

Let the trumpets sound, the angels in heaven rejoice, and the world fall into Spiritual Submission, for the Peace of the World is at hand; and it is there for the asking! Dear Lord, we pray for your Spiritual Beacon of Love. Help us to never detour from the correct pathway that you have chosen for each and every one of us. Pray for us that we will not fall by the wayside, Lord Christ, nor lose sight of our Rightful Destination in life. And, Lord Jesus, we ask that our destinies and passages on earth will lead us directly to you, Our Salvation Through Forgiveness, Our God, Our One and Only True Destination in this world and in the next, Our Crowned King Lord Jesus Christ!

Amen …

Chapter and verse that inspired prayer:

2 Samuel 22:2     And he said, The LORD is my rock, and my fortress, and my deliverer;

Revelation 3:12     Him that overcometh will I make a pillar in the temple of my God, And he shall go no more out: and I will write upon him the name of my God, and the name of the city of my God, which is new Jerusalem, which cometh down out of heaven from my God: and I will write upon him my new name.

# September Twenty-Three: "Seek Goodness And Virtue"

(As inspired from Daniel 2:20-21)

Lord Jesus, hear our prayer ...

Remarkable and Supreme is your Extraordinary Glory, words alone cannot even begin to describe your Infinite Holiness: Before the Light, there was only darkness; before knowledge, there was superstition,; before our Christian Enlightenment, our souls were lost! And now that you are in the world, Lord Jesus, all are saved!

Worship and prayer are not only reserved for the needy soul, but also for all who merely wish to speak to The Father, The Son, and The Holy Spirit! How enlightening it is, Lord Jesus, to know that everyone has the same ability to attain Eternal Life in your Heavenly Kingdom! How wonderful it is to know and understand the Sacred Truths of our Christian religion: To serve God with all of our heart through love and forgiveness! Blessed is your Heavenly Law, Lord God, that governs the natural course of all that exists, that establishes and withdraws all earthly powers, and that places Spiritual Understanding into the hearts of all who accept you, Lord Jesus Christ, as their Personal Savior and God!

From the beginning and through the entirety of all time, the irresistible force of your Compassionate Commitment to the human race, Lord Christ, is revealed in the Glorious Power of your Divine Will! And your Will, Lord Jesus, is the Only Way that we faithfully seek for the rest of our lives! Lord Christ, may our humble words of praise never be shallow, or empty, nor said in vain. May our reverences be sincere and our works pleasing to you. And may the Glory of your Loving Spirit, Lord Eternal, forever abide within us; protect us and pray for all of us, Lord Jesus Christ, to continually seek Goodness and Virtue in our lives. Blessed are you, Our Lord and Shepherd, Our Savior forever and ever!

Amen ...

Chapter and verse that inspired prayer:

Daniel 2:20-21    Daniel answered and said, Blessed be the name of God for ever and ever: for wisdom and might are his: (21) And he changeth the times and the seasons: he removeth kings, and setteth up kings: he giveth wisdom unto the wise, and knowledge to them that know understanding.

# September Twenty-Four: "Circle Of Love"

### (As inspired from James 5:16)

Lord Jesus, hear our prayer …

All that is impossible for us, as humans, whether it is out of reach or simply unattainable, is possible with you, Lord, because all things conceivable are achievable through you, Our Lord Jesus Christ: You changed water into wine, walked on waves, raised the dead, healed great infirmities, and have forgiven grave trespasses. With you, nothing is impossible, and with you in our lives, that which we pray for will be granted according to our sincerity of need. This is why we ask in your Name and through your Glorious Will, not our will, but yours, that all prayer requests will be met! Thank you, Lord Almighty!

Hear us and bless us, O Lord, whenever we pray to you with an open heart. And whether we pray for a family member or a close friend or even a stranger, we create a Circle of Love when we remember one another in our prayers; for in our hearts, Lord Christ, we aspire to live our lives according to your Righteous Word. Therefore, as we pray, all praise and all adoration are first given to you, Lord Jesus. And through the authority of prayer, our physical bodies are healed, our worries are removed, and our spiritual lives are redeemed! Thank you, Lord Jesus Christ, for the Commanding Might of your Love is made manifest through the power of constant prayer and through the sincerity of our Christian love that we have for one another: In your name, Lord God, we pray for our family and friends and for everyone in this vast and wonderful world!

We create a circle of life when we bless one another in prayer; a circle so Heavenly Powerful that nothing on earth can break it! Lord of Kindness, we pray for your Blessing to sanctify all who are in dire need of physical and spiritual renewal. Receive us, Lord God, as faithful and obedient members of your loving Christian family; for in all certainty, we abide in your Holy Word! And this, we openly and willingly and proudly confess in your Marvelous Name, Our Lord Jesus Christ!

Amen …

Chapter and verse that inspired prayer:

James 5:16    Confess your faults one to another, and pray one for another, that ye may be healed. The effectual fervent prayer of a righteous man availeth much.

# September Twenty-Five: "The God Of All"
### (As inspired from Ephesians 4:5-6)

Lord Jesus, hear our prayer …

O Lord Jesus, we believe in One God, One Faith, One Baptism, and we profess that you are the Vine of All Life, and we are the living branches of our Christian belief, and we cannot survive without you! Our Risen Lord, we beseech you, intertwine with our spirits that we may safely survive this world; for you are The God of All, The Father of Our Trust, The Patriarch of Every Family; and through you, by you, and for you, we live, we love, and we flourish! There is no doubt in our hearts, Lord Jesus, that the Bounty of your Love is Enormous and appears everywhere, everyday, in everyplace of the world! And throughout the year, we give special thanks and praise for our incredible blessings in nature: The winter snows, the spring rains, the summer sun, all the fauna and flora of the land, the waters, and the skies, the colors of the fall, and the rich soils of this good earth; for without these special blessings, the fruits of the world could not be grown and the autumn harvests would not be possible. Lord of the Bountiful Yield, we pray: For the seeds that are sown and for the crops that are grown, your faithful followers hope and pray that we will always be worthy of what we Sow in life. Lord Jesus Christ, may your Love Continually Shower Down Upon Us, may your Favor Magnify within us, and may your Divine Wisdom forever direct us that we will grow abundantly in our Christian faith and blessings.

Lord Jesus Christ, we openly avow: You are the One Lord, Our Only Faith, the True Baptism, Our One God and Father, The Holy Spirit Above All Life, and in All Souls, through which nothing exists without you! Amen!

Amen …

Chapter and verse that inspired prayer:

Ephesians 4:5-6    One Lord, one faith, one baptism, (6) One God and Father of all, who is above all, and through all, and in all.

# September Twenty-Six: "They Will Find The Light"

### (As inspired from 1 John 2:10-11)

Lord Jesus, hear our prayer …

The Sovereign Light of God shines brightly upon all who honestly love! Heavenly Father, we pray for every human on earth, for everyone is a brother or a sister to one another. And we pray that the entire world will realize this extraordinary inspiration and begin to treat each person they know as if they were warmly receiving a family member into their own life! Please hear us, Lord God, as we pray for the wanting souls of those who are lost and who have wandered from the True Light of the World. Through a sincere and heartfelt feeling of concern, and for the love and friendship among one another, we are united in our common goal, Lord Christ, and that is to pray for everyone that continually searches for but cannot find personal happiness in their life. O Lord, never finding what they want, they keep searching for something they already have. Never seeing what they have, they keep stumbling in the darkness of their own doubt. Lord Redeemer, we ask that you will end their search and help them to look within themselves, into the innocence of their own hearts. For there, they will find The Light of what your faithful have already found, and that is, You, Our Lord Jesus Christ, The Perfection of Peace and Radiant Love! And then, their searching will be no more; because you, Our Lord and God, are always there, with them, beside them, calling to them with outstretched arms from within the Tabernacle of your Holy and Eternal Radiance!

Dear Lord Jesus, please hear and accept our soulful proclamation of belief and faith: Into the Hallowed Security of your Sacred Heart do we place our lives and pray that you will safeguard our souls against all who attack peace and scorn love; thank you, Our Tender Lord, for the confidence and for the peace of mind that you have given us!

Amen …

Chapter and verse that inspired prayer:

1 John 2:10-11   He that loveth his brother abideth in the light, and there is none occasion of stumbling in him. (11) But he that hateth his brother is in darkness, and knoweth not wither he goeth, because that darkness hath blinded his eyes.

# September Twenty-Seven: "No Light Shines Brighter"

(As inspired from Ephesians 5:13-14)

Lord Jesus, hear our prayer ...

We have awakened from our spiritual slumber, O Lord, and we joyfully proclaim, from deep within our hearts, to all who will hear and accept the following Truth: All Pure Forgiveness comes from you, Lord Jesus; for in your Mercy is the Perfection of Perpetual Grace! No Light Shines Brighter than the Brilliance that Emanates from you, Lord Jesus Christ; because, without the Splendor of your Purity in the world, everyone would exist in spiritual darkness. No Compassion is Greater than the Mercy that is given by you, Lord of Mercies; for without your Love, the world would be in constant bitterness. And no Truth is More Resplendent than your Holy Word, God of Creation; because, without your Invincible Existence, the world would surely live in everlasting deceit! Lord of All Hope, without your Blessings of Love to inspire us, there would be nothing! We give thanks to you, Our Lord and God, for awakening a slumbering world to the Good News of your Divine and Unquestionable Truth and for allowing everyone and everything to exist in the Glowing Eminence of your Eternal Authority and Goodness!

Lord Jesus, you are The Lion and The Lamb, The Alpha and The Omega, The Son of God and The Son of Man, The Root of David, and we beseech you to write our names in the Book of Life, and reprove us not, but forgive each and every one of us, our own personal transgressions against your Holy Laws; for if we rend you from our lives, O Lord, we will live a godless life. If we remove you, Lord Christ, from our homes, we will live in a godless house. And if we do not have you deep within our hearts, Lord Jesus, we are not living, we are merely existing. Thank you, Lord Jesus Christ, for the Existence of Eternal Life, which is there for everyone who faithfully follows the precepts and teachings of your Veritable Gospels!

Amen ...

Chapter and verse that inspired prayer:

Ephesians 5:13-14    But all things that are reproved are made manifest by the light: for whatsoever doth make manifest is light. (14) Wherefore he saith, Awake thou that sleepest, and arise from the dead, and Christ shall give thee light.

# September Twenty-Eight: "Family And Friends"
### (As inspired from John 15:12-14)

Lord Jesus, hear our prayer …

Heavenly Father, that we may succeed in all that you Command of us though Bonding Fellowship, we offer the following words, which have derived from our Christian Values; Lord Jesus, a special prayer request from the heart, for our family and friends: We pray to you, Lord God, for those special people who share in our happiness, in our problems, and in our daily lives. We ask that you will enrich their lives and protect them from all harm and injury! Lord Christ, our friends are more precious to us than all the possessions and riches of this world! And we pray to you, Our True Lord of Great Compassion, that we will forever treasure every family member and every true friend that we have! May we never abuse nor lose the trusting love and fellowship that we have been so honored with! And may the Spiritual Blessings of The Father, The Son, and The Holy Ghost be forever upon each family member and upon each sincere friend that we have been rewarded with in life, now and forevermore!

Lord of Hosts, you have shown us that between good friends, as well as family members, there is a unique Spiritual Bond that graces all close relationships and causes all who are faithful to your Supreme Word, to be forever united under your Great Commandment of Love! Dear Lord, our friends are as family; therefore, we pray to you in total Christian unity! Hear us, O Lord of Peace, as we praise The Father, The Son, and The Holy Spirit, All of Whom are as One in a Heavenly Family of Peace: Blessed is the Trinity Godhead and Hallowed is the Blessing of Love and Friendship that has been bestowed upon us from the Greater Goodness of your Compassionate Love!

Amen …

Chapter and verse that inspired prayer:

John 15:12-14    This is my commandment, That ye love one another, as I have loved you. (13) Greater love hath no man than this, that a man lay down his life for his friends. (14) Ye are my friends, if ye do whatsoever I command you.

# September Twenty-Nine: "Our Spirits Are Restored"

### (As inspired from Micah 7:8)

Lord Jesus, hear our prayer …

You have shown us, Lord of Scripture, that all revenge is yours, that Deliverance and Salvation are yours to be given, and that all who truly love you, belong to you! How marvelous you are, Lord Jesus, for accepting us into the Good Graces of your Divine and Heavenly Love!

We will never rejoice in any opponent's downfall, rather, we will pray that God's Instruction will fill their hearts and lives to capacity, bringing them peace and calm. Lord, the Heavenly Realm of Your Goodness is indeed a steep mountain to climb, but it is a journey worth taking! Bless us, protect us, and keep us close to you, Lord God, within the Hallowed Sight of your Glowing Splendor; because the further we stray from the summit of your Light, the darker it becomes in our world! But the closer we come to you, Lord Christ, the more Enlightened we are, and the more we dwell in your Love! O Lord, please keep us in the safeguards of your Spiritual Emanation. Return us to a place in the Sun, far, far away from the worldly convictions of deceit and darkness!

Dear Lord Jesus, we pray for a daily blessing of your Spiritual Strength to occur within our individual lives. Enjoin our souls with yours, Lord God, to remain firm against the unfounded onslaughts of hostility, reproach, and distrust. Permit us, instead, Lord of The Enlightenment, to overcome and conquer any personal emotion that may subdue the Heavenly Reflections of our Spiritual Confidence; and help us, Lord of The Dawning, that we may proudly arise and stand tall in the Total Radiance of your Heavenly Compassion. Thankful are we, Lord Jesus Christ, to have your Celestial Light of Holiness in our lives; for with you, our spirits are restored and our world of shadows disappear in the Illumination from your Sacred Pinnacle of Purity!

Amen …

Chapter and verse that inspired prayer:

Micah 7:8    Rejoice not against me, O mine enemy: when I fall, I shall arise; when I sit in darkness, the LORD shall be a light unto me.

# September Thirty: "You Are The Power And The Glory"

(As inspired from Revelation 4:11)

Lord Jesus, hear our prayer …

You, Lord Jesus, are never lost, we are! This is why everyone, who aimlessly wanders through life, need not search any longer, for The Christ is Present, and may be found by everyone, simply, through acceptance and belief in you, Our Lord and Christ, The Promised Messiah! From one end of the creation to the other end, all life honors you, Lord God! We see, we agree, and we praise your Exalted Magnificence, Lord Jesus, for we acknowledge you in all that we do, in all that we are, and in all that we accomplish on earth! Lord Christ, we humble ourselves before you in thought and in deed; for all honor that comes to us belongs first to you! And we pray to you, Our Lamb of God, that we may never exalt ourselves in arrogant vainglory! May we forever remember that all the might and all the knowledge on earth and in The Kingdom above comes from you, Lord Jesus Christ! And may we never forget that you are the Power and the Glory in all things, in all ages, everywhere, forevermore, and throughout the passing of all time, from one end of infinity to the other end! Shepherd us, Our Good Lord Jesus, and pray for us to be strong and resilient against the forces that oppose the Might of your Blessedness, for all we really wish to do in life, Our Lord and God, is to return to the Heavenly Fold of your Loving Arms; where our souls are enriched through Blessings of The Holy Spirit! Therefore, we ask of you, Our Heavenly Father, to pray for us, so that everyone in the world will live a righteous life that is worthy of your Love and spiritually deserving in order to find their way home to your Great Mansion, our true destination on earth!

Amen …

Chapter and verse that inspired prayer:

Revelation 4:11   Thou art worthy, O Lord, to receive glory and honour and power: for thou hast created all things, and for thy pleasure they are and were created.

# October One: "Guardians Of Their Care"

### (As inspired from Genesis 1:28)

Lord Jesus, hear our prayer …

Every living creature on earth was created by you, Our Heavenly Father, and their purpose in this world is to serve and meet the physical, spiritual, and emotional needs of your blessed creation, us, your faithful multitudes, who have an inherent obligation to care for them; therefore, O Lord, a very special prayer request for our pets. We are so thankful to you, Lord God, for the blessing of innocent animals that are cherished, loved, and held so dearly in the hearts of your faithful. With obedience and loyalty, they dwell in our homes, share our lives, and accept us as we are, with an unconditional love. Lord Christ, may we all learn to protect and nurture this loving bond that exists between human and animal; for their trust in us becomes our promise of understanding and compassion. And through our understanding and patience, Lord Jesus, may their loyalty to us remain steadfast and trusting as we vow to become the guardians of their care, respect, and safekeeping. Lord Jesus Christ, inspire us that we may never destroy the innocence in the bond and trust that we have nurtured in our pets.

And now, to the One Who Shepherds All Souls, we offer a special prayer of thanks from those who have formed a loving attachment and bonding with God's creatures: Whenever we find a personal closeness, a companionship, an affinity with a domestic animal or creature, we are experiencing your fondness, Lord Jesus, for all life and for all blameless existence through innocent compassion! Blessed is the awareness of your Spiritual Trust throughout the creation, Lord God, and thank you once again for the ability to secure guardianships of trust and understanding with our beloved pets.

Amen …

Chapter and verse that inspired prayer:

Genesis 1:28    And God blessed them, and God said unto them, Be fruitful and multiply, and replenish the earth, and subdue it: and have dominion over the fish of the sea, and over the fowl of the air, and over every living thing that moveth upon the earth.

# October Two: "Your Word Has Delivered Us"

### (As inspired from Jeremiah 20:13)

Lord Jesus, hear our prayer …

O Lord of Compassion, your Gentle Word of Love delivers every poor soul into the Protective Hands of their Creator, into the Loving Embrace of your Mercy, Our Anointed One, Jesus Christ!

Lord of Our Salvation, you have liberated us from the terrible grips of all falsehood and you have revived our souls that we may forever exalt your name above all others as the complete fulfillment of God's Will upon earth! You are the Life Force of our immortal souls, and through the indisputable reality of your Divine Wisdom, Lord, our spirits joyfully sing out, for your Word has Delivered us and Sanctified us from the hands of all iniquity! All honor belongs to and is given to you, Lord God! And when we give praise, you know exactly what is in out hearts; therefore, we must be pure in mind and spirit when we confess the loyalty of our faith and love for you, Lord Christ! With boundless energy, we must elevate the vitality of our love to endlessly flow through the arteries of our Christian faith and through the heartfelt feelings of our acclaim for you! Lord Jesus Christ, our words of praise come deeply from within our hearts and they are as pristine as our love for you! Please, O Lord of Our Faith, see the purity in our hearts and the sincerity in our words of truth; for our words of innocence are spoken only to you, and only for you, Our Unquestionable Lord of Undeniable Compassion and Justice, Our Lord and God of Heaven and Earth; because we are Blessed, we are Loved, and we are Protected by the Spirit of your Never-ending Clemency!

Amen …

Chapter and verse that inspired prayer:

Jeremiah 20:13    … Sing unto the LORD, praise ye the LORD: for he hath delivered the soul of the poor from the hand of the evildoers.

# October Three: "Be Thankful For Every Blessing"

(As inspired from 2 Kings 19:15)

Lord Jesus, hear our prayer …

Night and day, in Benevolent Adoration, the Cherubim of Glory gaze upon the Radiant Face of the Holy Father; and with heart and soul, in great reverential respect, we also praise Him: You are God alone, Supreme Above All, Creator of Heaven and Earth, The Holy Spirit of Undeniable Presence, and we humbly ask of you, please, send your angels to protect the earth and all people who are against the enemies of your Heavenly Throne and your Blessed Creation!

Our prayer, O Lord, is a prayer for this world in which we live, for all human life that shares this Wondrous Blessing, and for all creatures, great and small, that survive and thrive on this beautiful planet! Lord Jesus, you are The Essence of Everlasting, and your Sacred Word dwells in heaven, on earth, and in every place of this vast universe! May the earth and all of its inhabitants continue in the Illuminating Glow of your Most Resplendent Love! And through the Holy Spirit of your Perpetual Presence, Lord Jesus Christ, we pray for nature to remain alive, forever: Permit all the rivers and streams to flow cleanly to our life-giving oceans; authorize the sun to continually warm the face of the earth and the rains to gently fall and nourish the soils therein; and may the multitude of life that exists on earth, from a lowly blade grass to a blessed human soul, Lord God, always be thankful for every blessing that is revealed through the Incredible Bounty of your Great and Generous Compassion that you hold for all life in a world without end! Lord Jesus, we ask that you pray for us to encourage one another, as individuals, to see and understand the paramount picture of earth's miraculous existence! And that heaven above may continually rejoice, we seek to perceive the knowledge of maintaining and keeping safe the very soul and essence of our living planet!

Amen …

Chapter and verse that inspired prayer:

2 Kings 19:15    And Hezekiah prayed before the LORD, and said, O LORD God of Israel, which dwellest between the cherubims, thou art the God, even thou alone, of all the kingdoms of the earth; thou hast made heaven and earth.

# October Four: "How Enduring Your Love Is, Lord"

(As inspired from Numbers 14:18)

Lord Jesus, hear our prayer …

In Perfect Peace is your Heavenly Kingdom; please, help the world to comprehend the simplicity of the Mystery of Life! Please, Dear Lord, help everyone to understand that you, Lord Jesus Our Anointed One, are The Solution, The Strength, The Answer to every single problem in life, no matter how simple or insignificant, nor how complex and complicated the situation may be; and all we have to do to find resolution, is to look towards you for a way out of any problem, and the door will open wide to show us the Way!

A blessing for the futures of our children and for all the children of the world. Lord Jesus, that all young people may receive gifts of the Holy Spirit, we ask for personal blessings of insight and forethought for one another as we pray for the end of world strife and iniquity; because, the wrong doings of a nation are inherited by its youth: Inspire us, O Lord, to regard our individual actions as lessons for everyone. Let us heed the warnings from Scriptural history and from the precepts of past generations that endured the words and Divine Revelations from prophets of old. And through acceptance and obedience to your Blessed Word, Lord Christ, we too will prosper and grow as Christians! How wonderful, how caring, how enduring your love is, Lord of Mercy! Thank you for your Compassionate Tolerance and Redeeming Grace over our misguided behaviors. How patient and longsuffering your love is, Lord of Forgiveness! And as a world, as a nation, and as a people of individual free will, we also ask of you, Lord Jesus Christ, to constantly guide our standards of behavior that we too may properly teach and direct our children and all future generations towards the Merciful Salvation of your Perfect Peace.

Amen …

Chapter and verse that inspired prayer:

Numbers 14:18    The LORD is longsuffering, and of great mercy, forgiving iniquity and transgression, and by no means clearing the guilty, visiting the iniquity of fathers upon the children unto the third and fourth generation.

# October Five: "Pour Out Your Blessings, Lord"

### (As inspired from Jeremiah 26:13)

Lord Jesus, hear our prayer …

Lord of Hosts, you are the Voice of Supreme Goodness, and your Words are heard in the consciences of those who desire to follow your Virtuous Ways on earth! We beg of you, Lord Jesus, surround us with moral judgment and a firm compulsion to always do what is right!

That we may amend our ways in life, we each personally ask for your forgiveness, O Lord, for any resentful feelings that we may have incurred through our own emotions of pride, prejudice, and intolerance of others. Inspire us, Lord Jesus, to always be happy for the blessings that others receive. Create in us, Lord God, the ability to discipline our emotions that we may show a True Compassion and Understanding over any loss or misfortune that others may suffer and endure. Encourage us, Lord Jesus Christ, to continually correct our ways by listening to the spiritual desires of the heart and soul, which you have so tempered through your Righteous Word! Dear Lord, we pray that any feelings of envy or spite will be removed from our hearts and replaced with your Compassionate Love and Mercy!

Pour out your blessings upon us, Lord God, that our spirits and thoughts will be fully restored, renewed, and kept away from any wrongdoings that may offend you. And as true Christians, we will now vow to improve our ways and our visions by giving total obedience to each Commandment of Our Lord and God: We vow to you, Lord of Souls, through daily prayer and renunciation of all transgression, to duly make right all thoughts and actions throughout the day, that we may become Genuine Reflections of your Goodness!

Amen …

Chapter and verse that inspired prayer:

Jeremiah 26:13    Therefore now amend your ways and your doings, and obey the voice of the LORD your God; and the LORD will repent him of the evil that he hath pronounced against you.

# October Six: "Lord, Your Love Is Forever"

(As inspired from 2 Thessalonians 1:11)

Lord Jesus, hear our prayer ...

You have revealed to us, Our God of Goodness, that you are pleased when our thoughts and actions become the fulfillment of your Righteous Commandments in all that we do and accomplish on earth! Please count us worthy as faithful Christians, O Lord, for we have amended our ways and duly follow the Timeless Teachings of your Holy Word of Compassion and Forgiveness!

All praise and glory to you, Lord God, for you alone have the power to heal through Compassion! Love is a living entity that cannot be seen nor accurately defined, it merely is, and by faith alone does its true essence exist in the souls of all who feel its heartfelt presence! Our Beloved Lord, we love you, and we have heard your calling to goodness and we faithfully promise to be obedient to your Wonderful Blessing of Virtue. Infinite and unceasing is your All-encompassing Love and Forgiveness, Lord Jesus! Unbounded is your Understanding and Compassion! Sacred and Hallowed is your Wisdom and Grace! Truly, we are blessed beyond our comprehension and in more ways than we will ever know. Lord of Heaven and Earth, we trust in you, we abide in you, and we seek to be spiritually deserving of all your blessings. Therefore, cleanse our hearts, our spirits, and our minds, Lord God, that we may come to you unstained by the corruptions and offenses of this world: Please, Lord Jesus Christ, count us worthy that we may proudly stand in the Impassioned Power of your Great Goodness! Dear Lord, your Love is Forever, your Word is Pure, and your Mercy Extends to All who ask for forgiveness. And only through you, Lord Supreme, is a True Spiritual Blessing of enduring faith possible! Pray for us, Our Beloved Lord, that each follower of your Holy Word will increase their individual faith and fulfill their rightful mission in life, and that is to find your Presence in their heart and soul everyday in their lives as Christians!

Amen ...

Chapter and verse that inspired prayer;

2 Thessalonians 1:11   Wherefore also we pray always for you, that our God would count you worthy of this calling, and fulfill all the good pleasure of his goodness, and the work of faith with power.

# October Seven: "Increase Our Wisdom, Lord"

(As inspired from Proverbs 3:35)

Lord Jesus, hear our prayer …

We praise you for our blessing of knowledge and discovery! We thank you for our modern conveniences and for all future inventions and creations that will benefit humanity! Pray for us, Our Lord and God, that we may exercise sound judgment in practical matters, sensible in behavior, and managing carefully our environment, keeping it safe from all harm, destruction, and pollution!

Spiritually encourage us, as individuals, to wisely contemplate our own personal thoughts and actions in life before proceeding forth; may we always ask ourselves if Jesus would think and do the same thing that we are about to do. O Lord, we pray that we will not be tempted nor drawn away from the Sacred Direction of your Heavenly Goodness. Strengthen our Christian convictions and increase our wisdom, Lord Christ, to know that only disappointment and dissolution reside in the shameful realms of transgression against your Word; pour out your Love that we may be lifted to a new Spiritual Awakening! And thank you, Lord Jesus Christ, for our individual blessings of conscience and conduct.

Above all creatures that exist, Dear Lord, you have empowered us with the Spiritual Enlightenment and the ability to choose between right and wrong, the light or the darkness, and to love or to abhor! Thank you, Lord of All Creation, for our inherent charge to watch over and protect the innocence of the creation; for nor animal or plant is capable of any iniquity or offense against the Laws of your Commandments, Lord God, only we, your blessed human creations of moral-conscience, have been given the right of freewill and choice! Therefore, Lord Jesus Christ, we choose the Way of Right, the Good Light, the Love of Your Divine Spirit and Might! Bless us and guide us, Lord of All Glory, in our personal decisions, discretions, and directions in life!

Amen …

Chapter and verse that inspired prayer:

Proverbs 3:35   The wise shall inherit glory: but shame shall be the promotion of fools.

# October Eight: "The Power Of Prayer"

(As inspired from James 5:15)

Lord Jesus, hear our prayer …

The Lord, in His Great Wisdom, can give answers to any mystery, even Heartfelt Questions, but there are times when the answers are forbidden to human knowledge; for sometimes, there are things in life that are Sacrosanct, and we are not privy to know why Mercy is Withheld.

Our Precious Lamb of God, you have revealed to us so many times in the Sacred Readings of the Bible that the power to heal anything comes from within the heart and soul of any person who sincerely calls upon your Holy Name, Lord Jesus, praying to you with intense faith and absolute belief!

O Lord, you have also shown us, through the blessed passages that are found in the Holy Scriptures that there is more power in a moment of sincere faith than a lifetime of doubt; for when we pray to you, Lord Jesus, we see the power of prayer through the Divine Intervention of your Magnificent Love! Lord of Heaven and Earth, we see and witness with our eyes, but through prayer, we witness with our hearts! And through Absolute Faith, our prayers will reach the Divine Authority of your Holy Spirit; for there is Heavenly Power in supplication and faith. And with the knowledge and assurance that our prayers will be answered by you, Lord Jesus Christ, we humbly submit our soulful requests in total faith and in complete trust: We pray that our words will be spiritually lifted up to you, Lord of Scripture, and be accepted by the Command of your Complete Love. And if our words of petition are found to be deserving, Our Most Gracious Lord, elevate our souls with your Redemption and our hearts with your Peace! Glory to you in the Highest, and with the highest of esteem, we, your faithful, proudly proclaim you as The True and Only Messiah, He, in whom the Word of God is promised and fulfilled: Holy Redeemer of Life, search our souls and find each one of us worthy to be called a Christian, a True Follower of your Immaculate Heart!

Amen …

Chapter and verse that inspired prayer:

James 5:15    And the prayer of faith shall save the sick, and the Lord shall raise him up; and if he have committed sins, they shall be forgiven him.

## October Nine: "In The Steps Of Your Righteousness"

(As inspired from Proverbs 12:28)

Lord Jesus, hear our prayer …

Speaking through the Apostles, Our Lord Jesus, you have inspired them to acknowledge to the flock that the wages of sin is spiritual death, but through forgiveness and constantly living one's existence through virtuous living, that all people have the same Promise to Eternal Life! Praised be to you, Lord Jesus Our Pure and Righteous King, show us the Pathway to your Sacred Heart!

There is a gentle peace that succumbs to the soul whenever the heart accepts the warm embraces of God's Tender Love, and we thank you, Lord Jesus, for sharing your Innermost Spirit of Compassion with us! Thank you, Lord, for our lives; worthy are you to receive the Power, the Glory, and the Devotion of all who worship and obey your Word of Love! It is our deepest ambition and prayer to be morally upright in accordance with your Holy Word, and to be just, honorable, and free from all trespasses! Make clear our journey through life, Lord God, for our pathway to you is but a spiritual and lifetime committal that we gladly follow! Bless us, Lord Jesus, that our travels through life may be that of a holy pilgrimage to the stairway of your heart; for only you, Lord Christ, can truly guide the way of one's life to a Perfectly Chosen Path. And, Lord Jesus Christ, we are ready to follow you! Inspire us to never transgress from our Christian faith, but to continually follow in the steps of your Righteousness. Encourage us to always remain steadfast in our spiritual convictions and never detour from our moral values. And at journey's end, Lord God, please allow our spirits to be rightfully welcomed into your Heavenly House; for you alone, Lord of All Honor and Virtue, will have guided our safe passage through life to the Holy Temple of your Great Love in the Heavenly Kingdom of saints and angels!

Amen …

Chapter and verse that inspired prayer:

Proverbs 12:28   In the way of righteousness is life; and in the pathway thereof there is no death.

## October Ten: "Holy And Divine Is Your Glorious Name"

(As inspired from 1 Chronicles 16:10-11)

Lord Jesus, hear our prayer …

Our hearts rejoice in the glory and in the might of your Heavenly Name known throughout the whole of the universe! And in a genuine reflection of our love for you, Lord Jesus, we will continually seek the Spiritual Strength that is only found through your Holy Name! For when there is a hollowness, a nothingness, a lack of purpose or direction in one's life, only you, Lord Christ, can fill an empty heart with love; only you can fill an empty spirit with joy; and only you can fill an empty life with a Spiritual Nourishment that is Pure and Unceasing! Holy and Divine is your Glorious Name, Lord Jesus Christ, and we pray to you: Bring peace to the world, fulfillment to all sincere prayers of faith, and a global determination to become a planet of goodwill! And this, Our Lord God of All People, we ask in your Sacred and Marvelous Name! For our eyes do not see what our spirits envision, our hands do not feel what our hearts may touch, and our lips do not speak the words that our souls want to say; because the Real Truth of Heaven is not found in our world of physical gratification, but only in the Spiritual Sphere of Prayer and Forgiveness!

Lord of Tender Graces, we seek your Beautiful Countenance, we seek the Ways of your Righteous Life, and we seek the Bountiful Glories of your Benevolence! O Lord and God, your Never-ending Love and Inspirations are continually before us, guiding us, showing to each faithful soul, their purpose, direction, and goal; but each one of us realizes that we must also do our own part by preparing the Way for your Divine Intervention into our individual lives. And through physical supplication and spiritual repentance, Lord God, your Spirit of Holiness is able to encompass our hearts and souls, healing all that is wronged! Blessed are you, Our Strength and Might!

Amen …

Chapter and verse that inspired prayer:

1 Chronicles 16: 10-11    Glory ye in his name: let the heart of them rejoice that seek the LORD. (11) Seek the LORD and his strength, seek his face continually.

# October Eleven: "Immersed In Your Heavenly Love"

### (As inspired from 1 Corinthians 12:13)

Lord Jesus, hear our prayer ...

Because all humans have the same Heavenly Father, we ask that you pray for us, Lord God, that everyone on earth will accept this fact and begin treating one another as brothers and sisters! O Lord, we have been lifted from the shadows of darkness into the Radiance of your Light through the mystery and majesty of faith, to bear witness, to accept, and to testify to your Glorious Presence found throughout our lives! All glory and praise is yours, Lord Jesus; for every person on earth is created and blessed in your Heavenly Image. And every person on earth shares a common bond, your Eternal Love and Mercy, Lord Christ! And no matter who we are or where we are in life, we are all born with a purpose; to find and to be united with the Divine Spirit of your Holiness! From mountain top to coastal waters, from woodland to prairie, from desert sands to green valleys, across every continent and body of water, and throughout the whole of this planet, all life was created by the Loving Generosity of your Spirit, Our Lord and God! And through your eyes, Dear Lord, every human soul is of one accord in the creation, created in the Spiritual Image of your Abundant Compassion. And together, everyone in the world shares the water, the land, and the air of our good home, our Blessing of Love from you, Lord of Creation! And we are truly thankful for our existence, for our lives, and for our earthly dwelling! Thank you, Lord Jesus Christ, for we are all immersed in your Heavenly Love, to share with one another, and to Perfectly Adore You, Our Lord and God!

Amen ...

Chapter and verse that inspired prayer:

1 Corinthians 12:13    For by one Spirit are we baptized into one body, whether we be Jews or Gentiles, whether we be bond or free; and have been all made to drink into one Spirit.

# October Twelve: "A True Reflection Of Your Goodness"

(As inspired from 2 Corinthians 3:18)

Lord Jesus, hear our prayer …

It is our prayerful agreement that every faithful Christian around the world, may proudly display a spiritual image that is in Holy Concurrence with your Blessed Spirit! Pray for us, Lord Jesus, that our souls will continually grow in your Perfect Direction, that our lives will each be filled with inward Goodness, and that our individual knowledge will be the Heavenly Fulfillment of your Hope and Good Heart that you so desire for us!

Your Holy Spirit of Compassion, Lord God, is a Gentle Caress of Love on earth that is alive and lives in Every Reflection of Goodness that is found in the whole of creation! And all that we believe in and all that we need, Lord, is reflected in the Glory of your Loving Spirit! As the moon reflects the sun's light, and as the oceans reflect the blueness of the sky, we too, Lord Christ, as followers of your Hallowed Name, desire to be a True Reflection of your Goodness; for all that is right and for all that is good, is a Precise Portrait of your Immaculate Heart! And it is our prayer, Lord Jesus, that we will be able to mirror and project an image that is worthy of our faith! Therefore, Our Lord of Life, we will continually place our faith and our trust in the direction of your Perfection! And as we will forever call upon your Sovereign Name, may our lives continually echo the sincerity of our deep Christian faith: Our Lord Everlasting, we entreat you, for it is our utmost desire on earth to be Spiritually changed into a Glorious Likeness of your Grand Resplendence; therefore, Lord Jesus Christ, we pray to be worthy of your Holy Name and Holy Spirit, Lord, through a faithful likeness of your Never-ending Love and Mercy! Bless us, Our Heavenly Father, and sanctify our spirits in this world so that we will be remembered in the next!

Amen …

Chapter and verse that inspired prayer:

2 Corinthians 3:18    But we all, with open face beholding as in a glass the glory of the Lord, are changed into the same image from glory to glory, even as by the Spirit of the Lord.

# October Thirteen: "You Are The Eternal Holiness"

### (As inspired from Habakkuk 1:12)

Lord Jesus, hear our prayer …

We testify to, and we believe in your Miracle of Love, Lord Christ. No other human or prophet nor self-proclaimed deity on earth, Lord Jesus, has ever walked on water, brought someone back to life after several days in a stone tomb, driven out legions of dark spirits from innocent souls, cured all forms of disease, illness, and affliction, forgiven sin, was then put to death, and after three days, emerged from a hewn vault, Glorified and Alive, except you, Our Lord and Christ! How is it possible for anyone to know these incredible facts and not believe in you, in your Miracles, or in your Pure Love for all humans, Our Lord and God! And it is for this reason, we offer a prayer for the whole world: Lord Jesus Christ, soften the hearts of all nonbelievers to accept you into their lives as their Only Salvation for Eternal Life!

Lord Christ, you are the Eternal Holiness! Your Word is Everlasting and we will live in the midst of your Redeeming Love forever and ever! And that we may never lose sight of you, Lord Jesus, we will always follow the calling of your Beautiful Word forevermore! We belong to you, O Lord! We are united as one heart and as one mind, in one thought, and in one knowledge that nothing and no one comes before you, Lord Jesus! Our hearts and our minds are filled with joy in knowing that we are of you, Lord Christ! For that which is not of you, Our Lord and God, cannot last; but that which is of you, Lord Jesus Christ, will last into the Forever, even into the Infinity of Holiness! You are The Living Spirit of the Everlasting, you are The Father, The Holy Spirit, The Anointed One, and in you there is Life, there is Redemption, and there is True Spiritual Salvation!

Amen …

Chapter and verse that inspired prayer:

Habakkuk 1:12    Art thou not from everlasting, O LORD my God, mine Holy One? We shall not die. O LORD, thou hast ordained them for judgment; and, O mighty God, thou hast established them for correction.

# October Fourteen: "In The Total Radiance Of Pure Light"

(As inspired from Job 22:27)

Lord Jesus, hear our prayer …

In your Exalted Name, Lord Jesus, we vow that you are The Way and The Door to all happiness on earth! Because, the mere mention of your Sacred Name chases away the shadows of darkness. The very thought of your Blessed Name brings joy to the heart! And just seeing your Prophetic Name in Scripture brings Absolute Assurance of Goodness to the lives of all who read and bear witness to the Gospels!

Lord, we cannot give anything to you that you do not already have, for you are the Creator of Everything! Therefore, we shall offer to you, Lord of Creation, the only precious possessions that we truly have: To you, Lord Jesus, we vow our sincere gifts of love, adoration, and obedience to your Holy and Commanding Word of Love! To you, Lord Christ, we vow that our individual prayers and praises are faithful and constant! And throughout this world, we acclaim and proclaim your Miraculous Victory of Life! From sunrise to sundown to sunrise again, we herald the Holy Power of your Great and Triumphant Love throughout all creation! And from the beginning of time until the end of all time, all life thanks you, Lord Jesus Christ, for the Crowning Majesty of creation, for the Incredible Wonders on this good earth, and for the Everlasting Kingdom of Heaven, which you are the Exalted and Enthroned Victor over all darkness and deception; for your Glory and your Might and your Kingdom, Lord God, exists in the Total Radiance of Pure Light and Absolute Truth! Blest are the praises offered to you, Lord Jesus, because you are worthy of all love and obedience from your faithful Christian followers!

Amen …

Chapter and verse that inspired prayer:

Job 22:27    Thou shalt make thy prayer unto him, and he shall hear thee, and thou shalt pay thy vows.

# October Fifteen: "Created Within Our Souls"

(As inspired from Obadiah 3-4)

Lord Jesus, hear our prayer …

Blessed is your Holy Image, O Lord, for in your likeness we were created. And in your eyes, Lord Jesus, no one person is greater than any other nor less than another. We are like branches of the same tree, standing in the Hallowed Brilliance of your Life Giving Sun, growing upon the spiritual foundation of your Merciful Love, forever united in a single Christian body, the Holy Spirit of your Word! Forgive us, Lord God, when haughty dreams deceive our visions. Absolve us, Dear Lord, of any personal arrogance or lofty regard. Humble our lips that boast, and deliver us from any false pride or pretense of the heart. And let us never fall victim to self-imposed honor and glory, but open our eyes that we may clearly see the Blest Reflection of your Most Holy Image all the days of our lives, Lord Jesus Christ, that you have created within our souls.

Forgive us, Our Prince of Peace, when we make trivial things in life important, and those things which are true treasures, insignificant: Overlook our personal insensitivity, Lord Almighty, when we ignore a radiant sunset, or take for granted the innocence of life, or brush aside a moment of heartfelt emotion; for it is because of you, Our Great Lord, that we have come to realize there are no wasted moments in life, only precious and personal moments that are wasted through missed opportunities.

Amen …

Chapter and verse that inspired prayer:

Obadiah 3-4    The pride of thine heart hath deceived thee, thou that dwellest in the clefts of the rock, whose habitation is high; saith in his heart, Who shall bring me down to the ground? (4) Though thou exalt thyself as the eagle, and though thou set thy nest among the stars, thence will I bring thee down, saith the LORD.

# October Sixteen: "Only You, Lord, Can Intervene"

### (As inspired from Isaiah 42:16)

Lord Jesus, hear our prayer ...

Your Sacred Love is Abundant and is freely given to every human on earth! Lord of All Righteous Ways, pour out your Lovingkindness into the hearts and minds and souls of all who inhabit this wonderful world. Humble the prideful spirit within, inspire the doubtful mind, and Spiritually Encourage the wayward to forever seek the Virtuous Path to your Loving Heart, which awaits every soul!

Intercede in our wills and intentions, Lord God, and let whatever we do in our lifetimes be done for your Unerring Will and not ours; and in this, we believe wholeheartedly! O Lord, we rejoice in our Heavenly Blessings of faith, but our Christian hearts are saddened for those who have lost their faith and are Spiritually defeated. Good Father, we offer a special prayer of resolution for those who cannot see the Glory of your Infinite Power and are unwilling to open their eyes: End their blindness, Lord Jesus, and clear their paths of all adversity and unrest! Allow them to witness the Spiritual Splendor of your Miraculous Love; for only you, Lord Christ, can give the disillusioned a will to pierce the veil of darkness that surrounds them. Only you, Lord, can intervene into the lonely lives of those who feel lost and alone. And only you, Our Chosen One, can give the confused a New Vision and the understanding to know what to do. Lord Jesus Christ, lift their spirits from out of the shadows of their uncertainty and bring them into the Lifesaving Knowledge of your Spiritual Enlightenment: And whosoever accepts you, Our Beloved Lord Jesus, as their own Personal Savior from all transgression, will suddenly realize a New Life, a New Hope, and a New Vision for their own future as a Born Again Soul; born into the Loving Care of Christianity!

Amen ...

Chapter and verse that inspired prayer:

Isaiah 42:16　　And I will bring the blind by a way that they never knew not; I will lead them in paths that they have not known: I will make darkness light before them, and crooked things straight. These things will I do unto them, and not forsake them.

# October Seventeen: "Blessed Are Your Gifts That Heal"

### (As inspired from 2 Samuel 22:7)

Lord Jesus, hear our prayer ...

During times of spiritual distress, we always call upon the Lord of Heaven and Earth to resolve our conflicts and to heal our emotions: This world is a wonderful blessing, and yet, a terrible temptation for all to delve into the shadows of false promises and allurement! Lord God, we pray: Give us strength to fend off the deceptions of all misrepresentations of goodness by giving us the Heavenly Knowledge that nothing in this world is free, that there is always a price to pay! Permit us, Our Great Lord, to always see the real intentions of those who pledge and insure the integrity of Righteousness! We thank you, Lord God, for our Spiritual Knowledge!

Pray for us, Lord, that we may always be strong during difficult and trying times; for only through your Spirit of Compassion are we delivered from our pain and suffering. And it is this wonderful knowledge, Lord Jesus, that is the promise of your Glorious Salvation! When darkness overshadows the mind and eclipses the spirit and enshrouds the body in doubt, we cry out from our earthly captivity to your Heavenly Love that towers over all that exists! Blessed are your gifts that heal our wounds and soothe our afflictions. In our distress, we call upon your Benevolent Mercy, Our God of Great and Tender Love: Lord Jesus Christ, rid our troubled lives of all sorrow and suffering! Guide us in our Spiritual knowledge! Allow the lessons of life to discipline our Christian faith and strengthen our character! And let our personal decisions in life be based upon common sense, sound judgment, and a total reliance upon your Redeeming Spirit of Mercy! We long for and pray for your Favor to bless us, Our Lord and God: We, your faithful followers, do implore the Radiant Goodness from within the Temple of your Heavenly Kingdom to come into our lives and fulfill our spiritual needs, to right all wrongs, and to heal all physical afflictions. Thank you, Lord God, for answering our prayers; for today, we have found freedom from the oppressive powers of spiritual tyranny!

Amen ...

Chapter and verse that inspired prayer:

2 Samuel 22:7   In my distress I called upon the LORD, and cried to my God: and he did hear my voice out of his temple, and my cry did enter his ears.

# October Eighteen: "Your Precious And Perfect Love"

(As inspired from 1 Chronicles 16:34)

Lord Jesus, hear our prayer …

The problems of the world often well up and cloud our thinking about the future! And within our earthly existence, there are times when we, as Christians, cannot resolve a troubling situation by ourselves. And it is for this reason that we praise you, Our Lord of Triumph: We give thanks to you, Lord God, because you are Good and your Compassionate Heart is Infinite! O Lord, we seek your Gentle Goodness! And throughout the nations of the world, there are people, everywhere, that are in soulful need and are searching for your Inner Peace and Spiritual Protection. Please, Lord Jesus, hear the loving prayers of your faithful multitudes!

From within the security of your Most Divine Kingdom, Our Great Lord, the dark shadows of hostility and turmoil do not exist; for Everlasting Peace and Unyielding Grace may only be found within the Tender Mercy and the Caring Assurance of your Loving Embrace! Therefore, Lord Christ, there is nothing more praiseworthy to us than the Quiet Strength of your Divine Spirit of Love! Throughout the day, throughout the year, and throughout our lives, we will cherish you, Our Good Lord Jesus Christ, and we will continually pray for and seek the Peace of your Precious and Perfect Love for the world as well as for ourselves! Lord God, it is our good intention in life to bring forth a great spiritual harvest from the fruits of your Heavenly Gifts of Compassion, and we ask of you to hear and place our resolution into the minds and souls of every human that exists, for there is no miracle too small nor too great that you cannot grant, because, all we need is faith: Peace on earth and goodwill to everyone!

Amen …

Chapter and verse that inspired prayer:

1 Chronicles 16:34   O give thanks unto the LORD; for he is good; for his mercy endureth for ever.

# October Nineteen: "Your Power, Lord, Radiates Truth"

### (As inspired from Jude 9)

Lord Jesus, hear our prayer …

Your Heavenly Angels guard and protect All That Is Good, merely by invoking your Name, Lord Jesus; and we too pray to you through your Infallible Name, that we, your faithful Christian followers, will never become clouds without rain, trees without fruit, but instead, we desire to become a downpour, a vast orchard of Spiritual Abundance whose harvest belongs only to you, Lord Jesus Our Good Christ!

O Lord, we pray: Please be patient with us, for as humans, we are weak and prone to backslide, but your Heavenly Authority, Lord God, is Immense and All Encompassing! And when there is total belief in your Commanding Presence, Lord Jesus, we know that strength and determination are added to our faith and our Spiritual Confidence becomes an indivisible shield against the attacks of doubt and disbelief! All Glory to your Supreme Knowledge, Lord Christ! Reach into the darkened depths of those who deny you, Our Lord Jesus, and rebuke their unfounded contentions, silence their disputes, and chase away the shadows of their ignorance! Inspire them to believe in the Enlightenment of your Unparalleled Perfection; for your Word and your Power, Lord, Radiates Truth and reaches deeply into the depths and realms of all darkness; your Might is in the Light of your Glorious Truth, where no shadows are allowed to exist! Consecrate everyone that believes in you, Lord Jesus Christ, Our King of Total Excellence; bless those who remain faithful and determined in their Christian beliefs; and sanctify your faithful followers who rebuke all transgression and follow your Most Holy Word of Life everyday of their life! Into your Unparalleled Power do we place our immortal souls for the Ultimate Protection of our Eternal Souls! Amen!

Amen …

Chapter and verse that inspired prayer:

Jude 9  Yet Michael the Archangel, when contending with the devil he disputed about the body of Moses, durst not bring against him a railing accusation, but said. The Lord rebuke thee.

# October Twenty: "Bless Our Household"

### (As inspired from Proverbs 3:33)

Lord Jesus, hear our prayer …

Everyday, Lord God, we ask that you will bring into our lives a peaceful quality within the hearts and souls of all who crossover our doorstep and come into our homes. Permit only those with God-fearing accord and good intentions to pass through the archway of our loving, Christian abode; Lord Jesus, bless our household and all people who enter into our lives. And that our spiritual confidence will continue to comfort and protect us, build within our lives a True Fortress of Courage! Fill our spiritual habitation, Lord Jesus, with the Undeniable Strength of the Holy Spirit, who will fortify and preserve all that is good and honorable! Hinder and foil the advances of all wrongdoers and wrongdoings. And whenever we are confronted by forces that challenge our Christian faith, Lord God, may we stand strong, as a tall castle in a storm, victorious and confident in our beliefs! And when we are surrounded by the shadows of uncertainty, allow the Supreme Knowledge of your Unmistakable Truth to cut through the knot of darkness and release us from our personal bondage. Permit us, Lord Christ, to obtain an inner quality of Spiritual Valor that will make us a Mighty Mansion of Heavenly Faith! Lord Jesus Christ, we thank you for blessing this house and all who abide within its sheltering fellowship: And may the Peace and Love of your Gentle heart, O Lord of Salvation, forever reside in this house and with all who live within!

Amen …

Chapter and verse that inspired prayer:

Proverbs 3:33    The curse of the LORD is in the house of the wicked: but he blesseth the habitation of the just.

# October Twenty-One: "In Your Name And Glory, Lord"

(As inspired from 1 John 5:1)

Lord Jesus, hear our prayer …

We, as humans, are beautiful creations of Heavenly Love, and we profess and strongly believe that you, Jesus Christ, are The Living God, Our Divine Creator, The Word and Spirit made Flesh, He, who was born to show us the Way out of darkness that all people may find Personal Salvation through your Immaculate Birth, Innocent Life, and Victory over death! All Glory to you, Our Wondrous Prince of Peace!

Blessed is the Enduring Love of our Lord and God, for it is forever! Lord Jesus, we continually celebrate the Miraculous Blessings of Life! How fortunate we are to be alive this day to represent the children of mothers and fathers from all the generations past. Through the millenniums of time, individuals have survived that we might be alive today! From the first two Living Souls in a garden paradise, the Hallowed Seeds of Life have been passed down. And every person that has ever been born or is born or is yet to be born, and loves the Spirit of Righteousness, is Formed and Immersed in your Name and Glory, Lord Jesus Christ! We pray for all the generations of the world, past, present, and future, that they may carry in their hearts the Seed of Love; the seed that will be imparted unto countless generations of humans yet to be borne of your Splendor and Acclaim! O Lord, you are the True Christ, you are the Scriptures of Love, and for millenniums yet to come, your Heavenly Truth will remain in the hearts of beautiful Christian souls who will one day take our place in future generations. Blessed are you, Lord God, and blessed are all people who follow Righteousness through your Glorious Namesake, for we are proud to be called Christians: earthly saints who are ever so dedicated in your Every Commanding Word of Compassion and Forgiveness!

Amen …

Chapter and verse that inspired prayer:

1 John 5:1    Whosoever believeth that Jesus is the Christ is born of God: and every one that loveth him that begat loveth him also that is begotten of him.

# October Twenty-Two: "You Are God Eternal"

(As inspired from 1 Timothy 1:17)

Lord Jesus, hear our prayer …

Timeless and permanent is your Majestic Word! We thank you, Lord God, for being so infinitely patient with us. One by one, the souls of the just turn towards you, Lord Jesus, and away from all worldly entrapments! Blessed are you, Our Crowned King, whose ceaseless forbearance will shepherd all who live and love through your Victorious Name!

All honor and glory is yours, Lord! And for all that we have received and and for all that we have been blessed with, our eyes turn towards heaven, our true home, and give praise and thanks! And although your Heavenly Form is indiscernible to human sight, Lord Jesus, your Virtuous Image will forever be found within the Divine Purity of your Great Compassion! Eternal is all love, Eternal are you, Our Lord and Christ Everlasting!

Unlike the mountains and hills, which will one day become plains and valleys, your Presence, Lord, is forever! Unlike the rivers and streams, which will one day cease their strength to surge, your Beautiful Spirit, Lord Jesus, continuously flows upon and through the creation. And unlike the forests and jungles, which will one day become desert and barren, your Infinite Word, Lord Christ, never changes and is always there for all to witness! Everlasting is your Love, Lord Jesus Christ, continuous is the creation, and forever, we will give you praise, Lord of Heaven and Earth, for you are God Eternal, Immortal, Invisible, and Ever Present in our Lives and in the lives of all people, everywhere, even in all the nations around the world!

Amen …

Chapter and verse that inspired prayer:

1 Timothy 1:17    Now unto the King eternal, immortal, invisible, the only wise God, be honour and glory for ever and ever. Amen.

# October Twenty-Three: "Through Every Moment Of Time"

(As inspired from 2 Peter 3:8)

Lord Jesus, hear our prayer ...

O Heavenly Father, you have taught us through chapter and verse: Our personal time on this planet is finite; but our time in heaven is infinite; that all life on earth eventually returns to dust and disappears; but all souls in heaven are forever fixed in the sight of God Almighty; and that love and adversity live together in this world; but in our Heavenly Kingdom, there are no shadows, because, Pure Love Flourishes Everywhere! All praise and Glory to you, Lord Jesus!

Incredible is any sunrise, wonderful are all the waking hours, and fantastic is the setting sun upon another day of living life through you, Lord Christ! Our time on earth is of a temporal nature, with a beginning and an ending, bounded in a limited amount of time, but your Existence, O Lord, is Endless and we give thanks to you for all the time that we, as humans, have been allotted upon earth! We pray: Let us never waste a single second of our precious life to bitterness or fear or sadness, but may we always keep your Cherished Word, Lord of Hosts, near; for all life is a blessing of measured moments in time. And through your eyes, Lord God, a thousand years could be but a day, and a day could be a thousand years. But if we live a thousand years or yet another day, we will forevermore, day by day, in a world without end, worship and adore you, Lord Jesus! For you alone, Lord Jesus Christ, are deserving of all praise and worship, now and forever, through every infinite passing of time!

Magnificent and glorious is each day that you create for us and for all living things! And we realize, Our Lord of Infinity, that there is no guarantee of a tomorrow for any one person; but we are absolutely certain that your Wonderful Love will be with us through every moment of time, today, and into all eternity! Holy and Sacred is each day of your love, Lord Jesus Christ, and blessed are your faithful who will one day, in time, return to your Loving Caress to live a new life in your Everlasting Flow of Endless Time!

Amen ...

Chapter and verse that inspired prayer:

2 Peter 3:8    But, beloved, be not ignorant of this one thing, that one day is with the Lord as a thousand years, and a thousand years as one day.

# October Twenty-Four: "The Way Of The Soul"
### (As inspired from John 14:6)

Lord Jesus, hear our prayer ...

From the Blessed Teachings of Christianity, we have come to know that there is a Hallowed and Sacred Passageway through which all souls must pass before entering into the Glorious Kingdom of God's Love; and it is you, Lord Jesus Christ, by whom all must find their Way! We humbly ask, O Merciful One, that you will pray for us and pray for all who search for your Undeniable Truth; because, the Way of the Lord is the Only Pathway that leads to an Eternal Life!

Lord God, your Word is Final! Only in you, Our Good Shepherd, do we place our complete trust and all of our love, for you are The Unblemished Truth of the Creation, The Holiness in All Life, and The Way of the Soul; and only through you, Lord Jesus Christ, are we able to inherit the Kingdom of God the Father! For when you walked the earth with your disciples, Lord, you gave them a New Commandment, to love one another as you loved them, and in doing so, the world would know them as True Followers of the Faith! O Lord, we too are proud to confess our love for one another, because we know that you absolutely love us; therefore, we are also True Followers, disciples of our wonderful Christian faith!

Dear Lord, our lives began the day that we were given life by you, and from that moment on, we have owed our physical and spiritual existence to you! We thank you, Lord God, for the Sacred Gift of Life, for it is the greatest blessing in the creation of the universe! And for the rest of our lives, we will repay our blessings of life through constant praise, reverence, and obedience to your Love, Mercy, and Glorious Name, Lord Jesus Christ Savior of All Nations and Peoples! And each day that we live, we will offer jubilant adoration to you and forever acclaim your Glory and Might! Triumphant is your Holy Spirit and Hallowed is your Immaculate Heart, Giver of all Life, Our Lord of the Way!

Amen ...

Chapter and verse that inspired prayer:

John 14:6     Jesus saith unto him, I am the way, the truth, and the life: no man cometh unto the Father, but by me.

# October Twenty-Five: "The Circle Of Faith"

(As inspired from Psalms 5:12)

Lord Jesus, hear our prayer …

Our Heavenly Father, we await for and pray for the day when every person on earth acknowledges their spiritual responsibility to create a heavenly atmosphere that will encircle the earth; creating a world that is filled with friendship, honest concern for one another, and a sincere desire to work for the common good of all people, of all families, and of all nations! We pray: Let us search our hearts for The Truth; and as we seek you, O God, we know that you will be found within us!

Shield us, Our Conquering King, with the Redemptive Resolution of your Merciful Grace! Bless all who search for and follow the peace that is within their own hearts! Dear Lord, we pray for all families on earth that they may grow in virtue and be Sanctified by your Love and Mercy; for when a new generation continues the Sacred Lineage of Love, the Christian family comes full circle! Blessed is your Wisdom, Lord Christ, for the family is the Complete Fulfillment of Life.

We give you thanks, Lord God, for the caring closeness and spiritual sharing of our mothers and fathers and brothers and sisters; we praise you, Lord Jesus, for allowing warmth and understanding to enter into the individual heart of each family member. And as loving relatives provide security and compassion for one another, we are forever joyous for everyone who becomes a faithful member in the family of your Heavenly Love; because, therein, begins the circle of faith! And through a daily reverence and trust in you, Lord Jesus Christ, we are thankful to be a part of your Heavenly Household, a loving lineage that is surrounded and shielded by a Halo of Hallowed Protection in the Glowing Circle of your Great Love for all your children on earth! And whether related or not, all Christians are united in Christ through a Fellowship of Kindred Blood, through the Sacrifice of Our Lord Jesus Christ, who gave up His Innocent Blood that everyone may be saved!

Amen …

Chapter and verse that inspired prayer:

Psalms 5:12   For thou, LORD, wilt bless the righteous; with favour wilt thou compass him as with a shield.

# October Twenty-Six: "You, Lord, Are The Giver Of Truth"

(As inspired from Daniel 2:22-23)

Lord Jesus, hear our prayer …

All praise to Our Heavenly Father and Teacher, for you have made known to us the secrets of life and all matters of how to inherit The Kingdom of Your Domain, which is to genuinely love one another on earth and to give our hearts completely to you, Lord Jesus Our Savior!

O Lord, all the knowledge in the universe stems from within your Holy Spirit! Blessed is your Name Forever into Eternity! You, Dear Lord, have made it possible for us, as humans, to look into the far reaches of space, to descend into the deepest seas, to climb the highest mountains, and to search the earth and unlock its mysteries; but wherever our quests may take us, our Christian faith will always remain with you, Lord Jesus! For we are able to look into our own hearts, search the depths of our own minds, and delve into the theories of life itself, but without the Guidance of your Great Wisdom, Lord Christ, we would remain in the darkness of our own ignorance and superstition. But as sincere and faithful followers of your Perfect Inspiration, Lord Jesus Christ, we will always seek your truth in all our journeys through life; because only you are the Giver of Truth! Therein, when we seek the Absolute Knowledge of the Absolute Truth, we need only search no further than our own love for you; and thereon, we will find the answer, Lord God, Our True Keeper and Giver of all Knowledge!

Amen …

Chapter and verse that inspired prayer:

Daniel 2:22-23    He revealeth the deep and secret things: he knoweth what is in the darkness, and the light dwelleth with him. (23) I thank thee, and praise thee, O thou God of my fathers, who hast given me wisdom and might, and hast made known unto me now what we desired of thee: for thou hast now made known unto us the king's matter.

# October Twenty-Seven: "If It Were Not For You, Lord"

### (As inspired from The Song of Solomon 1:1, 2:1)

Lord Jesus, hear our prayer …

Thank you for showing us, Our Almighty God, that where love is, there is True Creation! Where there is mercy, there is Heartfelt Compassion! And where there is forgiveness, there is Total Salvation! We cannot thank you enough, Our Lord So Merciful, for all that you have done for your faithful, for the world, for our souls!

Blessed is your Garden of Life, Our Most Gracious Lord, for you have filled it with the Bounty of your Love! Every imaginable variety of life exists upon and within this Planet of Existence! Be it plant or animal, you, Lord of Our Creation, in all your Wisdom, have created worlds within worlds, relationships that are dependent upon one another for their individual survival, and a multitude of unseen creatures whose very existence we rely upon for our own existence! All Glory, Praise, and Exaltation are yours, Our Lord of Life Jesus Christ!

O Lord, you are the beauty in the Rose of Sharon, you are the Perfect Accord in the Song of Songs, and you are the Innocent Purity in the Lily of the Valley. And if it were not for you, Lord God, our lives would be meaningless. Through your Great Love, our lives blossom and live! And through your Many Blessings of Love, our faith thrives and flourishes! Lord Jesus, you give us the needed courage when we are weak, you instill in us understanding when we are in doubt, and you fill us with Spiritual faith when all humanly hope seems lost! We thank you, Lord Christ, for the life that you have provided for us; for your Timeless Radiance extends far into the darkness of all uncertainty, your Merciful Salvation warmly touches every spirit on earth, and your Patient Love reaches deeply into the very soul of every heart! Blessed is the Compassion that you hold for us, Lord Jesus Christ, blest is the creation, and grateful are we to receive your Most Gracious Love!

Amen …

Chapter and verse that inspired prayer:

The Song of Solomon 1:1    The song of songs, which is Solomon's (2:1) I AM the rose of Sharon, and the lily of the valleys.

# October Twenty-Eight: "Reflections Of All That Is Righteous"
### (As inspired from 1 Corinthians 15:49)

Lord Jesus, hear our prayer ...

Because our world can be, at times, a quagmire of emotional existence, we pray for heaven on earth! Every scope and degree of negative feelings and attitudes seem to rob, detour, and deflect our True Reason for life, and that is to love you with all of our heart and soul, and to do unto others as we would have them do unto us. O Lord, we pray for heaven on earth, because your Blessed Kingdom, Lord Jesus, is serene, harmonious, and in perfect accord! Heaven is a Realm of Living Love, where age and time and tarnish do not exist! Your Sacred Domain is created from the Purity of Innocence, from which only peace and compassion are allowed to thrive! O Lord, we pray for heaven on earth!

Lord God, even though our physical bodies are of this earth, born of flesh, our infinite souls were created by you, God the Father, in our Home of Heavenly Hosts! Dear Lord, we ask for your Commanding Authority to govern and direct our visions and beliefs! Glory and praise to you, Lord of Creation, for you are the Divine Vision of Truth that is revealed and revered in the world; and we know that your Love will be with us now and forevermore! And that your Sacred Spirit will always remain in our lives, we pray that your Favor will forever guide us in our lifetimes. With your Love in our lives, Lord Christ, we become spiritually complete. With your Holy Spirit in our lives, Lord of Righteousness, our faith becomes whole. And with your Deep Mercy in our lives, Lord Jesus, we seek to fully understand and to live peacefully with one another. Therefore, Our Prince of Peace, that we, your faithful, may become Living and Loving Images of your Heavenly Compassion, allow the Great Power of your Word to subdue and overwhelm any earthly deception that may hinder the discernment of your glory from our eyes! Give us the strength and the knowledge to become True Reflections of all that is Righteous and Just! And allow us, Lord Jesus Christ, to become shining symbols of Christian Fellowship that is only found by accepting you, Lord God, as one's own Personal Savior and Lord!

Amen ...

Chapter and verse that inspired prayer:

1 Corinthians 15:49    And as we have borne the image of the earthy, we shall also bear the image of the heavenly.

# October Twenty-Nine: "We Beseech Your Mercy"

### (As inspired from Numbers 14:19-20)

Lord Jesus, hear our prayer …

Dear Lord, please, we beseech your Mercy and Amnesty: Forgive us and forgive all people who are sincerely sorry for having offended you in thought or in action! We pray that you will absolve those who blame you for their own misfortunes in life. Give remission to those who lack understanding and who carelessly use your name irreverently. And pardon those who denounce you, Lord God, for all the problems of the world; because, those who blame others for their personal misgivings are only blinded by their own shortcomings. We also pray for those who wrongfully curse you, Lord Christ, for they are deaf to their own words. And for those who cast accusations at you, Lord Jesus, for unfounded reasons, we pray that their personal insecurity will dissolve in your Spiritual Assurance. Lord Jesus Christ, we pray for those who willfully stand in darkness; for they cannot see your Light through their obscure veil of shadows.

Please, Lord of All Salvation, release all people from their self-imposed bondage and foolish iniquities. Absolve them, pardon them, and pass over their offenses, Lord God; because, they are ignorant of their ignorance! Please, Lord of All Enlightenment, make known in all minds and in all souls throughout the world, a True Knowledge of Spiritual Respect for your Glorious and Great Holiness! Fill all hearts, everywhere, with a Compassionate Desire to seek out and discover the Divine Beauty of your Merciful love! Lord Jesus Christ, please hear our prayer, as we pray for the world and for ourselves: Our dreams and goals are within reach when all belief and acclaim for you, Lord Jesus, is given in an earnest and assured understanding that the granting and attainment of one's personal prayer request is only achieved through your Perfect Will and Understanding, Our Lord of Goodness, and not through our own personal demands of what we believe is right! Bless us and pray for us, Our Lord of Forgiveness, that every soul on earth may obtain lasting understanding and patience!

Amen …

Chapter and verse that inspired prayer:

Numbers 14:19-20     Pardon, I beseech thee, the iniquity of this people according unto the greatness of thy mercy, and as thou hast forgiven this people, from Egypt even until now. (20) And the LORD said, I have pardoned according to thy word:

# October Thirty: "God Of All Redemption And Salvation"

(As inspired from Lamentations 3:25-26)

Lord Jesus, hear our prayer …

Enlighten the spiritual consciousness of every man, woman, and child, to fully comprehend that we, as humans, are completely responsible for all of our worldly troubles, spiritual problems, and physical ailments on earth because of transgressions and the lack of remorse; and that you, Lord Jesus Christ, are the Only Way that is needed to resolve all pain and suffering of the mind, the body, and the soul! We prayerfully plead to you, O Lord, for a World wide Revival of Christianity and the Complete Acceptance of you as our Lord and God Through Salvation and Forgiveness!

Our souls lament as we await the arrival of your Perfect and Merciful Compassion. Lord Christ, you are the True Messiah, and a day does not go by that we do not seek nor hope for the Cleansing Power of your Redeeming Grace. Save us, Lord Jesus, from the ignorance and sanctions of our personal transgressions and foolish mistakes, and forgive us our stumbling errors and wrongful misdeeds against others. And although we may not be worthy, Our Lord of Clemency, we offer our heartfelt praises to you as we thank you for Lighting the Way to our Spiritual Salvation through the Forgiving Embrace of your Great and Compassionate Love!

O Lord, you are the Perpetual Radiance in the heavens above, and whatever we do, or wherever we are, we know that you will not abandon us; only our freewill can move us away from the Light into the darkness; for in our hearts, we know that you will always be with us. And we know that you will forever remain our Constant Beacon to Forgiveness! Even if we slip or stray or lose sight of your Light, Lord Jesus Christ, we know that you will always have us in view. Blessed are you, Our Lord and God of All Redemption and Salvation!

Amen …

Chapter and verse that inspired prayer:

Lamentations 3:25-26   The LORD is good unto them that wait for him, to the soul that seeketh him. (26) It is good that a man should both hope and quietly wait for the salvation of the LORD.

# October Thirty-One: "You Are The Lord Of Holy Truth"

(As inspired from Revelation 7:12)

Lord Jesus, hear our prayer …

Your faithful family firmly attests to the following: We believe in you, we keep your Commandments, and we are proud to be called Christians, Followers of The Holy One! In our hearts, O Lord, we serve you night and day! And night and day, we give thanks to you, Our Lord God Almighty, for your Pure and Innocent Love that leads us away from deception and into the Resplendent Purity of your Crystalline Truth; for when the challenges come, we will stand firm in our secure Christian faith; when darkness surrounds us, we will still see your Most Radiant Glory; and when you approach, Lord Jesus Christ, we will race towards you with open arms giving Praise and Honor and Glory for your Great and Benevolent Love that Reigns Supreme throughout the whole of creation!

Lord of Heaven and Earth, with dignity, our voices proudly profess to the world: We will always believe in you! Through the cold, through the dark, and through every storm in life, our Christian faith will survive the forces of doubt and ignorance until your Magnificent Gospel is known and accepted by the whole world that you are the Lord and God of The Holy Truth! Inspire the nations of earth to seek your Flawless Grace, turn our streets of darkness into Light, let no one oppose your Might, and grant us the strength, Our Lord of Sublime Splendor, to meet every spiritual challenge forthright! And this we ask through The Holy Elegance of your Most Powerful and Honorable Name, lord Jesus Christ, Our Personal Savior and God! All power, all honor, and all praise unto you, Our Great and Wonderful Lord of All Life!

Amen …

Chapter and verse that inspired prayer:

Revelation 7:12    Saying, Amen: Blessing, and glory, and wisdom, and thanksgiving, and honour, and power, and might, be unto our God for ever and ever. Amen.

# November One: "Through Faith In Your Spirit"

### (As inspired from Genesis 1:1-2)

Lord Jesus, hear our prayer …

We praise you and give you thanks, Dear Lord, for the many blessings of the Holy Spirit: Heavenly Father, we prosper and we flourish through the Goodness of your Immaculate Heart; Hallowed and Pure are your blessings! And all that is good and all that is innocent, comes to us through faith in the Holy Ghost; Blessed and Sacred is your Holy Word! Lord God, in the beginning, there was only darkness, and then you brought Light into the world! You created the beginning of time, and as it was in the beginning, as it is now, and as it shall be forevermore, the Spirit of your Love moves upon the earth, through all souls, and throughout all time; Holy and Divine is your Great Spirit of Compassion! In your Most Honorable and Sacred Name, we individually denounce darkness as blameworthy for all the ills of this world, and we acclaim the Light of Jesus Christ as the Only Salvation for all the people of this world! Amen!

Lord God, there is so much to gain through faith in your Spirit; for the rewards of belief greatly outweigh the deceptions of doubt! Therefore, Lord Christ, we confess and we profess our sincere belief in your Holy and Divine Spirit! Lord Jesus, may every living creature in the creation bow in their reverence to your Glory and Greatness! Only to you, Lord God of Creation, do we owe our physical and spiritual lives for this wonderful world upon which we live, love, and learn! There is nothing in the known universe that you did not create! Hear the adulation of life, Lord Jesus Christ, as every creature and being in nature sings out their own innocent and individual praise to the Glory of your Greatness: Blest and Holy is your Spirit of Love, Blessed and Sacred is your Holy Spirit that exists forever unto eternity!

Amen …

Chapter and verse that inspired prayer:

Genesis 1:1-2    In the beginning God created the heaven and the earth. (2) And the earth was without form, and void; and darkness was upon the face of the deep. And the Spirit of God moved upon the face of the waters.

# November Two: "All Futures Begin Today"

### (As inspired from Deuteronomy 4:10)

Lord Jesus, hear our prayer …

Our Heavenly Lord, you have truly taught us, through the Blessed Scriptures, that a tree is known by its fruit, and that every good tree brings about good fruit! It is our prayer, Lord God, that the seeds we plant today, will one day give you a bountiful harvest! We have gathered together in good fellowship, Dear Lord, spiritually united in our belief that all young children are the future seeds; the future of creation, the future of life, the future of love, and the future of our Christian faith! And with genuine compassion in our hearts, Lord Christ, we offer our sincerest prayers for all children, everywhere in the world, that they will hear and learn the prophetic words of your Commanding Love! And that all people on earth will one day teach virtue and moral excellence to their own children, Lord Jesus, we pray that our young people will grow into adulthood, wise and strong in the ways of your Wisdom and Goodness. For when they acquire the Virtuous Knowledge of the Scriptures in their own hearts, their individual accord will lead them directly to a Spiritual Understanding that all futures begin today, with you as their Lord! Therefore, we ask that all children may learn to share in the words and works of your Righteousness: Lord Jesus Christ, we sincerely beg of you to keep safe all the young people of this planet and all the days of their lives and keep them Spiritually safe from the onslaught of darkness by placing their innocence in the Radiant Protection of your Never-ending Love!

O Lord, within the innocent heart of every child, is the blessed knowledge of love. Born to be cared for, children learn from their caregivers; therefore, we offer a special prayer for our greatest resource on earth, for all children: Lord, let the hands that feed them, never be raised against them in anger; may the arms that hold them, enfold them in gentle embraces; and we ask that you inspire the words that are spoken to them, be words of encouragement. In other words, Dear Lord, please sanction the care that all children receive on earth to be given with compassion, understanding, and patience.

Amen …

Chapter and verse that inspired prayer:

Deuteronomy 4:10    Specially the day that thou stoodest before the LORD thy God in Herob, when the LORD said unto me, Gather me the people together, and I will make them hear my words, that they may learn to fear me all the days they shall live upon earth, and that they may teach their children.

# November Three: "True Word Of Grace"
### (As inspired from Deuteronomy 15:7, 11)

Lord Jesus, hear our prayer …

Lord God, because of weak faith in the world, there are many who are disillusioned; poor people who are indigent in belief and impoverished in spirit! And it is for these lost souls for whom we pray: Permit the needy, in every nation, to come into the Full Richness of your Holy Spirit! Grant them the ability to discern those who try to deceive them, and allow them to also perceive all the ways that are used to lure their innocence away from Heaven's Light; and as we go about our daily lives, we will acknowledge and reflect a genuine heartfelt gratitude to you, O Lord, for continually feeding, clothing, and giving shelter to all who hunger and thirst for physical and spiritual nourishment. And by first giving thanks to you, Lord Christ, for the blessings that have been set before us, we in turn begin each day with a wonderful awakening in your Divine Protection and Grace that has been freely bestowed upon us by the Virtue of your Benevolent Love! And through your Loving Compassion, Lord Jesus, we are able to understand and experience a deep feeling of sharing and caring for others. As Christians, Lord Jesus Christ, we pray that you will prepare a grand feast for all who hunger. We ask that you will clothe all who are burdened and suffer from the forces of nature's elements. Our Lord and God, we pray that you will allow every person, great or small, who seeks spiritual or physical refuge, to clearly hear and sincerely believe in your True Word of Grace! Bless and heal every person who is physically, spiritually, and mentally poor; because, their needs can only be met through you and only by you, Our Lord of Heavenly Sanctuary!

Amen …

Chapter and verse that inspired prayer:

Deuteronomy 15:7, 11    If there be among you a poor man of one of thy brethren within any of thy gates in thy land which the LORD thy God giveth thee, thou shalt not harden thine heart, nor shut thine hand from thy poor brother: (11) For the poor shall never cease out of the land: therefore I command thee, saying, Thou shalt open thine hand wide unto thy brother, to thy poor, and to thy needy, in thy land.

# November Four: "Through The Darkened Barriers"

(As inspired from Zephaniah 3:5)

Lord Jesus, hear our prayer ...

Each new day begins with the Sun's Light; and proudly, Lord, do we follow the Righteous Course of your Sacred Teachings! Because, everyday, Our Lord of Heaven and Earth, you smile upon the just, you nurture the goodly cause, and you forever love the innocent heart. Shepherd us, Lord Christ, guide us and protect us from the iniquities of life. Sustain us, O Lord, against the adversaries of truth and from those who seek to cloud your existence. Teach us, Lord Jesus, to be wise in what we say, in what we think, and in what we do. Fill our hearts with Discerning Wisdom, O Lord, that we may remain insightful and not be blinded by unjust causes or by foolish convictions.

Lord Jesus Christ, your Judgments are Just and your Rewards are Exact; sanction your Sacred Writings to forever remain within the midst of our earthly Christian knowledge. And like the Crystal Clear Waters that flow from your Heavenly Throne, Lord God, direct your True Enlightenment to surge into our hearts that we will always be able to see through the darkened barriers of all unrighteousness! And with the setting sun and approaching darkness, we will, as Christians, begin each night in the serenity of your Loving Peace, as we await the Full and Radiant Morning Light of the Son! And then, with each new dawning, we pray to you. Dear Lord: Sanctify our lives against all that is contrary to your Holy Word, and enrich our faith with a Spiritual Awakening of Goodness! Allow the unjust to see their injustice towards others and towards your Holy Commandments! Release the world, Our Resplendent King, from all darkness and captivity. Place into every human heart, The Morning Star of Salvation, your Precious Word, Lord Jesus!

Amen ...

Chapter and verse that inspired prayer:

Zephaniah 3:5    The just LORD is in the midst thereof; he will not do iniquity: every morning doth he bring his judgment to light, he faileth not; but the unjust knoweth no shame.

# November Five: "To A New Freedom"

(As inspired from Luke 1:78-79)

Lord Jesus, hear our prayer …

A prayer request for ourselves and for every person in the world: Strengthen our individual characters and convictions that we will make correct and proper decisions in life! The woes of the world are upon our shoulders, Lord God, and we know and accept our human responsibility of spiritual disobedience and worldly pride, the same unrighteous infractions that led to the great downfall of all humanity; for no other creature on this planet has the moral obligation nor the understanding to commit a single act of transgression. We are but loving mortal beings endowed with the wonderful knowledge of what is right and what is wring, but all too often, through freewill, we choose the incorrect path. Pray for us and forgive us, O Lord of Justice, for our indiscretions; and through your Divine Inspiration, we will conquer all of our weaknesses!

Dear Lord, we call upon your Holy Name and you answer! We reach out to you, and you are there! Through you, Lord Christ, we fear no shadows, for you are The Sacred Harmony in life that leads the world to a new freedom, to a new understanding, and to a new way of life that will finally end all hostility and strife! We, who have miraculously found you, Lord Jesus, thank you for your Eternal Love and Tender Mercies! But for those who are still lost, still wandering with no purpose in their heart, still trusting in their false beliefs, we pray to you, Lord Jesus Christ, that their days of searching may soon be over. O God, we ask that those who are burdened with spiritual doubt will no longer thirst for proof. We pray that the curtain of darkness will fall from their view, allowing the Light of your Enlightenment to shine through, ending their years of captivity in the shadows of indecision and distrust. And we also ask of you, Lord God, that they will lift their eyes to spiritually see you as the True Light of The World that will direct them to the Splendor of your Loving Peace. Guide their minds, their souls, and their feet towards the faith of Christianity and to their own Personal Salvation!

Amen …

Chapter and verse that inspired prayer:

Luke 1:78-79    Through the tender mercy of our God; whereby the dayspring from on high hath visited us, (79) To give light to them that sit in darkness and in the shadow of death, to guide our feet into the way of peace.

# November Six: "Your Word Is Never Broken"

### (As inspired from Numbers 30:2)

Lord Jesus, hear our prayer …

Lord God, all truth comes from love, and all love comes from you, our Heavenly Creator! O Lord, your Holy Promise is a Stronghold of Virtue, and your Word is Never Broken! Hear our soulful confession, Lord Jesus: Your Sacred Vow is Everlasting, more permanent than the earth itself, more infinite than the ends of the universe, always remembered, and never forgotten, even unto eternity! Our Hallowed Lord, that we may never break our promise or go back on our word or purposely violate a solemn oath, we ask of you, Dear Lord, to remove from our hearts and from our minds and from our souls, any desire to state anything untrue, to give any falsehoods or false impressions, to perjure ourselves, to falsify any written or oral statement, or to knowingly forswear to you, Lord Jesus Christ, to others, or even to ourselves! Pray for us to develop sound principles, Lord Jesus, so that we will always do our best to honor all that we pledge or promise or vow to do in life!

Time heals all wounds, but not the scars. And it is of such experiences, Lord Jesus, that we pray to be released from: Remove all hurtful memories that we may have or that we may have given to others; we ask to be released from our transgressions and from our transgressors, in the name of The Father, The Son, and The Holy Spirit of Love! Lord God, you have given us the Ten Commandments to save our souls and to morally strengthen our personal convictions of self-discipline. And we clearly realize that all deception is wrong, for it not only hurts the deceived, but also the soul of the deceiver! Therefore, we ask of you, Lord: Spiritually inspire us to consider our actions before engaging ourselves in any pledge or promise; for a broken word has the ability to break a heart. Lord, pray for us that we may continue to be vibrant Christians, enduring in all that we commit to the heart and spirit! But most of all, Lord Eternal, help us, in our daily lives, to always be committed to the very real values of honesty, virtue, and in all that we avow as Proud Christians!

Amen …

Chapter and verse that inspired prayer:

Numbers 30:2    If a man vow a vow unto the LORD, or swear an oath to bind his soul with a bond; he shall not break his word, he shall do according to all that proceedeth out of his mouth.

# November Seven: "Fill Their Spirits To Capacity"
### (As inspired from Daniel 9:18)

Lord Jesus, hear our prayer …

There is such great love and praise in our hearts for you, Lord Jesus, because of your Wonderful Gifts and Blessings that you offer to us every day of our lives! And for this, we, as Christians, must thank you and give supplication for the salvation of all the people in the world who have not found you in their lives! To you, Our Lord, Our Spirit, Our Father in Heaven, we submit and surrender to the Holy Power and Authority of your Great and Compassionate Mercy! Hear the humble prayer requests of those who are destitute, Lord Jesus. Bless the weak and needy spirit that seeks fulfillment in your Name! Lord Christ, you fulfill the wants of all who are poor. And for all who pursue your Great Mercies, we ask that you will hear the soulful requests of those who are truly repentant in their hearts! Lord of All Forgiveness, we pray: Enrich the lives of those who suffer from the result of an impoverished spirit, poverty of vision, or a distressed heart. Into their lives, Lord Jesus Christ, pour out your Goodness and set their ambitions towards the Riches of Love. Remove the emptiness in their lives and fill their spirits to capacity with the Spectacular Atonement of your Great and Everlasting Mercy. Lord God, we ask that you will receive and give peace to all who seriously suffer in this world, to each person who soulfully prays to you, and to everyone that sincerely asks for forgiveness! End their personal problems and troubles, Our Prince of Salvation, and offer them a Life of Spiritual Tranquility, Heavenly Peace, and Unbounded Happiness, through the Fulness of your Holy Spirit!

Amen …

Chapter and verse that inspired prayer:

Daniel 9:18    O my God, incline thine ear, and hear; open thine eyes, and behold our desolations, and the city which is called by thy name: for we do not present our supplications before thee for our righteousnesses, but for thy great mercies.

# November Eight: "Our Lamp Unto The Darkness"

### (As inspired from 2 Samuel 22:29 and Isaiah 45:2)

Lord Jesus, hear our prayer …

Lord, we have the faith of the prophets, and there is nothing in this world nor in this infinite universe that is more powerful than your Merciful Love, and we praise you, Lord God, for our spiritual and physical protection: The Light of your Holy Redemption is continually set before us, shepherding us, making right the ways of your faithful souls. Lord Christ, what lies before us is always the uncharted unknown. And within the unknown, the snares of deception and misdeeds may lie in wait. However, within the center of our Christian faith is the Glorious Lamp of your Radiant Goodness that encourages and illuminates the path of moral virtue; and through your Divine Help, Lord Jesus, the pitfalls in life are seen and avoided. Our Gentle King and Lord, where there is belief in you, there is protection and safety through the Spiritual Trust and Wisdom of Sincere Faith! Please, Lord Jesus Christ, forever be our Lamp unto the darkness, light the path of uncertainty that lies before us, and help each one of us to be firmly established in our spiritual convictions; for with you in our lives, Our Living God, the stronghold of adversity is shattered and the crooked path is made straight! And no adversary of Goodness can ever be victorious when your Heavenly Protection is prayed for through a soulful remorse of repentance and a Spiritual Uplifting of faith! All Glory to you, Our Most Radiant Lord of Salvation; thank you for saving our spiritual and physical lives!

Amen …

Chapter and verse that inspired prayer:

2 Samuel 22:29    For thou art my lamp, O LORD: and the LORD will lighten my darkness.

Isaiah 45:2        I will go before thee, and make the crooked places straight: I will break in pieces the gates of brass, and cut in sunder the bars of iron:

# November Nine: "Together As One, In One Belief"

### (As inspired from Exodus 24:3)

Lord Jesus, hear our prayer …

We are grateful to you, Our Beloved Lord, for the physical and spiritual unity that is created whenever kindred souls share in the love and protection of the Christian Family. And in our physical and spiritual existence, there exists but one God, the Father of All Creation, the Spirit of all Love, the Son of All Hope, and it is you, Lord Christ Our Heavenly Host, that is the Heart and Center of everything! And through your eyes, Lord Jesus, the family is truly blessed. For the thankful family comes together as one, in one belief, in one voice to proudly proclaim that all the words and teachings that you have provided for us, Lord Jesus Christ, through the saints and prophets, will be faithfully followed by all who are devoted and obedient to the Authority of your Glorious and Continuous Word of Life!

Lord God, through the Commandments of your Blessed Writings, given to us from the Caring Goodness of your Sacred Heart, we receive and accept our lessons of life that will enable us to return to your Loving Favor in Our Heavenly Home! We ask of you, Lord Jesus, that you allow all families, throughout the world, to unify in your Magnificent Name: Encourage every mother and father and brother and sister and friend and stranger in the world to come together in spiritual peace and heavenly accord! And then together, as one voice in agreement, we will be able to offer a world of thanks to you for all the blessings of our vast global kindred! In the name of The Father, The Son, and The Holy Spirit, we entreat Spiritual Salvation and proclaim you, Lord Jesus Christ, as our Judgment and Reward on earth and in the Kingdom of Heaven!

Amen …

Chapter and verse that inspired prayer:

Exodus 24:3    And Moses came and told the people all the words of the LORD, and all the judgments: and all the people answered with one voice, and said, All the words which the LORD hath said we will do.

# November Ten: "The Truth Is Always Right"

(As inspired from Mark 10:15 and Deuteronomy 4:13)

Lord Jesus, hear our prayer …

Blessed and tender is the innocent heart of a child; and throughout your Heavenly Kingdom, O Lord, live the angelic, childlike innocence of your faithful souls. Lord Christ, we pray for world reform through the Divine Intervention of your Holy and Profound Wisdom! Impart into the minds and souls of everyone on earth the need to perceive and pursue the virtues of life's Ten Commandments. Illuminate the world through a Scriptural and Spiritual awakening, Lord Jesus, that will inspire people everywhere, to make clear and correct choices according to the sound judgments of right and wrong. And that everyone will forever desire the best for one another, empower our consciences to be guided and governed by the lessons of Goodness; Lord of Enlightenment, teach us to truly embrace the undeniable understanding of a righteous life. Remove from our hearts the insolence of arrogant pride and instill into everyone's spirit the heavenly knowledge that wrong is simply wrong and that the truth is always right! For just as little children perceive the world through innocent eyes, we too, Lord Jesus Christ, must follow the Perfect Path of your Righteous Word to the Kingdom of your Glorious Love; wherein, one day, everyone will enter through the Heavenly Gates of Goodness and be welcomed home by the Tender Mercies of our Loving Father! Therefore, whatsoever you Command in your Heavenly Kingdom, Lord Jesus, let it be written in stone that your Power and Might are known throughout all the realms and worlds of existence! Our hearts, our minds, and our souls have become Spiritual Scrolls for every Hallowed Word of your Authority over all that exists: Praise and Glory follow you, Lord Jesus Our Messiah, wherever you go!

Amen …

Chapter and verse that inspired prayer:

Mark 10:15          Verily I say unto you, whosoever shall not receive the Kingdom of God as a little child, he shall not enter therein.

Deuteronomy 4:13   And he declared unto you his covenant, which he commanded you to perform, even ten commandments; and he wrote them upon two tables of stone.

# November Eleven: "The Armor Of Our Righteousness"

(As inspired from Ephesians 6:10-11)

Lord Jesus, hear our prayer …

Our Good Lord of Heaven and Earth, there is no other energy, nor force, or entity that is capable of defeating your Hallowed Magnificence! You are All Powerful and we remain faithful and strong in our Christian conviction, that nothing in this world, or in any other world, will sway our belief in you or turn us aside from our Heartfelt Love that we have for you, Lord God! Thank you, O Lord, for your Great Spiritual Light! Thank you, Lord God, for always being right! Because, today, as with everyday, whenever we venture out into this world of uncertainty, it is our prayer that we may be victorious against the forces that oppose your Power and Might: Let us form an army of peace, whose sole armament is love, your Conquering Love, Lord Jesus, that has subdued, throughout the ages of time, the very hearts of your adversaries!

Our Lord and Protector, we beseech you, prepare us physically, mentally, and spiritually against the opponents of your Goodness: From the rivers of Truth and Justice, forge a double-edged sword that will go before us. Let one edge be that of Salvation and the other edge of Deliverance! Place the hilt into our palms, Lord Jesus, that we may be triumphant against the forces of oppression, ignorance, and all moral corruption! Lord of All Victory, permit your Unequaled Goodness to become the armor of our righteousness and shield us from the onslaught of darkness that we may always stand firm against the deceitful powers of worldly and irreligious allurements! Bless us, Lord Jesus Christ, and keep us safe in the Holy Vestments of your Spiritual Truth! And by truly following your Commandments throughout life, all people who firmly believe in your Hallowed Existence, Dear Lord, will remain strong in reputation and moral excellence, never having to defend one's character or principles!

Amen …

Chapter and verse that inspired prayer:

Ephesians 6:10-11   Finally, my brethren, be strong in the Lord, and in the power of his might. (11) Put on the whole armor of God, that ye may be able to stand against the wiles of the devil.

# November Twelve: "We Attest To Our Belief"

(As inspired from John 10:41-42)

Lord Jesus, hear our prayer …

Proudly, we attest to our belief in you, Lord God! And we thank you for your unceasing Miracles of Love! Lord Jesus, we know that devout belief comes from a personal acceptance within the innocence and purity of one's heart and soul. And through your Sacred and Timeless Words, O Lord, which are Faultless and Unblemished, all the hearts and souls of the world have no recourse but to turn away from their disbelief and accept absolute belief in you!

In true belief, there is Everlasting Life; therefore, we personally profess that there is no one else before us except you, Lord God our Father of Heaven and Earth, whose power reigns forever and ever!

In true confession, there is Mercy; therefore, we confess, Lord Jesus, that you are The Messiah and The Salvation of the world, in whom there is no other!

In true testimony, there is faith; therefore, we believe in the Holy Spirit and accept the Infinite Miracles of Unending Love and Forgiveness! Pour out your Spirit, Lord, to everyone on earth!

Only through you, Our Anointed One, will the world truly believe in and accept the genuine power of faith; for no power in heaven or on earth is greater than you, Our Lord Jesus Christ; we witness, we confess, and we profess that you are the Ultimate Goodness in all that has ever existed, exists, or will ever exist! Bless us, Lord of All Generations, of All Nations, of All Languages, and accept our words as sincere!

Amen …

Chapter and verse that inspired prayer:

John 10:41-42    And many resorted unto him, and said, John did no miracle: but all things that John spake of this man were true. (42) And many believed on him there.

# November Thirteen: "In Faith, We Trust"

(As inspired from Job 24:22)

Lord Jesus, hear our prayer …

Lord of Our Faith, we ask that you will bless our endeavors in life and clear our pathways of obstacles so that we may find the road ahead safe from all worry and concern! Heavenly Father, we pray for one another: Through positive supplication, we have secured our individual destinies through the Spiritual Comforter of your Consummate Concern for our futures!

Compassionate are you, O Lord, for helping us select all the Right Paths in Life. Through many challenges and individual choices, we harvest the fruits of faith and hope; blessed is the strength of our Christian belief, and blest is the Promise of Divine Grace! The certitudes in life are as assured as the uncertainties of life; for we live in a series of beginnings and endings: The known and unknown, birth and growth, weddings and funerals, changes that are warranted and unwarranted. But nothing in life, Lord Jesus, is more sure, more positive, more powerful than the Absolute Perfection of the Love that you have for each one of us! Great is your Love, fortunate are we to receive of it! In faith, we trust. In hope, we depend. But in your Grace, Lord Christ, we are Positive! Because only through you, Lord God, is Perfection Unrestricted; and we have complete faith in your Never-ending Love and Mercy. Thank you, God Almighty, for allowing us the freedom of Personal Will to select and choose our avenues in life; but we also thank you, Dear Lord, for your Divine Guidance that shows us the correct path that will deliver us to your Sacred Heart! Glory be to you, Lord Jesus Christ, Our Personal Savior and Deliverer from all worldly troubles and spiritual endangerment! Into your Hallowed Care, O Lord of Hosts, do we secure our futures through a silent confession of our individual transgressions: Thank you, Our Heavenly Lord, for receiving our personal words of remission!

Amen …

Chapter and verse that inspired prayer:

Job 24:22   He draweth also the mighty with his power: he riseth up, and no man is sure of life.

# November Fourteen: "Forever Shall Your Power Reign"

### (As inspired from Exodus 15:18)

Lord Jesus, hear our prayer …

We are of one accord and of one agreement: Heavenly Father, you are The Spiritual Lord and Our Living God, and your Authority shall reign in Heaven and on earth forever and ever!

Our Lord of Peace, we pray that you will prepare the way for our spiritual victory over all the temptations of this world. In your Triumphant Name, through the shedding of your Innocent Blood, and by your Stripes, we rebuke the shadows of darkness and all who oppose your Divine Authority and Might; because, you are The Lord Jesus, The Spirit of God made flesh! And we are humbled, Lord of Majesty, by the forces of nature that are submissive solely to the Authority of your Word. All earthly powers are temporal, only the Heavenly Love that is borne of you, Lord Jesus, is forever! The riches and wonders of this world will come and go; for everyone and everything is consumed by the passing of time: The delicate flowers of the field blossom in their beauty and then they wither; the intense brilliance of a scarlet sunset is but a fleeting farewell in the eye of the beholder; a gently falling rain momentarily touches the essence of all life before slowly moving on; and even the rule of Kings and Queens and Heads of State will reign in authority for a mere moment in time. But in you, our Lord Jesus, exists the Eternal and Endless Limits of All Time! Your Hallowed Powers, Lord Jesus Christ, are Unlimited and Endlessly Divine! Our Lord Jesus, you are forever, and forever shall your Power Reign! Blessed are you, Lord God, Our Blest Savior, You, who defeated death and is the True Resurrection and Life of The Eternal Everlasting; pray for us, Dear Lord, that your chosen faithful, each and every one of us, will one day unite in the Eternal Mansion of your Everlasting Grace and Gentle Love!

Amen …

Chapter and verse that inspired prayer:

Exodus 15:18    The LORD shall reign for ever and ever.

# November Fifteen: "You Touch Each Life"

(As inspired from 1 Peter 3:8-9)

Lord Jesus, hear our prayer …

O Great and Merciful Lord, it is written, "Vengeance is mine; I will repay, saith the Lord;" for we, as true Christians, must never retaliate nor seek spiteful reprisal, instead, we are to honor your Words and pray for those whom are ignorant of their actions and your Commanding Love: O Lord, give us strength by softening the heart of all who are hardened against your Compassionate Peace.

We, your loyal Christian followers, do pray for an Inheritance of Goodness to be empowered within each and every one of our individual souls, Lord God, for the purpose of reflecting your Hallowed Righteousness; and thus, bringing the world together in a universal belief of you, Our King and Lord Jesus Christ!

We beg of you, Our Lord, do not allow the emptiness of spite, malice, and selfishness to fill our hearts. Instead, please, encourage each one of us to share the many Blessings of Love that you have shared with us. Lord Jesus, your Wonderful Gifts are Unconditional, and we know that you want everyone in life to be happy and to be completely fulfilled; and through you, Our Lord Christ, everyone will find Everlasting Love, Joy, and Calm within their lives. It is not impossible, for as Christians, we believe that all lives are meant to have meaning and to be meaningful to the lives they touch, because all things through you, Dear Lord, are possible! And as you touch each life in a very special way, Lord Jesus Christ, sanctify all people to also show compassion, fellowship, and generosity in the lives they touch! And through the kindness of thought and deed, everyone in the world, one day, will reflect your Heavenly Goodness, Lord of All That is Right! For if everyone truly accepts and believes in the ways of peace, then all people, everywhere, will one day exhibit a true understanding of your Unending Love that you have for us, Our Lord of Great Mercies!

Amen …

Chapter and verse that inspired prayer:

1 Peter 3:8-9     Finally, be ye all of one mind, having compassion one of another, love as brethren, be pitiful, be courteous: (9) Not rendering evil for evil, or railing for railing: but contrariwise blessing; knowing that ye are thereunto called, that ye should inherit a blessing.

# November Sixteen: "All Paths Lead Directly To You"

## (As inspired from Matthew 3:3)

Lord Jesus, hear our prayer …

From the wilderness of worldly despair, please, hear our soulful prayers, O Lord, as your faithful call out to you for Spiritual Redemption: That our lives and souls will be on constant alert, ready to answer your calling, we pray to you, Lord Jesus, that our wants and ways will always be a journey filled with your Tender Love and Forgiveness. To have you, Lord Christ, in one's life is to have the Kingdom of Heaven within reach; for your Kingdom of Love, Lord God, is wherever you; and wherever you are, Lord Jesus Christ, all paths lead directly to you, your Sacred Heart and Holy Spirit!

Where there is love and devotion in one's heart, you are there, Lord Jesus! Where there is peace and harmony in one's life, there you are also, Our Lord! And where there is kindness and mercy in one's spirit, you will forever be found there! All Glory to you, Our Lord of Vision and Truth, for you are always before us, guiding us, showing us The Way!

And whenever or wherever the sincere qualities of compassion prevail, Our Lord Jesus, your Heavenly Powers are made known. Lord God, your Goodness and Greatness and Majesty are Exalted Above All, and your Glory will Forever Rule Supreme in the Heavens above and on the earth below and deeply within each and every obedient heart and soul that faithfully pursues the True Way of Salvation! Bless us and pray for us, Lord of Redemption, that we will make our paths straight: Heavenly Father, we have prepared The Way for your Goodness to enter our hearts through atonement; thank you for the blessing of Forgiveness, Our Lord Jesus Christ of Great Mercy!

Amen …

Chapter and verse that inspired prayer:

Matthew 3:3   For this is he that was spoken of by the prophet Esaias, saying, The voice of one crying in the wilderness, Prepare ye the way of the Lord, make his paths straight.

# November Seventeen: "Defeat The Enemies Of Truth"

(As inspired rom Colossians 1:16)

Lord Jesus, hear our prayer …

By you, Our Hallowed Father, are all things created. You heal with a thought, your Holy Spirit engulfs the universe, and your Blessed Heart goes out to all who worship, give thanks, and are completely obedient to your Heavenly Authority: All praise and thanks are yours, Our Divine Jesus and Lord!

In our thoughts, in our hearts, and in our souls, we are with you, Lord Christ! Bless us and deliver us, Our Lord and God, from the seen and unseen misfortunes that come to us in life. Lord Jesus, we believe that all worlds and powers, visible and invisible, belong to you! We believe that all things are possible through the Presence of Absolute Faith. We believe that all wrongs are righted through your Ever Redeeming Forgiveness! And we believe that all needs are fulfilled through a constant obedience to your Almighty Will! Help us, Lord God Our Christ, to defeat the enemies of truth and to conquer the dominions of doubt! Bless us, Lord Jesus Christ, in your name and inspire us to proudly carry the banner of your Victorious Love throughout our lives!

There is not a single day that passes, Lord Jesus, when you are not in our thoughts! Daily, Lord, we exalt and pay homage to you for the table that you have set before us in life; and our table is always filled with acknowledgment and praise! Through steadfast supplication and continued obedience to your Commanding Will, we show our thankfulness to you, Lord Jesus, for our continued blessings in life! And through your Abundant and Hallowed Benevolence, Lord Jesus Christ, Heavenly Gifts, seen and unseen, are bestowed upon us through your Immutable Love!

Amen …

Chapter and verse that inspired prayer:

Colossians 1:16   For by him were all things created, that are in heaven, and that are in earth, visible and invisible, whether they be thrones, or dominions, or principalities, or powers: all things were created by him, and for him:

# November Eighteen: "Given A Special Gift"
(As inspired from Daniel 1:17)

Lord Jesus, hear our prayer …

O Lord, we dream of the day when all people, in all corners of the world, will be united in friendship. We believe in the Power of Prayer; therefore, whatever may be envisioned, will inspire the heart to be fulfilled: And through our dreams, visions and inspirations, Lord God, we pray that your Divine Intervention will forever bless our individual futures to be all that you so desire for us! We praise you for our spiritual and physical gifts, Our Lord, for we believe that you touch and bless the Christian lives of your faithful followers in so many different ways; and there are so many ways that each person has received a blessing through your Benevolent Love. Lord Jesus, we believe that every individual has been given a special gift at birth, a special blessing that must be understood, accepted, and glorified! And through diligent prayer and perception, each one of us will realize our own unique talent or ability in life and use it to its fullest! And we also believe, Lord Christ, that whenever sincere thanks are given to you for our personal blessings, your Heavenly Grace and Glorious Name are given high praise and honor! Therefore, Lord Jesus Christ, we pray that you will allot us, according to our needs, the wisdom to see and to comprehend our Spiritual Gifts; we also ask of you, Lord, to endow us with the needed knowledge to use our gifts according to the Glory of your Encompassing Will and Glorious Compassion! Blessed is every blessing, Lord God, and Blest are you, Our Holy and Beloved One, He, who has the key to all Eternal Understanding of Visions and Dreams!

Amen …

Chapter and verse that inspired prayer:

Daniel 1:17   As for these four children, god gave them knowledge and skill in all learning and wisdom: and Daniel had understanding in all visions and dreams.

# November Nineteen: "Make Our Hearts Pure And Good"
### (As inspired from 2 Peter 3:18)

Lord Jesus, hear our prayer …

It is our solemn oath to you, Our Lord and Savior, to continually grow in our beautiful Christian faith and loyalty to your Holy Word of Promise and Love! Through our daily supplications, Lord God, we ask you to give special counsel to our petitions of prayer. Lord Jesus, if it is your Blessed Will, please consider our words of need: We come to you, Lord Christ, to ask for your Spiritual Grace and Guidance; because, without the Fullness of your Love in our lives, we perceive and realize that only a lonely and wanting life is possible. But with your Hallowed Love in our lives, all hollowness becomes whole, all voids are filled, and we rejoice in complete joy for a life that is meaningful and no longer empty. And with your Heavenly Influence in our individual lives, Lord Jesus Christ, your Grace will touch our souls and make our hearts pure and good. Glory to you in the highest, Lord of Heaven and Earth, You, Who Shall Reign Until Everlasting!

When we are lost, we are bewildered. When we stand in the shadows of doubt, our direction is obscured. When we are saddened by loneliness, our emotions and spirits become empty. But when you are with us, Lord Jesus, all darkness becomes the Fullness of Light, all direction becomes known, and we can clearly see our way; for we are no longer lost and alone! O Lord, we acclaim and testify to your Everlasting Holiness and to your Everlasting Presence in our lives! And with unspeakable joy, we will forever rejoice in our Christian faith through the Glory of your Blest Name, Lord Jesus Christ, Our Savior of All Humankind!

Amen …

Chapter and verse that inspired prayer:

2 Peter 3:18    But grow in grace, and in the knowledge of our Lord and Savior Jesus Christ. To him be glory both now and for ever. Amen.

# November Twenty: "Award Us Peace Of Mind"
### (As inspired from Romans 12:19)

Lord Jesus, hear our prayer ...

Revenge gives birth to retaliation, vengeance is the pay back for retribution, and all vendetta completes the circle of malevolence. But through your Mighty Love and Mending Mercy, Lord Jesus, Forgiveness ends the cycle of chaos! Pray for us, for the world, for all families and nations to end their thirst for vindictiveness.

A prayer for reconciliation: Lord God, when we have been wronged, we will seek justice, not revenge! And when we pray to you, Lord Christ, for any injustices or any offenses that may have been done to us, we will offer up prayers of atonement to The Highest Law in the world, to the Supreme Court of Truth, to the Greatest Judge of Life, to you, Lord God Almighty, Judge of the Heavens and Earth, whose judgments are final and just! O Lord, your Law is a law that cannot be appealed nor acquitted; for your Law Governs all Truth and all Justice! Lord of Mercy, we beseech you, help us to put aside our personal feelings of anger and vindictiveness. To you, The Highest Law in the Universe, we appeal and pray for a Solemn Healing and Atonement of the Soul! Please, Lord Jesus, judge not our emotions but our hearts. Award us peace of mind and Spiritual tranquility in all that we do and in all that has been done to us. We praise and accept the wisdom of your decisions, Lord Jesus Christ: Into your hands we place our troubles and we thank you for your Peaceful Resolution that has resolved and atoned our transgressions and transgressors! And From this moment on, Lord Jesus Our Divine Protector, remove from all of us, any bitterness that may linger in the heart, withdraw all spiteful emotions that plague the spirit, and pardon our angry thoughts with a True Enlightenment of Heavenly Love from your Holy Spirit, which will fill the void and become the dominating force and focus within our individual lives, now and forevermore!

Amen ...

Chapter and verse that inspired prayer:

Romans 12:19    Dearly beloved, avenge not yourselves, but rather give place unto wrath: for it is written, Vengeance is mine; I will repay, saith the Lord.

# November Twenty-One: "You Are The Crowned Glory"

### (As inspired from Jeremiah 4:2)

Lord Jesus, hear our prayer …

Through countless examples in the Bible and throughout life, your Spiritual Instruction has directed our personal and individual knowledge to understand and appreciate the many lessons that we have learned and have yet to learn! And as a people, morally driven by our Christian convictions, we know that you bless the nations and the people who outwardly honor and love your Commandments of Love, in life, for all lifetimes!

In God we trust, always! Bless this land, bless the people of this Great Nation, and bless us, O Lord, for by your Blessings of Love, we, as a Christian people, as individuals, are delivered from all abomination. Our Lord Jesus, the Strength of your Love is incapable of being overpowered by the dominion of darkness. The Glorious Might of your Unconquerable Will is Invincible to all violence! And the Direction of your Truth cannot be stopped by any false witness. You are The Crowned Glory over all that is, over all that was, and over all that will ever be! You cannot be defeated! You will always be Victorious; and in this, we wholly and completely attest to! Lord God, into your hands we entrust our lives, our souls, and our destinies! Please, Lord Jesus Christ, bless this wonderful generation and all the generations that venerate and honor the Majesty of your Hallowed Holy Spirit of Divinity!

Lord Jesus, you are known by many beautiful names: Jehovah, Yahweh, Son of David, The Nazarene, The Good Shepherd, all of Whom are One in Victory, in Truth, in Judgment, and in Righteousness! Blessed and Sublime is your Glory, Dear Lord, and we ask you to inspire us that this generation and all the generations to follow, may learn to trust in your Never-ending Wisdom. And may everyone, everywhere in the world, Lord Jesus Christ, celebrate your Insurmountable Power and Perfection from generation to generation, now, and until the end of all generations!

Amen …

Chapter and verse that inspired prayer:

Jeremiah 4:2    And thou shalt swear, The LORD liveth, in truth, in judgment, and in righteousness; and the nations shall bless themselves in him, and in him shall they glory.

# November Twenty-Two: "We Have Humbled Our Hearts"

(As inspired from James 4:10)

Lord Jesus, hear our prayer …

O Lord Jesus, you were born into this world without sin, and you never sinned in mind, body, or Spirit, not because you feared punishment, but because you are incapable of impurity; for you know that all transgression is an abomination to Goodness! Please, Lord God, help us, and help everyone in the world to see and understand that doing wrong is wrong, and doing right is honorable, simply, because doing Your Will is the correct and virtuous thing to do in God's eyes! Lord God, we have weighed our spiritual needs, we have searched our consciences, and we have humbled our hearts in your sight! And as we offer our complete love and total obedience, look into our souls, Lord Eternal, and see the truth of our belief; for through our Christian faith, we know, Lord Jesus Christ, that we are unconditionally loved and forgiven by you! To you, Lord of Salvation, we surrender our lives.

Dear Lord, we are humbled by your Immaculate and Glorious Love that you have for us, and we realize that real happiness can only be attained through sincere love and constant devotion; therefore, we perceive and accept that only our deepest heartfelt love and our steadfast devotion to you, Lord Jesus, will bring forth your Infallible Blessings of Love and Mercy from above! And as you are Eternally Perfect and True to us, Lamb of God, so must our prayers and intentions be towards you; for then, our spirits and words will be lifted heavenward, Lord Jesus Christ, and we will receive your Immutable and Undisputable Answers for all of our spiritual and worldly needs in life! Blessed are you, Our Lord of Heavenly Hosts, He, who can see into the depths of our hearts and perceive the authenticity of our individual souls and intentions!

Amen …

Chapter and verse that inspired prayer:

James 4:10    Humble yourselves in the sight of the Lord, and he shall lift you up.

# November Twenty-Three: "Our Past Generations"
## (As inspired from Ezekiel 18:4)

Lord Jesus, hear our prayer …

Every stage of life is important and critical to our personal achievement of your Heavenly Kingdom. We are born as blank slates, develop into inquisitive children, grow independently as adults, mature, and eventually return to our Heavenly Home. And by all of our deeds, thoughts, and accomplishments, we will be judged by you, Our Lord and God! Pray for us and inspire us, Lord of Eternity, to understand and to believe in The Everlasting; because, as humans, we exist and live our lives in a world of finality, beginnings and endings, whereas, the true comprehension of infinity often eludes our individual understanding. Encourage everyone on earth, Lord of Life, to realize the depth and consequence that our actions on earth have on our immortal souls. We pray for your Holy Spirit, Lord God, to pour out, onto the world of humans that we may not parish, Our Lord of Universal Reasoning; instill into all ages, in all nations, the knowledge and ability to correctly judge and choose right over wrong!

Bless us, O Lord, as you have blessed our mothers, our fathers, our grandparents, and all the generations of family and friends that have come before us. Bless us, Lord Christ, and keep us morally right and spiritually just; for our physical lives are subject to the elements of the earth, but our immortal souls will forever belong to you! And as we venture forth with each new day, we venture forth with the Divine Spiritual comfort that you, Lord Jesus, at all times, watch over and direct all physical and spiritual paths; for you have guided and protected our parents and their parents and all the loving souls of our past generations, and we thank you, Lord Jesus Christ, for their spiritual safekeeping!

We thank you, Lord God, for all the health and happiness that we have received throughout our lives. And in our travels, far and near, we pray that you will guard and protect us from all injury and harm, keeping us safe and sound for our eventual return to our Eternal Home! Therefore, only through the Faultless Guiding Force of your Everlasting Love, Lord of Holiness, do we remain spiritually safe for that appointed day and hour of our Heavenly Reunion with all the loving souls of everyone who came before us! Thank you, Lord Jesus Christ, for our spiritual safekeeping.

Amen …

Chapter and verse that inspired prayer:

Ezekiel 18:4    Behold, all souls are mine; as the soul of the father, so also the soul of the son is mine: the soul that sinneth, it shall die.

# November Twenty-Four: "Show Compassion And Tolerance"
### (As inspired from Zechariah 7:9-10)

Lord Jesus, hear our prayer …

Through you, Lord Jesus Christ, we will individually execute good judgment and show spiritual compassion to every person we meet and know! Furthermore, we will never oppress any person, people, or nation, or imagine any form of transgression or personal revenge. As Christians, we will pray for our Brothers and Sisters in Christ, and trespass not against family member, friend, or even stranger! Amen!

In our prayers, O Lord, we thank you for all of our blessings in life; but we also ask of you, Lord Jesus, to turn us away from any feelings of apathy, lack of concern, or any display of personal disinterest for the dismal plights of others that live and exist throughout the world. Please, Lord Redeemer, change our inner emotions and the emotions of others to an outflowing of Spiritual and Personal Compassion. Our Lamb of God, we turn to you for wisdom and for judgment and for the spiritual and physical fulfillment of every person in every part of this great planet! Provide for those who hunger and for those who suffer misfortunes in life; Lord Christ, we beg of you to feed and clothe them in the Soothing Caresses of your Kindly Concern! And please, give refuge to all people who seek shelter and protection from the physical elements of life; consent to their needs through your Unceasing Mercies and Infinite Love! Lord Jesus Christ, we furthermore ask that all who search for fair-mindedness in life will find their rewards through your Eternal Truth and Justice; let no one, Dear Lord, suffer the oppression of heartless spite, but let all people, everywhere, show compassion and tolerance towards one another; and with deep reverence, we pray: Inspire the powers that be, to execute fair judgment and understanding; let all people realize that whatever they do for others, they also do for themselves! We thank you, Lord of Hosts, for your blessings of Spiritual Love and your Unfailing, Compassionate Understanding!

Amen …

Chapter and verse that inspired prayer:

Zechariah 7:9-10    Thus speaketh the LORD of hosts, saying, Execute true judgment, and show mercy and compassion every man to his brother: (10) And oppress not the widow, nor the fatherless, the stranger, nor the poor; and let none of you imagine evil against his brother in your heart.

# November Twenty-Five: "Let All Conflict End"

### (As inspired from Esther 9:22)

Lord Jesus, hear our prayer …

We have come together this day, in a Spirit of Loving Friendship, and ask of you, Lord God, to bless this home, bless this family, and bless all who come together in a heartfelt celebration of Thanksgiving! And throughout the world, whenever or wherever family and friend gather in your Name, Lord Jesus Christ, we pray that you will bestow Great Blessings of Peace and Love upon all who give thanks for their blessings and to all who freely assemble in the name of Christianity! We also thank you this day, Our Lord and Good Shepherd, for all the food that you have apportioned to us, and for this peaceful dwelling that we abide in. But we especially thank you, Lord Jesus, for all the wonderful family members and friends that share in our good fortune through the Holiness of your Good Name!

O Lord, on this day, and every day of giving thanks, we petition you from our souls for harmony throughout the world: Let all conflict end and your Beautiful, Ultimate Peace begin! Turn all earthly sorrow into Heavenly Joy, and all personal doubt into a Spiritual and Holy Awakening of your Truth. We pray to you, Lord Supreme, divert all divisions of the heart, the mind, and the soul into a Blessed Christian Unity of Love! Lord Jesus Christ, empower all people, everywhere, to sit down together at the Feast of your Table of Peace and share in your Bountiful Gathering of Compassion and Accord! We pray for every human alive, because we all share in this Blest Planet of Life and Goodness: Remove the shadows of uncertainty, and encourage all souls to begin a New Age of Love and Trust!

Amen …

Chapter and verse that inspired prayer:

Ester 9:22    As the days wherein the Jews rested from their enemies, and the month which was turned unto them from sorrow to joy, and from mourning into a good day: that they should make them days of feasting and joy, and of sending portions one to another, and gifts to the poor.

# November Twenty-Six: "Lord, Enable Us To Grow As Individuals"

### (As inspired from 2 Chronicles 20:21)

Lord Jesus, hear our prayer …

Beyond all pomp and circumstance, whether it be formal or traditional, the only thing that really counts in our Wonderful Christian Religion and Belief, is your concern for our souls as witnessed in the last two Commandments that you gave us to follow on earth: To love God with all of our heart, and to love our neighbors as we would love ourselves. Thank you, Lord Jesus, for if we could just learn to follow these Two Wonderful Commandments, then what else in life would truly matter! We praise you, Lord, in word and deed as we surrender our hearts and spirits to the Heavenly Authority of your Conquering Love! No nation, no army, nor is any one person able to oppose the Commanding Power of your Divine and Encompassing Compassion! And as we proudly yield our total obedience to you, Lord Jesus, we also give to you our greatest of praises for your Spiritual Strength that continually combats the forces of deceit and darkness; because only through your Heavenly Protection and Compassionate Care does a person, a family, or a nation prosper and survive! Lord Jesus Christ, please, bless us and surround us with your Immaculate Love; for it is truly written and believed by all Christians: In God We Trust!

Our eyes are the windows to our souls! And we ask of you, Lord, enable us to grow as individuals and as sincere members of our Christian faith. Grant us the bounty of your Great Holiness to adorn our innermost being so that it will be reflected in and through the brightness of our individual visions! And then, Lord Jesus, our spiritual growth will surely become an outward reflection of your Deep Love and Benevolent Care, which will be clearly seen by all! And because right is right, and wrong is wrong, your Perfect Virtue and Goodness will forever prevail! Lord Jesus, as a vast, worldwide multitude of Christians, we proclaim to be soldiers in your Heavenly Army of Peace! Proudly, we carry your Banner of Love to all nations and to all peoples as an offering of Harmony and Fellowship in Christ All Mighty!

Amen …

Chapter and verse that inspired prayer:

2 Chronicles 20:21   And when he had consulted with the people, he appointed singers unto the LORD, and that should praise the beauty of holiness, as they went out before the army, and to say, Praise the LORD, for his mercy endureth for ever.

# November Twenty-Seven: "Our Fears Are Conquered"

### (As inspired from Nahum 1:3)

Lord Jesus, hear our prayer ...

You are slow to anger, patient with your children, and unequaled in power and strength; and it is this wonderful acknowledgment, Lord God, that you are forbearing with your faithful and that you are eager to forgive the repentant soul that has become the Divine Driving Force in our spiritual existence! All praise and thanks to you, Lord, for our wonderful lives on earth! We have been greatly blessed by the Goodness of your Venerable Spirit of Love and Kindness, which is unlimited through your Hallowed Might over all things seen and unseen, Lord Jesus! Even when dreams seem lost and visions are clouded by the shadows of doubt, we swiftly find solace through the presence of our faith! When whirling winds whisper and storm clouds gather, we quickly find peace in the protection of prayer! And during the darkest nightfall, when all things seem lost, all hope is restored, Lord Jesus Christ, as we embrace the Visible Love of your Dawning Radiance! We praise you and glorify you, Our Lord and Light of the World, for the splendor of your Enduring Spirit that is always there for us during all difficult times and in times of need: Through you, Lord of Peace, our fears are conquered and the ill winds of our spiritual distress and unrest become reassured and tranquil. Thank you, Lord God Almighty, for this wonderful blessing of life! And thank you, Our Lord of Presence, for removing all the shadows and the clouds of darkness that hinder our direction towards you. In you, Our Prince of Peace, our souls are Greatly Blessed!

Amen ...

Chapter and verse that inspired prayer:

Nahum 1:3    The LORD is slow to anger, and great in power, and will not at all acquit the wicked: the LORD hath his way in the whirlwind and in the storm, and the clouds are the dust of his feet.

# November Twenty-Eight: "Lord, You Transcend Time And Space"

(As inspired from Exodus 15:11)

Lord Jesus, hear our prayer …

Blest are you, Lord God, for creating this great planet upon which we all live, love, and learn. Lord of Eternal Light, as promised through Scripture, your Grand Creation will endure and continue for ever and ever, for there is no end to your Sacred Love! There are no limitations and there are no boundaries that confine or encompass your Almightiness! Lord Jesus, you are the Infinite and Eternal Holiness of Life! And we beg of you, Lord God, to reach down from your Heavenly Kingdom and touch our very souls that we may receive your Sacred Redemption and Salvation!

O Lord, you transcend time and space, for you have always been and you will always be! No foreign power or entity of darkness is able to eclipse your Magnificent Majesty, Our King of Glory, for all other greatness is dwarfed before you! May the whole world acknowledge and submit to the Holiness of your Supreme and Absolute Existence! And we ask through prayer, that you will endow everyone with the power to believe in you and to accept you as their Lord and God! Return to us now, Lord Jesus, and soothe all anguish and worldly sorrow.

Lord Christ, you are King of Kings, and nothing can overthrow your Magnificent Authority Over All Life nor destroy your Spiritual Glory; because, you are in all truth, Flawless in Every Way! Therefore, as all creation receives your Complete and Redemptive Light, we ask that our sincere prays of praise will be received and accepted into the Purity of your Holy and Radiant Virtue! Bless us, Lord Jesus Christ, in all that we do; for all that we do, Our Lord of Great Wonders, we do for you!

Amen …

Chapter and verse that inspired prayer:

Exodus 15:11   Who is like unto thee, O LORD, among the gods? Who is like thee, glorious in holiness, fearful in praises, doing wonders?

# November Twenty-Nine: "Your Benevolent Goodness"

(As inspired from Ephesians 5:20)

Lord Jesus, hear our prayer …

Heavenly Father, as we prepare to partake in the bounty of this land, we will always remember to pause and reflect upon our Bountiful Blessings on Earth.

We acclaim and give you thanks, Lord Jesus, for all things! And that we may resound joyfully in our praises and continually receive of our joyful blessings throughout life, permit us to individually show you our deepest and sincerest appreciation, Lord Christ, for your Faultless and Unselfish Compassion! Therefore, daily, through prayer and spiritual devotion, we will forever extol the Immensity of your Benevolent Goodness; for without you, Lord Eternal, a living, loving existence is not possible. And with every beat of our heart, and with every breath that we take, we, as Christians, will forever remember, Lord Jesus Christ, that it is you who gives Spiritual and physical life to our world and to our very existence!

Dear Lord, we live our lives according to your Beautiful Word, for you are the Spiritual Strength and the Way of our Faith Convictions; for you make our paths unerring and straight! What a Wondrous Blessing it is, Lord God, to know that your Holy Word continues forever and ever in all who trust in your Heavenly Will! Lord Jesus Christ, we pray: Fortify and maintain all people around the world, in all nations, who sincerely believe in the Paramount Authority of your Divine Word; become the Unequaled Tenderness in their heart, the Goodness in their soul, and the Guiding Force of their Christian Principles! And for those who do not understand your Living Presence within their lives, we ask you to endow their hearts with your Perfect Knowledge of Acceptance through Faith!

Amen …

Chapter and verse that inspired prayer:

Ephesians 5:20    Giving thanks always for all the things unto God and the Father in the name of our Lord Jesus Christ;

# November Thirty: "King Of Kings"

(As inspired from Revelation 19:16)

Lord Jesus, hear our prayer ...

Lord of All Compassion, this prayer is dedicated to the One we love most on earth! In our heart of hearts, deep within our souls, we offer to you, Our Lord Christ, this prayer of love: Throughout our individual lifetimes, there will always be relationships, commitments, and responsibilities toward others, but none is more deserving of our total commitment in heart and soul, than you, Lord Jesus! Dear Lord, it is our spiritual responsibility to give all honor and acclaim to you, Our Lord of Creation, because, it is our individual desire to develop a deep and personal relationship with Our Beloved Savior, with you, Lord Jesus Christ, forever and ever into eternity!

Lord God, from sunrise to sunset, from dusk to dawn, there is a deep spiritual belief, held by your faithful multitudes that circumnavigates the globe: Eternal and Infinite is Heaven's Wisdom! And it is your Incredible Love for us, Lord Jesus, that is the Hallowed Promise that directs the destinies of all true believers in you, Jesus Christ, as Our Lord and Savior! From the smallest of seeds there have grown the mightiest of trees, and from the humblest of births, there has risen the Greatest of Kings; you, Lord Jesus Christ, you are the King of Kings, The Unquestioned Authority that Reigns Supreme in heaven and on earth!

O Lord, you are the Eternal Truth and the Eternal Light that Radiates from within every soul on earth! Only your Great Love, Lord God, can awaken a world and stir everyone's soul from its spiritual slumber to rise up again, engage, and conquer the terrible enemies of Righteousness! Allow it to begin today, Our Lord of Total Salvation, within the heart of every person, the Conquest of Life's Fulfillment, the Will to Live Spiritually, and The Strong Desire to Lead a Whole Life in Peace and Harmony; and through your Matchless Truth, Lord Jesus Christ, the world will learn to exist in Everlasting Faith and Virtue! And then everyone, everywhere, will acclaim you as their God, their Holy and Divine Word of Perfection, their Lord of Lords, and cry out with great happiness: Blessed be this Day of The Beginning!

Amen ...

Chapter and verse that inspired prayer:

Revelation 19:16    And he hath on his vesture and on his thigh a name written, KING OF KINGS, AND LORD OF LORDS.

# December One: "May The Quest For Peace Begin"

### (As inspired from Genesis 4:8-9)

Lord Jesus, hear our prayer …

Our Heavenly Host, we pray that you will inspire all people to realize that we are all brothers and sisters on this planet. And the land upon which we stand is the same earth upon which everyone is born, lives, and exists! Pray for us, Our Lord and God, to see and understand that all humans, everywhere, in every nation, has but One God, One Father, One Holy Spirit, One Son of Man, and it is you, Our Lord Jesus Christ, that Surmounts and Prevails Over All!

Dear Lord, as we enter into the final weeks and days of this year, may we begin this month with a special prayer: On this day, Lord Jesus, we pray for world harmony, spiritual calm, and individual accord. We pray for your blessings of peace, Lord Christ, to be like the winds of a storm and rush outward to rescue every troubled and embittered soul! Lamb of God, become the Intercessor in our lives whenever problems arise between family or friend. We beg of you, O Lord, to intervene on behalf of individual unity and world agreement! Calm the raging heart and restore the peaceful spirit by permitting your Spiritual Tranquility of Love and Friendship to fill the emptiness that is created by hostility and anger. Lord of Lords, allow the Enlightenment of Serenity to fill the void in all who are affected by trouble and turmoil in their lives. And within our own individual hearts, may the quest for peace begin now and radiate outward to one another in a world where you are forever in our midst; and from this day forth, Lord Jesus Christ, we will proudly answer Cain's question, "Am I my brother's keeper?" with a resounding, "Yes, we are our brother's and sister's keeper of compassion for one another!" Glory be to you, Our Beautiful Prince of Peace, Our Renowned King of Heaven and Earth!

Amen …

Chapter and verse that inspired prayer:

Genesis 4:8-9   And Cain talked with Abel his brother: and it came to pass, when they were in the field, that Cain rose up against Abel his brother, and slew him. (9) And the LORD said unto Cain, Where is Abel thy brother? And he said, I know not: Am I my brother's keeper?

# December Two: "May We Continue To Spiritually Grow"
### (As inspired from Proverbs 3:1-2)

Lord Jesus, hear our prayer …

Throughout the years, Our King of Kings, we learn, we teach, and we retain the words of your Most Holy Commandments. Throughout our lives, our spirits embrace the Unflawed Laws in the Goodness of your Glorious Word! And from our hearts, we hold dear all who keep your teachings of Love and Peace. Lord Jesus, we pray that our days on earth will be long and fruitful, that wisdom will pervade our years, and that our lives will be filled with good health and individual compassion and concern for one another!

May we continue to spiritually grow in your knowledge, Lord God, and be of good character to those around us. And through the inherent wisdom of our years, may we honorably attain the respect of family, of friends, and of those around us; blessed are those who have lived long and have learned well the lessons of a virtuous life.

Only through your Unceasing Love and Patient Understanding, Our Ever Enduring God of Abraham, do we learn the true values of life; where there is selfishness, let there be selfless charity; where there is anger, let there be unending forgiveness; and where there is darkness, let there be the Glowing Light of your Goodness! We thank you, Lord Christ, for all our wonderful years of life; and we pray to you, Our Lord Jesus Christ, that our years will be many and be prosperous and be guided by the Wondrous Sanctification of Salvation through Christianity, as we proudly confess: We believe in the future through hope, confidence, and a new life in Christ Jesus Our Savior and Lord!

Amen …

Chapter and verse that inspired prayer:

Proverbs 3:1-2 My son, forget not my law; but let thine heart keep my commandments: (2) For length of days, and long life, and peace, shall they add to thee.

# December Three: "Blessed Are The Moments Of Truth"

(As inspired from Luke 1:46-47)

Lord Jesus, hear our prayer ...

All things in existence, on this planet, and throughout the universe have been set in motion and continue to subsist by the Will of God! Thank you, Lord for Divine Intervention, for the wondrous events that change our individual lives forever; thank you for the Revelations that produce lifelong memories of joy! Blessed are the Moments of Truth, our Spiritual Inspirations, and the Reverent Lessons of Life! Lord Jesus, from out of darkened worlds we flee the confines of our stressful inner doubts, our groundless suspicions, our unmerited insensibilities, and follow the Lucent Path of your Beckoning Call. And when we receive the Heavenly Glory of your Holy Word, we seize the Moment of Truth and embrace your Spirit of Love! Our hearts rejoice and our souls magnify you, Lord Jesus Christ, as we joyfully accept you into our individual lives as our God and Personal Saviour! Blessed is a life fulfilled by your Glory!

You engulf our lives, Lord God, as the abundant waters that encircle the world; for our hearts are eternally quenched and our immortal souls are forever saved by the Silent Teachings of your Holy Spirit! Lord Jesus Christ, please, permit your faithful ones to continually hear and follow the unspoken Spiritual Words of your Heavenly Inspirations! Remove the veil of silence that separates Good Tidings between heaven and earth and empower us to always be aware of your Loving Presence and your Continuous Intervention into our Christian lives, now and forevermore! Lord Jesus, our souls are magnified by the Immense Power of your Holy Spirit of Love, and greatly do we rejoice in our Heavenly Blessings! Thank you for all that we have and for all that we are!

Amen ...

Chapter and verse that inspired prayer:

Luke 1:46-47   And Mary said, My soul doth magnify the Lord, (47) And my spirit hath rejoiced in God my Saviour.

# December Four: "Whatever You Bless, Is Blessed Forever"
### (As inspired from 1 Chronicles 17:27)

Lord Jesus, hear our prayer …

All life is a cherished blessing from the Everlasting Goodness of your Heavenly Magnificence; and here we are, Lord God, living beings of your Complete Love! Bless us, Lord Jesus! Bless every single member of our Christian family and all of our friends! Bless our homes and our lives, Lord Jesus Christ; because, whatever you bless, is blessed forever! And with the deepest of respect in our words, Lord Eternal, permit us to openly express our truest feelings of how wonderful you are; for when we venerate you, O Lord, please know that our praises come from the absolute center of sincerity that is found within our souls! Blest are your blessings, Our Most Honorable King, and blest are you forever! Into your Redemptive Arms of Salvation, Our Messiah, do we long to be! Please, receive each and every one of us as true and sincere believers!

Thank you, Lord Jesus, for our happiness! Thank you for bringing joy into our hearts! We proclaim from our spirits and testify with our words that you, The Son of God, are the only one worthy of being revered with the Greatest of Respect and Devotion! For only you, Lord Jesus Christ, are worthy of Profound Reverence and Total Adoration! Only you, Our Holy Spirit, are worthy of Everlasting Exaltation! And only you, Our Heavenly Father of Love, are truly deserving of All Veneration for blessing earth with the creation of life and the Hallowed Gift of Spiritual Deliverance! And just as our wonderful King David danced in prayerful celebration of you, Lord God, we too, as grateful Christians, celebrate our blessings of life through spiritual dance and joyous song whenever the soulful melody of love sojourns within and touches our very souls, for the heartfelt verse becomes a True Reflection of Life, which is, simply, to be happy in God!

Amen …

Chapter and verse that inspired prayer:

1 Chronicles 17:27    Now therefore let it please thee to bless the house of thy servant, that it may be before thee for ever: for thou blessest, O LORD, and it shall be blessed for ever.

# December Five: "We Confess This Truth As Absolute"
### (As inspired from 1 John 4:2)

Lord Jesus, hear our prayer …

O Lord, as the moon revolves around the earth, and the earth revolves around the sun, all the love and all the glory of life that has ever been brought into existence, revolves around you! Lord Jesus, you are the heart and the soul of all that originates, you are the essence of the universe, and you are the center of every individual's life, throughout life, for all lifetimes! And let it be known throughout the entire world, that we will not deceive our hearts nor bare any false witness to the Perfect Truth, Lord Jesus Christ, that you are truly, the Uncorrupted Innocence of All Love, the Holy Spirit of All Souls, and the Flesh of Our Heavenly Father! To ourselves, and to everyone around us, we confess this Truth as Absolute, as a Christian Doctrine from The Gospel of Our Forever Living Lord Jesus Christ! Hear, accept, and live for all eternity!

Protect us, Lord Christ, from everyone who sets their heart to deceive. Entitle our spiritual instincts to discern those who have harmful intentions. And safeguard our destinies from all misfortune in life! Glory be to you, Lord Jesus Our Living God of Pure Light!

As it is during the light and as it is during the darkness, your love, Lord of All Who Exist, is the center of our lives; for all there is in life, begins with you, Lord Jesus Christ! May our thoughts and reflections as Christians, continually revolve around the Glory and Grace of your Great Power and Love, now and for the rest of our lives on earth, as it is done in heaven for all eternity!

Amen …

Chapter and verse that inspired prayer:

1 John 4:1-2    Beloved, believe not every spirit, but try the spirits whether they are of God: because many false prophets are gone out into the world. (2) Hereby know ye the Spirit of God: Every spirit that confesseth that Jesus Christ is come in the flesh is of God:

# December Six: "Judge The Worthiness Of Our Needs"
(As inspired from 1 Timothy 4:10)

Lord Jesus, hear our prayer …

The answers to all questions and to all mysteries belong to our Living God in Heaven! Lord Jesus, you know every secret, for you are able to see deeply into the truth of all hearts. Therefore, Lord All Knowing, we ask you to hear our silent prayers of intention; for our thoughts are true and stem from within the heartfelt sincerity of our faith and trust in you! Lord Jesus Christ, we ask that you will listen to the inaudible pleas of our Personal Petitions. We pray that you will peer deeply into the depths of our hearts and hear the requests of our individual wants. Lord God, we beseech you to judge the worthiness of our needs and sanction your will, not our will, to be justly served through the spiritual truth of our solemn supplications. And now, Lord God, we quietly and individually, as one body, unified in Christ, do ask of you our personal prayer requests: Thank you, Lord Jesus, for hearing our spiritual voices, and for answering our requests!

Only through you, Lord Savior of All Humankind, does complete belief and understanding of Personal Salvation begin! Lord Jesus, encourage the joys of our Christian beliefs to fill our knowledge with the faithful assurance that you are forever, and Forever Faithful is your Love for us! Pray for us, Lord Jesus Christ, that our hearts will be strong and that our spirits will endure; and through soulful prayer, and your Spiritual Assistance, Lord Jesus Christ, we will be able to avoid all the entrapments of this world!

Amen …

Chapter and verse that inspired prayer:

1 Timothy 4:10   For therefore we both labour and suffer reproach, because we trust in the living God, who is the Saviour of all men, specially of those that believe.

# December Seven: "In You, We Trust"

### (As inspired from Numbers 15:28)

Lord Jesus, hear our prayer …

Forgive us, O Lord, by the Compassionate Authority of your Hallowed Name, as we make spiritual atonement for our personal transgressions, which we have knowingly or unknowingly committed against the Commandments of your Holy Word: Please, cleanse and purify our souls, our hearts, and our thoughts! Into your hands, Lord, do we place our love and obedience. Shield us, Lord Jesus, from all injustice, release us from the bonds of biased forethought, and free each one of us from the servitude of our own ignorance; for only through you, Lord Jesus, do we believe in the Power of Total Redemption!

In you, we rely! Embrace us, Lord of Divine Right, as you deliver us from the darkness and enshroud us in the Light of your Great Holiness!

In you, we trust! Lord of Everlasting Peace, we extol and acclaim your Great Mercy! Worthy of all glory and honor are you, Lord Christ, for in your Spiritual Embrace does our Personal Salvation and Eternal Life begin!

In you, we live! Lord Almighty, we exalt and worship the Heavenly Influence of your Wondrous Wisdom! All deserving of reverence and devotion are you, for in your hands, the chains of doubt are broken, the stumbling block of spiritual ignorance is removed, and our vision is clearly restored that we may see the Incorruptible Light of the World and be saved by your Beautiful Radiance, Lord Jesus Christ!

Amen …

Chapter and verse that inspired prayer:

Numbers 15:28    And the priest shall make an atonement for the soul that sinneth ignorantly, when he sinneth by ignorance before the LORD, to make an atonement for him; and it shall be forgiven him.

# December Eight; "You Are All That We Need"

### (As inspired from Philippians 4:19)

Lord Jesus, hear our prayer …

Willingly, we are spiritually and emotionally submissive to the Holy Command of your Great Authority; please, accept our personal profession of obedience: Dear Lord, a day does not pass that we do not speak to you or call upon your Glorious Name; you are forever in our thoughts! Lord Jesus, you are the Realization and the Fulfillment of all Hope and Promise! Just as the sun and the stars are ever present, and just as the air we breathe is always with us, your Sacred Love, Lord Christ, has become the Ever-flowing Source of Energy that is found within the center of our lives! Your Holy and Eminent Love is our passion for existence, and we humbly submit our hearts and souls to you, Lord of Glory, as we pay spiritual tribute for the wonderful blessings that you have accorded us! How marvelous and wondrous it is, O Lord, to have your blessings in life, day after day! Through you, all voids are filled, all prayers are answered, and all shadows disappear in your Sacred Brilliance! Lord of Radiant Beauty, you are all that we need in in life, we want for nothing more!

Lord Jesus, through the fulness of our Christian faith, we possess Countless Riches of Spiritual Wealth that can only be found through belief in you! Lord God, you supply all needs, you answer all questions, and you provide all that is necessary to achieve Life Everlasting! Glory to you, Christ Jesus Our Living and Present God, He, who suffered and died for us that we may attain Spiritual Salvation and live eternally in the Kingdom of Heaven; and with all the angels, Lord of Glory, we Praise your Holy Name forever and ever into eternity!

Amen …

Chapter and verse that inspired prayer:

Philippians 4:19    But my God shall supply all your need according to his riches in glory by Christ Jesus.

# December Nine: "In Your Name, Lord, There Is Victory"

(As inspired from 1 Chronicles 29:10-11)

Lord Jesus, hear our prayer …

Our hearts have become an altar unto you, Our Holy Trinity, and only words of peace will be our offerings from this moment on, to you, to one another, and to The world! Blessed is the Lord God of Israel, our Heavenly Father, He, The Son of Man, The Holy Spirit of Love, who is exalted above all others, do we pledge our lives, our souls, and our destinies on earth!

May our praises be as pure as a child's soul. May our needful prayers be sincere. And may the power of our Christian faith, Lord Christ, be as one mind, as one spirit, and as one voice proudly proclaiming to the world of your Great Glory and Goodness! In your name, Blest Lord, there is Victory over darkness! Through your name, Lord God, there is the Blessing of Hope! And with your name on our lips, Lord Jesus, we forever acclaim and testify to the Flawless Perfection of your Infinite Majesty! For all that is in heaven and on earth, belongs to the Profound Prominence of your Divine Glory, Lord Jesus Christ, Lord God of All that exists!

Lord, that our prayers will be heard, we praise your name continuously! That our praises will be received, we believe and worship every word of Scripture! And that our adoration will be accepted as genuine and sincere, we will forever proclaim your Excellence and Infinite Majesty, Lord Jesus Christ, to all of heaven and earth and to all who will listen! Lord God, we pray: Surround us and protect us with blessings of Heavenly Love! Into your Compassionate Care do we deliver our hearts and souls for your safekeeping! Please, O Gracious Lord Our King, do we claim Victory in your Name; deliver us from all who oppose your Righteousness, your Glory, your Power, and your Triumph over all that is worldly! Who can deny the Greatness of your Hallowed Existence!

Amen …

Chapter and verse that inspired prayer:

1 Chronicles 29:10-11   Wherefore David blessed the LORD before all the congregation: and David said, Blessed be thou, LORD God of Israel our father, for ever and ever. (11) Thine, O LORD, is the greatness, and the power, and the glory, and the victory, and the majesty: for all that is in heaven and on earth is thine; thine is the kingdom, O LORD, and thou art exalted as head above all.

# December Ten: "The Will Of Your Holy Spirit"

(As inspired from Acts of the Apostles 2:4)

Lord Jesus, hear our prayer ...

The True Fulfillment of Life is beyond the spoken word or any possible human understanding. Whenever a new soul is borne of your Spirit, Lord Jesus, the Love in the Kingdom of Heaven above bursts open in a Great Heavenly Utterance of Joy! And throughout the world, all the many tongues reveal the same Spiritual Praise that your Love is Everlasting and created for all! Hear us, Lord Christ, for our hearts will not be stilled! Like zealous children, we loudly call out your beautiful name: Glory to Our Lord Jesus Christ! Help us, Lord Jesus, to live our Christian lives according to the Will of your Holy Spirit! Without a doubt, no truth in the creation burns brighter than your Truth, Our Lord Emmanuel! For you are The Way, you are the Everlasting Life, you are the Forever Flame of Goodness! Lord Jesus, your Spirit is our pathway to all salvation, and all that we do, we do according to your Perfect Plan; which was designed for us long before the beginning of time! Glory be to you, God Almighty in the Highest! Fill our hearts, our minds, and our spirits with the gifts of the Holy Spirit that we may witness and share our Salvation with others!

To you, Our Holy Spirit of Immeasurable Compassion, do we offer Untold Words of Respect and Reverence! Please, hear our heartfelt praises, for you are truly the Spiritual Essence of Love and Purity, Profoundly Hallowed, and Ever Present in the lives of all who confess and profess that our Heavenly Father's Glory resides within Our Savior Lord Jesus Christ! And to everyone who firmly believes that Salvation is readily at hand, Life Eternal begins with the Acceptance and Absolute Belief in Jesus Christ, He, who was born by The Word of God made Flesh!

Amen ...

Chapter and verse that inspired prayer:

Acts of the Apostles 2:4    And they were all filled with the Holy Ghost, and began to speak with other tongues, as the Spirit gave them utterance.

# December Eleven: "In The Name Of Your Love"

(As inspired from Isaiah 65:25)

Lord Jesus, hear our prayer …

Throughout the millenniums of change, Lord God, you have delivered the human race and guided the world through countless ages of existence: Through Primitive Ages, the Stone Age, the Bronze Age, the Iron Age, the Dark Ages, and the Nuclear Age! And now, through the Spiritual Guidance of your Goodness, the world reaches out and prays to you that we may enter into the Enlightenment of Righteousness! Lord Jesus Christ, in your Glorious Name we pray: Allow the Age of Accord to begin today!

All the peaceful hearts of the world cry out to you, Lord of Hosts: Heal the wounds of hostility! Lord Jesus Prince of Peace, we pray for the day when the hawk and the dove will nest in the same tree. We pray for the day when everyone, everywhere, will be able to resolve their strife and conquer their fears! Oh, Dear Lord, how we pray for the day when conflict and confrontation between people and families and nations will cease to be! Our Lord of Immutable Mercy, let that day begin today! Empower everyone, Lord Jesus, to stand shoulder to shoulder upon the Holy Summit of your Redeeming Word! We pray for peace: Quicken the day of Total Amity, Lord of Mercy, and plant the seeds of calm and accord throughout the world. Let an affinity grow between peoples and nations, and let the branches of your Love and Resolution reach out to cover all who struggle in the name of justice, in the name of harmony, and in the Name of your Love, Lord Jesus Christ! Permit us, Lord God, to approach your Holy Mountain of Redemption that we may ascend to the Summit of your Majestic Might, where we may worship and pay tribute to your Glorious Existence!

Amen …

Chapter and verse that inspired prayer:

Isaiah 65:25   The wolf and the lamb shall feed together, and the lion shall eat straw like the bullock: and dust shall be the serpent's meat. They shall not hurt nor destroy in all my holy mountain, saith the LORD.

# December Twelve: "Your Eternal Power"

### (As inspired from Romans 1:20)

Lord Jesus, hear our prayer …

Lord God, your faith in our Personal Salvation is staggering to our senses! Every day, every hour, every minute of life, we are given the opportunity to individually choose, through freewill, which direction in life that we wish to follow. And without a doubt, Lord Jesus, we deeply desire to follow only you, Lord; for your blessings are like the stars in the heavens above, too numerous to number! And we are overwhelmed by your Benevolent Concern and Never Ending Care for all that you have created. Please, favor us with your Blessings of Faith and instill into our consciences, Lord Jesus, a total understanding of all that is right! Lord of Judgment, we seek to be worthy of your faith that you have in us. And we realize that faith does not necessarily rely upon absolute physical proof. For we cannot see the wind, but it moves constantly through our existence; we cannot touch time, but it passes before us; and of the first seed or tree, we know not which came first, but we will harvest the nourishment of its branches and be content with our bounty! Sow the Grains of Discernment into the wisdom of all hearts, Lord Christ, for we are Christians who witness and confess, through faith, to your Majestic and Hallowed Existence! Thank you for our many blessings, Lord Jesus Christ, and praiseworthy is the knowledge of any person who can believe without seeing! For your Eternal Power generates all the Life-giving Energy that is in the universe, in our souls, and in your Great Heavenly Kingdom; because you, Our Living God, without question, are The Reason and Existence of All Creation!

Amen …

Chapter and verse that inspired prayer:

Romans 1:20    For the invisible things of him from the creation of the world are clearly seen, being understood by the things that are made, even his eternal power and Godhead; so that they are without excuse:

# December Thirteen: "From Darkness To Light"

(As inspired from Deuteronomy 32:39)

Lord Jesus, hear our prayer ...

Our Hallowed Father and King of Glory, there is no other god with you: Blessed is the Divine Might of your Immense Power! Only you can create life, Lord God, only you can heal all suffering, and only you, Lord Eternal, can deliver us from harm's way. We, your faithful, who understand so little, seek your Everlasting Wisdom and Unremitting Patience, Lord Jesus. Help us to overcome our earthly burdens through prayer, and help us to rise above our spiritual failures through repentance. We need your Holy Guidance, Lord Jesus Christ, for only you have the unequaled forbearance and understanding to lead a nation, a people, or even a single individual from their personal darkness into the Radiant Light of your Enlightenment!

As you have showered your mercy down upon your faithful throughout the ages, Lord Christ Our Redeemer, have mercy on us. Please, Lord Jesus, help us to become sincere in our understanding and in our compassion of the world, of one another, and of ourselves. Grant us knowledge of the Spirit that we may clearly see the path to Spiritual Salvation is achieved simply by moving from darkness to Light!

Inspire us, Dear Lord, to individually mend our ways in life that we may obtain the Priceless Fulfillment of Eternal Life! Please, Lord God of All Ages, help each one of us to defeat our personal shadows of ignorance; bring us back into the Brilliance of your Unerring Wisdom! We, who understand so little, seek your Everlasting Love and Mercy, Lord Jesus Christ, that we may one day live forevermore with you in your Heavenly Kingdom of Heavenly Hosts!

Amen ...

Chapter and verse that inspired prayer:

Deuteronomy 32:39   See now that I, even I, am he, and there is no god with me: I kill, and I make alive; I wound, and I heal: neither is there any that can deliver out of my hand.

# December Fourteen: "In Your Name And For Your Glory"

(As inspired from Romans 1:4-5)

Lord Jesus, hear our prayer …

Why cannot the entire world perceive and accept the Healing Power that you, Our Lord and Holy God Jesus Christ, has so ordained from the beginning of time! Please, Lord Merciful, hear our deepest prayer request for all people, for all the inhabitants of earth to become an Integrated Whole of your Holiness: Through the Sacred Purity of the Holy Spirit, we ask of you in prayer, Dearest Lord, to bless us and protect us this day with the Overpowering Authority of your Hallowed Almightiness; open the hearts and minds of every person around the world, Lord Jesus, to personally accept you as the Living Embodiment of God Their Savior!

How blessed it is to know that every man, woman, and child who fully believes and follows the Testaments of Christianity is an Apostle to Jesus Christ Our Lord, according to The Resurrection and the Hallowed Gifts of The Holy Spirit of Life!

O Lord, your Almighty Power does not rest nor does your Holy Radiance darken! Your love is here, your love is there, your love, Lord Christ, is everywhere! Lord God, your Sacred Powers are declared by the heavens above, by the earth below, and there is no greater intensity in the universe, in the world, or in any one individual than the Everlasting Strength of your Eternal Love! And as Christians, we realize that there is no mightier force within us than the inner strength that is forged by our love for you, Our Lamb of God; for it is in the Divine Influence of Love that all life is created! And it is from this Gift of Love, Our Lord of Spiritual Restoration, that we humbly yield our hearts, our souls, and our total obedience to the Absolute Authority of your Immaculate Love, in your name, and for your Glory, Lord Jesus Christ The True Son of The Living God, now and forevermore, among all nations and tongues!

Amen …

Chapter and verse that inspired prayer:

Romans 1:4-5    And declared to be the Son of God with power, according to the spirit of holiness, by the resurrection from the dead: (5) By whom we have received grace and apostleship, for obedience to the faith among all nations, for his name:

# December Fifteen: "Your Words Of Life"

### (As inspired from Colossians 3:16)

Lord Jesus, hear our prayer …

Through the teachings of the Holy Bible, we have come to understand, Lord God, what one generation accepts as their standard of behavior, the next generation will always take it a step further. And for this reason, Lord Jesus, we beseech you in prayer: Please, soften the hearts of all future generations to be temperate in their language, in their song, in their dress, and in their mannerism, but be full of fire and passion for their Christian beliefs, which are established by the Rich Passages from the Glorious Son of Man!

We celebrate the benevolence of your Most Merciful Heart, Lord Christ; for truly, we are blessed in all things! And as we freely receive of your wonderful blessings, Lord Jesus, we joyously celebrate and extol the Spiritual teachings of the Scriptures formed by your Sacred Word. And by instructing one another in the virtues of accepting and believing in your Ageless Truths, we, as Faithful Followers, firmly abide in the Wisdom of your Wondrous Words! Lord Jesus Christ, through soulful searching, we have found the Eternal Truth of Knowledge in your chapter and verse, in your Psalm and Proverb, and in the Old and New Testament: Peace and grace reside in our hearts, love and song are on our lips, and your Words of Life dwell within our souls, Lord God! And beyond a shadow of doubt, we are blessed in all things by your Holy Spirit of Love and Forgiveness; blessed is Our Anointed One, Our Redeemer of Souls, Our Good Shepherd and Teacher, you, The Son of God, Our King and Glorious Lord Jesus Christ!

Amen …

Chapter and verse that inspired prayer:

Colossians 3:16    Let the word of Christ dwell in you richly in all wisdom; teaching and admonishing one another in psalms and hymns and spiritual songs, singing with grace in your hearts to the Lord.

# December Sixteen: "The Heavenly Chimes Of Joy"

### (As inspired from Deuteronomy 30:2)

Lord Jesus, hear our prayer …

Receive our prayers, O Lord, as we gather together to give you thanks for our blessings of love and happiness! Lord Jesus, we live our lives for your Unparalleled Love! Today, tomorrow, and into forever, our hearts sing out spiritual praises that reach to the very ends of the universe! And for your glory, Lord Jesus Christ, permit the heavenly chimes of joy to ring loudly throughout your living creation! And throughout every loving heart and soul on earth, allow us to sing our praises of elation to the Triumphant Goodness of Our Creator, to you, Lord God Almighty! Blest is the Healing Power of your Holy Name, Our Lord and Savior Jesus Christ, for all eternity!

Please, Dear Lord, gather your faithful into your loving arms and fill our spirits with the Rhapsody of your Compassion! Return us, Lord Christ, from an eternity lost, to a time of innocence, to an age of total love and absolute trust! Restore us, Lord Jesus, to your Ultimate Truth, to your Perfect and Pure Love, to the Garden Paradise that we lost forever. And from this day forward, in our hearts and in our souls, we vow complete obedience to every Commanding Word of your Holy Spirit! Lord God, you are The Door, The Way, The Light of the World, and we beg of you, please, deliver us from ourselves: Purify our souls, strengthen our personal beliefs in all Christian principles, and clear the path for Goodness to enter into everyone's heart! And then, the whole world will joyfully cry out to you, Lord Jesus Christ, in Rapturous Song and Praise!

Amen …

Chapter and verse that inspired prayer:

Deuteronomy 30:2    And shalt return unto the LORD thy God, and shalt obey his voice according to all that I command thee this day, thou and thy children, with all thine heart, and with all thy soul;

# December Seventeen: "Your Evangelizing Love"

(As inspired from Mark 1:17)

Lord Jesus, hear our prayer …

From the darkened shores of life, you have summoned us to follow you into the Radiance of your Evangelizing Love! Lord Jesus, when you beckon to us, we answer; for your voice, Lord Christ, is the heartfelt call that we quietly hear from within our souls! Night or day, day or night, our lives and our spirits we owe to you, O Lord; because, that which comes from you belongs to you! And willingly, Lord God, do we submit our entire beings to you; for our salvation can only come through your Divine Deliverance. Thank you, Lord Jesus Christ, for the rich blessings that have been portioned out to us in life, and we also give thanks to you for allowing us to share our wonderful Christian blessings with others so that they too may find the Soul Saving Salvation of your Infinite and Far-reaching Grace!

Dear Lord, you have shown us through the Blest Scriptures that we are not in this world alone as solitary individuals, that we all belong to an earthly and heavenly family of living and loving souls. And in this world, everyone, in one way or another, is somehow dependent upon others. But only through you, Precious Lord, is the well-being of the earthly family totally blessed! You have given our lives purpose and meaning; for without you, Lord Jesus Christ, the purpose of life would have no meaning. Lord of All That Is, you are The Bread of Life, you nourish the soul to perfection and maintain the significance of existence, which is to find love and forgiveness in our hearts and to forever follow you throughout the duration of our lifetimes! Blessed are you, Lord Almighty!

And now, as we cast our nets upon Your Crystal Clear Waters of Goodness, Lord Jesus, the bounty of the catch is too enormous for any one person to gather alone: Your Generosity is overwhelming, our souls and lives are filled to capacity with your Magnificent Blessings of Love! Thank you, Our Lord Christ, for making us Fishers of Fellowship in your Name!

Amen …

Chapter and verse that inspired prayer:

Mark 1:17   And Jesus said unto them, Come ye after me, and I will make you fishers of men.

# December Eighteen: "Love Is Unconditional"

(As inspired from Haggai 1:5, 2:5)

Lord Jesus, hear our prayer …

The Living Force of The Holy Spirit is Always Alive, All-powerful, and Unstoppable! Remember us, Our Lord, as we, your Christian followers, individually choose to make our personal lives better: Help us to learn from our mistakes and errors in judgment, strengthen our moral convictions that we may each realize the Enormous Strength in your Word, which you gave to former generations, is Forever Meaningful!

Heavenly Father, we have considered our ways according to the Commandments in which Christianity is rooted, blessed is the Spirit of the Word, and blessed are you, Lord God, for your Glorious Love is Unconditional. The Royal Signet of your Absolute Reigning Power, Lord of Hosts, has released and raised up a people from out of a captive land millenniums ago. And from all nations, Our Lord of Preservation, your faithful have sustained the full and perpetual message of your Enduring Love! From generations, now long forgotten, your Beautiful Word was carried from person to person, from age to age, and from soul to soul into present day; and today, your Wonderful and Holy Promise of Salvation remains with us! Lord Jesus, from deep within our hearts and souls, we have considered our ways in life, and we are in complete agreement about our destinies: Into your hands, Lord Christ, we entrust our faith, our love, and the futures of all Christian generations yet to come! No one else can lead us from the unknown reaches of darkness into the Brilliance of your Radiant Perfection! Forever, we will follow only you, Lord Jesus Christ. And through the passing centuries, our faces and names will also, one day, be lost in time, but your Powerful Message of Mercy and Love will still continue, forever, unconditionally to one and all, through the hearts and souls of your heavenly and earthly faithful, until the end of times!

Amen …

Chapter and verse that inspired prayer:

Haggai 1:5, 2:5    Now therefore thus saith the Lord of hosts; Consider your ways. (2:5) According to the word that I covenanted with you when ye came out of Egypt, so my spirit remaineth among you: fear ye not.

# December Nineteen: "The Blessing Of Innocence"
### (As inspired from 1 Timothy 4:12)

Lord Jesus, hear our prayer …

Throughout the Old and New Testaments, we, as God's children, are continually asked to repent of our trespasses, that all shall be made whole and pure again! Unblemished and Incorruptible is the Supreme Spirit of Our Heavenly Father! Blest is the Virtue of your All-encompassing Heart, Lord God, the Magnificence of your Endless Love, and the Greatness of your Perfect Judgment. Lord Jesus, we thank you for the Blessing of Innocence that tenderly exists in our lives; a Sacred Virtue that is truly found within the hearts of those who daily renounce and regret all personal offenses against the Word and Will of God! Thank you, Lord Jesus, for the simplicity of Forgiveness, for the Graces of Salvation, and for being Our Lord and Personal Savior!

Lamb of God, we pray that all people, young and old, everywhere, in every part of this great world, will be Spiritually Motivated to grow forthright in mind, in body, and in their soulful quest to embrace virtue through righteous living! And to everyone who is entrusted with the well-being and the enormous responsibility of teaching Christian values, we ask of you, Our Prince of Peace, that you will bless them with patience and understanding as they instruct our lives and guide us on our paths; for it is through your Holy Spirit of Love and Long-suffering that the foundation of the world was created!

Lord Jesus Christ, please, receive the sweet savor of our innocent praises that so clearly rings out through the forgiven hearts and pure spirits of your children on earth, we, who love and adore you: Glory be to you, Our Lord and God, Hosanna in the Highest!

Amen …

Chapter and verse that inspired prayer:

1 Timothy 4:12    Let no man despise thy youth; but be thou an example of the believers, in word, in conversation, in charity, inspirit, in faith, in purity!

# December Twenty: "The Season Of Challenge"
### (As inspired from 1 Kings 8:57-58)

Lord Jesus, hear our prayer ...

As this season winds down, our hopes and aspirations in you, Lord God, continue to grow by leaps and bounds! Never before have we ever aspired to be so uplifted and fulfilled by the Word of God then now, at this time and gathering of family and friends. And we pray to you, Our Spirit of Good Counsel: Please, permit our souls to become the Spiritual Sheaves that you call Your Own among the many nations and peoples of this world; for our faith and our strength come from you, O Lord. And with unbounded certainty, we know that you will never forsake us nor abandon us during any tribulation or trial or testing of faith! Lord Jesus, as the time of harvest ends, and the trials of winter are about to begin, we anxiously await the season of challenge; because it is a time of endurance, of survival, and of what has been gained and realized in our personal commitments to the Righteous Words of your ageless Commandments! Inspire our hearts, Lord Jesus Christ, to never lose confidence in the convictions of our Christian faith; for you are always there to strengthen our hopes and aspirations during all troubling times!

Dear Lord, we pray that we will have stored up our faith for the trials of life that are to follow. For only through your lessons, Lord God, and through the testing of faith do we prove and assure our worthiness and the sincerity of our devotion to you! And only through faith and the testing of faith do we ensure and warrant a future of personal and spiritual growth. Lord Jesus, teach us what we must know to endure any season of trial and tribulation!

Amen ...

Chapter and verse that inspired prayer:

1 Kings 8:57-58    The LORD our God be with us, as he was with our fathers: let him not leave us, nor forsake us: (58) That he may incline our hearts unto him, to walk in all ways, and to keep his commandments, and his statutes, and his judgments, which he commanded our fathers.

# December Twenty-One: "We Will Follow You"

(As inspired from Matthew 19:21)

Lord Jesus, hear our prayer ...

Through the Hallowed Halls of your Glorious Kingdom echo the innocent chants of constant praise: All are welcomed by the One That Has Always Been, Our Father, The Anointed One, He, who came to earth in the Spirit of God and was made flesh by the Holy Spirit, lived among us, teaching, healing, and forgiving our trespasses, was falsely accused, put to death, and was Gloriously Resurrected by the Faith and Love of Holiness, now stands in the Gateway of Heaven, allowing all who believe in His Word of Compassion to pass through into the Halls of His Heavenly Kingdom, there, to live forever in His Infinite Love!

O Lord, beyond all earthly wealth, the treasure of an eternity awaits all who are faithful to your Word! The full bounty of your Great Love, Lord Jesus, is Eternal and Pure and is worth more than all the riches of the world! Lord of Compassion, your love is an Unequaled Love, a Love that is Unblemished and Unconditional, a Love that is True and Sincere, a love that cannot be bartered for nor purchased. Your Love, Lord of Mercy, is freely given to the world, and freely the world accepts your Love! Lord of Total Forgiveness, your Radiance Shines Brightly upon all creation, you are the Spirit of Understanding, the Giver of All Light and Enlightenment! To you, Lord God, belong the heavens and the earth and all the wonderful life that exists therein. And faithfully, Our Good Shepherd of Peace, we will follow you, today, tomorrow, and everyday that we live! Your Great and Holy Goodness has captured us, Lord of Our Salvation, and for all eternity, we will treasure your Love and praise you as Our Lord Jesus Christ, God of All That Is: Comfort and heal our wounds and scars, Lord Eternal, that we may find peace at the end of the day, at the end of all days, and at the end of our existence here on earth!

Amen ...

Chapter and verse that inspired prayer:

Matthew 19:21    Jesus said unto him, If thou wilt be perfect, go and sell that thou hast, and give to the poor, and thou shalt have treasure in heaven: and come and follow me.

# December Twenty-Two: "True And Perfect Adoration"

(As inspired from Psalms 51:10-11)

Lord Jesus, hear our prayer …

We sincerely ask of you, Our Lord and God, to establish a Covenant of Love with each member of your loving flock: Create within us, O Lord, a clean and pure heart! Renew our souls and make permanent your Holy Spirit in our lives!

Lord God, through your Faultless Spirit of Knowledge, you have inspired a confidence within those who faithfully follow every Word that is ordained in the Greatest Book Ever Written! And we cannot thank you enough, Our Precious Lord, for creating the Gospels of the Holy Bible, because it gives us Guidance, Truth, Laws, and a Full Realization of who we are in relation to the creation! We are all sons and daughters of Our Living God, of you, Our Lord and Christ, Jesus, The Messiah; He, Who was Promised; He, Who Came; He, Who Rose from the Dead; He, Who Exists as Pure Love! He, whose reflections of Encompassing Compassion are seen everywhere; for you are clearly known in the eyes of all who truly love you as Our God of Life! Because, wherever and whenever an impassioned vision is revealed upon earth, it is there, Lord Jesus, that you may be found!

Blessed is this world, for we know that you, O Lord, may be established on the highest of mountain peaks, or in lush green valleys, upon the sweeping prairies, in the driest of deserts, in a rustic countryside, on great ships that sail the seas and lakes, in the skies above, in crowded cities, in the deepest reaches of the universe, and even on the lonely shores of life. Lord God, you have created each of us in your image, please, also create in each one of us, the passion to establish a pure heart with a Spiritual Vision, that wherever we are, we will reach out with honorable and perfect adoration to praise the Impeccable Discernment of your Holy Spirit in our daily lives! Lord Jesus Christ, only you can restore the broken heart and renew an empty life with your Unremitting Love and Grace; for you are always there, Our Good Shepherd, with outstretched arms, waiting for us to return to your Loving Embrace!

Amen …

Chapter and verse that inspired prayer:

Psalms 51:10-11    Create in me a clean heart, O God; and renew a right spirit within me. (11) Cast me not away from thy presence; and take not thy holy spirit from me.

# December Twenty-Three: "Home Again For The Holidays"

(As inspired from Acts of the Apostles 20:35)

Lord Jesus, hear our prayer ...

A special prayer and blessing for all who enter into our homes and into our lives, and not only during this time of year, but also during all the times of the year: Our Heavenly Father, may the Reverent Peace of Christmas engulf everyone's spirit to joyfully give of their innermost feelings of compassion and friendship to family members, to friends, and even to strangers.

Dear Lord, as the days grow shorter, and the shadows cast longer, the frozen wintry falling is a gentle reminder from the heavens above, as the warmth of our holiday season settles upon us again. And during this special time of year, Our Spirit of All Wisdom, how brightly your Word shines, for you have taught us that it is truly more blessed to give than to receive! For once again, Lord Jesus, we have come together through family honored traditions, with fellowship, and celebration in our hearts, bearing gifts of peace, hope, and love for one another: Christmas, the warmest and fullest of all occasions, Lord Christ, brings us home again for the holidays and becomes your Hallowed Promise for family and friend to renew old passions of giving and sharing. We thank you, Our Immanuel of Prophecy, for this wonderful time of the year, and we ask that you bless and encourage all who gather in your Name to develop a loving and giving spirit that will not end, but will continue throughout the entire year! And throughout the year, Lord Jesus Christ, may everyone learn to carry your Blessing of Life in their heart and truly share your Most Precious Gift of Love with one another. Glory be to you in the Highest, for you have given greatly, O Lord, of your Prayers, of your Life, and of your Love for us!

Amen ...

Chapter and verse that inspired prayer:

Acts of the Apostles 20:35    I have showed you all things, how that so labouring ye ought to support the weak, and to remember the words of the Lord Jesus, how he said, It is more blessed to give than to receive.

# December Twenty-Four: "We Await The Birth Of Peace"

(As inspired from Daniel 7:14)

Lord Jesus, hear our prayer ...

Our Promised One, you are the Good Shepherd who is born to lead your people away from the tribulations of this world into the calm, green pastures of Love and Peace! All Praise and Glory to your Immaculate Birth!

O Lord, we pray for and we await the birth of peace on earth! And therefore, we wonder, Dear God, what in the world would happen if all the nations, West and East, laid down their arms and refused to war. And the rulers of the nations, great and small, began to treat their citizens with understanding. And the citizens unified into communities of fellowship. And from these communities, there arose safe neighborhoods, and neighbors became as friends, and friends became as family. And from within the family, borne to each member, a deep respect formed for one another. And each individual, in one accordance, began to love peace. And that individual peace was outwardly magnified to every nation, city, and hamlet; and then the world would wonder, Lord Jesus Christ Our King and Savior, what in creation happened.

And now, we pray that your Spirit of Absolute Authority and Power, Lord Jesus, will sweep through the nations, through the people, and through all the languages of the world, proclaiming Everlasting Dominion in your Wonderful Name! And all who believe in you, who follow you, and who do your will, will never be lost, but will find an Eternal Heavenly Home by the Holy Throne of your Existence! Blessed are you, Lord Jesus Christ, and blest are all people who accept you into their hearts and into their lives as their Lord and God and Personal Savior! Hallelujah! Hallelujah! Hallelujah!

Amen ...

Chapter and verse that inspired prayer:

Daniel 7:14    And there was given him dominion, and glory, and a kingdom, that all people, nations, and languages, should serve him: his dominion is an everlasting dominion, which shall not pass away, and his kingdom that which shall not be destroyed.

# December Twenty-Five: "Peace On Earth"

(As inspired from Luke 2:13-14)

Lord Jesus, hear our prayer …

Bless this morning and the evening to come, Lord, as this day becomes a Most Hallowed Celebration filled with warm greetings of a festive Christian season. And for one Sacred Moment, from a distant past, a mysterious force brings all people together for just one day; for on this Glorious Dawning, Lord Jesus, the Season of Love is Born! And to everyone, each in their own way, this day belongs to all! And for all eternity, this Wondrous Moment will be a time held special for family and friends; thus, a time to remember, a time to share, and a time to embrace life; for once again, for just one day, the world gives freely of its love! For the secret of this season is held forever in its Spiritual Inspiration of Hope! And only through the eyes of childlike innocence can a world truly begin to understand your message, Lord Jesus Christ, which is an Eternal Truth, heralded by angels and shepherds: Peace on earth, and goodwill towards everyone; and Merry Christmas to every Christian and non-Christian, and to every soul and person that exists, a very happy new year to come, and may it be filled with love, blessings, and good tidings for all!

Amen …

Chapter and verse that inspired prayer:

Luke 2:13-14   And suddenly there was with the angel a multitude of the heavenly host praising God, and saying, (14) Glory to God in the highest, and on earth peace, good will toward men.

# December Twenty-Six: "Fill The World Forevermore"

(As inspired from 1 John 4:18)

Lord Jesus, hear our prayer …

Good Shepherd, remove all doubt from our thoughts and fill our hearts to capacity with the confidence of your Never Ending Love and Assurance! For if we consider fear and concentrate upon it, then we are not thinking of you, Lord God! Please, we beg of you, keep our attention and thoughts directed only upon your Glorious Ability to remove all suffering and pain: Into your Calming Hands, Lord Jesus, we place our trust and love, knowing perfectly well that your Peace will quell the troubled heart!

O Lord, if it were not for your blessings of Perfect Love, turmoil and torment would prevail everywhere, and all life would be bitter, and all futures would be bleak; we pray continuously to you, Our Lamb of God, for your Unbounded Compassion to fill the world and to fill everyone's heart! Lord Jesus, if it were not for the blessings of your Heavenly Salvation, our world would be doomed, our spirits empty, and our prayers lost in the darkness of fear!

Lord God Almighty, warrant your Glorious Light of Holiness to continually fill the world forevermore and permit your faithful to follow and prosper in the brilliance of your Redeeming Deliverance! Lord Christ, if it were not for you, there would be nothing in our lives. But with you in our hearts, Lord Jesus Christ, we have everything; we are whole, our world is complete, and our spirits are filled with the Perfection of your Endless Love and Mercy! All adoration and praise to you, Our Lord of Perfect Love, for coming into our world and saving our lives!

Amen …

Chapter and verse that inspired prayer:

1 John 4:18   There is no fear in love; but perfect love casteth out fear: because fear hath torment. He that feareth is not made perfect in love.

# December Twenty-Seven: "Lord, You Chose Us"

### (As inspired from Deuteronomy 4:32)

Lord Jesus, hear our prayer …

God All Powerful, redeem us from selfish intentions and worldly entrapments, for it is our Spiritual Desire to do unto others as we would want others to do unto us! And that we will succeed in our Christian endeavors, we will place your Compassion into our emotions, your Forgiveness into our hearts, and foremost, your Never-ending Love into our lives! For without a single doubt, you have surely blessed us, Lord God, because we are able to behold and understand our world around us! Heavenly Father, your creation of life is a wonderful blessing, and when we look across this wondrous land and into the heavens from horizon to horizon, and realize that it was all created out of love, we are truly humbled! Everything was created from your Compassionate Heart for us to enjoy, to cherish, and to give thanks! How glorious your love is for us, Lord Christ! Among all of your creations, O Lord, you chose us to perceive your Divine Greatness, to embrace your Anointed Love, and to be fully aware of your Supreme Magnificence that is found throughout creation! Lord Infinite, it is a Wondrous Blessing that we are able to realize and know that you are the Creator; for no other living creature has the ability to know, to love, and to praise its Creator! And how fortunate we are to be aware of your Heavenly Compassion, Lord Jesus Christ, because all that is radiant and beautiful is designed from the Splendor and the Glory of your Never-ending Love! Therefore, from this day forth, we will eternally remember and acknowledge that every single creation is wonderfully blessed and comes from you, Lord God Creator of All!

Amen …

Chapter and verse that inspired prayer:

Deuteronomy 4:32    For ask now of the days that are past, which were before thee, since the day that God created man upon the earth, and ask from the one side of heaven unto the other, whether there hath been any such thing as this great thing is, or hath been heard of like it?

# December Twenty-Eight: "We Denounce All Worldly Possessions"

(As inspired from Matthew 6:24 and Corinthians 4:15)

Lord Jesus, hear our prayer …

Thank you, Lord God, for the blessings of discernment and knowledge! Through Scripture, we, as Christians, have learned that no one can serve two masters: That a life filled with confusion and doubt is a life divided and cannot possibly pursue the One and Perfect Direction of God's Will!

Bless us, Lord Jesus, and all who come together in your Blest Name, for we desire to serve only you! May the authority of your Merciful Salvation be upon all who are truly deserving; and through a silent, solemn, individual repentance, we abjure and renounce the ways of the world. And from a deep committal of adoration and constant obedience to you, Lord Christ, please permit us to prove the sincerity of our devotion to the will of your Word, as we proudly proclaim: Through personal sacrifice and spiritual commitment, we denounce all worldly possessions and material wealth as having no Spiritual significance in our lives, and we pray earnestly for your Holy and Divine Guidance! O Lord, we ask that you redound our lives with blessings of Love and Mercy; therefore, in mind, in word, and in spirit, we deny, forgo, and forfeit all that is temporal for all that is Holy and Good! Lamb of God, we pray for your Infinite Wisdom and Eternal Blessings of Love and Forgiveness! We believe in the sanctified power of your Never-ending Love, Lord Jesus Christ, as we praise the bounty of your Endless Grace! And we vow our immortal souls to serve the Absolute Perfection of your Everlasting Spirit of Promise and Hope! Bless us, Our Lord, and all who openly confess and witness to the Grandeur of your Great Glory on earth as well as the heavens above!

Amen …

Chapter and verse that inspired prayer:

Matthew 6:24       No man can serve two masters: for either he will hate the one, and love the other; or else he will hold to the one, and despise the other. Ye cannot serve God and mammon.

2 Corinthians 4:15   For all things are for your sakes, that the abundant grace might through the thanksgiving of many redound to the glory of God.

# December Twenty-Nine: "Your Benevolent Spirit"

(As inspired from Joel 2:12-13)

Lord Jesus, hear our prayer …

The Lord's Greatest Blessing from Heaven to Earth is Love, and all who receive of its Beautiful Endowment must always cherish and nourish Life's Spiritual Emotion; for Love is the center of All Life, and Life truly begins when one finds True Love in self and others; and today, let us Resolve to Love One Another!

Through heartfelt contrition, over all transgression that offends your Almighty Word, Lord God, we turn towards you with tears of joy, knowing full well that your Forgiveness is Forever with us, merely for the asking! O Lord, as the end of the year draws near, our thoughts turn to the Graces of your Benevolent Spirit. We shall remember always to reflect upon all the Heavenly Gifts that you have bestowed upon us throughout the year; but mostly, Lord Jesus, we give thanks to you for your Blessings of Kindness. We pray: Allow your Unyielding Spirit of Love, Lord Christ, to continually fall upon this good community and upon all who live within its borders. May our praises of gratitude for your Compassion reach your attention and pleasure, Our Radiant Light of the World, and gloriously fill this household, fill our hearts, and fill the lives of all who gather as family and friend within the Circle of your Love. And may we, as faithful Christians, personally and individually give thanks to you, daily, Our Good Shepherd, for the many Wonderful Accounts of your Gentle Mercies that we have received through your Boundless Bounty of Love! Lord Jesus Christ, sanctify your Gracious Blessings to continually fill our hearts and our Spirits! And may the Spiritual Joy that we embrace become an Endless Song of Love and Praise for you throughout the year, throughout our lives, throughout the world, and throughout all eternity! Blessed are you, Our Glorious Prince of Peace!

Amen …

Chapter and verse that inspired prayer:

Joel 2:12-13     Therefore also now, saith the LORD, turn ye even to me with all your heart, and with fasting, and with weeping, and with mourning. (13) And rend your heart, and not your garments, and turn unto the LORD your God: for he is gracious and merciful, slow to anger, and of great kindness, and repenteth him of the evil.

# December Thirty: "The Word Of Your Anointed Love"
(As inspired from 1 Timothy 1:4-5)

Lord Jesus, hear our prayer …

Our Beautiful Lord and Christ, you have taught us through the Gospels that our Heavenly Father is Boundless, Incapable of Error, and is not subjugated to the physical laws of humankind nor nature! Our God and Father is oblivious to all constriction of thought and awareness; He is Omnipresent and cannot be bordered by the human confines of space and time; Glory to His Infinite Presence!

Blessed are the Scared Writings of your Word, Our Gentle Lord, and blessed are those who live by your Commandments! And that we may learn a more reverent and deeper awareness of all that you have shared with us, inspire us, Lord Jesus, to avoid empty discussions and trivial matters of little Spiritual concern or contention. Instill into our hearts, Lord Christ, a profound desire to refrain from senseless arguments, foolish questions, and pointless details concerning our Christian faith that only take away from the True Meaning of your Godly Edification! Allow our prayers and affairs to innocently and sincerely flow from an enlightened heart. Instruct our souls, Lord Jesus Christ, to abide within and perceive your Heavenly Encouragements and Inspirations. Inspire us to not base our beliefs upon a singular passage but upon the entire message of your Holy Word, and that is to love one another as we love God and ourselves; for then, Lord God Almighty, we will be true to ourselves and faithful to the One and Only True Word, the Word of your Anointed One, Our Lord and Messiah, Jesus Our Christ and Personal Savior, He, who resolves all mysteries through the Understanding of Love: One Perfect Love, One Infallible Love, One Infinite Love, All United in the Purity of Love!

Amen …

Chapter and verse that inspired prayer:

1 Timothy 1:4-5    Neither give heed to fables and endless genealogies, which minister questions, rather than godly edifying which is in faith: so do. (5) Now the end of the commandment is charity out of a pure heart, and of a good conscience, and of faith unfeigned:

# December Thirty-One: "Gathered Together Under One Roof"

### (As inspired from Revelation 21:4)

Lord Jesus, hear our prayer …

Tonight, we anxiously await and welcome in the new year! Today, we give thanks and praise for the entire year and all our blessings! And now, Dear Lord, this day, this last day of the year, becomes, for this year, our final prayer for world peace; but tomorrow also becomes our first resolution for a new year of world accord! Lord Jesus, may the new year that is about to begin, bring unbounded peace to all people, of every race, color, and creed! And it is our prayer and resolution, our Anointed Savior, that all people, of all nations, and of all religious convictions, will one day unite in a solitary belief, a sublime acceptance in the Divine and Holy Power of your Unconquerable Love! And from this single belief, there will come a great outpouring of Heavenly Peace. And from this Great Harvest of Love, there will be constructed an undivided faith of Pure Harmony, one that will tower over and conquer all fear and ignorance! And from this universal Faith of Fellowship, there will grow a Spiritual Strength that will sweep through the hearts and souls of all peoples and all nations of this good earth! Lord God, we pray that the world will one day be united in faith; for then, Lord Jesus The True Son of God, countries will come together as one family under the constant outpouring of your Magnificent Compassion! Oh, what a glorious day that will be, Lord Protector, when all your children are gathered together under one roof of Heavenly Belief, praising and singing: Glory be to you, Lord Jesus Christ Our Promised Messiah, Hosanna in the Highest!

Amen …

Chapter and verse that inspired prayer:

Revelation 21:4    And God shall wipe away all tears from their eyes; and there shall be no more death, neither sorrow, nor crying, neither shall there be any more pain: for the former things are passed away.

CPSIA information can be obtained
at www.ICGtesting.com
Printed in the USA
LVHW061702260323
742643LV00014B/1293